WE ARE CUBA!

WE

HELEN YAFFE

HOW A REVOLUTIONARY PEOPLE

ARE

HAVE SURVIVED IN A POST-SOVIET WORLD

CUBA!

For information about this and other Yale University Press publications, please contact:
U.S. Office: sales.press@yale.edu yalebooks.com
Europe Office: sales@yaleup.co.uk yalebooks.co.uk

Set in Adobe Garamond Pro by IDSUK (DataConnection) Ltd
Printed and bound by CPI Group (UK) Ltd, Croydon, CR0 4YY

Library of Congress Control Number: 2019956581

ISBN 978-0-300-23003-1

A catalogue record for this book is available from the British Library.

10 9 8 7 6 5 4 3 2 1

CONTENTS

LIST OF FIGURES AND TABLES

ACKNOWLEDGEMENTS

This book owes its existence to the Cuban people whose principled intransigence and revolutionary resilience sustained their system into the post-Soviet world. I am grateful to the Cubans who gave me interviews and answered my questions with patience and candour; to those who did talks and presentations which they allowed me to record; and to those who shared their analysis and materials. I thank the individuals and institutions in Cuba who facilitated my research: Vilma Hidalgo, Vice-Rector of Research at the University of Havana; Raúl Rodríguez and Ernesto Domingo López in the Centre for Hemispheric and United States Studies, which is attached to the same university; Jesús Pastor García Brigos and the Institute of Philosophy in the Ministry of Science, Technology and the Environment; and Kenia Serrano, formerly president of the Cuban Institute of Friendship with the Peoples. My time in Cuba is always enriched by my family and friends on the island, a crowd which has grown each time I return.

The research carried out in Cuba was facilitated by the support of individuals and with funding from academic institutions in Britain. At the London School of Economics (LSE), Nick Kitchen collaborated to secure seed funding from an Institute of Global Affairs/Rockefeller fund, which took me to Havana to carry out the first set of interviews in December 2016 and to New York in March 2017. As a Visiting Fellow at LSE's Latin America and Caribbean Centre (LACC), I contributed to two academic seminars hosted by the University of Havana, in summer 2017 and December 2018, which provided further opportunities for research and for expanding my networks in Cuba. I am grateful to LACC director Gareth Jones and to Álvaro Méndez, co-director of the LSE's Global South Unit, for facilitating my participation. Michael Maisel, who, prior to studying a master's degree at LSE, worked for the coalition Engage Cuba in the United States, invited me to join the excellent programme of talks he organised in Havana for LSE students in spring 2018.

I am also grateful to Ray Stokes and all my colleagues in Economic and Social History (ESH) at the University of Glasgow, where I began as a Lecturer in January 2018. ESH funding took me to Cuba in spring 2018 and freed me from other responsibilities so that I could complete the manuscript in 2019. All academics know how precious, and how rare, these windows of concentrated time are. Special thanks are due to Malcolm Nicholson, recently retired Professor of the History of Medicine in ESH, for commenting on drafts of both medicine-related chapters, and to Professor Reinaldo Funes Monzote, Cuban environmental historian and President of the Cuban Society for the History of Science and Technology, for doing likewise with the chapter on the Energy Revolution. Ann Yaffe accompanied me through the process with enthusiasm, patience and a deep compassion for the subject, while David Yaffe and Paul Bullock cast their critical eyes over the manuscript.

My appreciation goes to John Kirk, Cuba expert and professor at Dalhousie University, for sharing his publications and sources; he is among a group of non-Cuban scholars with the integrity to go against the grain to generate a more balanced discourse in Cuba studies. Recognition is due to the peer reviewers of this manuscript whose comments pushed me to sharpen my arguments. I am indebted to Taiba Batool for launching me on this book-writing project before her departure from Yale University Press, leaving me in the capable hands of Julian Loose and the great team there. It has been a pleasure to work with them.

It has been a long journey, exhausting and exhilarating, and I am grateful for the support I have received from friends and *compañeros/as* in Britain and around the world and, most decisively, for the love, intelligence and encouragement of my family which has borne me through it.

INTRODUCTION
'¡SOMOS CUBA! ¡SOMOS CONTINUIDAD!'

A crowd gathers in the bright sun in front of a multi-coloured colonnade on a main street in the city of Pinar del Rio, capital of Cuba's westernmost province. There is an air of excitement, some chanting and dozens of arms extended with smart phones to capture the occasion for social media. It is not one of the many international celebrities who have recently visited the island that draws their attention. It is not Fidel or Raúl Castro, or any other veteran of the Cuban Revolution. They are meeting their new president, Miguel Díaz-Canel, who strides confidently down the middle of the road, shaking hands and kissing cheeks, lightly flanked by security guards in short-sleeved guayabera shirts. 'He is following the steps of our Comandante,' a woman tells the reporter from Latin American broadcaster Telesur. 'Meeting with the people, to know what people think, to know how people live. A wonderful experience, I actually shook hands with him. I feel very happy and very lucky.'[1] Over her shoulder another woman nods emphatically with her lips puckered in agreement. The comparison is intended: 'We are Cuba! We are continuity!' is the slogan adopted by Díaz-Canel and others in contemporary Cuba to demonstrate their enduring commitment to the socialist revolution.[2]

It is mid-September 2018 and, since becoming president in the spring, Díaz-Canel has plunged in among the Cuban people, across the length and depth of the island, visiting workplaces, communities, schools and other centres. He has urged all Cuban leaders to get closer to the people, and to ensure that local development strategies relate to each community's culture and history, to the aspirations, motivations and opinions of local people. Implementation, he has pointed out, will depend on their support and participation.[3] In Pinar de Rio, a province famous for its tobacco production, the president visited a fruit canning factory, an agricultural polytechnic institute, a store for construction materials, and held meetings in the Provincial

Assembly of Peoples' Power, where he was told about problems obstructing economic progress and social programmes. 'He is demonstrating that he is one of the people,' agrees another young man in the street, 'that he is someone who is addressing problems, the situation, the things that most concern Cuban society. I think that is most important.' The tall, grey-haired Díaz-Canel leans in close to address a circle of Cuban women: 'There are things that can be solved quickly; and there are other things that we will be proposing in our economic plan from next year,' he explains.

'Next year' is 2019: it marks 60 years of Cuba's revolutionary government. The Revolution is older than the new head of state. President Díaz-Canel is entirely a product of Cuban socialism. He is the son of a mechanic and a school teacher, born in April 1960 in Placetas, a small city in central Cuba founded by Spanish colonists in 1861 as a sugar town and known as 'the villa of the laurels' for its wild laurel trees. As a beneficiary of Cuba's free, universal education policy, in 1982 Díaz-Canel graduated in engineering at the Central University of Las Villas, where, in 1959, Che Guevara had declared that the university 'should paint itself the colour of workers and peasants . . . the colour of the people, because the university is the asset of no one but the people of Cuba'.[4] After three years of mandatory military service in Cuba's Revolutionary Armed Forces (FAR) Díaz-Canel returned to his alma mater to teach. He went on an internationalist mission to Sandinista Nicaragua in 1987, and the same year joined the Union of Young Communists (UJC). Soon he was second secretary of the UJC's National Office in Havana and in 1993, the hardest year of Cuba's post-Soviet economic crisis, Díaz-Canel joined the Cuban Communist Party (CCP). One year later, he was leading the party in his home province of Villa Clara. He subsequently transferred to the same role in Holguin province, later being nominated as the government's Minister of Higher Education, then Vice President of the Council of Ministers, and then First Vice President in 2013 – the first person born after the Revolution elected to that position.

In April 2018, with a not-quite unanimous vote from the National Assembly of People's Power, he took over from Raúl Castro as President of the Council of State, a post which was redesignated as President of the Republic in the new Constitution, which was approved in February 2019.[5] His ascendency is one of history's conundrums solved: the end of the Castro reign did not signal the end of the Cuban Revolution.[6]

For years, students of Cuba were conditioned to believe that the Revolution's trajectory could only be understood by reference to Fidel Castro's biology or psychology. Then Fidel ailed, he resigned, he died, but the Revolution lived on.

Raúl Castro took over. He was referred to as the 'brother', as if that explained his governance; the 'reformer', as if a peaceful transition to capitalism was assured. Raúl came, he reformed, he resigned, and the socialist system prevailed. So, if it wasn't the 'Castro-brothers' who explained the endurance of the system, then other factors must account for its survival into the post-Soviet world. Have we been too distracted by all the talk about what the Revolution was doing wrong to enquire about what it was getting right and how?

For 60 years, Cuba has defied expectations and flouted the rules. It is a country of contradictions: a poor country with world-leading human development indicators; a small island that mobilises the world's largest international humanitarian assistance; a weak and dependent economy which has survived economic crises and the United States blockade; anachronistic but innovative; formally ostracised, but with millions of ardent defenders around the world. Despite meeting most of the Sustainable Development Goals set by the United Nations in 2015, Cuba's development strategy is not upheld as an example.[7] These contradictions require explanation. 'Cuba is a mystery,' Isabel Allende, Director of the Higher Institute for International Relations, told me in Havana, 'it is true, but you have to try to understand that mystery.'[8]

Historians like anniversaries: they help to mark the passage of time and to provide perspective to its passing. 2019 marked 60 years since the Rebel Army seized power from the Cuban dictatorship of Fulgencio Batista; but at the halfway point was another useful marker. It was 30 years since Fidel Castro publicly declared that, were the Soviet Union to disintegrate, the Cuban Revolution would endure. He said that on 26 July 1989, 18 months before the USSR collapsed and four months prior to the fall of the Berlin Wall.[9] For three decades, the survival of Cuban socialism was attributed to Soviet aid. Today, the Revolution has existed in the post-Soviet world for longer than it did under the Soviet sphere of influence. How on earth did Cuban socialism survive?

This book begins to tell that story: how Cuba's revolutionary people survived into a post-Soviet world. It traces the historical roots of contemporary developments, extending the focus of my previous book, *Che Guevara: The Economics of Revolution*, about Guevara's contribution to Cuba's economic transformation and to socialist political economy debates in the early 1960s.[10] Each area examined here shows how decisions made in a period of crisis and isolation since the late 1980s onwards have shaped Cuba into the twenty-first century in the realms of development strategy, medical science, energy, ecology and the environment, culture and education. Many of these developments have taken place 'under the radar', astonishing outsiders such as Dr Kelvin Lee,

Chair of Immunology at a New York cancer centre, who described the achievements of Cuban biotechnology as 'unexpected and very exciting'.[11]

By emphasising political aspects, many scholars of Cuba have inevitably focused on Fidel and Raúl Castro, or on 'dissidents', 'entrepreneurs' or other sectoral interests. This book, however, frames the discussion of contemporary Cuba in relation to both its political economy and its economic history. It focuses not just on the policy, but on the restraints and conditions that shaped each course of action and the motivations, agendas and goals behind them. It brings out an essential element that has been understated in most commentary on Cuba: the level of engagement by the population in evaluating, critiquing and amending policy changes and proposed reforms, through representative channels, public forums, national consultations and referenda. Therein lies the voice of the revolutionary people. In socialist Cuba, the relationship between the 'government' and the 'people', through their organisations, is extremely permeable. Cuban socialism has survived with the backing of the revolutionary people and failure to recognise this leads to distortions and misconstructions about the legitimacy of the revolutionary government and the balance of power.

This is not to deny the indefatigable leadership and authority of Fidel Castro, and the subsequent dominance of Raúl Castro, which the following chapters elucidate. But as military historian Hal Klepak has pointed out, 'neither the FAR [Revolutionary Armed Forces] nor even important police resources were ever needed in an internal security role' to quell civil unrest.[12] The projects the Castros initiated were dependent on their ability to get the Cuban people behind them. Hence the need to constantly go to the people, to explain, urge, debate and win consent in order to mobilise people to action.

The label 'revolutionary people' in the title of this book does not just mean communist militants, government leaders and state administrators. It includes the communities and 'ordinary' Cubans who just got on with the art of living, pulling together through the Special Period of economic crisis: the city dwellers who became urban farmers to provide food for themselves and their neighbours; the 'disconnected' youth who became the Citizens' Army in the Battle of Ideas; the environmentalists pursuing sustainable development and renewable energies; the medical personnel who left behind their homes and families to serve the world's poorest and most neglected communities; the medical scientists who worked tirelessly to produce medicines the island could not import because of the United States blockade or the international market price; the social scientists who warned policy-makers that Cubans were being left behind in the drive for efficiency; and the millions of Cubans who turned out time and time again to debate the proposed policies and reforms which would affect them. But the label 'revolutionary people' can also include the malcontents and critics of government policy, those who 'pilfer' state resources, work illegally or live off foreigners, the self-employed and private farmers, the marginalised youth without work or study. In the cycle of revolutionary regeneration any of these groups can and have been reincorporated into the socialist project, as this book shows.

Cuban political scientist Rafael Hernández complained: 'Cuba is not the transfiguration of a doctrine, nor the reification of a totalitarian philosophy. It is a country. Little is written and even less is published about this real country.'[13] My endeavour is to write about Cuba as a 'real country', without the cynicism or condescension that characterises so much of what is written about the island by outsiders, and to highlight episodes and developments about which little is known outside Cuba, except perhaps by well-informed solidarity activists and specialists in those areas.[14] These episodes include the Battle of Ideas from 2000, the Energy Revolution from 2005, the acceleration of Cuban medical internationalism and the development of Cuba's biotechnology sector. I am also concerned with the political economy of development in different stages: during the period of 'Rectification' in the late 1980s; the economic crisis of the 1990s known as the 'Special Period'; reforms from 2008 under Raúl Castro's mandate; and more contemporary debates over economic efficiency and social justice. Today, the socialist development path is in the balance and, whilst being wary of attempts to predict the future, history can help us assess the internal and external factors which *will* determine the outcome.

The information is drawn from speeches and articles, documents, scientific, technical and financial reports, data sets, and books and articles about Cuba read over many years, in English and Spanish.[15]

As it is written for a broader audience, this book avoids some academic conventions. There is little examination of the existing literature or analysis of debates within that. Specific references are given to texts from which I have drawn directly, but without expansive lists of previous publications by the scholars cited. Clearly a far broader body of work has been consulted over the years in which I have studied Cuba, including classic texts in the field which have contributed to my knowledge and shaped my analysis, even if they are not cited.

In addition, for each chapter I sought interviews with Cuban leaders, thinkers and activists: insiders who could give a Cuban perspective to each story. For example, I had the inside view of the Battle of Ideas from Cubans who were youth leaders closely identified with the era: Hassan Pérez, President of the Federation of University Students (FEU); Kenia Serrano, another national FEU leader; and Enrique Gómez, First Secretary of the Union of Young Communists (UJC) in Havana. Regarding the Energy Revolution, I talked to scientists who are leading advocates of renewable energies and sustainable development: Luis Bérriz, President of Cubasolar, and Alfredo Curbelo Alonso from Cubaenergía. For Cuban medical internationalism, I spoke to Jorge Pérez Ávila, former director of Cuba's hospital for tropical diseases, the IPK, which has been central to Cuba's overseas medical interventions: he prepared Cuban doctors for their mission to combat Ebola in West Africa in 2014–15. Concerning Cuban biotechnology, I consulted Agustín Lage Dávila, then director of the Centre for Molecular Immunology (CIM), a key character in Cuba's biotechnology story, and Dr Kelvin Lee, the US medical scientist cited above.

Regarding relations between Cuba and the United States, in Havana I interviewed two top Cuban negotiators who had led official and secret talks with the US: Ricardo Alarcón, who headed Cuba's US policy from 1962, holding top posts in both the Cuban government and the United Nations, including as President of Cuba's National Assembly for 20 years from 1993; and Josefina Vidal, who led the island's US policy from 2013, handling the secret negotiations with the Obama administration which led to the brief rapprochement announced by the Cuban and US presidents on 17 December 2014. Vidal is now Cuba's Ambassador to Canada. In New York, I met with Cuba's Ambassador to the United Nations, Anayansi Rodríguez Camejo, who returned to Havana in January 2019 to serve as Vice Minister of Foreign Relations. With regard to Cuba's broader international relations, I spoke with Isabel Allende, cited above, and Alberto Navarro, the European Union's High Representative (Ambassador) in Havana.

For the economic history and political economy chapters on the challenge of development and Rectification, the Special Period, Raúl's reforms and the contemporary Cuban tightrope, I consulted Cuban economists, sociologists, political scientists and other specialists, including José Luis Rodríguez, Minister of the Economy from 1998 to 2009, and a former Vice President of the Council of Ministers and member of the Council of State.[16]

To object that because the interviewees have links to the government of Cuba they are somehow distinct from 'ordinary people' is to impose a false dichotomy.[17] The political representatives, heads of scientific institutions, youth leaders and others whose voices are represented here do not hail from an elite or aristocracy any more than Díaz-Canel does. Over the years in Cuba I have visited the homes of former ministers, of diplomats, political leaders, intellectuals and other professionals who live in 'ordinary' homes lacking luxury, and who share the daily deprivations of their neighbours. As state sector employees, many of my interviewees receive low salaries, even by Cuban standards, notwithstanding their qualifications and the responsibilities of their post. In summer 2019, employees in the political organisations of People's Power and a group in public administration received their first pay rise since 2005.[18]

Before the Revolution, Allende told me, her family's 'big dream' was for her to work as a secretary in the US-owned Cuban Electric Company. Instead she attended university, became an ambassador and is today director of an important institute which trains diplomats and academics. 'I am not a millionaire, I do not have any of that, but from the point of view of what I did in my life . . . Could that have happened before the Revolution? No. That is due exclusively to the Revolution.'[19] Likewise, Pérez, the son of a bus driver, became the head of a world-renowned medical institution. These are 'ordinary' people given the opportunity to do extraordinary things by the Cuban system. Given that the state controls most institutions and organisations in Cuba, it would be difficult indeed to find people in significant roles, contributing to Cuban development, who have no links to the government.

I have also drawn on previous interviews carried out with leading veterans of the Cuban revolution, *compañeros* of Che Guevara in the field of industry, and with the former president of Ecuador, Rafael Correa. In addition, I consulted non-Cubans from foreign interests dealing with Cuba.[20] I also benefited from the insights of non-Cuban specialists on the country, particularly for the final chapter concerning the Trump administration's Cuba policy.[21]

The analysis also draws on my own experiences of visiting and living in Cuba frequently since the mid-1990s when I first stayed on the island as a teenager with my sister, who is two years my senior. This was an austere time during the Special Period; we saw how Cubans dug deep to survive, as individuals and as a socialist society. It was a transformative experience. I have returned to the island regularly: for world festivals, solidarity brigades, research trips and field work, personal visits, academic seminars and more research trips.

Our first trip to Cuba from Britain turned everything we knew on its head, introducing us to new precepts and concepts, values and priorities, social relations and hierarchies, aspirations and cultural norms, means and ends. The experience taught me the value of an 'immanent critique': instead of judging socialist Cuba based on the internal logic of the capitalist system, greater insight and appreciation are possible by evaluating the island on the basis of its own strategic objectives, while acknowledging the challenges the island has faced. Scholars of Cuba, particularly from the Cubanologist school of interpretation, have so often struggled to explain or account for developments in Cuba precisely because they fail to engage with the Cuban Revolution on its own terms. The issue is ideological, an aspect of the political confrontation between capitalism and socialism.

The key tenets of Cubanology are that the revolution of 1959 represented a rupture; and Fidel and Raúl Castro have personally dominated domestic and foreign policy since, denying Cuban democracy and repressing civil society. Thanks to their mismanagement of the economy, growth since 1959 has been negligible. They simply replaced pre-revolutionary dependency on the United States with dependence on the Soviet Union until its collapse in 1991, and subsequently on Venezuela.[22] These ideas have shaped international political and media discourse on Cuba.

The caricature is problematic. First, because it obstructs our ability to see clearly what goes on in Cuba and, by depicting the Cuban people as an amorphous and pacified mass, fails to account for the Revolution's endurance and achievements. Second, because it is premised on neoclassical economic assumptions, which entail abstraction, a negation of history and 'path-dependence'.[23] By stressing economic policy over economic restraints, critics have shifted responsibility for Cuba's poverty on to 'the Castros' without implicating successive US administrations that have imposed the suffocating US blockade. The crippling effect of the blockade on every sector in Cuba has been ignored or dismissed by many commentators who blame shortages and inefficiencies on 'mismanagement' or even cynically credit it with keeping the Castros in power.[24] In the developing world there is greater appreciation for Cuba's revolutionary resilience. In 2009, then president of Ecuador Rafael Correa told me: 'It is impossible to judge the success or failure of the Cuban model without considering the [US] blockade, a blockade that has lasted for 50 years. Ecuador would not survive for five months with that blockade.'[25]

Third, poverty and material deprivation were not introduced to Cuba with the socialist Revolution: they have been structurally inherent since the island was 'discovered' by Christopher Columbus. Fourth, the accepted discourse hides political bias behind a veil of objectivity. Cuban-American sociologist Nelson Valdés complained that: 'The literature on Cuba has been permeated by so much political polemic that scholars have preferred to remain silent about the method they have utilized or the paradigm guiding their investigation and analytical logic.'[26]

This is clearly seen on the issues of democracy and human rights, both of which are contested terms. Put simply, observers who accept parliamentary liberalism – the form of political organisation preferred in the advanced capitalist countries – as synonymous with 'democracy' will find it missing in Cuba and conclude that there is no democracy on the island. There is no need here for either a gratuitous censure of socialist Cuba for the absence of multiparty elections, nor for a defensive foray into explaining how the Cuban system of participative democracy actually functions. Many scholars of Cuba have addressed this question quite adequately.[27] Likewise, addressing the issue of human rights involves philosophical questions about the nature of freedom: from what, to do what, for whom? The United Nation's Declaration of Human Rights recognises two distinct sets of rights: 'economic, social and cultural rights' and 'civil rights and political liberties', without prioritising either set morally or legally.[28] The extent to which these rights are entirely congruent is another debate. Liberal capitalist countries, most vociferously the United States, highlight civil rights and political liberties, while socialist Cuba prioritises economic, social and cultural rights. The choice is determined by which rights are compatible with the economic system.

For the Cuban Revolution, the commitments to social justice and independence are integral, not supplementary, components of the revolutionary project.[29] Failure to understand or accept this facilitates a narrative about economic 'mismanagement' and 'inefficiency'. 'The social objective of the economy is not growth for the sake of growth, but for the social implication of that growth,' insists Geidys Fundora Nevot, a young Cuban doctoral student I interviewed.[30] 'Growth is a condition for development, but it is not development,' adds former Cuban Economy Minister José Luis Rodríguez.[31] Indeed, the government avoids certain measures of improving efficiency or gross domestic product (GDP) that would be harmful to the well-being of the majority of the population. As US academic Al Campbell points out: 'This different goal clearly has the potential to cause Cuban policy-makers to act differently than their capitalist counterparts would.'[32] So it is problematic to apply the yardsticks of capitalist economics, focusing on GDP growth or money-wages per day, to measure 'success' or 'failure' of the Cuban economy, while paying little attention to the social and political priorities of the island's development.[33]

SPECULATION ABOUT CUBAN SOCIALISM

Following the restoration of diplomatic relations between Cuba and the United States in summer 2015, Havana became the place to be for veteran rock bands, pop stars, politicians, film-makers and the fashion industry. President Obama visited Cuba in March 2016, followed swiftly by the British Foreign Secretary, the French president and other European ministers. They were trailing behind Russian, Chinese and Latin American heads of state. The sharp edges of the US blockade were chipped away through licences for trade and investment issued to US companies by the Obama administration.

Meanwhile, since 2008, major internal developments have been underway in Cuba: the distribution of 2 million hectares of state land to private farmers; the *Guidelines for Updating the Economic and Social Model*, approved in 2011 and updated in 2016, reduced state control of the economy and cut government spending; the Mariel Special Development Zone and a new Foreign Investment Law of 2014 sought to channel foreign capital into Cuba; hundreds of thousands of workers were transferred from state jobs to cooperatives and self-employment, prompting a rise in remittances and the emergence of private enterprises; and Cubans were permitted to sell their homes and cars on an open domestic market for the first time in thirty years.

While the Cuban government insists that these measures are necessary to preserve the socialist Revolution, the process has led many commentators to conclude that, intentionally or not, Cuba is reintroducing capitalism. Where does the truth lie? The market openings gave US policy-makers a pretext to initiate a change in US–Cuba policy under the Obama administration, while the anticipation of western policy-makers, analysts and academics was evidenced in the plethora of conferences and publications on 'Raúl Castro's reforms'. There was speculation about whether we were witnessing an Eastern European style transition to capitalism, or a gradual economic liberalisation under existing centralised state structures, the 'Chinese model'.

Like a castle made of sand, rapprochement was washed away with the Trump administration's default to hostility. But the Cuban reforms continued, hesitantly, in fits and starts, leaving many to wonder if Raúl Castro had pulled the reins in before dismounting the horse. Now Díaz-Canel is responsible for overseeing the extremely complex process of 'updating' the Cuban system. The reforms are an economic imperative but also constitute a political risk. They create expectations and interest groups which will exert increasing pressure on the socialist system for further concessions to market forces. These challenges will be explored in the following chapters from the perspective of the revolutionary people of Cuba who, ultimately, will have to meet them.

Chapter 1 locates Cuban economic history and post-1959 political economy in relation to the 'challenge of development' faced by all underdeveloped or developing countries: how do they receive the capital they need to be able to invest in domestic developments and social welfare for their people without jeopardising their sovereignty? The lack of consensus among Cuban revolutionaries about how to overcome the structural components of the island's underdevelopment, whilst in transition to socialism and facing hostility from US imperialism, explains why the economic management system has been changed so frequently, even prior to the Soviet collapse. Decisive measures were taken during the period known as the Rectification from the mid-1980s, which pulled Cuba back from the Soviet model and arguably contributed to the survival of Cuban socialism. The Cuba which emerged in the post-Soviet world was determined by the policies and constraints faced in these earlier periods and the lessons drawn from them.

Chapter 2, on the Special Period, shows how the economy was restructured for reinsertion into global capitalist markets without relinquishing socialism, while the planning system was restored and adapted to the new conditions. The disintegration of the USSR could not eliminate the island's structural dependence on foreign trade but forced it to find new partners.[34] The chapter discusses the grave socioeconomic impacts of the crisis, the measures taken to alleviate them and the enduring impact of those measures on the island's social fabric. It explains how state farms were handed over to cooperatives and families to work, while agricultural production shifted to organic farming, revitalising traditional techniques, and an urban gardening movement emerged.

Chapter 3 explains how the struggle to return the little shipwrecked Cuban boy Elián González to his father grew into the Battle of Ideas, catalysing ambitious socioeconomic and educational programmes with youth as the principle protagonists and beneficiaries. In the face of escalating US hostility, the Battle of Ideas sought to strengthen socialist consciousness whilst tackling material deprivation on the island. **Chapter 4,** on the Energy Revolution, explains how efficient new power generators were installed in a 'distributed' system, replacing worn-out Soviet power stations, while old durable goods were replaced with energy-saving equipment. It discusses the programmes underway to promote greater energy efficiency and renewable energies, and shows how research into these technologies began far earlier than assumed. **Chapter 5**, on medical science, describes how science and technology were prioritised, even when the budget was tight, to find endogenous solutions to domestic problems and to the scarcity manufactured by the US blockade. Cuban advances in biotechnology have placed it at the forefront of an emerging global field for the first time in the island's economic history.

Chapter 6, on medical internationalism, shows how the nature of Cuban internationalism shifted from military to medical missions, as hundreds of thousands of Cuban health care professionals travelled to impoverished communities throughout the world and tens of thousands of foreigners were trained or treated on the island. It describes how a new export strategy was forged to reap the benefits of the Revolution's investments in health care and education. **Chapter 7**, on Cuba–US relations, shows how the island withstood renewed hostility from the United States and its allies, determined to see the demise of Cuban socialism in the post-Soviet era, and how the island broke out of its political and economic isolation following the collapse of the socialist bloc, building new alliances which in turn generated pressure for a change in US policy on Cuba, at least until Trump entered the Oval Office.

Chapter 8 provides an account of the reforms introduced under Raúl Castro's mandate from 2007, framing the measures in terms of the problems they were intended to address and the results attained. It shows how the reforms sought to improve efficiency and productivity, opening a space for market mechanisms within the socialist framework. It highlights the national and sectoral debates that accompanied the process, encompassing the entire population, seeking consensus to legitimise the new measures. **Chapter 9** discusses the contradictions being introduced into Cuban socialism with the reform process, and the debates and critiques they have fuelled. It highlights the role of investigators and policy-makers who kept checking who had been left behind, devising targeted programmes of assistance, and reigning in economic 'progress' when it sacrificed social justice. **Chapter 10** was added as the book was being edited to incorporate the return to hostility under the Trump administration, particularly from early 2019. As Cuba enters a renewed period of difficulties, the developments outlined over the following chapters will be decisive if the socialist Revolution is to survive into the post-rapprochement period.

1

★ ★ ★

THE CHALLENGE OF (SOCIALIST) DEVELOPMENT

How do countries develop? Is the operation of the free market or state action decisive? Where can developing countries get the capital they need to invest in domestic infrastructure and social welfare? This is particularly problematic for smaller economies with a limited capacity for domestic accumulation. How can foreign capital be obtained under conditions that do not obstruct such development or undermine sovereignty? How can international trade be used to produce a surplus in a global economy which, many argue, tends towards unequal terms of trade? These are among the pivotal dilemmas facing the majority of the world's nations, those labelled as developing, emerging, underdeveloped, less developed, Third World, global south, or low- and medium-income countries, among other expressions. There are many descriptors for these countries, and even more theories explaining their 'backwardness' relative to the first industrialised nations.[1]

Different ideologies and schools of interpretation have produced divergent formulas to address the challenge of development: from classical and neoclassical theories of free markets and comparative advantage in international trade;[2] to Karl Marx's observations about the impact of the capitalist countries on their colonies;[3] to Marxist–Leninist theories about imperialist exploitation (which serve as a guide to revolutionary political action);[4] to Latin American 'structuralism' from the 1940s, which described the unequal terms of international trade between the industrialised 'centre' and the primary product-exporting 'periphery' countries; to more radical dependency theories of the 1960s and 1970s, concerned with 'metropolis' exploitation of the 'satellite', the 'development of underdevelopment' and its impact on social structure in the periphery;[5] to the 'Dual Sector Model', which explains development in terms of the transition of the labour force between subsistence (agricultural) and capitalist sectors of the domestic economy; to

13

Gerschenkron's theory about the active role for government and large banks in addressing economic backwardness; and to Walt Rostow's anti-communist stages of economic growth in which all countries follow the path of the industrialised nations to 'high mass consumption'. Fundamentally, these theories of the development process can be juxtaposed by the function they assign to the state, versus the market, in the development process.

More recently, economic historians concerned with why the former Spanish colonies of Latin America were 'left behind' the former British territories of the United States and Canada have debated alternative explanations: initial environmental or geographical factors ('factor endowments' such as climate and agriculture, and the availability of land, labour and capital); the institutional legacy of colonialism (British institutions and laws implemented in North America, versus Iberian institutions and laws in Central and South America); and embedded inequality (resulting from the subjugation of indigenous peoples, the importation of enslaved Africans and the enduring control over power and policy by a small oligarchic elite). However, this debate tends to stay within the framework of neoclassical economics, adopting its key assumptions that free markets, private property and individual material incentives generate efficient economic outcomes. Meanwhile, the enduring impact of imperialism barely features.[6]

For the Cuban revolutionaries of the 1950s, US imperialism was *the* principle explanation for the island's structural weaknesses. US economist Edward Boorstein opened his account of working as an adviser to the Cuban government in the early 1960s by asserting that US imperialism had locked Cuba into a structure of underdeveloped, mono-crop dependency:

> The central fact about the Cuban economy before the Revolution was neither its one-crop concentration on sugar, nor the monopoly of most of the agricultural land by huge *latifundia* [plantations], nor the weakness of national industry, nor any other such specific characteristic. Until the Revolution, the central fact about the Cuban economy was its domination by American monopolies – by American imperialism. It was from imperialist domination that the specific characteristics flowed. Unless this is recognized, the Cuban revolution cannot be understood.[7]

Thus, the Revolution of 1959 faced two real alternatives: it could renounce all fundamental changes, beyond expelling the dictator Fulgencio Batista, so that it would be acceptable to Washington; or it could pursue the deep structural changes necessary to address the island's socioeconomic ills and dependent development, which would bring hostility from the United States.[8] That is, it either operated within the limits imposed by Cuba's subordination to the United States, at most bolstering Cuban national capital, or it broke that dependant relationship and built real sovereignty, confronting both US imperialist interests and the Cuban 'bourgeoisie' which was allied to them. The Cubans opted for the latter, initially under the banner of Fidel Castro's Moncada Programme and subsequently adopting socialism as the only viable alternative. The revolutionary government expropriated the private sector and adopted a centrally planned economy and state ownership because they perceived that path to offer the best answer to Cuba's historical development challenges. However, the commitment to operate within a socialist paradigm implied additional restraints and complications, particularly in the context of the Cold War and given both the island's structural dependence on, and geographical proximity to, the world's leading capitalist power.

THE DEVELOPMENT OF UNDERDEVELOPMENT IN CUBA[9]

The United States' historical determination to colonise Cuba had a strong economic and political rationale before it occupied the island in 1898. The Cuban sugar industry was globally dominant by the 1820s and attracted capital accumulated in the United States seeking profitable sources for investment. In 1823, when US president James Monroe announced the 'Monroe Doctrine', staking a claim for control over the Americas to the exclusion of European powers, the US Secretary of State John Quincy Adams wrote that Cuba, like a ripe apple, should gravitate naturally to the US when cut off from Spain.[10] Throughout the nineteenth century the notion that the United States must annex Cuba was a recurring theme; in 1848, President James K. Polk's offer to buy the island for USD 100,000,000 was rejected by Spain.[11]

A network of US companies was formed to operate with and on the island. Thousands of US citizens established residence in Cuba as investors, traders and corporate representatives, increasingly influencing the island's economy and augmenting Cuba's importance for US elites and vice versa. Meanwhile the destruction of property and commerce during the Cuban Independence Wars (1868–1878, 1879–1880 and 1895–1898), and the embargo ordered in 1869 by the Spanish government for any person associated with the independence struggle, opened space for increasing US ownership in Cuba. By the 1870s, 75 per cent of Cuban sugar was shipped to the United States.[12] In

1895, the total value of US investments in Cuba was estimated at USD 95 million.[13]

Hence, the economic relationship between Cuba and the US was determined by the logic of the expansion of US corporate capitalism, or emerging imperialism, and the subordination of Cuban industries to its interests. Absorbing Cuban estates and factories at an increasing rate was part of the expansion of the vertical integration of productive processes under corporate management, a trade mark of US capitalism and a major factor in its transition to a hegemonic position. From the geopolitical perspective, Cuba was in a key location to serve as a base to protect New Orleans and Florida, and to control Central America and the interoceanic communication vital for the US economy. Building a power structure in the region was a necessary step in the process of transforming the United States into the centre of the world system. Thus US strategic imperatives were to wrest control of Cuba from Spain and stop other European powers from establishing control of the island. The war with Spain and the occupation of Cuba, Puerto Rico, the Philippines and a few Pacific islands were elements of this strategy.

In 1898, when Spain was losing control of Cuba to the independence movement, the United States intervened, effectively preventing the triumph of a social revolution. The United States subsequently managed the construction of a Cuban Republic in which the traditional elites, threatened by the radicalism of the intended independence, maintained a privileged position.[14] The Cuban oligarchy was willingly incorporated as a subordinated component in a US-centred power structure, becoming in the process a key tool in producing and reproducing US hegemony. The Republic of Cuba which came into being in 1902 was shaped by mechanisms created to secure US domination over the new nation – namely the Platt Amendment, which was incorporated into US law and the new Cuban constitution, in return for granting Cuba 'independence'. It set up US control over Cuba's foreign relations and public finances, established two US military bases on the island and gave the US the right to intervene in Cuba when it chose. Hero of the independence movement General Juan Gualberto Gómez said it 'reduced the independence and sovereignty of the Cuban Republic to a myth'.[15] Under its provisions, US troops returned to the island from 1906 to 1909, again in 1912, and from 1917 to 1923.

Domination over the Cuban economy was reinforced through the Trade Reciprocity Treaty of 1904, which granted Cuban agricultural products exported to the United States a 20 per cent tariff discount. In exchange, a long list of US goods received up to 40 per cent tariff discount in Cuba. By the

1920s, US companies controlled two-thirds of Cuba's sugar production. US banks made huge loans to Cuban sugar producers, generating the speculative boom known as the 'Dance of the Millions'. When this collapsed, the US banks foreclosed passing the assets into United States ownership.[16] By 1929, US investments in Cuba had soared to USD 919 million, 62 per cent of which was invested in agriculture, mainly the sugar industry.[17] The majority of imports flowing into Cuba came from the United States, including 95 per cent of capital goods and 100 per cent of spare parts.[18]

With the Great Depression, US capital retracted and the Cuban sugar industry increasingly fell into domestic ownership. Between 1929 and 1932, falling prices and output saw the peso value of Cuban sugar production collapse from around USD 200 million to USD 40 million. The impact on Cuba was traumatic, leading to a period of political upheaval: strikes took place and workers' 'soviets' were established in sugar mills throughout the island, culminating in the overthrow of General Gerardo Machado's dictatorship with the Revolution of 1933 and the 'Sergeant's Revolt', which brought Batista to the centre stage for the first time. In January 1934 Batista, in coordination with US envoy Sumner Wells, removed President Ramón Grau San Martín and his progressive One Hundred Day Government. In May that year, the US government introduced a quota system for controlling sugar imports, under which Cuba was allocated a percentage of total US imports.[19] This acted as an instrument of political and economic control over the Cuban government as the quota could be, and was, adjusted.

Cuba was the largest producer and exporter of sugar in the world; sugar production and all its by-products accounted for 86 per cent of Cuban exports in the late 1940s, 80 per cent of which were shipped to the United States. Sugar companies controlled 75 per cent of the arable land, half of which they left fallow, and employed a quarter of Cuba's workforce, but only 25,000 full time, with up to 500,000 workers hired for the labour-intensive harvest lasting two to four months and afterwards dismissed for the *tiempo muerto* (dead season). Poverty, unemployment and underemployment were inherent aspects of the island's sugar-dominated society, forcing an army of unemployed workers to sell its labour cheaply as cane cutters.[20]

After the Second World War the Cuban sugar industry was stagnant; the US-imposed sugar quota acted as a disincentive to investment while sugar workers resisted attempts at mechanisation. Thus, when US investment poured back into Cuba it was channelled principally into public utilities and to a lesser extent into petroleum, manufacturing, mining and other industries.[21]

Consequently, in the 1950s Cuba's power, railway, highway, port and communications facilities were among the most developed in Latin America.[22] Cuba was the third greatest recipient of US direct investments in Latin America, receiving USD 713 million of direct investment in 1955. US investors controlled 90 per cent of the telephone and electric services, 50 per cent of public service railways and 40 per cent in raw sugar production.[23]

After seizing power in a military coup, once again with US support, in 1952, the dictator Fulgencio Batista encouraged foreign investment in the mining sector, in tourism, on public work projects and in the cattle industry. But this increase in foreign investment did not mean that the Cuban economy was 'taking off' with capitalist development.[24] For example, oil refineries owned by Standard Oil, Texaco and Shell, which together added over USD 50 million per year to Cuban output statistics, employed fewer than 3,000 people, and the majority of their higher positions were held by foreigners.[25] Most of the wealth from foreign corporations was repatriated. As French philosopher Jean-Paul Sartre remarked: 'What I took to be signs of wealth, were, in fact, signs of dependence and poverty. At each ringing of the telephone, at each twinkling of neon, a small piece of a dollar left the island and formed, on the American continent, a whole dollar with the other pieces which were waiting for it.'[26] Meanwhile, less than 20 per cent of imports were consumed by the mass of the people – mainly foodstuffs and medicines – while the remaining 80 per cent, which totalled USD 770 million in 1957, went to Cuban elites and large corporations.[27]

From a development perspective, the most striking phenomenon of Cuba's economy was the inequality between the conspicuous consumption of Havana and the rest of the island. In 1957, the Catholic University Association reported: 'Havana is living in extraordinary prosperity while rural areas, especially wage workers, are living in unbelievably stagnant, miserable, and desperate conditions.'[28] Nearly 35 per cent of the working population was unemployed. 'The specter of unemployment affects all thinking on labor and manpower problems in Cuba,' noted a US government report, adding that 'Cuba has been fortunate that chronic unemployment has not created a more critical situation.'[29] Only 3 per cent of rural Cubans owned the land they worked and the average annual income of the largely rural population was USD 91 – one-eighth of that in Mississippi, the US's poorest state. Inevitably, given massive unemployment, low salaries and little access to land, only 4 per cent of Cubans in the rural areas ate meat, only 1 per cent ate fish, 3 per cent ate bread, 11 per cent had milk after weaning and less than 20 per cent ate eggs.[30] More than 75 per cent of rural dwellings were wooden huts, and only

2 per cent of rural Cubans had running water and 9 per cent had electricity.[31] Some 24 per cent of the population was illiterate, life expectancy was 59 years and infant mortality was 60 per 1,000 live births.[32] Racist discrimination was rife and institutionalised.

THE CHALLENGE OF SOCIALIST DEVELOPMENT

The new revolutionary government seized power, formally on 1 January 1959, but incrementally over the following months as old institutions were dismantled and replaced by new ones, and as the old elites were replaced by inexperienced and unqualified young revolutionaries who took over as the managers and administrators of the country. The new government had only national savings and tax revenues to draw on for investments, severely limiting the capacity for public spending and private investments. Wealthy Cubans were leaving the island, taking their deposits and taxes with them. How was the new government going to carry out the ambitious socioeconomic reforms outlined in the Moncada Programme without financial resources? Moreover, it had to do so while transforming the economy to address the island's historic dependence on sugar and on trade, as well as endemic unemployment and socioeconomic deprivation, whilst inverting the balance of power in favour of the impoverished classes.

1959–1962 was a tumultuous period during which the country experienced nationalisations, an almost complete shift in trade relations, the introduction of state planning, new institutions, new social-relations of production, the mass exodus of managers and professionals, imposition of the US blockade, sabotage and terrorism, invasion and the threat of nuclear conflagration. The revolutionary government's first redistributional measures spurred a period of economic growth, but by 1962–3 national output and worker productivity began to decline as the shocks of profound structural change set in. This was also the result of the rash implementation of policies whose consequences had not been fully analysed. For example, eager to industrialise their way out of mono-crop dependency, the revolutionary government neglected the sugar harvest, but the fall in export earnings, exacerbated by the US blockade, reduced Cuba's capacity to import the raw materials and spare parts required for industry. Labour shortages in the countryside led to increased reliance on voluntary labour for agricultural work.

The challenge for revolutionary Cuba was to solve these practical problems within the broader framework of a socialist transition: to increase productive capacity and labour productivity in conditions of underdevelopment and in transition to socialism, without over-reliance on capitalist mechanisms (market forces, the profit motive, competition, material incentives) that undermine the formation of a new consciousness and social relations that are integral to socialism. But what strategies are best to build socialism in a blockaded and trade-dependent island? How can production and productivity be stimulated while maintaining a development process focused on human well-being? How can growth be obtained alongside equity and social justice? Who should own and who should control production and distribution? What should be the balance between private and social accumulation – the plan versus the market – are they complementary or contradictory? What democratic structures should exist? What is the role of culture and consciousness?

Consensus on these issues has never been achieved in Cuba. The debate, which is as old as the Revolution, continues today, as discussed in Chapter 9. The search for solutions to these questions explains why so many different approaches to economic management have been adopted under the Revolution, five different systems in the first three decades alone: the Budgetary Finance System, the Auto-Financing System, the Registry System, the Soviet Planning and Management System and the 'Campaign of Rectification of Errors and Negative Tendencies', known as Rectification.[33] Each system reframed the relationship between market mechanisms and the state plan in accordance with the economic and political imperatives of the period and international conditions.[34]

EARLY 1960s: CHE GUEVARA REBELS AGAINST THE SOVIET MODEL

As Minister of Industries from February 1961, Ernesto 'Che' Guevara developed a unique system of economic management for the socialist transition known as the Budgetary Finance System.[35] It was the fruit of a dynamic interaction between theory and practice, emerging first as a practical measure to solve concrete problems in industry, but gaining a theoretical base as he studied Marx's analysis of the capitalist system, engaged in contemporary socialist political economy debates and investigated the technological and administrative apparatus of the capitalist corporations nationalised in Cuba. Guevara used the Budgetary Finance System to test his assertion that it was possible and necessary to raise consciousness and productivity simultaneously, even in an underdeveloped country, in the process of socialist construction. He believed that failure to do so, focusing exclusively on economic development fostered through market mechanisms, would lead to the restoration of capitalism.[36] On this basis he criticised the Soviet's 'hybrid' system as socialism with capitalist elements. This lacked the efficiency of the 'free market', with its aggressive fight for profits, because the state plan and legally defined relations of production prevented exploitation and capitalist accumulation, whilst also failing to foster the collective consciousness in workers which Guevara believed was a precondition for socialism and communism.

Meanwhile, other Cuban ministers and planners rejected the audacity of Guevara's challenge to Soviet orthodoxy, opting to adopt the tried and tested Soviet economic management system, known in Cuba either as Economic Calculus or the Auto-Financing System. They blamed the economic deterioration of 1962–3 on what they saw as excessive centralisation and the lack of financial incentives to individuals and enterprises associated with Guevara's economic management model. This was the period that saw increasing integration into the socialist bloc via trade and human exchange: Cuban students went to Eastern Europe on scholarships while the socialist countries sent technicians and economists to Cuba. Socialist bloc advisers advocated the Soviet's Auto-Financing System with decentralisation and financial autonomy for enterprises, which functioned as independent accounting units responsible for their own profits and losses and, in the case of the National Institute for Agrarian Reform (INRA), was similar to the *khozraschet* model of cooperative farms in the USSR.

Thus, as the dust settled in the early 1960s, revolutionary Cuba had two competing economic management systems, operating under one Central Planning Board (JUCEPLAN), one central bank and one treasury. Guevara's Budgetary Finance System operated in the Ministry of Industries (MININD), the Ministry of Transportation and the Ministry of Sugar, founded in 1964. The Auto-Financing System was implemented in INRA and the Ministry of Foreign Trade. All ministries received a state budget allocated by JUCEPLAN, but the economic management system they applied had practical implications affecting their organisational structures, policies, the financial relations between state institutions, relations between producers and consumers, and so on.[37]

This introduced operational contradictions within the new revolutionary state and created the institutional conditions for what became known retrospectively as the 'Great Debate' about which economic management system was appropriate to Cuban conditions.[38] The dispute was aired openly through institutional journals where articles by participants met retort or support from other contributors. However, it also took place internally at the highest levels. Tirso Saenz, one of Guevara's deputies in MININD, told me that witnessing arguments on the government's Economic Commission and the Council of Ministers was 'like watching a boxing match'.[39] Defending the Auto-Financing System corner was Carlos Rafael Rodríguez, pro-Soviet communist leader and head of INRA. Guevara was the challenger in the Budgetary Finance System corner. The Great Debate established a tradition of open discussion, within the socialist paradigm, in the search for solutions, consensus and legitimacy. The two sides of the debate have also served as a reference for understanding the pendulum swing of alternative systems between the 'plan' and the 'market' since then.

LATE 1960s: MISINTERPRETING GUEVARA'S SYSTEM

There were neither winners nor losers in the Great Debate. It ended when Guevara departed from Cuba in 1965. However, in 1967, both systems were supplanted with a new Registry System which was implemented across the economy. From April 1967, the state budget was eliminated, while charges and payments between ministries and enterprises were abolished and replaced with a system of 'economic records'. In 1968, the correlation between production and remuneration was severed, and the last forms of taxation abolished. University studies in socialist political economy and public accounts were closed down. In March 1968, the Great Revolutionary Offensive was launched to put an end to the non-agricultural private sector. Over 58,000 small private businesses were nationalised within one month – they too joined the Registry System.

Cuba's then president, Oswaldo Dorticos, claimed this system was consistent with Guevara's economic ideas. In reality, it abandoned key premises of the Budgetary Finance System: economic analysis, cost controls, and the focus on productivity and efficiency. A member of JUCEPLAN at that time, Alfredo González Gutiérrez, told me that to associate the Registry System with Guevara 'is a great historical injustice, because if there was someone in this country who was concerned for costs and for efficiency it was Che'.[40] As Minister of Transport, Faure Chómon Mediavilla was among those instructed to implement the Registry System. Chómon had been a co-founder of the Revolutionary Directorate, one of the three main revolutionary organisations which overthrew Batista's dictatorship on 1 January 1959. He described how: 'Everyone made their own interpretation of how to apply the basic elements of the Registry System. Many interpreted it incorrectly deciding that they could produce without concern for costs . . . At that time we did not fully understand Che's ideas and the compañeros who proposed the System did not prepare specialists in the productive and services sectors of the country. It was pure idealism in which, logically, Che's absence was felt.'[41]

Reflecting on this period from the mid-1970s, Fidel Castro said that the failure to analyse whether the Budgetary Finance System or Auto-Financing

System was most appropriate in Cuba led to the 'less correct decision' of inventing a new system. 'When it might have seemed as though we were drawing nearer to communist forms of production and distribution, we were actually pulling away from correct methods for the previous construction of socialism.'[42] The annual budgets could not be monitored or controlled. One consequence was that during the mass mobilisation of labour for the campaign to harvest 10 million tons of sugar in 1970, the disruption to other sectors of the Cuban economy resulting from the drain of resources was not sufficiently perceived or monitored. Fidel Castro had staked a lot on a record-breaking harvest and when the result fell short, and with the rest of the economy approaching chaos, he consented to the adoption of the Soviet Planning and Management System, which Guevara had opposed, to reverse the fall in production and productivity and reintroduce economic controls.

1970s TO 1980s: THE CUBAN–SOVIET EMBRACE

Implementing the Soviet Planning and Management System would enable Cuba to become a full member of the Council for Mutual Economic Assistance (CMEA), the trading body for the Soviet bloc countries. This would formalise the international trade and exchange already taking place between Cuba and other CMEA members, and permit longer-term contracts on the basis of complementary national plans. It integrated Cuba fully into the socialist bloc international division of labour, as a producer and exporter of sugar, nickel and citrus, and an importer of fuel and food. In 1976 a beneficial bilateral deal with the Soviets indexed the prices of imports and exports between the two countries to counter the deteriorating terms of trade – a global phenomenon between industrialised countries and the global south. According to the Cuban economist who became the Minister of the Economy and Planning in the mid-1990s, José Luis Rodríguez: 'This gave Cuba fair treatment for the first time in the history of its foreign trade.'[43] The result was a 50 per cent growth in Cuba's purchasing power, compared to world market prices. When we discussed this in Havana, Rodriguez said that Cuba resisted pressure to follow the 'heavy industries' development model promoted within CMEA and, from the 1980s, sought to develop branches that were not priorities for the Soviet bloc, mainly biotechnology and computing. 'It was not an easy task, because Cuba had interests in developing several branches that were not priorities of CMEA.'[44]

According to some critics, Cuba's integration into the socialist bloc simply substituted the island's pre-1959 dependence on the United States for dependence on the USSR. Responding to that view in 1973, US Marxist Paul

Sweezy outlined how the relationship with the Soviet states was different: 'The Russians do not own any Cuban enterprises or means of production, and their economic support of Cuba takes the form of grants and loans.'[45] Likewise, many commentators dismissed the Revolution's economic and social welfare achievements as merely the fruit of Soviet subsidies, a notion refuted by US economist Andrew Zimbalist:

> First . . . the magnitude of this aid is vastly overstated by false methodology. Second, even if the exaggerated aid figures were accepted, on a per capita basis Cuba would still be getting less in [CMEA] aid than many other Latin America economies receive in western aid. Third, if one is attempting to disentangle the sources of Cuban growth and to isolate its domestic and foreign components, it is hardly sufficient to consider only the beneficial effects of Soviet aid. One must also consider the monumental and ongoing costs to Cuba of the US blockade.[46]

Rodríguez agreed that 'the higher prices only partially offset the economic damage to Cuba caused by the US blockade, losses that amounted to USD 30 billion by 1990'. The prices were also beneficial for the USSR, he pointed out, below the cost of domestic production or imports on the international market. 'The large nickel deposits the Soviets had were in the Arctic circle,' he explained, 'getting nickel out in those conditions would have cost a lot more than buying the mineral from Cuba.' Likewise, getting citrus from Cuba was cheaper than importing it from Morocco.[47] Others have pointed out most sugar trade internationally was under preferential agreements: the United States pre-1959 sugar quota had a premium 80 per cent over the world market price, while Soviet prices for Cuban sugar were not so high compared with British prices for sugar imported from the Caribbean.[48]

The Cubans implemented a 'slightly simplified version' of the Soviet system which had operated prior to the Soviet reforms in the 1960s. 'Well, this model introduced order to the Cuban economy,' says Rodríguez: 'The national accounts were revised, a new planning system was created, and it had a number of positive aspects.'[49] In 1978 non-agricultural self-employment was first permitted and more flexible regulations were introduced in the early 1980s, with permission for state entities to hire such workers. Private enterprise emerged, including small manufacturers who sold products to state enterprises, set up their own shops, obtained raw materials, used machinery and hired workers to expand production and distribution. Some 10,000 private truck owners transported products from the manufacturers and private farms, and even carried passengers, for example to the beach on Sundays. However, self-employment peaked at just 1.2 per cent of the labour force.[50]

In 1980 private farmers' markets were established, with unregulated prices, and in 1982 foreign direct investment was legalised and a more decentralised state enterprise management system was introduced. Private housing construction and sales were authorised. Of the nearly 400,000 housing units built from 1981 to 1986, 63 per cent were constructed privately by the people.[51] The economic results were positive, with an annual average growth of 7.3 per cent between 1981 and 1985 (compared to Latin American GDP which fell by almost 10 per cent between 1981 and 1984) and with high rates of investment and relative growth of the industrial sector. Marginal industrial sectors, such as electronics, were expanded and new ones were established, including biotechnology and, less successfully, computing.[52]

Cubans of a certain age recall this period with nostalgia as a time of plenty and rising standards of living. Isabel Allende, Director of the Higher Institution of International Relations, recalled: 'I lived that prosperity in the 1980s . . . People had money and people went on holidays. There were no tourists here. The hotels were for Cubans . . . We went on our honeymoon with money. I went to the Hotel Seville, I went to the Hotel Capri, I went to the Hotel International in Varadero. A hotel cost 20 pesos a room.'[53] Salaries rose, especially for skilled workers, leading to increased consumption, while social security and housing improved.[54] Workers received multiple workplace 'motivation bonuses' for over-completion of production 'norms' or standard output. Meanwhile, the benefits of state investments in social welfare since the early days were being reaped, as Cuban welfare indicators soared to first world standards, surpassing many Latin American and industrialised socialist countries in key indicators such as life expectancy and infant mortality.

Despite the economic benefits, problems also emerged, including immense bureaucracy and 'excessive' material incentives, which Rodríguez described as placing a 'heavy burden' on the Cuban economy. 'Incentives' schemes overlapped, so workers were rewarded several times for the same tasks: for example, for over-fulfilment of the plan, and again if it was an export good. It cost too much and generated the tendency in entities to focus on activities which provided the most incentives or gave most material prizes.'[55] It was derailing socialist production and corrupting socialist consciousness and social relations.

Fidel Castro viewed developments with growing unease. One of Guevara's closest collaborators in the Ministry of Industries, Edison Velázquez, attributed this partly to Guevara's forewarning that the Soviet's 'hybrid system' threatened the return of capitalism: 'Fidel is not stupid and he had a lot of affinity with Che . . . He began to prepare for events. He couldn't say it publicly because we were receiving everything from the Russians, but he prepared financial reserves for when the Soviets disappeared, otherwise we would not have been able to survive the collapse.'[56]

Already in 1980, Fidel Castro was warning the Cuban people about the spread of 'bad habits' and a mechanistic approach to socialist construction:

> Perhaps it was felt that the institutionalisation of the country's socialist legality, the creation of People's Power [system of representation] and the progressive implementation of the Economic Planning and Management System would, in themselves, perform miracles and then everything would get much better automatically without the essential, basic efforts of man.[57]

Political work was being subordinated to economic mechanisms, he believed, negating the role of the Communist Party, and generating a mechanical approach to socialist transformation.[58] The growth of private activities by private farmers, street vendors, middlemen, truck drivers, small manufacturers, personal-service workers and house-builders in the first half of the 1980s was leading to the creation of 'a wealthy class in Cuba, as large or larger than the bourgeoisie which the Revolution expropriated', complained Fidel Castro. This 'new stratum of rich people' had money to buy everything, and created inequalities and irritation in the population. He cited examples of people earning between 30,000 and 150,000 pesos a year, labelling them a 'new bourgeoisie with capitalist attitudes', this 'spoiled lumpenproletariat [who were] corrupting the masses'.[59] In 1982, the state cracked down on 'abuses' in the private farmers' markets: exorbitant prices unaffordable to low-income groups, excessive middleperson profits, resources diverted from the state sector. But by 1984 the private markets had flourished again, at greater expense to the state sector.[60]

Thus, from 1984, before Mikhail Gorbachev became the Soviet premier and launched glasnost and perestroika, Fidel Castro began seeking consensus within Cuba to reform the system. The purpose? To rectify 'the errors and negative tendencies' associated with the Soviet system. Essentially, it was a parting of ways: as the Soviets were liberalising, opening up to market mechanisms, the Cubans were radicalising, falling back on the plan and political mechanisms.

THE SOVIETISATION THESIS

The 'stages of the revolution' narrative about post-1959 Cuba describes the 1970s to the mid-1980s as the 'Sovietisation' period because of the economic integration described. However, in domestic politics and in foreign policy, the Cuban Revolution demonstrated greater independence and political radicalism. In 1976 the Organs of People's Power were set up, significantly improving grassroots representation and participation in decision-making. The new system incorporated a non-party system of delegate elections.[61] Accountability was embedded into the system, with delegates expected to 'render accounts' at regular intervals to their constituents, who had the right to recall. To prevent the emergence of career or professional politicians, delegates continued in their existing employment with no change in salary.[62] The local budgets for People's Power grew from 21 per cent of the total state budget in 1978 to 33 per cent in 1984. This compared to a budget for local administration in the Soviet Union of 17.1 per cent.[63]

Meanwhile, as material incentives were increasingly emphasised domestically, appeals to 'revolutionary consciousness' saw thousands of Cuban medics, soldiers, educators and development aid workers volunteer for tough missions in poverty stricken, far-flung places, particularly in Africa, as Chapter 6 outlines. From 1975, Cuban military and civilian professionals poured into newly independent Angola to defend it from the invading armed forces of apartheid South Africa. At the Angolan president's invitation, some 36,000 Cuban soldiers and 200 Cuban healthcare workers served in Angola between November 1975 and March 1976. This was an independent foreign policy initiative which, by 1991, had seen altogether 350,000 Cuban soldiers and civilians serve in Angola.[64]

MID-1980s – RECTIFICATION: THE CUBAN REVOLUTION FORGES ITS OWN PATH

Rectification came with a party programme and a long-range development plan. It was the Revolution's fifth new political and economic management system. Within a few years it was swept aside by the Special Period as the struggle for survival in the post-Soviet world took precedence. Nonetheless, Rectification is important for the clues it holds about how and why the Cuban Revolution outlived the Soviet bloc. Was it responsible for extricating Cuban socialism from the line of falling dominoes? It certainly demonstrates the disposition of the Cuban leadership to take the island on an independent path and to preserve the historic commitment to sovereignty and social justice, dating back to the late nineteenth-century independence movements, even at the expense of economic growth.

In 1984, a 'Central Group' was set up with top government and party leaders to take over functions from the Central Planning Board (JUCEPLAN), including those of investment and trade planning.[65] The Central Group modified the 1985 economic plan and took leadership over preparing the plan for 1986 to 1990 and subsequent annual plans. Fidel Castro met with state enterprise directors in Havana to discuss the problems identified.

The issue came to a head in 1986 with the third Congress of the Cuban Communist Party (CCP) in February when the Rectification of Errors and Negative Tendencies was officially launched. Two major themes emerged in the Congress debate: the growing gap between party leaders and rank and file members, and the deterioration in export performance and economic efficiency of the Cuban economy.[66] Dramatically, it was decided to defer the Congress session for ten months to enable more time for a broader consultation about the roots of the problems and the nature of the new approach to economic management that was to replace the Soviet Planning and Management System. Debates took place in local branches of the Communist Party and the Union of Young Communists, and in workplaces. From these debates emerged thousands of proposals, ideas and suggestions, hundreds of which were approved and incorporated into the Communist Party programme. The deferred session of the Congress met between 28 November and 2 December 1986. Clearly exhilarated by the process, Fidel Castro described it as 'possibly one of the best political meetings we have witnessed throughout the history of the Revolution'.[67] The process of Rectification was in full throttle.

Were the Cuban people surprised by the 'ferocity of the official criticisms of the economy' given the previous decade of growth and rising living standards?[68] What were the errors and negative tendencies it was introduced to address? On 8 October 1987 in Pinar del Rio, Cuba's westernmost province, at a special event to mark the twentieth anniversary of Che Guevara's death, Fidel Castro cited the contemporary transgressions that 'would have horrified Che'. Voluntary work had become almost a formalism; a swamp of bureaucracy had emerged, along with inflated payrolls, anachronistic norms, tricks and lies. There were companies that were profitable because they stole, that fulfilled the plan and distributed prizes for fulfilling the plan in 'values' but not in supplies, that produced for profit, not in order to meet production needs. Monetary bonuses for surpassing work norms were designed to be easy, so that: 'on certain occasions, almost all of the workers met them twice and three times'. Bonuses were paid without regard to increased or terminated production. Workers were corrupted by the pursuit of money, even moving jobs in pursuit of the highest incentives. He slammed a group of companies, 'plagued by shoddy capitalists – as we call them – who are playing with capitalism . . . forgetting about the country, forgetting the town, forgetting about the quality, because the quality did not matter at all, but the heap of money. . .' He concluded:

> I'm telling the truth, Che would have been horrified, because those roads will never lead to communism, those roads lead to all the vices and all the alienations of capitalism. Those roads, I repeat, and Che knew this very well, would never lead to the construction of a true socialism, as a previous stage and transition to communism.[69]

Under the Soviet Planning and Management System, production was directed towards tasks that were awarded higher 'values' for the purpose of calculating results, instead of being directed towards the completion of goods or projects. The pursuit of material awards was undermining the social function of production. So, for example, because under the plan for construction the work of moving earth and erecting columns were afforded higher 'values' than other activities, buildings were not being finished. Construction teams were directed to complete 'tasks', not works. Fidel Castro raged about the thousands of millions of peso invested:

> Fourteen years to build a hotel! Fourteen years burying bars, sand, stone, cement, rubber, fuel, work force, before a single penny came into the country through the use of the hotel. Eleven years to finish our hospital here in Pinar del Río! It is true that it was finally finished, and with quality, but things like that should never happen again.[70]

There was nothing socialist or revolutionary about this state of affairs.

In the 1970s, specialist contingents of workers had been formed, the so-called 'microbrigades', to build houses, schools and medical institutions at speed and with flexibility. These were eliminated with the introduction of the Soviet Planning and Management System; dismantled, according to Fidel, by theoreticians and technocrats who did not believe in man, but who were committed to market mechanisms. 'Thus, there was no longer any force to build houses in the capital; with problems accumulating, tens of thousands of houses propped up and at risk of collapsing and sacrificing lives.'[71]

These practices contributed towards the economic stagnation which had begun, in the mid-1980s, to replace the growth of the previous period. The slowdown was also largely due to external economic factors which in turn exposed Cuba's continuing structural weaknesses: foreign debt, falling revenues from sugar exports and deteriorating terms of trade with the USSR.

EXTERNAL PROBLEMS

In 1984, Cuba's overall trade deficit increased by a record 155 per cent and international reserves fell by 21 per cent.[72] To arrest this deterioration, imports were reduced, exports promoted, import substitution pursued and efforts made to reduce the island's dependence on the Soviet Union and CMEA, particularly by increasing domestic oil production. There was also Cuba's external debt to deal with. In the early 1960s, Cuba pulled out of the International Monetary Fund (IMF), the World Bank and the Inter-American Development Bank. With US pressure on its capitalist allies to isolate Cuba, the government struggled to get access to credit in hard currency. Most loans were obtained on favourable terms from the socialist countries. However, the 1970s oil shocks and the accumulation of 'petrodollars' in private European banks changed the scenario for Cuba.[73] With the massive spike in private loans to developing countries, even Cuba could tap into these funds. 'With the push to recycle petrodollars in the 1970s,' explains Rodríguez, 'Cuba also was able to obtain significant financing from capitalist countries.'[74] The second oil shock from 1979 led to steeply rising deficits for non-oil producing developing countries exacerbated by the US interest rate hike and appreciation of the US dollar, leading to an explosion of outstanding debt in developing countries – from USD 68 billion in 1970 to USD 546 billion by 1982. By 1985, foreign debt in Latin America alone had soared to over USD 360 billion.[75]

Cuba was also now exposed; its external debt in convertible currency rose from USD 291 million in 1969 to USD 2.9 billion by August 1982. The government successfully renegotiated with the Paris Club of debtors for a manageable repayment plan between 1982 and 1986; this represented 36 per cent of the island's convertible currency debt. However, in 1986 the Paris Club began to demand adjustments to Cuba's internal financial policy. Cuba rejected their demands and broke off negotiations. Consequently, 'We stopped receiving credits from more or less "normal" organisations from 1986' explained Rodriguez.[76] By 1989 the debt in convertible currency had risen to over USD 6 billion because of the devaluation of the Cuban peso against the US dollar in 1986, the very high interest rates (and priority repayment terms) Cuba had to pay for the small amounts of credit in convertible currency it still obtained, and the relatively weak performance of the Cuban economy in the second half of the 1980s.[77]

In the mid-1980s, Fidel Castro was vociferously calling for a complete cancellation of the 'unpayable' debt, or a debt strike by the developing nations. 'The formula proposed by Cuba is simple, understandable and perfectly feasible: that the governments of the developed creditor countries assume the debts of the Third World countries, with their own banks, and that 12 per cent of what is now invested in military expenditures be used to pay off the debts.'[78]

Meanwhile, in 1983, the Soviet premier Leonid Brezhnev shredded the defence guarantee, operative since the Cuban Missile Crisis of October 1962, that Soviet armed forces would defend Cuba.[79] This, together with the ratcheting up of aggression under the US presidency of Ronald Reagan from 1981, saw the Cuban government double the share of the state budget allocated to 'defence and international order' from 5.4 per cent in 1980 to 10.8 per cent in 1988.[80] As head of the Cuban armed forces, Raúl Castro began to reorganise Cuban defence along the lines of a people's war to resist a possible US attack.[81]

In 1985, Gorbachev took over as premier of the Soviet Union and the following year began to terminate all special deals between the USSR and other socialist countries. This included unilaterally ending the indexing between Cuban exports and USSR exports; the price paid for Cuban sugar exports was cut from 900 peso per ton to 850 (5.5 per cent). The international market price of sugar, at which Cuba sold a small proportion of its exports, had also plummeted after 1981. Soviet payments for Cuban nickel were similarly reduced, seriously impacting the island's revenues. Cuba suffered a 21 per cent decrease in terms of trade with the USSR. Exchange earnings fell by 50 per cent. Fidel Castro sought accommodation: in 1987 he went to the USSR and signed a communique with Gorbachev expressing mutual satisfaction over relations. Two years later in Havana, Gorbachev signed a 24-year 'Treaty of Friendship and Co-operation' in Havana. It was not worth the paper it was written on.

The situation in CMEA was described as 'critical' by Rodríguez who represented Cuba at the institution's meetings. The other member states proposed to follow the Soviet example and move to world market prices. 'This was being proposed in CMEA!' he exclaims. The Cuban representatives argued strongly against these proposals. 'I remember well the last meeting of the CMEA that took place in Czechoslovakia in 1991; the representatives of other countries practically paid no attention to the discussion, they started reading newspapers, chatting over here and over there. There was total decomposition.

There was practically no CMEA – there was no commitment, none!'[82] In August 1990, the USSR announced that trade and economic relations in general were to be conducted in free currency and at market prices from 1991. The decision was unilateral. The fate of CMEA was sealed. 'We jumped from preferential prices to market prices, from roubles to dollars. For Cuba this was a rupture, practically a cataclysm,' explains Rodríguez.[83] Cuba faced the additional burden of the US blockade to obstruct trade and access to financial resources. As a consequence, during Rectification the Cuban system underwent changes to the internal management system and its foreign economic relations simultaneously. The accumulation of all these factors produced a serious financial contraction between 1986 and 1990.

RECTIFYING CUBAN SOCIALISM

The journalist and historian of Cuba Richard Gott explained that:

> The new programme addressed three problems: the immediate need to deal with the foreign exchange crisis; the longer term need to restructure the economy to reduce the country's dependence on exports; and a more controversial and political need to rectify the previous strategy, replacing material incentives with the moral incentives once advocated by Che Guevara. The first and second problems involved technical solutions: the service of foreign debt was suspended, mechanisms were devised to re-establish centralised control of foreign trade and a campaign to promote non-traditional exports was started, as was an austerity programme.[84]

The third problem was a political one.

The 'austerity' programmes involved cuts in government spending: a reduction on state subsidies for electricity, transport and food, reduced food and textile supplies, cuts in meal provisions for government employees and 'rationalisation' of nursery meals, cuts in rural school transport, cuts in television broadcasting and a reduction in the interference caused by workplace meetings, sport and recreation. There were also cuts for state officials' quotas of petrol, cars, expenses and hard currency spending money whilst abroad.[85]

The Cuban state began to recentralise control over the economy, affording it greater capacity to economise on the use of foreign exchange and bring existing investment projects to completion.[86] In 1986, the private farmers' markets were closed down and farmers were instructed to sell produce to the state collective agencies (called *acopio*). A programme was introduced to increase state-controlled domestic food production, with the aim of both substituting food imports with locally grown produce and replacing the private farmers' markets' with food sold directly to the population at lower prices via state-run farmers' markets. By 1989, the growth of state markets had more than compensated for the loss of the private ones.[87] Private manufacturers and street vendors were stopped. In 1988 the National Assembly modified the housing law to curb profiteering by making the state a compulsory partner in the buying and selling of homes.[88] Homes could now be exchanged under a system of '*permuta*', with monetary compensation levels for differences in value determined by the state. Three million labour 'norms' and 14,000 job grades were revised.[89] Wages were increased, by 10 per cent for the lowest income bracket, which constituted 5 per cent of the workforce; pensions were raised for most of Cuba's pensioners – some 725,000 people. In 1988, 1,500 economists visited 370 loss-making state enterprises to seek solutions to high production costs and low efficiency.[90]

An important component of the Rectification process, explains Rodríguez, 'was to develop policies that addressed the deeper issue of searching for a more balanced means of managing the economy that combined economic mechanisms with appropriate political mobilization of workers'.[91] Essentially, it involved a return to *Guevarista* notions about moral incentives, consciousness and political participation, including the return to voluntary labour.[92] In 1987, around 12 per cent of the workforce (some 436,000 Cubans) carried out 40 hours of voluntary labour each.[93]

The construction microbrigades were resurrected to deal with the serious backlog of social infrastructure and residential housing needed by the population. In 1987, state entities (factories, enterprises or offices) were asked to send excess personnel to join them; one in eight workers were considered to be superfluous. Their colleagues who stayed put were expected to maintain output and meet the plan, despite the reduction in personnel, inevitably raising individual productivity in those workplaces. Each microbrigade had around 40 members, some full-time and others participating after the work day or at weekends. The state reimbursed the factory with the salary of the *microbrigadistas*, but instead of working 5 or 6 hours in their usual workplace, the *microbrigadistas* worked 10 or 12 hours a day, raising their own productivity and completing projects with a social function – mainly housing, but also nurseries, healthcare facilities, special schools and so on. Half of the housing units built went to the enterprises for their own workers. The state distributed the rest.

In October 1987, Fidel Castro announced that there were already 20,000 *microbrigadistas* in Havana. Sardonically, he declared: 'Our shoddy capitalists cannot say that their enterprises are being ruined; on the contrary, they can say: "they are helping the company, I am producing with 30, 40, 50 less men, I spend less salary". They can say "I will be profitable, or I will be less unprofitable, I will distribute more prizes and bonuses now since I have reduced the salary expense".' As a result of the microbrigades, he claimed, 'so many extraordinarily useful things are being done today, and the State promotes all these works without spending a penny more on salary'.[94]

Hammering the point, he stated:

You could ask the *mercachifleros* (market-lovers), the shoddy capitalists, those who have blind faith in the mechanisms and categories of capitalism: Could they perform that miracle? Could they build 20,000 homes in the capital without spending one penny more in salary? Could they build 50 nurseries in a year without a penny more in salary? When before that only 5 were planned for the 5-year period and they were not built, and when 19,500 mothers were waiting for a nursery that would never arrive because at the pace, the rhythm at which that enrolment capacity would be reached – we would need 100 years! By which time they would have died long ago.[95]

He declared that in 2 years 100 nurseries would be built in Havana and in 3 years over 300 would be built throughout the island, increasing childcare places to 70,000 or 80,000 without spending a penny more on salaries.[96]

Rectification also saw an acceleration in the transformation of private farms into cooperatives which had begun in 1977 with the Agricultural Production Cooperatives (CPAs), set up for private farmers who voluntarily joined lands and resources in order to raise efficiency. By late 1987, 71 per cent of non-sugar private farms had been be converted into collective forms; the proportion of the labour force made up by small private farmers had fallen slightly to 2.9 per cent.[97]

Cuba experienced some success at diversifying its trade and partners. The share of sugar and its by-products in Cuba's total exports declined from nearly 86 per cent in 1979 to just over 74 per cent in 1987.[98] On the assumption that relations with the USSR would continue to deteriorate, the government decided to open up to tourism in 1986, despite being wary of its social and political costs.[99] In 1988, the first joint venture with foreign capital was established, six years after the foreign investment law had entered the statute books. Annual average growth fluctuated in the second half of the 1980s, but the average between 1986 and 1989, when the Special Period was launched, was 0.6 per cent.[100] With the subsequent collapse of the Soviet bloc, obliterating 86 per cent of Cuba's trade and investment, things could only get worse.

In 1988, in the midst of Rectification, the People's Councils, a new institutional form of grassroots participation and engagement, were piloted before being rolled out nationally four years later. And, also in 1988, Fidel Castro inaugurated the Neighbourhood Transformation Workshops in Havana, organised by the Group for the Comprehensive Development of the Capital. The Workshops gathered half a dozen professionals, including architects, planners, social workers, to identify the main problems (usually housing) in their location and mobilise the neighbourhood and outside resources to address them.[101] This demonstrated an approach which became essential to monitor the state of Cuban communities, maintain a dialogue between them and state institutions and help direct resources to get them through the Special Period of economic crisis.

RECTIFICATION: A STEP TOWARDS SURVIVAL?

Colombian novelist Gabriel García Márquez apparently once said that the explanation for Cuba is that Fidel Castro is both head of the government and leader of the opposition: a fitting description for his role during Rectification. Did pulling away from the Soviet model prevent Cuba falling into 'the dustbin of twentieth-century socialist experiments'?[102] The emphasis on political mobilisation, on socialism as a conscious process of construction and self-transformation, the renewal of the link between the Cuban Communist Party and the people, were all key elements which pulled the revolutionary people of Cuba through the Special Period of economic crisis in the post-Soviet world. Had Fidel Castro not kicked back against the elevation of the profit motive and material incentives, how would the Revolution have fared when there was hardly a peso to spend on basic salaries, let alone incentives, and with the fiscal deficit rising to 35 per cent of GDP by 1992?[103] Had the state not endeavoured to substitute the private farmers' markets with state markets after 1986, would the hunger experienced by Cubans in the early 1990s have actually meant starvation? Had the most corrupt members of the Cuban Communist Party not been purged, had Fidel Castro not harangued Party militants, insisting that workers were at the centre of the socialist Revolution, might not the revolutionary people have turned on their leaders in revolt? Had Rectification not undermined the material basis of the rising 'new rich', could their economic clout have manifested as political opposition, a counter-revolution? Had Cuba not introduced tourism and biotechnology, begun diversifying trade partners and exports, initiating foreign investment, increasing its international reserves, would the economic catastrophe that resulted from the collapse of the Soviet bloc have been enough to tip the Revolution over the edge? Rectification reaffirmed the Cuban resolve to turn to state action, not market exchanges, as the best solution to Cuba's historical development challenges. In doing so it highlighted one of the durable paradoxes of the Cuban Revolution: relative political stability and resilience, along with continual reinvention and change.[104]

The process of Rectification may well explain *why* Cuban socialism was in a position to withstand the collapse of socialist regimes in the USSR and Eastern Europe, but to understand *how* the revolutionary people survived in a post-Soviet world we need to look at what happened during the 'Special Period in Time of Peace'.

2

★ ★ ★

SURVIVING THE CRISIS
THE SPECIAL PERIOD

Dusk was falling when Cuba's Commander in Chief took the podium in Agramonte Square, Camaguey, in summer 1989. Thousands of Cubans had gathered, despite the evening drizzle, for the annual 26 July celebration. Fidel Castro began by commenting on the threat of rain, a metaphor for the stormy times he foresaw ahead. Noting that US president George H. W. Bush had recently visited Poland and Hungary and was speaking in triumphant terms about the end of socialism, he declared: 'If we were to wake up tomorrow or any other day to the news that there had been a large-scale civil war in the USSR, and even if we were to wake up and learn that the USSR had disintegrated – something that we hope never happens – even under those circumstances, Cuba and the Cuban Revolution would continue struggling and resisting.' Nobody expected the Cuban Revolution to survive if the socialist world disappeared, he admitted, foreseeing a total blockade of the island that would not allow 'even a litre of fuel to enter, nor a morsel of food [to] enter the country'. In such a scenario, he affirmed, 'we know we would resist . . . In the event of invasion or occupation of the country by Yankee troops, we know how we could resist, how we could fight, and what we would do . . . we learned a long time ago how to count only on our own strength.'[1]

José Luis Rodríguez described Fidel Castro's words on that day as like a 'lightning bolt in a clear sky'. At that time, Rodríguez studied the Soviet Union at Cuba's Centre for Research into the World Economy (Centro de Investigaciones de la Economía Mundial – CIEM).[2] Despite his expertise, he told me that 'no one expected things to reach that point'. Events were fast moving, however. 'First to go was Poland in August 1989, one month after Fidel Castro spoke. In November 1989 it was the Berlin Wall. And then we had the domino effect among the countries of Eastern Europe, and the crisis of the USSR accelerated.'[3] On 19 August 1990, the Communist Party's daily newspaper *Granma* informed readers that the USSR had failed to deliver a number of essential contracted imports, especially oil, and that consequently a Special Period of extraordinary measures would be implemented to face the pending crisis.[4]

Thus, the island lurched into what is euphemistically known as the Special Period in Time of Peace, or the 'Special Period' for short. This implied a kind of war-footing, or crisis management, without military confrontation. While the Special Period is commonly described as a consequence of the disintegration of the USSR, it was actually introduced 16 months prior to that in response to Soviet premier Mikhail Gorbachev gradually withdrawing military and economic cooperation with the island. Gorbachev's successor from summer 1991, Boris Yeltsin, was completely hostile to Cuba. The socialist trading bloc, the Council for Mutual Economic Assistance (CMEA), was dismantled in autumn 1991.

The very survival of the socialist system was at stake. Cubans dug deep to find what they needed to survive, as individuals and as a socialist society. 'The whole community helped each other,' my teenage sister Susan wrote in 1994 after staying with a poor Cuban family in Marianao, just outside central Havana. 'But they're finding it harder to survive and to keep up their good will – it's the grinding point now, after five years of the Special Period. The black market is the only way to survive as rations decrease. There's hardly any food in the shops, to buy with pesos, and the monthly rations aren't enough.'[5] She described run-down buildings, street vendors everywhere, people selling homemade cakes, neighbours sharing a single tap of running water, growing class divisions based on access to dollars. The situation had slightly improved by autumn 1995 when, aged 18, I went to live in Cuba with my big sister until summer 1996. Like our Cuban neighbours, we sweated through 10-hour electricity blackouts, had our water supply switched off, cycled around Havana, hitch-hiked between provinces, breakfasted on stale bread rolls, lost weight, wearily wandered through near-empty farmers' markets, held on to plastic bags and biros like special possessions. Even with hard currency we struggled to find supplies.[6]

From the outset, the Cuban government ruled out the option of a transition to capitalism. Remaining socialist meant retaining a planned economy; it meant maintaining '*los logros*', welfare achievements, of the Revolution in health, education, public infrastructure and social services. But how to achieve this when the economy is in free fall, the US blockade is tightened and the island is politically isolated? The closer the Special Period is examined, the more remarkable the Revolution's survival into a post-Soviet world appears.

From the comfort of wealthy, consumerist countries, many commentators have struggled to accept or appreciate that, while the Cuban people suffered extremely difficult conditions, most Cubans did not seek the restoration of capitalism. Despite the scarcity and exasperation at inequalities introduced via access to dollars, 'they were prepared to live with it', as my sister observed. She noted that Cubans with better housing and more resources 'were more anti-Fidel and more angry at their current economic situation' than poorer Cubans. 'I was surprised how pro-Fidel many people without access to dollars were – they realise it's worth preserving the things they have.'[7]

In 1995, a university teacher invited Susan and me to give a talk to university students, historically a sector from more privileged backgrounds. We wrote about the experience: 'It was immediately obvious that they had a selective [positive] image of capitalism . . . They acknowledged the benefits of Cuban socialism but saw the introduction of capitalism as a means of regaining the circumstances they had lost [since the onset of the Special Period].' Meanwhile, the workers we spoke to in factories, schools or on the newly created cooperative farms remained committed. We asked some young workers in Coppelia ice-cream factory if they were prepared to accept capitalism: 'They told us they would not because they would lose everything – their jobs, social provisions and their dignity. One female engineer of 26, the head technician in the factory of 167 workers, told us: "I don't want capitalism, not even as a gift!"'[8]

Explaining the lack of notebooks for the pending school term, a primary school head teacher told us that 'the few resources we have are always shared equally between everyone' and was proud to point out that 'not one school in the country has been closed, and educators have tried to . . . elevate the quality of education'. The doctor at a children's day-care centre highlighted the importance of international solidarity and donations from other countries: 'We are blockaded but not isolated,' and another worker said the 'majority of Cubans will continue to fight so as to preserve and save all the gains of the revolution and freedom we have now'. Referring to the recent economic reforms, a farmer at one of the new agricultural cooperatives created out of state land told us: 'Some people thought that because of the changes Cuba would leave socialism. But this is a real revolution and real independence.' Our report concluded: 'Life in Cuba has begun to improve. Through our visits we have seen the determination of most of the Cuban people to overcome the current crisis and accept these changes in order to preserve the gains of the revolution.'[9]

Rodríguez attributes this resilience to political consciousness:

> a strong commitment to national sovereignty with an understanding of the
> benefits thirty years of the socialist Revolution had brought to Cuba in
> comparison with neighbouring third-world countries. This awareness was at
> the heart of the population's ability to tolerate extremely difficult economic
> conditions while remaining committed to building socialism, which they
> saw as the only road to authentic economic and social development in a
> world dominated by large capitalist powers and as necessary to maintain real
> national sovereignty.[10]

Cubans were close witnesses to the devastation wreaked on Latin American
populations during the military regimes which swept over the region from the
1970s and the neoliberal 'lost decade' of the 1980s to the 1990s. And, vitally
important, in the front trench was Fidel Castro, cajoling, explaining, persuading,
warning and rousing the revolutionary people of Cuba.

The Special Period became an enduring feature of Cuban reality. The austerity
and restraints that characterised it became the norm for Cubans on the island,
while millions of Cubans born since the 1980s are too young to understand
the nostalgia of the older generation whose personal narratives are divided into
the pre-Special Period time of plenty and post-Soviet life of sacrifice since then.
This chapter portrays the wide-ranging trauma incurred in the economic, social,
political, cultural and agricultural realms, examining how Cubans responded to
such an intense crisis and with what results. This recent past has moulded Cuban
development; deep scars have been left on the fabric of Cuban life, but the
calamity also impelled innovative advances which have shaped Cuba on its voyage
into the future. Thus, developments in contemporary Cuba can only be fully
understood with reference to both the crisis and the measures taken to address it.

There is no consensus about when the Special Period ended or, indeed, to
what extent it has ended. However, new campaigns and projects began to
define the Cuban experience with the Battle of Ideas initiated in 2000, so this
chapter recounts how the Cuban Revolution survived up to the turn of the
Millennium.

THE STATE OF THE CUBAN ECONOMY IN 1990

The structure of the Cuban economy made it particularly vulnerable to the
collapse of the socialist bloc and the USSR.[11] Cuba was among the most state-
controlled economies in the Soviet bloc, with a rigid planning system, state

ownership of most enterprises and only a handful of joint ventures between Cuban state and foreign firms.[12] One-fifth of the agricultural sector was in the hands of small private farmers and cooperatives and a tiny proportion of workers were self-employed, some 15,000 people. The state controlled prices and the financial sector, and had a monopoly on foreign trade. Cuba was heavily dependent on CMEA for trade and finance, most of which came from the USSR. CMEA supplied over 87 per cent of Cuba's imports and took over 86 per cent of its exports. Sugar accounted for 80 per cent of export earnings in 1990 and Cuba received three times the world market price within CMEA – generous, but a massive disincentive to diversify internal production and exports.[13] The island was heavily dependent on imports, including for 90 per cent of its oil needs, 80 per cent of its machinery and equipment and two-thirds of its foodstuffs. Oil and food imports accounted for 40 per cent of total import spending in 1990. Cuba's GDP per capita was below the CMEA average.[14]

Relations with CMEA had disguised internal structural problems in the Cuban economy and protected the island from the impact of the US blockade. Prior to that, Cuban access to the latest technologies developed in capitalist countries may have been frustrated, but the population could meet its basic needs through imports from CMEA. Almost overnight, Cuba became fully dependent on an international capitalist market dominated by a hostile superpower, the United States. The US blockade constituted a severe, additional economic constraint. According to Cuban estimates, it cost the island USD 15 billion dollars just between 1990 and 1995.[15] Hoping to topple the Revolution, the United States tightened the screws, approving three new punitive laws in 1990, 1992 and 1996 to strengthen the blockade, and expanding its extraterritorial imposition to prevent trade and financial relations between Cuba and the rest of the world, as outlined in Chapter 7.[16] This was the triumphant moment of western capitalism, described by US scholar Francis Fukuyama as 'the end of history'; few countries or companies could afford to defy US mandates in the world economy.

IMMEDIATE IMPACT

The extent of the crises cannot be overstated. GDP fell 35 per cent in three years, the scale of collapse usually associated with war, famine or a natural disaster. Between 1990 and 1993, manufacturing capacity was down by up to 90 per cent, construction down 74 per cent and agriculture 47 per cent. Overall imports fell by 75 per cent; imports of machinery and transportation equipment fell by 91 per cent, manufactured products by 70 per cent, fuels and lubricants by 65 per cent and food and oils by 51 per cent. Government spending nose-dived, on investment by 86 per cent, and on defence by 70 per cent. State administration was slashed with the elimination of 15 ministries. Real wages fell 50 per cent between 1989 and 1993 and both household consumption and average calorie intake fell by one-third.[17]

Meanwhile, nominal spending on health and welfare payments was maintained and there was a steep rise in the burden of subsidies to ensure the population's supply of basic goods and to protect employment. To shield Cubans from the shock, the government kept official prices, wages and the exchange rate fixed. Spending above their means was unsustainable, but it was also politically essential. Inevitably, with expenditure outstripping revenue, the fiscal deficit rose dramatically, from 10 per cent of GDP in 1990 to around 33 per cent in 1993.[18] This was the cost of preserving the socialist character of the Revolution. The government had no access to external finance and no domestic financial market. The deficit was fully monetised.[19]

By 1992, oil imports from Russia were reduced to a trickle: 1 million tons, down from 13 million tons imported from the USSR in 1989.[20] After that, not a drop of Russian oil was delivered. What country can operate without fuel? Inevitably, as Rodríguez says, 'This created an enormous crisis from 1992; blackouts, factories paralysed.'[21] Investment projects were abandoned, fuel allocations cut and public transport slashed. The planning system was thrown into chaos; supplies failed to arrive and enterprises had to stretch resources or concoct alternatives. Long-term planning was abandoned, although by 1993 medium-range planning resumed and proved essential in harvesting scarce resources and directing them to mitigate the social crisis through the distribution of materials, welfare and employment.[22] With production reduced and workers kept on the payroll, absenteeism soared and productivity nose-dived. The informal economy ballooned, creating opportunities and incentives for black market activities and for pilfering goods from the state sector. The greatest immediate beneficiaries were those engaged in illegal activities or in receipt of remittances from émigré families. The informal sector undermined the government's control over the allocation of scare goods and services.

The value of the Cuban peso (CUP) collapsed. With official prices fixed, the poorest Cubans suffered a reduction in the supply of state-allocated basic goods and services, but were not affected by price rises. In the informal economy, the value of the CUP fell by 95 per cent between 1990 and 1993, so the small proportion of Cubans who principally bought goods in hard currency faced a CUP inflation rate of around 2,000 per cent.[23]

'RESOLVIENDO'

The Cuban government responded to the crisis with emergency mobilisation to facilitate an organised collective response, a set of stabilisation policies and economic restructuring. In 1990, the Economic Defence Exercise involved factories, offices, households, schools and hospitals in rehearsing emergency responses to the loss of electricity and water supplies.[24] In December 1990, a Food Programme was launched to expand local food production for self-provisioning. In December 1991, the 'forum for spare parts' was re-established, 30 years after its creation by Che Guevara in the Ministry of Industries, for sharing local initiatives to recycle machinery and make substitutes for imported spare parts. In January 1992, an Energy Plan instructed households, enterprises and local authorities to cut fuel consumption. Agriculture was restructured and organic and urban farming introduced, as discussed below. Foreign trade was decentralised and many state exporting enterprises became self-financing, responsible for sourcing and paying for imports directly through export sales. Their surpluses were still used by the state to fund social services and imports for non-exporting productive enterprises. Decentralisation went further with new public stockholding companies set up to circumvent the US blockade.[25] The Communist Party was mobilised to organise a politically coherent response to the crisis.

Outside Cuba, economists argued that economic collapse was imminent and transition to capitalism inevitable. As Cuba's fiscal deficit soared, an informal delegation of IMF officials who visited the island concluded, in October 1993, that the 'time frame for decisive action' was up to six months and warned of hyperinflationary catastrophe if the required stabilisation measures were not introduced.[26] However, the Cuban government did not impose any package of reforms until seven months later, in May 1994, following months of nationwide debate to seek approval among the Cuban people. The much espoused 'shock therapy' was rejected outright.

MARKET MECHANISMS AND DE-DOLLARISATION

'We cannot guide ourselves by the criterion of what we like or dislike, but rather what is and is not useful for the nation and the people . . . We have said that we are introducing elements of capitalism in our system, in our economy, that is a fact. We have talked even of the consequences that we see from the use of such mechanisms. Yes, we are doing it,' announced Fidel Castro in 1995.[27]

Measures introduced between 1990 and 1994 sought to open space for market mechanisms to reactivate the economy but without renouncing its socialist tenets. Liberalising and stabilising reforms included: legalising the US dollar, fiscal adjustment, joint ventures with foreign capital, expanding tourism, converting state farms into cooperatives, opening private farmers' markets, and increasing self-employment, all of which are discussed below. 'All these measures,' explains Rodríguez, 'had clearly designed economic and political objectives that constrained their application: they would meet those objectives and go no further . . . the measures were always to be controlled so that they would not develop a momentum of their own that would gradually reintroduce capitalism, as the opponents of the Revolution hoped.'[28] Subsequent regulations in the 2000s that withdrew or modified many of these reforms vindicate Rodríguez's assertion.[29]

At his annual 26 July speech in 1993, the worst year of the Special Period, Fidel Castro announced that foreign currencies, specifically the US dollar, would be legalised.[30] Possession of the US dollar had been prohibited in Cuba since 1979. He made his distaste clear, warning of emerging inequalities as those in receipt of remittances would enjoy 'privileges that the rest do not have', something 'we are not used to'.[31] The black market use of the dollar was so widespread by 1993 that the government had concluded that prohibition was unworkable. Legalisation would transfer the benefits of using the dollar from individuals to the state, so everyone could benefit. It was a necessary component for opening up the tourism industry and harvesting dollars from tourists. Furthermore, with so many Cubans having relatives in the United States, the inflow from remittances could bolster the ailing economy. However, remittances also exacerbated historically rooted racial and class inequalities, as most recipients were white and better off, with relatives who had left in earlier, more politically motivated waves of emigration and were well established in the United States, or Europe, with adequate resources to send money back to Cuba.

US dollar transactions were permitted in the domestic economy and for personal use. Most basic necessities continued to be purchased in CUP, but luxury goods and supplementary basic goods available outside the ration card allotment were sold at 'hard-currency collection shops' (*tiendas recaudadoras de divisas*), known as 'dollar shops', at prices that included steep taxes.[32] Remittances fostered consumerism and the CCP Central Committee warned of the 'ideological contamination' introduced via dollars.[33] 'Cubans can now hold dollars,' wrote my sister in 1994, 'but they get secondary treatment in tourist shops. They're not allowed into hotels alone . . . mistaken for a Cuban I was sent to the back of the queue . . . they felt it's hard to be treated as second class citizens in their own country, but understood it was the only way to save Cuba in the face of the increasingly hard-line blockade.'[34]

Throughout the island, the government set up state-run 'exchange houses' (known as *cadecas*) which adopted the informal exchange rate of CUP 150 = USD 1 at the outset in February 1994. By mid-1996 this gap had fallen to CUP 18 = USD 1, and subsequently stabilised around CUP 24 to USD 1. The recovery of the CUP had an immediate impact on relative incomes, as the CUP value of USD 100 a month was reduced from 50 times to 10 times the average wage between 1994 and 1996.[35]

In the enterprise sector, accounting and exchange operations continued to function with an official exchange rate of CUP 1 to USD 1. This became problematic because it obscured losses and surpluses from their accounts, and removed incentives to increase exports. The enterprises' economic results appeared the same whether their produce was sold internally for CUP or exported for hard currency, even though the monetary value to the Cuban government was significantly different. For example, if a cigar factory sells 100 cigars for CUP 5 each within Cuba, it earns CUP 500 or USD 20. However, if it exports 100 cigars for USD 5 each, it earns USD 500. Foreign exchange transactions, meanwhile, continued to be controlled by the state and its trading enterprises.

In 1994, the Cuban government introduced a new convertible Cuban peso (CUC) to substitute the US dollar for use in Cuba at an exchange rate of one to one. The CUC was printed and controlled by the Cuban Central Bank. Gradually, use of CUCs outstripped US dollars, which were removed from circulation in 2004. The dual currency remained, however; dollars could be received and held but had to be exchanged for CUC to be spent in Cuba.

The dual currency divided the economy into two parts. Which branch any Cuban operated within depended on whether their income was exclusively from a state salary paid in CUP or they had access to dollars or CUC. Many Cubans had a foot in each sector. A Foreign Currency Incentive System allowed some workers to receive part of their pay in CUC.[36] By 1998, 35 per cent of Cuban workers received some remuneration in CUC.

Legalising the dollar deflated the black market and significantly increased hard currency inflows, which Cuba needed to operate on the international market.[37] The government scooped up hard currency through taxes and dividends from sales in state-owned US dollar shops. Sales mirrored the growth in remittances, which were estimated at between USD 400 and USD 800 million per year.[38] The dual currency also reassured foreign investors considering entering the Cuban market as they would be insulated from problems with the domestic currency.[39]

However, it also entrenched inequality and broke the link between work and remuneration. Incomes no longer depended on skill level, or the quantity or quality of formal work. Those with access to dollars could buy subsidised peso goods for a fraction of their market price *and* consume additional goods from dollar shops. Those dependent on peso incomes could not afford non-subsidised markets. State workers, including the most highly skilled, earned the lowest incomes.

NEW AGRICULTURAL COOPERATIVES

In 1993, state ownership of arable land was reduced from 75 per cent to 33 per cent as state land was distributed to workplaces and public institutions – enabling them to produce food for their own cafeterias and sell it cheaply to their workers – and to cooperatives and individuals. By 1996, over 43,000 individuals had been given land to farm in 'usufruct', a rent-free loan conditional on productive use.[40] Most state land, however, was converted into Basic Units of Cooperative Production (UBPCs), incorporating 272,400 members and occupying 42 per cent of the arable land by 1997; it was the first time since the Agrarian Reform Law of 1959 that the state had transferred land to the non-state sector.[41]

As cooperatives, the UBPC's retained a social character. They received land in usufruct, but owned what they produced. The state controlled the allocation of inputs and supervised employment. The UBPCs were obliged to sell set quotas to state entities at fixed prices, but from 1994 could sell surpluses in farmers' markets. Converting unprofitable and heavily subsidised state farms into cooperatives was intended to provide incentives to increase production in the context of food scarcity. Following the restructuring of land tenure, there were ten different forms of agricultural organisation in Cuba: four kinds of state farms, two types of collective non-state farms, three forms of individual non-state farms, and the mixed sector of joint ventures with foreign partners.[42] Foreign capital was only permitted in the state sector.

Despite the changes, Cuba's agricultural performance remained insufficient to enable a significant reduction in food imports. The reluctant introduction of the farmers' markets in 1994 was an additional incentive to increase food production during the Special Period.

FARMERS' MARKETS

The private farmers' markets, opened in 1980 to sell directly to Cuban consumers, had fostered the emergence of unproductive 'middlemen' who hiked up prices. Vehemently opposed by Fidel Castro, the markets were closed in 1986 during Rectification, as explained in Chapter 1. In the context of food scarcity in the early 1990s it was proposed to reopen them. The option was rejected at the Fourth Congress of the CCP in 1991 and the National Assembly of December 1993. Then, in September 1994, Raúl Castro suddenly announced that farmers' markets would be re-established.[43] It was a measure of desperation, coming one month after the (only) violent anti-government protest in Havana, which is described below. Farmers could sell produce surplus to their state quotas, an incentive to increase production. The markets were heavily regulated, inspected and taxed, with price restrictions to avoid the price hikes of the 1980s.[44] Competing state markets were established, including military-run ones, which undercut prices in the private markets. By March 1995, around 20 per cent of all agricultural products were sold through farmers' markets; informal exchange and prices had fallen.[45] Prices in the farmers' markets more than halved in the first five years. Nonetheless, food purchases could still account for two-thirds of the average Cuban salary by 2000.[46]

SELF-EMPLOYMENT

In September 1993, the number of activities in which Cubans could be self-employed was raised from 41 to 158. Licences were strictly controlled by the Ministry of Labour and renewed every two years. Priority was given to retirees, the disabled and the poorest applicants.[47] Self-employment shot up from 15,000 people to 208,000 within three years, sliding down to 157,000 by 2000 – around 4 per cent of the workforce. It offered a vocation to workers the state could no longer employ, tasked them with providing services the state could no longer offer, and formalised part of the informal economy so it could be taxed and regulated. Rodríguez explains: 'Legalising, regulating and taxing their employment meant that instead of these individuals being the only beneficiaries of their illegal economic activity, all of society would benefit'.[48] Self-employed workers paid one-third of their income in taxes. Income tax had been abolished for a generation in Cuba, now the state had to quickly re-establish a taxation apparatus.

Where did the self-employed get their supplies? The state had a monopoly on foreign trade but did not offer wholesale provision to the non-state sector. As Morris points out, the self-employed largely depended on the informal economy for supplies in the form of goods stolen from the state, diverted from the subsidised distribution system or brought into the country by visitors. Effectively the state was unwillingly subsidising the self-employed, who

47

generally had far higher incomes than workers in the state sector. In 2003, the self-employed earned nearly five times more, after tax, than workers in the state sector.[49]

Following the national consultation of 1993, measures were taken to improve the country's fiscal balance without introducing severe cuts to '*los logros*' (welfare programmes) of the Revolution. Subsidies to unprofitable enterprises were reduced, from CUP 5.4 billion in 1993 to less than CUP 800 million in 1995. The prices of, and tariffs on, some non-essential goods and services, such as tobacco and alcohol, were raised, generating a two-thirds growth in total revenue from sales taxes (an increase of CUP 2.7 billion). The new tax system also raised revenues for the state.[50] Cuba's fiscal balance was quickly restored, so that, from 1996, spending was allowed to rise in line with revenues.[51] By 1999, Cuba's budget deficit had fallen to 2.4 per cent of GDP, from 33 per cent five years earlier.[52]

FOREIGN INVESTMENT

Foreign investment is a particularly politically charged issue in Cuba. In the 1950s, US investors had controlled 90 per cent of the telephone and electric services, 50 per cent of public service railways and 40 per cent of raw sugar production.[53] In opposing foreign control, the revolutionary organisations of the 1950s bound the question of national sovereignty to anti-imperialism. In 1960, foreign properties, mostly of US interests, were nationalised. The Cuban Constitution of 1976 established that all land belongs to the state, except farmers' small holdings and agricultural cooperatives. In 1982, foreign investment was legalised, but only for joint ventures with the Cuban state, and it was another six years until the first mixed enterprise was established.

With the collapse of CMEA, Cuba had to turn to foreign investors for capital to replace depleted infrastructure and equipment. Raising capital from bonds and stocks was ruled out as they would expose the economy to international financial manipulation, especially given US economic aggression.[54] Foreign direct investment (FDI) was the cheapest way to raise capital and the only source available to Cuba, which is outside the IMF, the World Bank and other international financial institutions.[55] Thus, FDI was the only form of private capital inflow permitted. However, since 1986 there had been a moratorium on foreign debt repayments in freely convertible currency. Recognising that it would be difficult to secure FDI without renewing these debt repayments, the Fourth Congress of the CCP in 1991 agreed to seek negotiations to reschedule Cuban debt.[56]

Despite little progress being made in rescheduling existing debts, by late 1991 fifty joint ventures had already been set up and foreign investors were keen to enter what they assumed would be the next post-communist emerging market. It was possible to negotiate FDI contracts under the radar of the US blockade, which threatened legal action and fines levied against investors anywhere in the world. In July 1992 the Cuban Constitution was amended to state that mandatory state ownership applied only to the 'fundamental means of production'. Privatisation of public assets remained ruled out; only joint ventures with Cuban state companies were permitted. 'To ensure adherence to the economic development and national sovereignty objectives, each business deal was approved on a case-by-case basis [by the Council of Ministers or its Executive Committee], the subsurface and marine property rights of the Cuban state were reserved, and forms of economic association that would not compromise the sovereignty of national assets were extensively used,' explained Cuban economist Nancy Quiñones.[57] Foreign partners were expected to contribute the capital, new markets or technology and expertise, which Cuba lacked. FDI was to be controlled within the framework of the national development plan. In September 1995 a new investment law codified the new framework.

An employment agency was set up for Cubans working in joint ventures with foreign enterprises. Foreign partners paid state enterprises in hard currency, but Cuban workers received their salary, mostly in CUP, from the state. There were other perks, however: 'Access to technology, office supplies, and comforts (such as air conditioning) . . . firms would often award workers with needed "extras" that were hard to come by during the Special Period, such as clothes, toiletries and some specialty foods . . . [some] enterprises offered workers – both under the table and legally – at least part of their salaries in dollars,' wrote Miren Uriarte in a report for Oxfam.[58] Corruption increased with the penetration of foreign businesses and hard currency.

In 1997, the Fifth Congress of the CCP endorsed the existing policy, but reiterated that health, education and the defence sectors were out of bounds to foreign capital. With experience, Cuban negotiators imposed increasingly demanding criteria on foreign investors and there was a strategic shift away from less profitable contracts with smaller companies, or those considered insufficiently beneficial, towards larger, more capital-intensive projects, for example in mining, energy and infrastructure. Effectively this limited the sphere of operation of capitalist mechanisms introduced via foreign capital, diminishing their impact on Cubans as producers and consumers, whilst simultaneously strengthening the state's economic resources based on higher value-generating activities. Net FDI inflows were substantial, totalling USD 1.93 billion between 1993 and 2000 according to official figures.[59] Contracts came from Spain (23 per cent of contracts), Canada (19 per cent), Italy (9 per cent), France (4 per cent), demonstrating Cuba's success in diversifying trade partners.[60] The first 100 per cent foreign-owned enterprise was a Panamanian power plant. Joint ventures transferred technology, managerial skills and business knowledge to Cuba, all of which were essential for operating in the capitalist world market. The potential was massively obstructed by the US blockade, and the impact largely restricted to industries and products related to international trade, such as nickel, oil and tourism.

Despite having one of the world's three largest reserves of nickel, the collapse of CMEA resulted in a 60 per cent fall in Cuba's nickel earnings between 1990 and 1993. To reverse this, in December 1994, the Cuban government signed a joint venture with Canadian company Sherritt International, which provided capital and the new technology required to modernise, upgrade and expand industrial capacity. Nickel production and earnings were restored to pre-crisis levels within two years and were 50 per cent higher by 2000.[61] By then, Sherritt International had formed another joint venture with Cuba's state oil company, CUPET, to raise domestic oil production, which met only 6 per cent of the island's domestic needs in 1990. Oil imports accounted for 38 per cent of total import spending in 1994, thus import substitution was urgent to save scarce hard currency. Sherritt provided the cleaner technology which the government required to exploit its oil reserves without contaminating the nearby tourist resort of Varadero. By 2000, domestic oil production met over 35 per cent of Cuba's needs in oil and gas, saving some USD 850 million in import costs.[62]

For many Cubans, the pre-1959 tourism industry symbolised the island's humiliating semi-colonial status, facilitating exploitation, prostitution, gambling, corruption and racism. While there was little enthusiasm for developing tourism, there were strong incentives to do so. First was the attractiveness of Cuba as a destination; second, the sector is less capital-intensive than other options and generates rapid returns on investment bringing in foreign exchange and attracting foreign capital to build the industry more quickly than Cuba's capital resources would allow; third, it provides substantial employment. So the industry was begun in earnest and between 1998 and 2003 tourism was Cuba's largest source of foreign revenue. Gross revenue in 2000 from the tourist industry alone accounted for 40 per cent of total earnings from goods and services.[63] The sector diversified to foster health, solidarity, cultural and eco-tourism. Within the decade, tourist arrivals had soared from less than 250,000 to nearly 2 million despite the US government maintaining its ban on tourism in Cuba.[64]

Direct foreign ownership proved to be a red line for the Cubans: a proposed law giving foreign investors ownership rights in Cuba was rejected after consultation with trade unions and CCP members in 2000.[65] Meanwhile, the lifespan of four free trade zones established between 1997 and 1998 to foster and diversify manufacturing for export and provide employment was cut short after it was found, in 2004, that only 1 in 15 participating companies were manufacturing enterprises. The zones were redesignated as 'development zones' promoting productive, rather than commercial, activity, and non-productive companies operating there were closed down or moved away.[66]

ECONOMIC RESTRUCTURING

'Qualitatively, in less than twenty years the Cuban economy radically transformed itself,' wrote Cuban economist Quiñones.[67] While resisting a transition to capitalism, the Cuban government undertook a major structural transformation of the economy. The island had to be reinserted into the global economy on the basis of new export products and markets developed almost from scratch, with restricted access to external financing and with the US blockade strengthened. Within one decade sugar exports fell as a proportion of all goods' exported from 80 per cent to 26.7 per cent, and to just 4 per cent of all exports when services are included.[68] Sugar was replaced by mining, tobacco and medical products.[69] The export of Cuban services soared, from 10 per cent of total exports in 1990 to 70 per cent by 2005.[70] Initially this was due to tourism, a service export, but from the early 2000s, the export of medical and other professional services, mainly to Venezuela, soared.[71] Simultaneously, the shift in trade partners was almost total. In one decade, Cuban exports to non-CMEA countries increased from 10 per cent to 90 per cent of total exports.

The banking and finance system was restructured to facilitate the introduction of market mechanisms domestically and interaction with international capitalist markets.[72] One of the few financial experts with experience in global financial markets, Francisco Soberon, was appointed head of the National Bank of Cuba in 1994. In 1997, this became the Central Bank and a new financial system was established with a set of 'autonomous' state-owned banking corporations, competing for business domestically and able to form joint ventures with foreign partners. The overdue debt was placed on the books of a separate bank, so the new ones started with a clean slate.[73]

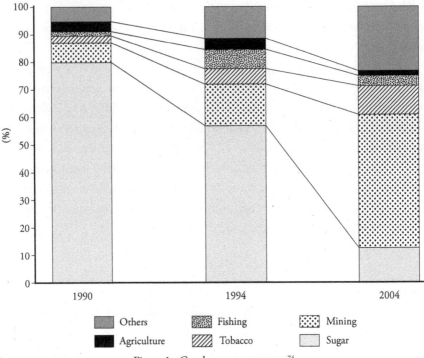

Figure 1. Goods exports structure[74]

The shift from the Material Product System of national accounts, used by the socialist planned economies, to the United Nations System of National Accounts, with profit and loss and GDP measurements, required extensive retraining for ministry officials and enterprise managers. Subsidies to enterprises had been cut by up to 90 per cent, leaving many without capital, equipment, energy and inputs. A group of enterprises were transformed into semi-autonomous profit-seeking state corporations open to FDI. In August 1998, the Enterprise Perfection System (EPS) of economic management expanded nationally. This had been developed within the Ministry of the Revolutionary Armed Forces (MINFAR) enterprises during Rectification. Enterprises had to meet a checklist of specific modern operational criteria. They had greater autonomy in planning and securing imports, while the old Central Planning Board (JUCEPLAN) was replaced in 1995 with a new slimmed down Ministry of the Economy and Planning, with half the number of employees.

EMPLOYMENT

The importance of employment in revolutionary Cuba is more than an economic question. First of all, low monetary wages do not determine the standard of living, or level of consumption, because the state provides and heavily subsidises so much of what in most countries must be purchased with a wage.[75] Second, in the context of socialism, the political and social functions of employment are as, if not more, significant than the remuneration. Work is a means of political participation, of contributing to social development and of distributing social benefits. Employment facilitates an individual's links to society. This explains the decision, during the Special Period, to avoid mass redundancies. With most workers in the state sector, the government had tight control over employment, but policy had to be coordinated with the important national trade union confederation (Central de Trabajadores de Cuba, or CTC), which brings together 19 formerly independent trade unions, representing almost all workers. Cuban trade unions have leverage over policy.

The decision was taken to keep state workers on the payroll, or temporarily laid off on 60 per cent of their salaries until alternative employment could be found. The burgeoning tourism industry absorbed excess workers, including employees of the armed forces and the Communist Party, the first institutions to undergo severe cuts. Spending on the military was halved between 1989 and 1993, with personnel slashed to one-fifth by the end of the decade.[76] Military historian Hal Klepak explains: 'Air force pilots were given tasks as pilots for tourist firms, army drivers for car hire companies, and naval personnel for yacht hire. More officers were sent to rapid courses in management techniques before being sent to head companies.'[77] The number of central government administrative bodies was cut from 50 to 30.[78]

Inevitably, with workers kept on payrolls while production ground down, labour productivity plummeted, except in sectors where FDI raised efficiency, such as tourism and nickel. Equipment no longer attainable was replaced by manpower in some sectors, such as agriculture and health. Incredibly, between 1990 and 1993, while GDP fell 35 per cent, employment in Cuba actually rose by 40,000 and the official unemployment rate fell from 5.4 to 4.3 per cent.[79]

This unprecedented profile (shown in the graph below), unlikely to be seen in any capitalist economy, can only be understood in terms of the function of employment in a socialist country. The policy also mitigated against internal migration.[80] Salaries necessarily remained very low, to facilitate near-full employment. This acted as an incentive for Cubans to enter either the informal

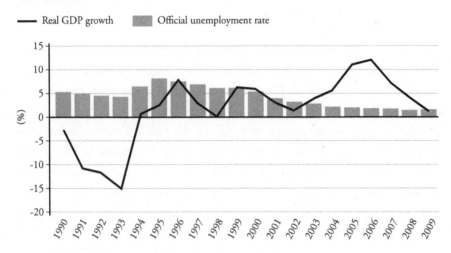

Source: Oficina Nacional Estadísticas.

Figure 2. Unemployment and real GDP growth

economy or the formal non-state sector; employment in the latter rose to 22.5 per cent of total employment by 2000.[81]

Women are invariably most adversely affected by austerity. Many Cuban women left employment because they considered the cost of getting to work and the increased burden of domestic tasks outweighed any salary incentives.[82] In 1995, the Federation of Cuban Women (FMC) began training courses in economics for women. A specialist in the women's economy, Blanca Munster, explained: 'We realised that women themselves had to be transformed, women themselves had to be trained ... From women intellectuals to farmers, to industrial workers – we have seen a radical change and a new kind of involvement in the transformation process: they are more active, not passive subjects.'[83] Child labour never emerged, although by hassling tourists for money in the street a child could take home more in one day than their parents' state salary in one month.[84] 'Children kept asking us for chewing-gum and baseball caps in the streets,' wrote my sister in 1994, noting that it was not food they asked for, but 'the kind of commodities they thought tourists would have'.[85]

Cuba's economic contraction was halted and reversed by 1994. The fiscal deficit was reduced from 33 per cent in 1993 to around 2 per cent by 1996 and access liquidity was rapidly reduced.[86] Growth averaged 4 per cent in the second half of the 1990s.[87] Still, living standards had not recovered their 1990 level by the end of the decade, productive capacity, infrastructure and public services had been crippled, and the dual economy and price distortions had skewed incentives and entrenched inequalities. The economic contraction generated a social crisis. Cuts in food consumption, utility supplies, basic goods and transport led to malnutrition, emigration, inequality and illegality. However, the allocation of basic goods and the labour market continued to operate under a central plan, delivered through existing state institutions to alleviate the crisis.

THE SOCIAL SPHERE

'Where Cuba differed from other countries undergoing liberalising reforms, was the political will to shield the population from the most pernicious of these effects as well as from the impact of the crisis itself,' observed Uriarte. 'Cubans sought to maintain the basic values of the Cuban social policy: universality, equitable access, and government control.'[88]

Compelled by conditions, the Cuban revolutionary government had introduced the ration, or *libreta*, in March 1962 and for nearly thirty years it provided the basic basket of goods at highly subsidised prices that were affordable even to the poorest Cubans. During the Special Period, the content of the *libreta* was slashed and by 1993 nutritional intake had dropped by one-third per person and the average adult lost 5.5kg in weight.[89] Half of all children aged between 6 and 12 years suffered from iron deficiency, according to UNICEF. However, the most severe weight loss was experienced by those who could most tolerate it; so, while the proportion of the population underweight rose from 8 per cent in 1991 to 10.3 per cent in 1995, the fall in obesity was sharper: from 14.3 per cent of the population to 7.2 per cent by 1995.[90] The silver lining was a decline in diabetes and heart disease accompanying that weight loss.[91] While hunger was widespread, state distribution of resources and services prevented starvation. There was, however, a 50 per cent increase in deaths from infectious diseases (tuberculosis, typhoid and diarrhoea) and parasites between 1990 and 1993.[92] Immune systems were weakened by malnutrition, producing an epidemic of neuropathy which hampered the vision and affected the legs of over 50,000 Cubans.[93]

Housing construction and repairs were paralysed. Deteriorating conditions and overcrowding became a feature of life, particularly in Havana where growing families draped curtains across a single room to provide the semblance of privacy. Regular electricity blackouts lasted 8 to 12 hours, leaving families in the dark and humid heat without air fans, televisions or working fridges. Students did homework by candlelight, when candles could be found. The immense stress all this placed on families is evident in the sudden rise in divorce as the crisis peaked.[94] To avoid fatalities, architects visited all buildings, ready to move families out of houses in danger of imminent collapse. Living there at this time, we would occasionally notice the skyline had changed after a building collapsed, although we never heard of casualties.

Public transport was decimated in cities and rural areas. Cubans walked miles to work and back under the searing sun. The government imported 1.2 million Chinese bicycles and manufactured half a million more, distributing them to a Caribbean population with no tradition of cycling. Professionals, party officials, factory workers – everyone got to work on a bike. It was not unusual to see two policemen, workmates or a family of four balanced on the frames and back wheel racks.[95] An official system of collective hitch-hiking, or carpooling, was established; state-owned vehicles were obliged to pick up passengers at highway junctions. Less formal hitching became a way of life throughout the country; hitchers lined the main roads in Havana waiting for a ride. Old trucks were converted into buses with metal benches and steps welded onto the back. In cities, trucks were melded with buses, to make the famous camel buses, which could cram in 300 people. In small towns and cities, people turned to horses for transportation.

Always resourceful, Cubans increasingly sought imaginative solutions to scarcity and need, known as *inventos*: 'Nothing was wasted . . . old construction nails were straightened for reuse; every scrap of wood was saved . . . "*No es facil*" (it's not easy), a favourite phrase, took on a whole new meaning.'[96] As a substitute for toilet roll, which was often scarce or too expensive, most Cubans used the daily newspapers or ripped out pages from old books. Plastic bags, pens, notebooks were precious resources and knowledgeable foreign visitors brought them, along with soap, toothpaste and multivitamins, for Cuban friends.

It was in the context of this deprivation that thousands of Cubans risked the choppy, shark-infested waters in makeshift rafts (*balsas*) to reach the United States, where Cuban immigrants held a privileged status. In 1990, 467 Cuban rafters were picked up at sea by the US Coastguard. In 1993, 3,656 rafters were picked up. In the summer of 1994, thousands of Cubans launched themselves into the precarious waters. On 5 August that year, two policemen were killed stopping hijackers from seizing a ferry in Havana harbour, sparking the most significant anti-government demonstration in Cuba since 1959. Crowds gathered on the Malecon, the broad esplanade, roadway and seawall that runs along the Havana coast. My sister happened to be there and reported: 'We heard people smashing windows, and police shooting into the air to disperse the crowd. When we came back, there were two groups of maybe 600 people. One group was those who'd had enough of the problems – there'd been a real tension in Havana, and it was as if it had burst. The others were workers from the rural areas who'd parked their vans in the streets to stop too much movement and were all set to stop the trouble. The police were there, but participated less than the workers . . . It was all shown on television.'[97] The event became known as the 'Maleconazo'.

Fidel Castro headed to the scene, ordering his bodyguards not to fire.[98] Footage shows him addressing the crowd: 'We are in a Special Period . . . one of the most difficult periods of our history. Why? Because we've been left alone to confront imperialism. Alone. What is needed to confront imperialism alone?' People in the street and on balconies shout 'unity', Fidel continues: 'It requires unity. It requires courage. It will need patriotism, it requires revolutionary spirit. Because a weak people, a cowardly people, surrenders and returns to slavery. But a dignified people, a courageous people, like ours, does not surrender, will never return to slavery.'[99] That same day, Fidel Castro called on the people to come out in remembrance of the policemen who had been killed. 'So on the Sunday morning the CDR (Committees for Defence of the Revolution) across the road got the whole community around and we went down there with thousands of other people, young and old,' my sister wrote.[100]

Following another deadly hijacking several days later, Fidel Castro announced that Cuban police would no longer stop people leaving Cuba unless they were hijacking boats or planes. LeoGrande and Kornbluh explain what happened next: 'Now free to go, Cubans streamed to the beaches with small boats, rafts, inner tubes, and cars outfitted with pontoons in place of tires, to set out on the perilous ocean journey. Their numbers were staggering . . . the *balsero* crisis was under way.'[101] The US administration panicked about the influx and announced that, for the first time since the 1960s, Cuban rafters picked up at sea would not be immediately permitted into the United States. Instead they were to be taken to the US Naval Base in occupied Guantanamo Bay to be processed. The announcement failed to halt the exodus. In early September 1994, the United States and Cuban governments reached an agreement to halt the crisis. The United States would issue 20,000 visas annually for Cubans to travel to the United States legally, plus 6,000 additional visas to Cubans on the long waiting list, and Cuba would restore its coastguard operations to prevent illegal departures from the island.[102]

The rafters' crisis took Cuba's most impatient and restless citizens, mostly young males, off the island. Over 45,000 Cubans arrived in the United States between 1990 and 1994, including those processed through Guantanamo Naval Base, plus 15,675 who travelled to the US with a temporary visa but never returned.[103] However, the Maleconazo and the rafter crisis never spiralled into a political revolt as military historian Hal Klepak pointed out, 'Neither the FAR [Revolutionary Armed Forces] nor even important police resources were ever needed in an internal security role.'[104] A decisive factor was a 34 per cent increase in the share of Cuba's GDP spent throughout the 1990s on social programmes, cushioning the population from the worst effects of economic crisis.[105]

ALLEVIATING THE SOCIAL CRISIS

From the outset, the revolutionary government's response to the crisis put social need at the centre. The Food and Nutrition Surveillance System (Sistema de Vigilancia Alimentario y Nutricional) monitored nutrition, allocated supplementary rations, and maintained a network for mothers and babies after a slight rise in low-birth-weight babies was detected from 1992 and of pregnant women with insufficient weight gain during pregnancy.[106] State welfare agencies worked within the new Peoples' Councils (Consejos Populares), established in 1991, to identify 'at risk' households and individuals in order to administer relief programmes.[107]

While GDP contracted by one-third, total government spending rose from an already high 68 per cent to 90 per cent of GDP between 1990 and 1993. Spending on social security and welfare increased by 29 per cent between 1990 and 1994.[108] There was a rise in subsidies for employment protection and food security. The prices of essential goods were fixed, despite the shortages, and the cost of the ration was affordable even to those on minimum social security allowance. In 1994 my sister recorded that: 'On ration day there was a carnival atmosphere. I was woken up early, given a glass of water and sugar, and we went by bike to pick up the allowance of bread, coffee, sugar and other goods. It was also washing day, because the ration of soap had come.'[109]

In the 1930s, Cuba had been among the first Latin American countries to introduce a state pension. Under the revolutionary government this was completely state funded. The retirement age was 55 for women and 60 for men. There were also disability pensions. By 1995, some 1.35 million Cubans were receiving a state pension, over 12 per cent of the population, and it was raised from CUP 83 in 1990 to CUP 107 in 1997, so the decline in real terms was less steep than for those earning wages. The government also provided targeted social assistance through cash subsidies and special services to the most vulnerable sectors of society.[110]

Cubans are proud to say that no school or hospital was closed during the Special Period. Nonetheless, the structural conditions of public infrastructure deteriorated in the absence of construction materials and investment funds. Medical equipment broke or became obsolete, medicines and disinfectants were scarce. An effort was made to compensate for this with increased medical personnel. Health spending rose 13 per cent and 15,380 medical professionals joined the service between 1990 and 1994, raising the doctor to patient ratio from 1 for every 276 inhabitants to 1 for every 202. Between 1990 and 2003, the number of Cuban doctors increased by 76 per cent, dentists by 46 per cent, and nurses by 16 per cent.[111] Remarkably, infant mortality declined from 10.7 per 1,000 in 1990 to 7.2 in 1999, while life expectancy rose from 75 to 75.6 years despite the crisis.[112] Meanwhile, education spending declined by 18 per cent, leading to falling school attendance and a reduction in the numbers of teaching staff; university enrolment fell from 21 per cent in 1990 to 12 per cent in 1996.[113] In two years, 1993 to 1994, 8 per cent of teachers left education for the tourist industry.[114]

INEQUALITY AND ILLEGALITY

The principles of Cuba Socialista were eroded by a palpable rise in inequality, crime, prostitution and individualism. While the majority of the population suffered a fall in their standard of living, a minority benefited from the market openings. They were not Communist Party or military officials, nor bureaucrats; the highest paid officials could afford little beyond the basic basket. Prior to the Special Period, Cuba's highest salaries, earned by professionals such as doctors or engineers, were 4.5 times those of the lowest-paid workers.[115] During the crises, however, as Cuban economist Vallejo wrote, 'The most negatively affected segments of the population were precisely those most connected with the essence of Cuban socialism.'[116] The monetary value of their qualifications fell, causing dissatisfaction and frustration.[117] Many highly qualified Cubans left their professions for jobs with access to CUCs and a higher level of consumption such as tourism, taxi driving, the black market or joint ventures. The beneficiaries were those operating in the informal sector and those with access to hard currency. By 1993, a Cuban receiving USD 100 a month in remittances could exchange their income for 40 times the average nominal monthly peso income. A black-marketer could earn ten or more times this amount – a massive incentive to operate illegally.[118] The result was socioeconomic fragmentation and the emergence of new social groups with high levels of income and consumption relative to the average levels in the population.[119]

Legislation was introduced to limit the potentially destructive impact of the material competition entering Cuban relationships at the grassroots level and to prevent exploitation or the accumulation of capital. For example, to prevent the emergence of a sex-tourism industry, Cubans were prohibited from staying in hard currency hotels unless married to a foreigner. The phenomenon of illegal and semi-legal activities known as *jineterismo* became widespread in tourist destinations as 'hustlers' and opportunists sought hard currency or consumption goods from tourists. This became conflated with prostitution, which also spiked. While alarming, these activities were effectively tolerated by the state, the police and the population. A new decree in August 1997 criminalised pimping, but not prostitution: 'A person who sells his or her body will not be punished, but those making personal gain or benefiting in any way from acts of prostitution will face sanctions.'[120] The problem of pimping was exposed in the daily newspaper of the Union of Young Communists (UJC), *Juventud Rebelde*. The Cuban Women's Federation (FMC) and Committees for Defence of the Revolution (CDR) worked with prostitutes to retrain and reintegrate them to their home communities; it was estimated that 70 per cent of those in Havana came from other provinces.[121] Those suspected of being in Havana to work as prostitutes or otherwise hustle tourists were often asked by police to show their identity cards to reveal their permanent place of residence. This was part of an attempt to stem the tide of internal migration and prevent illegality, but it also led to accusations of police harassment and discrimination.

CULTURE SHOCK

Since its beginning, wrote the US poet and writer Margaret Randall, Cuba's revolutionary government invested in, and nurtured participation in, the arts, establishing cultural houses in every town and city. 'Cuba,' she says 'fought the US cultural blockade with the same tenacity it fought its diplomatic and economic counterparts. It established important cultural institutions, hosted conferences and symposiums and invited intellectuals and artists from around the world to visit the island, and supported its own creative minds.'[122] Cuban artists were insulated from the pressures of commercialisation through state support. Cuban director, Gerardo Chijona, described Cuban filmmakers as 'the spoiled children of Latin American cinema'.[123] The state guaranteed financial backing for cinema production, including salaries, while affording creators a degree of autonomy. The situation was replicated throughout the arts.

During the Special Period, cutbacks in state support and resources, along with the introduction of market mechanisms, impacted upon Cuban culture.

'Filmmakers with no experience in the funding process outside the state subsidy system had to adapt, learning to navigate international partnership and financing systems,' explained Cristina Venegas.[124] The proliferation of hard currency and tourism shaped sexual and business relationships and was reflected in emigration and remittances. The question of ownership over Cuban cultural identity was complicated with a growing diaspora benefiting from the globally rising popularity of that identity. In 1997, the Buena Vista Social Club album was released by US and British music producers to worldwide acclaim; it starred an ensemble of 'forgotten' Cuban musicians resurrecting music from pre-revolutionary Cuba. Cuban music had found an international mainstream market.

Writing about Cuban culture in the Special Period, Hernández-Reguant referred to 'Havana's new showbiz elite' that had emerged with the increasing marketisation of culture, while artists and artisans were among those who 'got richer' by being 'plugged into transnational economic networks'.[125] In the state-owned publishing sector, the sudden and severe lack of resources saw an implosion of publications. A tension emerged between 'true literature' and 'literary tourism' for voyeuristic consumption by foreigners. Even the increase of religious observance over the Special Period was partly connected to the new economic openings, according to Kevin Delgado who observed that the practice of Santería (an Afro-Cuban religious tradition) in cities was particularly subject to commercialisation, as 'some Cubans convert spiritual and cultural capital into financial capital'.[126] When foreigners paid to participate, financial exchanges commodified the practices of Santería. Meanwhile, the emerging Cuban hip hop movement was given space to breathe by the new young Minister of Culture Abel Prieto, who bought the 'counter-culture' into the Cuban cultural mainstream with state support for forums and artists.[127] Prieto afforded Cuban artists more autonomy in licensing their works abroad and travelling internationally, and in promoting art and culture which could be understood as critical or challenging to the status quo.

FROM INDUSTRIALISED AGRICULTURE TO URBAN AND ORGANIC FARMING

By the 1980s, Cuban agriculture was the most industrialised in Latin America, using more fertiliser proportionally than the United States. The island had adopted the 'Green Revolution', a model of mechanised agriculture practised on its predominant state-farms, relying on natural-gas-based fertilisers, oil-based pesticides and diesel-powered machinery, almost all of which were imported. The island used 90,000 tractors.[128] Yields were high, but production was directed towards exports (sugar, tobacco and citrus), while two-thirds of foodstuffs consumed by Cubans were imported.[129] Under this model, the island was unable to feed its own population. And *then* the crisis hit.

The dramatic fall in imports, including fuel, agrochemicals, agricultural equipment, spare parts, seeds, animal feed and vaccines, had a catastrophic impact on food production, which fell to 55 per cent of pre-crisis levels by 1994.[130] Food imports were also halved. How was the island to feed itself? Even when families had food, electricity blackouts rendered fridges useless for preserving it.

The first goal was to keep the population alive. This was facilitated by the existing means of distribution: the ration book, reduced but maintained, and *vias sociales* (social means), including free meals in workplaces and health and educational facilities. By the end of the decade, the *libreta* provided two to three weeks of basic consumption based on United Nations minimum monthly caloric intake, with subsidised food in workplaces raising this from three to four weeks.[131] Vulnerable groups received additional or specialised supplements. While food imports and formal food production halved, average calorie intake fell one-third between 1990 and 1993. The disproportional decrease reveals that informal food production and markets had expanded.[132]

While their tractors rusted without fuel or parts, Cuban farmers returned to the use of oxen for turning soil and planting crops. Experienced older farmers set up training schools and in just over one year most cooperatives had someone training in the use and breeding of oxen.[133] Cuban research centres had begun studying sustainable agriculture before the crisis, so the state quickly channelled this work into replacing the chemical inputs no longer available with locally produced biopesticides and biofertilizers.[134] In 1961, the Association of Small Farmers had been set up to organise, represent and assist farmers in the non-state sector, providing training, resources and sharing new approaches. In 1996, it added 'sustainability' to its goals and promoted agro-ecological farming techniques nationwide.

ORGANIC AND URBAN FARMS

Visiting the Armed Forces Horticultural Enterprise in December 1987, Raúl Castro had been impressed by how 'the engineer Anita' was growing vegetables without using petrochemicals. Anita had constructed an '*organopónico*'; a rectangular walled construction, thirty metres by one metre containing raised beds of a mixture of soil and organic materials. The method was subsequently adopted in armed forces' facilities.[135] The first civilian *organopónico* was set up in Havana four years later, just after the breakup of the USSR.[136] *Organopónicos* are a Cuban invention, ideal for growing crops on poor soils in small urban spaces, be they building sites, vacant lots, roadsides or sloping lands. The raised beds can produce vegetables all year round and achieve good yields.[137]

Meanwhile, Cubans without prior experience took over vacant land in the city to grow food, launching the local 'urban gardening' movement, which saw parcels of wasteland, many informally used as rubbish dumps, transformed into lush green productive areas. In city gardens the soil is planted directly. The process brought neighbours together and, subsequently, gave purpose and employment to thousands. Cubans converted their own backyards to grow fruit, vegetables and condiments and raise small animals, such as poultry. Cubans without access to land, or time to cultivate it, began growing food on balconies and rooftops.[138] The government endorsed the movement, encouraging its expansion and providing training to improve yields.[139]

In 1994, an Urban Agriculture Department (UAD) was formed to work with provincial and municipal organisations to secure an adequate and sustainable supply of food to urban areas, particularly Havana. The UAD aimed to provide fresh, low-cost, healthy food, encourage community activities, create a safe urban atmosphere, generate employment and economic growth, and to reduce energy and oil usage, pollution and waste output.[140] The motto was 'produce while learning, teach while producing, and learn while teaching'.[141] An urban agriculture representative from the Ministry of Agriculture was incorporated into every one of Cuba's 1,400 Peoples' Councils. The use of agrochemicals in urban gardens was prohibited by law.

Among the most successful *organopónicos* was Vivero Alamar, created in 1997 on abandoned wasteland 8 kilometres east of Havana's centre. Monty Don, the BBC television presenter of *Gardeners' World*, described the Alamar *organopónico* as a vision of heaven, 'wonderful vegetables grown organically, it looks beautiful, people all working together from the community, growing them, earning a living, eating them and caring about it'.[142]

Havana led the way and, in 1998, the National Urban Agriculture Group was set up to promote local food self-sufficiency nationally. Urban agriculture programmes had 28 sub-programmes, in crops, animal husbandry, organic manures, seeds, irrigation and drainage, marketing and technical education. Within 12 years, 350,000 new, paying and productive jobs (some 7 per cent of the workforce) were created through those programmes, including for retirees, mothers or young people, who would otherwise have been unemployed.[143]

Being local and smaller scale, urban agriculture minimised machinery use and reduced transport costs. The idea was 'food production in the neighbourhood, by the neighbourhood and for the neighbourhood'. The quantity of land cultivated and yields rose quickly. Production of vegetables and fresh herbs jumped a thousand-fold from 4,000 tons in 1994 to 4.2 million in 2005. The produce was sold directly to consumers from local stands and farmers' markets. Tons of food were donated to schools, old peoples' homes, maternity homes, other local social institutions and neighbours in need. The savings made with the switch to organic vegetables was estimated to be USD 39.5 million per tonne of produce, while the cost of pest control fell to 9 per cent of its previous level.[144] By the early 2000s Cuba was exporting biopesticides and biofertilisers to Latin America.

By 2006, when Cuba was recognised as the only nation in the world living sustainably, 80 per cent of the island's agricultural production was organic and the annual use of chemical pesticides had fallen from 21,000 tonnes in the 1980s to 1,000 tonnes (a 95 per cent reduction), with petrochemicals used only in sugar, potatoes and tobacco production.[145] Researcher Sinan Knoot concluded that Cuba had become the only country in the world to produce most of its food locally, employing agro-ecological techniques for production.[146] Urban agriculture accounted for nearly 15 per cent of national agriculture, occupied 87,000 acres of land and was meeting over 50 per cent of the total vegetable needs of Havana's population of 2.2 million inhabitants.[147] In smaller cities and towns, urban agriculture met 80 to 100 per cent of the population's fruit and vegetable requirements. Calorie intake had recovered its pre-crisis level by 1999 and continued to rise. Monty Don concluded: 'The Cubans have created a working model for the future we all face. In the middle of a large city, with practically no money and no resources, they are producing fresh, organic fruit and vegetables by and for local communities, not industrially, but in the garden.'[148]

POLITICAL PARTICIPATION AND COMMUNITY MOBILISATION

The Cuban leadership recognised that survival of the Cuban Revolution depended on securing commitment to the socialist project from the general population. That commitment, and the sacrifices implied, could not be induced through repression. The leadership could draw on three decades of voluntary mass participation in revolutionary transformation, from the literacy campaign of 1961 to Cuba's military role in Angola. The bond between 'the people' and the state had to be strengthened; political, military and bureaucratic cadres could not become an elite detached from the masses and their daily suffering. Policy-makers must share in the hardships. And they did, as I witnessed first-hand.

A dual process was developed involving both the creation and expansion of existing community and grassroots organisations, alongside increasing public participation in official policy-making processes. Peoples' Councils and Transformation Workshops were new community-based organisations which worked alongside existing grassroots institutions to mobilise social support, particularly in urban areas. Uriarte observed, for example, how the CDR provided recreation at the block level and organised community clean-up, while the FMC distributed vitamins to every household and advised on how to cook meals with limited ingredients. 'Mass organizations also participated in the prevention of crimes and delinquency at the community level by activating the neighbourhood watch and organizing activities for youth. This continuous work at the community level is clearly an important element that allowed Cuba, and especially Havana, to weather the crisis,' she wrote.[149] In Havana, Neighbourhood Transformation Workshops encouraged community participation in addressing specific neighbourhood problems, mobilising local and outside resources in projects involving construction, environmental issues, small-scale economic development projects and social service activities. By 2002, Havana had 20 Transformation Workshops.

In 1991, new People's Councils were set up as 'aggressive advocates of local issues' in every neighbourhood.[150] Members were volunteers, local delegates elected directly by their neighbours, and local representatives from the main economic, social and political institutions, including the CDRs and FMC. Council delegates elected their own president, who worked as a full-time employee, investigating problems and bringing them up for discussion and resolution. The Councils had a reputation for efficiency, managing and alleviating the impact of the crisis, restoring a sense of community to the tattered fabric of Cuban neighbourhoods. In 1992, the Constitution was amended so that the people ratified delegates to the National Assembly, who required over 50 per cent for approval.

The Fourth Congress of the Cuban Communist Party (CCP) in October 1991 was preceded by six months of nationwide debates about economic policy: discussions were organised in hundreds of local and workplace CCP branches, in meetings organised by the new Peoples' Councils and at the national congresses of the UJC and National Association of Small Farmers (ANAP) in April and May 1991. Three and a half million Cubans participated.[151] This became the modus operandi, extensive public consultations prior to significant economic reforms.[152] It was repeated with 'Workers' Parliaments' established between January and March 1994, prior to the National Assembly, which introduced important economic reforms. Three million workers (85 per cent of the workforce) met in multiple sessions in 80,000 workplaces to discuss the issues their delegates would debate.[153] The Workers' Parliaments shaped the reforms that were subsequently implemented, for example rejecting the proposal to impose income taxes or social security contributions on state employees.

As a member of the National Committee of the Federation of University Students (FEU) between 1993 and 1998, Kenia Serrano recounted how student leaders were also consulted. Once the reforms had been prepared, she said, 'the Comandante called the leaders of FEU from around the country to the Convention Palace to sit down with him and other government Ministers. He then asked them to explain to us the measures that would be taken and asked us to give our opinions.' Serrano lived with 16 other FEU leaders and younger students from the Federation of Middle School Students (FEEM) in a student house in Havana. Fidel Castro frequently visited the students, she recalled, often turning up at dawn. 'Fidel was always reflecting with us about the causes of the crisis in the socialist camp and he was very concerned that our generation should understand why the socialist camp had fallen.'[154]

Throughout the Special Period, as Cuban economist Rita Castiñeiras García notes:

> Discussions concerning fairly severe and fundamental government-proposed economic belt-tightening measures were organised in neighbourhoods and workplaces throughout the country. These heavily attended meetings led to large numbers of revisions to the original proposals. But beyond that, they represented a step towards making men and women into the subjects, not the objects, of the process of social development.[155]

This unique participatory process created some sense of public ownership of policy, contributing towards the acceptance of economic reforms and their consequences.

DEEP SCARS OF THE SPECIAL PERIOD

A report by the United States Central Intelligence Agency (CIA) circulated on 1 August 1993 concluded that Fidel Castro's government was likely to fall within the next few years. It recognised the devastating impact of the collapse of CMEA: 'Food shortages and distribution problems have caused malnutrition and disease, and the difficulties of subsisting will intensify.' The analysts predicted 'regime-threatening instability' occurring at any time'.[156] By the end of the decade, however, Cuban socialism had survived the Special Period. Its economic structures had been radically transformed, the social structure had stratified and its international relations had entirely shifted. The scars were deep and indelible. Survival had entailed the introduction of market mechanisms which had intensified the contradictions between the plan and the market that are inherent to the process of socialist transition. Cuban policy-makers were fully aware of these tensions, but saw no alternatives in the context, as Rodríguez explained:

> Adopting market mechanisms while failing to understand that they contradict socialism would propel Cuba towards capitalism. At the same time, market mechanisms are necessary in socialism as long as the forces of production are insufficient for the collective nature of labor to express itself without mediation. Failure to understand this, particularly in the specific context of a small open economy in crisis in a world thoroughly dominated by capitalism, would have led Cuba to reject the market mechanism necessary to survive its economic crisis and hence also would have brought about the end of its revolutionary project.[157]

Put crudely, it was a case of damned if you do, damned if you don't.

Cuba cautiously opened to foreign capital, restructured the economy, integrated into the global capitalist market, joined international trade bodies, including the World Trade Organization in 1995 and the Latin American Integration Association in 1999. Fidel Castro temporarily ditched his military fatigues, donning a business suit in international forums. The Cubans fought hard against the extension of the extraterritorial character of the US blockade, and against a campaign of terrorism directed by Cuban exiles and former CIA operatives, who targeted the island's burgeoning tourism industry, as shown in Chapter 7. At the turn of the century, the region was swept up by the 'Pink Tide' of progressive left governments, bolstering Cuba's economic and political relations with Latin America, providing greater room for manoeuvre and augmenting Cuba's regional and global influence.

The measures implemented to mitigate the impact of the crisis on the island's population, saw its key human development indicators improve. In 1999, Cuba was ranked fifth best out of 92 developing countries in terms of human poverty – astonishing given how the economic crisis had impoverished the country.[158] The measures taken to aid economic recovery and to protect the population from the human costs of the Special Period generated new contradictions whose resolution was necessarily postponed, in many cases until the present. For example, the decision to protect employment generated the cycle of low productivity, low salaries and low incentives which remains today. Changes to the employment structure announced in 2010 were designed to break this cycle by reducing the number of state employees and expanding the non-state sector. That measure led in turn to the need to legalise private business, as discussed in Chapters 8 and 9. The dual currency has endured for a quarter of a century, despite plans for monetary reunification, entrenching inequalities and further breaking the correlation between work and remuneration, social contribution and reward. While some of these economic measures endured, the most severe deterioration of Cubans' standard of living was addressed much earlier during the Battle of Ideas launched with the new millennium, and the focus of the next chapter.

3

★ ★ ★

FIDEL CASTRO'S CITIZENS' ARMY
THE BATTLE OF IDEAS

The shocking photo flashed around the world. A child's small terrified face peers out from a wardrobe and over the arm of a man who clutches him. A United States federal agent in a helmet and body armour points an automatic rifle close to the boy's chest. I see the image on a small, wall-mounted television in the rural town of Caimanera, a place particularly sensitive to the activities of the US military as the Cuban town closest to the US Naval Base which occupies Guantanamo Bay. Around me there is a wave of collective horror, relief and anticipation. The child is Cuban: he is Elián González and the story of the struggle over his custody has become big international news over the previous months. On one level, this is just a tragic tale of a divided family, a distressing maternal death, a traumatised boy and a complex custody battle. But if ever there was a story that proved that the personal is political, this is it. Within the United States, the battle over Elián González was to lose sympathy for Cuban exile groups; around the world it galvanised international support for Cuba, and on the island it snowballed into a nationwide, redemptive Battle of Ideas, which came to define the post-2000 era, and was characterised by the programmes for young social workers and teachers examined in this chapter.

Cuba's revolutionary people had survived into the post-Soviet world, but the vision of social justice and equity had been warped with the economic reforms reluctantly introduced. Fidel Castro launched the Battle of Ideas to reconsolidate socialist principles and redefine 'progress' in revolutionary Cuba. Progress was not economic liberalisation, but its retraction. Progress was strengthening state control over the economy, de-dollarisation and government programmes to reduce socioeconomic inequalities. Progress was to reduce private investment from capitalist corporations in favour of bilateral projects with fraternal states such as China and Venezuela. It was opposing neoliberal free trade by creating an alternative trade and cooperation bloc within the Bolivarian Alliance for the Americas (ALBA).

The Battle of Ideas invoked a return to Che Guevara's concept that education and culture are essential to create commitment to socialism, but that these remain abstract if the standard of living does not alleviate daily concerns for survival. Material improvements should not be achieved by promoting market exchanges and encouraging private enterprise, but by central planning, state control over finances and state investment in skills training and education, fostering industry, exploiting endogenous resources and investing in research and development.[1]

The Battle of Ideas cultivated new revolutionary protagonists, drawn from the youngest, poorest and most racially diverse sections of Cuban society, and incorporated them into a 'Citizens' Army' to combat the Revolution's enemies within (the 'new rich') and without (imperialism). It bore Cubans through the perilous era of the United States Bush presidency, with its wars and occupations, threats and impositions (see Chapter 7). Having ditched the business suit for his guerrilla uniform, Fidel Castro was back at the helm and this era bears his stamp. In response to internal pressure from Oswaldo Paya's Christian Liberation Movement and external aggression from the Bush administration, in June 2002 8 million people, almost the entire electorate, approved a constitutional modification that made the socialist system irrevocable.[2] The mass, voluntary mobilisation of this period was reminiscent of the revolutionary fervour of the early 1960s. The story of how and why the battle for Elián González became the Battle of Ideas is told in this chapter.

THE BATTLE FOR ELIÁN GONZÁLEZ

Elián González was five years old on 22 November 1999 when his mother, Elizabeth Brotons Rodríguez, took him on an aluminium fishing boat with a faulty engine, setting out at 4 a.m., in a bid to reach the United States. They left from their home town, Cardenas, in Matanzas province, two hour's drive east from Havana. Elizabeth's boyfriend and a dozen others were on board.[3] It was a perilous journey that tens of thousands of Cubans had risked, and an unknown number had not survived. After two days the engine failed, a storm raged and the boat filled with water. Elián was placed in a truck inner tube for safety and drifted out at sea, being rescued on 25 November by two US fishermen, who handed him over to the US Coastguard.[4] Only two other passengers survived; his mother and her boyfriend were not among them.

70

Elián's parents were divorced and his father, Juan Miguel González Quintana, was remarried with a new baby boy, but still cared for Elián. Discovering that his ex-wife had taken his son, without his knowledge, Juan Miguel alerted his uncle in Miami, Lázaro González. The United States law known as 'wet-foot, dry-foot' stipulated that Cubans found at sea (with 'wet feet') must be repatriated but those who made it to shore, or crossed the Mexican border (with 'dry feet'), were granted US residency. Elián and the other survivors should have been sent back to Cuba. Instead, after a day in hospital, US authorities handed him over to Lázaro González in Miami. Against his father's wishes, and backed up by the powerful Cuban American National Foundation (CANF), Cuban-American politicians and the right-wing Miami exile-community, Elián's great-uncle declared that he should stay in the United States.[5]

On 27 November, Juan Miguel faxed Cuba's Foreign Minister requesting help to return his son.[6] He had every right: international law decrees that a child is the charge of their parents. The Ministry immediately contacted the US Interest Section in Havana (the substitute for an Embassy) stating that the father of the little boy found at sea was demanding his immediate return. The next day, the Union of Young Communists (UJC) daily newspaper *Juventud Rebelde* reported on Elián's 'kidnapping', calling it 'a new crime by the United States against the Cuban people'.[7] It blamed the deaths of migrating Cubans on the US Cuban Adjustment Act, which encourages illegal emigration from Cuba.[8]

Juan Miguel, who was a member of the Cuban Communist Party (CCP), turned down bribes offered via his Miami family to emigrate to the United States to be reunited with his son.[9] On 29 November he told Fidel Castro that he would neither travel to the United States nor negotiate, nor would he agree to discuss his rights over the child's future in the corrupt courts of Miami.[10] On 4 December Fidel Castro publicly stated that if the US administration did not return the boy within 72 hours, Cuba would launch a campaign for Elián's return.[11] When the deadline passed, the Cubans prepared for battle.

'I had the privilege of participating in this process from the very beginning,' said Hassan Pérez who was President of the Cuban Federation of University Students (FEU) at that time.[12] 'I already knew about the Elián issue,' Pérez told me in the crumbling grandeur of the University of Havana where he now lectures. At dawn on 4 December, Pérez arrived in Havana with the Cuban delegation returning from Seattle, where 400,000 demonstrators had mobilised outside the World Trade Organization's conference.[13] 'During the reception, Fidel said that the United States had an obligation to return Elián immediately,

71

based on the rights of his family, or Cuba was going to start a great battle for his freedom, a battle in the field of ideas.'

The next day, 1,600 Cuban Youth Technical Brigade members meeting in the capital's Convention Palace carried out an impromptu march to the US Interests Section on the Malecon, the sea-wall in Havana, and held an open rally (*tribuna abierta*) to demand Elián's return to his father in Cuba.[14] 'And that's when the rallies began,' explained Pérez. On 6 December, while Fidel Castro visited Elián's school in Cardenas where his peers were marking his sixth birthday in his absence, another rally outside the US Interest Section was attended by 20,000 Havana youth and students. Rallies over the subsequent two days mobilised 40,000 and 50,000 young Cubans respectively. On 9 December, a 300,000-strong march was held by the organisations of Pioneers (7- to 14-year-olds), High School students (FEEM) and FEU. The ball was rolling. On 10 December, 2.2 million Cubans participated in rallies organised with staggered start times and televised live in 15 cities and towns around the country, from Guantanamo to Pinar del Rio.[15] Millions of T-shirts and placards were printed with the face of Elián; the little boy became the face of a revolutionary nation as it changed gears from 'resisting' to 'insisting'. International solidarity activists carted box loads of the T-shirts back to their own countries where they demonstrated for Elián's return to Cuba.[16]

Between 5 December 1999 and 28 June 2000, when Elián finally returned to the island, 106 open rallies were organised in municipalities across the country, from small towns to provincial capitals. The events were essentially cultural acts, almost celebrations, interwoven with a political message. The live national broadcasts strengthened both the sense of collective identity, '*Cubanidad*', and local pride, shining a national spotlight on local talent and traditions; artists and performers, dance troops, singers and musicians, many of them children. There was even a resurgence in 'repentism', a rural tradition of public improvisation to music.[17] Eleven huge marches were held in those seven months, as well as 84 *Mesa Redondas* (round tables), a new format of daily live televised discussions which took over prime time Cuban TV.[18]

Elián's image also saturated US television: showered in toys, paraded round Disney World, meeting with US politicians and the Cuban-American exile powerbrokers.[19] Those images were broadcast on Cuban state TV. 'There was so much aggressive media around Elián that many of us worried what the psychological and pedagogic impact of all this would have on him,' explained Kenia Serrano, then a leading member of the UJC, who chaired a *Mesa Redonda* on this issue in January 2000.[20]

The battle for Elián took on huge political significance in Cuba. It was translated as a battle for sovereignty and an ideological battle, pitting the consumerism of Elián's Miami experience against a poor socialist country where childhood is not commodified and every child has access to free education, health care, culture and sport. Led by Cuban youth organisations, the campaign to demand Elián's return involved all sectors of Cuban society: artists, intellectuals, workers and athletes. Such extensive popular engagement raised the stakes for the Cuban leadership. After the demoralising trudge through the Special Period in the 1990s, the battle for Elián reignited a spark among the Cuban people. The revolution could not afford to lose. And for once they had majority support in international opinion.[21]

In the United States, meanwhile, the case produced an institutional power struggle pitting Washington against Miami. This conflict was exacerbated by the pending US presidential elections in which the votes of the Miami Cuban exile community were decisive for the national result. The Bush family had close ties to powerful Cuban exiles, links which were cultivated as Jeb Bush took over as Governor of Florida in January 1999 and George W. Bush announced he would run for president in summer 2000.[22]

First, on 1 December 1999 the US Immigration and Naturalisation Services (INS) stated that Elián's father must present his custody claim at the family court in Florida. Then, on 5 January 2000, after interviewing Juan Miguel in Cuba, INS officials announced that he was the biological father and legal custodian of Elián. President Bill Clinton and Attorney General Janet Reno agreed with the INS. But five days later a Miami judge completely undermined the decision, granting guardianship of Elián to his great uncle Lázaro. Later that month, Reno met with Elián's grandparents, who US authorities had permitted to travel from Cuba. They were able to see him briefly just once, but their visit galvanised public opinion in favour of Cuba's claim.

INS authority was further undermined in mid-February when one of its senior officials, Mariano Faget, was accused of spying for the Cuban government after being fed false information unrelated to Elián, and a Cuban diplomat, who had been instructed to leave the United States after also being accused of spying, announced a hunger strike, was arrested by the Federal Bureau of Investigation (FBI) and deported to Canada.[23] An exasperated Juan Miguel wrote to Reno: 'It is really surprising that all the authority of INS is reduced, apparently, to depending on the good will of the kidnappers.'[24] By late March 2000, the case had reached a legal and political stalemate in the United States. Hoping to win those decisive Florida votes, the Democrat presidential candidate, Vice President Al Gore, broke with the White House to say Elián should stay.[25] A Florida judge dismissed a petition for asylum made on Elián's behalf by his Miami-based relatives, who vowed to appeal, while a Miami-Dade county mayor and other civic leaders announced that local authorities would not cooperate with Federal agencies to repatriate Elián. Janet Reno declared that Elián was authorised to return to Cuba, and that his father could speak for him. INS warned the Miami family to expedite the appeal process or lose custody of Elián. Meanwhile, the claim that Fidel Castro was too scared of Juan Miguel defecting to let him travel to the United States was tested when Juan Miguel flew there with his wife and baby boy on 6 April. He did not defect, despite allegedly being offered USD 2 million in front of his lawyer. By then, 80 per cent of the US public believed Elián should be returned to his father.

The Justice Department ordered Lázaro to reunite Elián with his father at 2 p.m. in Miami airport on 13 April 2000. The deadline came and went, and Lázaro's formal custody over Elián was withdrawn. Six days later, an Atlanta Court of Appeals ruled that Elián must stay in the United States until his Miami relatives had appealed the asylum ruling, in May. Lázaro's house where Elián resided was surrounded by an international media circus, police and Cuban-Americans, including armed and criminal elements, 'protecting' Elián from Federal forces.[26] Finally, at dawn on 22 April, 130 heavily armed officers surrounded and stormed the house to remove Elián. Associated Press photographer Alan Díaz snapped his Pulitzer prizewinning photo mentioned at the start of this chapter.[27] Within four hours, Elián was reunited with his father, step-mother and half-brother. A new image hit the front page of *Time* Magazine; Elián was smiling joyfully in the arms of his father. It was the same boy with a very different face.[28]

Elián was stuck in the United States for two months, while the Miami family exhausted their legal processes. He was joined by his cousin, his pre-school teacher, four classmates with their parents, and a doctor who travelled from Cuba. They set up a mini-school so Elián could catch up with his studies and reintegrate with his peers.

Back in Cuba, the marches, rallies and the *Mesa Redonda* programmes continued. A permanent assembly space, named the 'anti-imperialist tribunal', was constructed outside the US Interest Section in Havana, with a statue of Cuban national independence hero, José Martí, clasping a child protectively and pointing an accusing finger towards the US building. The space was filled with 200,000 Cuban Pioneers who marched there on 22 June. Finally, on 28 June, the US Supreme Court rejected a further appeal from Lázaro, and Elián was free to go. As Elián's flight was in the air, the Cuban people were informed, via television, that there would be no official statement or public mobilisation.[29] Hours later, Elián was received at the airport by a crowd of his family, school peers and teachers chanting his name and waving small Cuban flags. Elián was not to be a war trophy, declared Fidel Castro, who did not meet him until the end of the school year two weeks later when he visited Elián's home in Cardenas, gifting him a book of children's stories by José Martí.[30]

Inspired by Juan Miguel's loyalty to the Revolution and the symbolism of the embattled child, the Battle for Elián had seen a return to the mass mobilisations reminiscent of the early 1960s. US journalist, Ann Louise Bardach claimed that, by the time she got to Cuba in February 2000, 'Elián fatigue' was a nationwide epidemic.[31] Having arrived in Cuba two months later, in April 2000, I cannot agree. Young Cubans I knew, who had previously been disengaged, had rediscovered their militancy and spoke with urgency about the need to mobilise, to demand justice, as if Elián's plight was a metaphor for the history of Cuba's subjugation by the United States. That momentum had to be maintained.

FROM THE BATTLE FOR ELIÁN TO THE BATTLE OF IDEAS

Against the backdrop of mass mobilisations and public denunciations, Elián's case spurred a self-critical evaluation of the deep socioeconomic scars left on Cuban society by the Special Period, and of the structural problems inherited from a colonialised society and not yet resolved. There were two precursors to this awareness. First, a high-profile conference of the Union of Cuban Writers and Artists in 1998, attended by Fidel Castro, which warned against 'cultural invasion' and called for action to raise cultural levels and re-democratise access to culture.[32] Second, a study the following year of 500 youth prisoners in Havana, most of whom were found to have low educational levels and be from 'socially disadvantaged families' from the city's poorest neighbourhoods, revealed that 58 per cent had committed their first crime by the age of 20, only 2 per cent had parents who were university graduates, and 64 per cent had abandoned their studies and were not working when sentenced.[33] The existence of social inequality was officially recognised. For the first time in many years the term 'poverty' was used in Cuban political discourse, and it was by Fidel Castro, who insisted that as most crime has social causes it is avoidable.[34] 'Building a new society is much harder than it might appear,' he told Ignacio Ramonet, explaining how pre-revolutionary class and racial privilege was unwittingly perpetuated by the merit-based education system post 1959. 'The parents' educational level, even after we've made the Revolution, continues to

75

have a tremendous influence on the children's later outcomes,' he said.[35] This conclusion pinpointed education and culture as mechanisms for obstructing inherited privilege in revolutionary Cuba.

At the outset of the campaign for Elián's return, Fidel Castro convened a group of youth leaders, from the UJC and the FEU, including Hassan Pérez, Kenia Serrano and Enrique Gómez, who were interviewed for this chapter, to address these problems at their roots. Why would a Cuban mother risk the life of her young child to get to the United States? Clearly, the pull factor was the US Cuban Adjustment Act, which gave Cubans permanent residency within one year of arriving in the world's wealthiest nation. But what were the push factors? What were the conditions in those poor barrios, in the homes and schools? What resources were lacking?

Did Fidel Castro forge this select group of youth leaders to bypass existing institutions he saw as deficient or bureaucratic, I asked them. Pérez replied, 'Fidel worked as he had in the guerrilla struggle: general command, advance, add, multiply and integrate. But he never disregarded the institutions; on the contrary, he was aware that it was the existing structures which had to carry out the tasks.' Serrano described the group around Fidel Castro as 'reinforcement for his leadership style and methods' and concluded 'evidently it was a catalyst to solving problems'.[36] 'While Ministries work from 8 a.m. to 5 p.m.,' Pérez pointed out, 'the youth organisations could work around the clock.'[37] Fidel Castro understood that the existence of a *nomenklatura*, a bureaucratic caste, had corrupted the Soviet Union and was the subject of justifiable grievances and he sought to harness the energy and creativity of Cuban youth leaders to prevent this happening on the island.

Traditionally Cuban university students dedicate two weeks of their summer vacation to social or productive projects. In summer 2000 in Havana their contribution was organised through newly established University Social Worker Brigades (Brigadas Universitarias de Trabajo Social, or BUTS). Their task was to investigate how many young people were outside work and employment in the Municipality of Plaza in central Havana and identify the causes of youth unemployment. The BUTS study encountered thousands of young people who had completed pre-university exams, in the twelfth grade, but not secured a university place.[38] Cuban university entrance exams were demanding, competition was tough and university places had fallen dramatically during the Special Period.

As First Secretary of the UJC in Havana at that time, Gómez told me how strongly Fidel Castro criticised the UJC cadre for their lack of information about, or engagement with, young people who were not in work or study.

'Fidel complained that the Ministry of Work had no record of these youth and the Ministry of Education said they are in schools.'[39]

For a year, BUTS 'shock brigades' investigated the socioeconomic reality of Cuban individuals. 'It was a fabulous thing,' Pérez recalled. 'Every weekend, 6,000 students from all the universities in Havana City participated. With the Comandante we designed a programme to visit, for example, 75,000 children who we had detected as living in vulnerable conditions.' He described how their findings led to 'an explosion of work in many fields', generating some 200 'programmes of the Revolution' under the umbrella of the Battle of Ideas. Most were designed to engage Cuban youth in revolutionary society. By 2000, around 300,000 young people, up to 20 per cent of the youth population, were 'disconnected', that is, outside work or study. They either operated in the informal sector, hustled or hung around bored.[40] However, programmes were extended to all vulnerable or disadvantaged sections of society, spanning the fields of education, health, culture, employment and prisons.

YOUTH SOCIAL WORKERS

If the intensity and breadth of social work was to continue, a more professional structure was needed. But how to achieve this without losing the energy and exuberance of an organised youth force such as BUTS? The approach adopted attempted to transform 'disconnected' young people from the problem into the solution by training them as social workers to work in their own communities. A social worker school was established in Cojimar, Havana, and, in September 2000, 650 students who had just completed twelfth grade were enrolled. The first course lasted one semester. In early 2001 it was repeated, but this time the students were recruited from among 'disconnected' teenagers, not recent school graduates.[41]

From September 2001, enrolment rose to 7,000 with the opening of three new social worker schools, attached to local universities, in Villa Clara, in central Cuba, and Holguin and Santiago in the east. The course now lasted ten months, with a curriculum incorporating elements of law, psychology, sociology and social communication. Social workers in Cuba had no previous experience of professional education.[42] There were social workers within the Ministry of Public Health, some 4,000 mainly working in psychiatric services, and 800 more within the Ministry of Work and Social Security. The latter were incorporated into the new social worker programmes, while the former were left in the healthcare sector but, like the new social work graduates, were given the chance to study at university level.[43]

Social work was not an easy option. Initially, students boarded at the school, rising at 6 a.m. for classes from 7 a.m., followed by guided activities until 10 p.m., with practical work in the community on Saturdays. On graduation they were guaranteed 400 pesos monthly, a comparatively good wage for a young person, were exempt from military service and could study for a university degree, choosing from 22 courses, without having to pass the competitive entrance exam. That meant combining a full-time social work job with university studies for a minimum of six years.[44] For those enrolling as social workers, access to a university course was a principle motivation, given the valued status of higher education in Cuba. Above all, it gave young people a revolutionary responsibility reminiscent of the youth who participated in the literacy brigades of 1961, or the volunteers who fought in Angola against the invading army of apartheid South Africa in the 1970s and 1980s.

Gómez categorises the social work training programme into three stages: 2000–2003, investigating and relaying information to the state about the socioeconomic problems detected; 2004–2008, carrying out tasks designed by the programme; and 2008–2011, developing a professional practice.[45] The social workers began by visiting over 6,500 'disconnected' under-21-year-olds in Havana to enquire about their situations, with the ultimate aim of keeping them out of prison. Mirroring the young prisoners studied before, many of these youths had left education during or on completing secondary school. Only 2.5 per cent had professional parents, 69 per cent had families in 'unfavourable social situations', 37.8 per cent lived in 'marginal' neighbourhoods, 263 had already been to prison and 165 were prisoners.[46] Given the deterioration in the value of Cuban salaries during the Special Period, instead of registering in Cuba's employment offices they had sought incomes through the informal sector or illegal activities. Importantly, however, 80 per cent of them said they would like to return to study, or enter employment.

Armed with this information, the revolutionary leadership sought to tackle the problem. Again harking back to the 1960s, study was offered as an employment option for disconnected youth.[47] A new Comprehensive Improvement Course was established nationwide from 1 October 2001, with students paid to study computer science, English, geography, history and mathematics in three-hour classes, four times a week. 'The goal is for these young people to acquire knowledge and culture' explained an information leaflet, 'to have the opportunity for upgrading, study, social integration and participation in production or the provision of services.'[48] In the first academic year, almost 74,500 young people aged between 17 and 29 were enrolled in

333 schools with 4,812 instructors – about 15 students per teacher. Almost two-thirds of the students were young women and one-quarter had children.[49]

From March 2001, the first group of social work graduates continued the investigation started by BUTS, visiting 197,282 under-15-year-olds in Havana. Material conditions were found to be 'critical' in 898 homes with 1,520 children. The social workers and university students returned to those homes with financial and material aid delivered by the state. This demonstrated to ordinary Cubans the state's political will to address the problems of the most vulnerable families on a case-by-case basis. Institutions were mobilised to tackle the causes of these household's deprivation by finding employment for parents, meeting educational needs and granting social assistance, pensions and other help.[50]

Between March and December 2001, the social workers assumed a huge project: to measure and weigh every Cuban child up to 15 years old. The point, Gómez said, was to go beyond the numbers to alleviate the causes. He recalled Fidel Castro insisting:

I don't need statistics, I need the name and surname, and the reason the child is underweight. Who knows this? Who is looking after the child? I cannot sleep peacefully and you tell me that it is 3 per cent, that it is 1 per cent, that it is low in this country; that we have improved. No, no! Who is that child, what are the causes and what should be done?[51]

The social workers were assisted by members of the Cuban Communist Party (CCP), the Cuban Women's Federation (FMC), the Committees for the Defence of the Revolution (CDRs) and government officials, and accompanied by nurses and technicians to recalibrate the weighing equipment. 'Everyone participated,' said Gómez, who was by then leading the social worker plan nationally, 'the country mobilised.'[52] Across the island, over 2.2 million children were weighed and measured.[53] Children found to be below the average scores were visited at home and their family situation was evaluated to determine possible causes. Subsequently a programme of food assistance was rolled out to 97,733 children and regular check-ups organised. The situation of 28,517 minors was described as critical, catalysing coordinated action from the institutions caring for them.[54]

In 2001, over two weeks of the summer holiday, 5,000 BUTs and 1,000 university professors set out to put a finger on the pulse of every home in Havana, how they lived and what they thought. They were armed with an open survey addressing issues from health and education, to the work of social organisations and the quality and uptake of television programmes. Later, 1,000 social workers completed the work in the homes not reached by the university students and staff. For the state, this was an important means of feedback about the daily reality of people's lives, their problems and aspirations. It strengthened the Cuban leadership's commitment to the development of the social worker programme. 'The results of the survey produced new programmes which constituted a real revolution in the fields of education, health and culture,' Gómez explained.[55]

New investigations were launched into the situation of the elderly and disabled people. In 2001, retirees and pensioners with the lowest incomes were assessed. In Havana this was led by BUTS, but in the rest of the country it was implemented by social workers, coordinating with the Ministry of Work and Social Security. The elderly had suffered the greatest deterioration of living conditions during the economic contraction of the 1990s. The project raised awareness nationally of the ageing population, and fostered new social policies. Pensions were increased, physical rehabilitation services reanimated or expanded, food supplements extended, a programme for 'satisfactory longevity' was set up by the Ministry of Public Health and the University for the Elderly programme developed. Meanwhile, specialists devised a comprehensive 'Psychosocial, Pedagogic and Clinical-Genetic Study' which they took on visits to 366,864 people with major disabilities, of which 16,223 were evaluated as 'critical social cases'.[56] Between summer 2001 and spring 2003 these cases were followed up and programmes in health, medical genetics and ear implants were developed to assist them. Policies were devised to incorporate disabled people into work, where feasible, including providing training, with local formulas to implement support. Further investigations assessed the social and biological factors affecting learning in children. Families were advised about hereditary diseases, and over 6,000 mothers were allocated a salary to provide full-time care for children with serious disabilities.[57]

The *content* of social work in this period was mainly limited to carrying out visits and conducting surveys, tasks which Gómez describes as corresponding to a welfare and bureaucratic conception of social work.[58] The *form* was a mobilised youth force which intervened in emergency situations to confront tasks prioritised by the revolutionary leadership, from opinion surveys to mosquito eradication campaigns.

By 2004, 14,000 young people had trained as social workers. They began to design their own tasks and programmes. Building on the 2001 experience of weighing and measuring under-15-year-olds, a more comprehensive study of Cuba's child population was initiated with specialists from relevant ministries and institutions.[59] Evaluating each child's 'bio-psycho-social' situation, they sought to identify anything, beyond nutrition, affecting normal development. They considered school results, conduct, school relationships, family communication with the school, family concern for the child, plus biological factors. All 2,143,995 under-15-year-olds in the country were assessed; nearly 250,000 of them, 11.7 per cent, were identified as needing systematic attention and were assessed further. In this second stage the context in which each of those children lived was analysed: 181,375 children, 8.5 per cent of all Cuban children, were categorised as being in 'at risk' personal, family or social situations. These cases were discussed with the relevant institutions, which adopted measures to monitor their health status systematically. Some children in rural zones faced long journeys to school which impeded their access and attendance. Consequently, micro-schools were founded, with teachers travelling daily to teach a handful of children and, in several cases, a single pupil.

With the Ministry of Work, the social workers evaluated the country's employment situation, categorising informal employments and their territorial specificity. They identified shortcomings in work centres' efforts to recruit recent graduates of technical courses and universities, those leaving compulsory military service, people with criminal records on parole, and other unemployed adults up to the retirement age. They reviewed the System for Family Care, guaranteeing food to people with low incomes, the construction of social housing, care for patients with low-prevalence diseases, and so on. A study into households struggling to meet their survival needs identified 43,480 family units in a 'critical state', and programmes of assistance were designed with resources centrally approved.

Two significant aspects to these social worker programmes were, first, that with a return to economic growth, resources had become available to provide material assistance, and, second, that moving beyond the established principle of universal access, they incorporated the concept of personalised and differentiated provision based on need.[60] Given the ongoing scarcity of resources, explained José Luis Rodríguez, who was then Minister of the Economy, these programmes sought the highest economic and social outcomes possible at the lowest cost.[61]

As the Cuban economy continued its recovery, a series of regulations introduced from 2003 recentralised the country's financial resources, providing the state with funds for investment and social expenditure and enhanced government control of finances and monetary policy in general. Internal motives included the lack of financial discipline in self-financing enterprises, which failed to resolve the country's foreign-exchange constraints, and the threat of an energy crisis in 2004 as Cuba's ageing power stations fell into disrepair (see Chapter 4). 'The situation required massive hard-currency investments to rebuild the power grid,' explained Rodríguez.[62] The external motive was aggressive action by President Bush's administration to halt hard currency revenues to Cuba discussed in Chapter 7.

In 2003, the number of Cuban enterprises authorised to operate with US dollars was reduced and US dollar payments between Cuban enterprises were replaced by payments in Cuban convertible pesos (CUC), a currency pegged to the US dollar but printed and controlled by Cuba's Central Bank since 1994. Enterprises had to swap the convertible peso for US dollars or other convertible currencies held by the Central Bank to pay for imports, thus recentralising control of this activity. US cents were removed from domestic circulation and replaced by CUC coins. From November 2004, the US dollar was no longer accepted in domestic commerce. 'De-dollarisation' had become an imperative after the Bush administration set up the Cuban Assets Targeting Group to stop US dollar flows into and out of Cuba. In the three weeks Cubans were given to swap their US dollars for CUCs, the sum deposited in the island's banks was greater than deposits over the previous ten years. CUCs were now the only convertible currency accepted in Cuba's 'dollar shops'.[63] In December 2004, Resolution 92 centralised all foreign currency transactions in the Central Bank, introducing a degree of financial centralisation not seen since the early 1960s.

Also in December 2004, Venezuela and Cuba accelerated the exchange of medical and educational services for oil and together launched the Bolivarian Alliance for the Americas (ALBA). This provided Cuba with an alternative export strategy that was consistent with its socialist principles, reaped the benefits of the Revolution's welfare-based development strategy and was not obstructed by the US blockade. The number of smaller private foreign investors in Cuba was cut, so mixed enterprises decreased by 41 per cent from 2002 to 2006. Meanwhile, the government consolidated large investments in major infrastructural and development projects in strategic sectors such as mining and energy, establishing joint ventures with state companies from fraternal countries, Venezuela and China. The result was to limit the sphere of operation of capitalist mechanisms, introduced via foreign capital, diminishing their impact on Cubans as producers and consumers, whilst simultaneously strengthening the state's economic resources based on higher value-generating activities, for example in nickel and oil production.

Debt repayment agreements were reached with several governments, facilitating Cuba's access to new investment capital. Cuba's current account and balance of payments were positive in 2004 and 2005. GDP grew an average 8.1 per cent between 2002 and 2007, peaking at 11.2 per cent in 2005 and 12.1 per cent in 2006. Significantly, the proportion of Cuba's international trade carried out with Latin America rose from 5 per cent in 1989 to 35 per cent in 2006.[64] This economic boost facilitated the scale of imports and state subsidies required by the Energy Revolution, in which the social workers played a key role.

SOCIAL WORKERS IN THE ENERGY REVOLUTION

The Energy Revolution was a major state initiative to improve energy security and energy efficiency through the installation of new power generators, increased use of renewable energies, progressive electricity tariffs and the replacement of old durable goods with energy-saving equipment (see Chapter 4). This last aspect was carried out by some 13,000 social workers. For most Cubans the first indication of the Energy Revolution was in July 2005, when social workers arrived at their door with backpacks of energy-saving fluorescent light bulbs, which they delivered and installed for free. They took away every incandescent light bulb.[65] Within just six months, 9.4 million light bulbs had been replaced, making Cuba the first country in the world to complete the switch.[66] During these visits, the social workers made inventories of the ageing and inefficient electrical equipment in every household. Next, they returned with new, more efficient household appliances imported from China. From fridges to televisions and rice cookers, some 30 million electronic items were distributed house by house.[67]

The social worker programme had been created to address the deprivation and marginalisation of the revolutionary population as it emerged from the Special Period. But the flip side of this post-Soviet period was the emergence of a 'new rich' who benefited from access to dollars or hard currency, via tourists, remittances, illegal activities or joint ventures with foreign companies. A certain proportion of the population benefited from the free welfare and education provision without contributing back to society. Fidel Castro referred to 'several dozens of thousands of parasites who produce nothing'. Low salaries and scarce material goods generated widespread pilfering of state resources. This problem had always existed under socialism, as Fidel Castro pointed out, 'Don't think for a moment that stealing resources and materials is just a present-day illness . . . The Special Period aggravated it, because in this period we saw the growth of much inequality and certain people were able to accumulate a lot of money.' He sought to confront this reality through the Battle of Ideas: 'We invite everyone to take part in a great battle . . . against larceny, against all types of theft, anywhere in the world.'[68]

Most social workers came from non-professional families and 72 per cent of them were women. Gómez explains how they became immersed in the battle over energy resources, pitted against the 'new rich' and 'parasites' whom Fidel Castro perceived as an existential threat to the Revolution. Cuba's oil supply was running low and, in the context of the war and occupation in Iraq, international oil prices were rising. 'Cuba was in danger of electricity blackouts again, the Guiteras thermoelectric plant was broken and we couldn't get spare parts,' explained Gómez.[69] It was vital to avoid a return to the blackouts of the 1990s.

Fidel Castro devised a plan to tackle what he called, 'the dirty little crooks selling [stolen] gasoline to the new rich'. It required the element of surprise. First, 150 social workers gathered in a school around an old fuel pump and were given a few minutes each to practice operating it. 'They were motivated,' explained Gómez, 'because they knew it was an important task, but they did not know what they were going to do.'[70] Then, at dawn on 10 October 2005, Fidel Castro met with the social workers and explained their role, before they boarded buses that took them straight to the petrol stations in Pinar del Rio province, two hours' drive west of Havana. They were joined by local government officials and members of the CCP, mobilised at the last minute. It was a national holiday, so the regular petrol station attendants had been given the day off; the social workers took over the pumps.[71] The result? Fuel sales doubled in one day – evidence that half of the petrol supply was being stolen by the regular attendants. This programme was extended across the island. Fidel Castro announced: 'We started in Pinar del Rio to ascertain what was happening in the gas stations that sell gas in dollars. We soon discovered that there was as much gas being stolen as sold.'[72] The action was not a deterrent, however; more fuel was subsequently stolen from pumps in other provinces as 'people took advantage down to the last minute before the social workers arrived'.[73] By 5 December social workers were operating every petrol station on the island.

Next, social workers were sent to refineries to accompany fuel distribution trucks. The results were rapid and tangible. Fidel Castro described how the social workers 'get on board the trucks that carry 20,000 or 30,000 litres [of petrol] and they watch, more or less, where that truck goes, and how much of the oil is rerouted. They have discovered private gas stations, supplied with oil from these trucks.' Gómez explains that the outdated technology and lack of control over the fuel distribution system made stealing from the state easy. In the midst of the economic crisis, every institution had created their own petrol stations, lacking standardisation or security. 'In one agricultural area in Pinar del Rio, fuel was distributed in boots – rubber wellies! It was not litres, or anything like that, but boots of fuel.'[74]

For ten months, more than 10,400 social workers worked full time at petrol stations located outside their own provinces, rotated regularly to avoid them being corrupted by local 'crooks'. This was not real social work, Gómez admitted, but it was decisive social action. 'The social workers were an organised youth force and this was an important task for the country. It was an emergency situation, and it was tackled within one year because with the extra revenue collected, the state imported the digital technology necessary to ensure greater control in all the service centres.'[75] By then, Fidel Castro had become ill, but the social worker programme carried on.

In the 2008–2011 period, the social workers promoted solutions based on community self-development, which, as Gómez pointed out, 'constitutes an alternative to the paternalistic and top-down concept that had prevailed'.[76] Postgraduate training for professional social work was developed; over 2,200 social workers enrolled on five postgraduate courses, with vocational courses in every municipality. In 2011, a new investigation into the situation of cohabitation in Cuban families had evaluated 3,071,987 homes, 85 per cent of all the homes in Cuba. Problematic situations requiring attention were registered in 530,014 households, 17.3 per cent of the total family units visited. The main problems were alcoholism, 'unsociable behaviours', difficulties in educating children, lack of care for the most vulnerable family members, and domestic violence.[77] Importantly, 85,018 families (2.8 per cent of the total) were identified as vulnerable to the economic reform process initiated since 2008 under Raúl Castro's presidency, with the reduction of staff payrolls, elimination of free provisions and the fall in subsidies. This finding contributed to the pushback against the 'economism' of the reforms (see Chapter 9), and for a greater balance between the drive for economic efficiency and the need for social justice.

By 2011, 43,000 young people had qualified as social workers: 'a mass of youth and women' and a high proportion of them non-white. Many young women dropped out as they became mothers, while others left as the professional demands increased. Some fell in love with the profession, said Gómez, but others were not interested: they had entered the programme for the university degree. Nonetheless, some 35,000 social workers were professionally active from

2006 to 2009, 1 for every 320 inhabitants. Then, suddenly, in September 2011 the entire programme was ended by government decree. Just 8,000 social workers formed under the Battle of Ideas passed over to the Ministry of Work, the rest were found employment in other areas.[78]

What has Gómez to say about rumours that the social worker programme was ended because the young recruits had become corrupted? He pointed out that these young people are shaped by daily social realities and adds that only around 100 social workers faced disciplinary measures for corruption of any sort. This does not detract, he said, from the value of the general conduct of the social workers and the tasks they carried out. 'They were young people, who had material needs, handling resources with a high market value.' As an illustration he recounted the story of a teenage social worker tasked with accompanying an oil truck. The young man had a difficult situation at home and the truck driver began to help him out, bought him lunch, gave him rice to take home and so on. But it was manipulative, not caring. When the driver stole fuel, the social worker felt indebted to him and thus unable to report it. He hid from the driver to avoid accompanying him again. When the authorities found out, the social worker was not punished: he was removed from the programme, although permitted to continue his studies. The driver, on the other hand, faced a tough prison sentence for corrupting a state official, as well as for theft.

Other examples involved social workers prioritising their own friends and families with the distribution of electro-domestic equipment. Gomez reflected that:

> Most interesting is the trust that the revolutionary process had in these disconnected youths to become better people. The Revolution had the capacity to mobilise young people who were not elites, youths who were often in the barrios without studying or working, to carry out fundamental tasks, to contribute to the construction of society. That must have marked them as a generation. The importance of that process was not just the actions carried out, but who the protagonists were.[79]

The social workers were a large part of Fidel Castro's Citizens' Army in the Battle of Ideas. But there were other groups of youths mobilised with different tasks, among them thousands of teenagers recruited as teachers and known as *Maestros Emergentes*, which can be translated as either 'emergent' or 'emergency' teachers. In this case, both translations are appropriate.[80]

EDUCATION REVOLUTION

The Elián González case led Fidel Castro and the youth leaders working with him to interrogate the state of the island's schools, as well as Cuban homes and neighbourhoods. Serrano said, 'We asked ourselves about the ability of the Cuban educational system to reinsert Elián quickly at the social level when he returned.'[81] Cuban schools had deteriorated over the Special Period. Thousands of teachers had left the profession seeking better incomes in tourism, self-employment or other jobs. Those who remained were overstretched and underpaid, classrooms were overcrowded, school libraries emptied, resources and materials depleted and buildings falling apart. 'UJC cadre went to visit the homes of all the teachers in the capital,' recalled Gómez, 'to identify which neighbourhoods they lived in, how they lived, how many students they had.' In Havana, classes had swelled to 35 or 40 students. With reference to the 1999 investigation into youth prisoners, Fidel Castro began to speak about 'student number 40' as a candidate for prison. 'The teacher was worn out and lacked the energy and ability to give differentiated attention to 40 students, especially those who had most difficulties,' he surmised.[82] The education system clearly needed revitalising. Thus the Battle of Ideas incorporated a revolution in education.

No primary school teacher should have more than 20 students, it was concluded, and no secondary school teacher more than 15 students.[83] This would strengthen relations between teacher and student and, through regular home visits, the student's family. But where would the extra teachers come from? The answer was the Emergent Teacher Training Plan.

EMERGENT TEACHERS

For primary schools the emergent teachers were 16- and 17-year-olds who had dropped out of school after completing tenth or eleventh grade. They enrolled on an eight-month intensive training course, followed by two months working in a school in their own neighbourhood, alongside a mentor. The following academic year, they entered the classroom as teachers responsible for 20 children. They wore their own school uniform, as they were simultaneously finishing their secondary education on Saturdays. They signed up to work as teachers for eight years. Like the social workers, once they had completed pre-university studies they could continue on to university degrees with exemption from the difficult entrance exams.[84] Demands on the emergent teachers were even greater than on the social workers. The teenage teachers arrived at school around 7.30 a.m. to teach a full timetable, supervising children at breaks, completing their preparation and marking at home, attending schools on Saturdays or evening university courses, attending teacher training methodology classes, and carrying out home visits to each of their 20 pupils at least once a month.[85] By January 2002, over 5,500 16- and 17-year-olds were training as 'emergent' teachers for primary schools.

Emergent teachers for secondary schools were called Comprehensive General Teachers. They often left their home province to teach students aged 12 to 15 years, only a few years younger than themselves. Over 6,500 of them trained alongside 41,200 existing teachers being retrained to fit the new scheme, although existing professionals could opt out of the new system, becoming mentors to the new young teachers instead.[86]

Secondary schools at that time had a specialist teacher for each subject; each student had 11 teachers, and each teacher had 100 students. However, Gómez explained, Fidel Castro began to argue that, as secondary school was, for young people, the age when they were drawn towards drugs and crime, they needed more than just a teacher: they needed a 'perceptor', a mentor, an educator in the full sense. He proposed the Plan for Comprehensive Teachers in Secondary Basic, which transformed Cuban schools. Under the new system, students had one teacher who knew them and their family well. Specialist classes were delivered by experts via the television, so all Cuban students would have access to the best teachers on each topic. These 'audio-visual classes' were pre-recorded. The class teacher then 'leads and accompanies the student in that learning process'.[87] The school day was extended from half day sessions, which left students hanging around, to a 'double session', with additional hours of computing and language training. The Plan faced resistance from the Ministry of Education, explained Gómez. 'Fidel met with education officials, he went to schools, he debated with teachers, he went on television. He battled to defend these programmes.' Ultimately, Gómez said, 'when there was a debate Fidel Castro had the most authoritative voice'.[88] The Plan was implemented.

Three additional requirements for the implementation of this Plan led to additional programmes under the Battle of Ideas. First, the need to repair school facilities and construct additional classrooms. The School Repair Plan was launched in Havana where schools were in the most critical condition and population density put extra pressure on facilities. State entities mobilised materials and human resources, while teachers and parents contributed voluntary labour over the summer holidays. In summer 2002, 799 schools were repaired with 30,000 builders on the job.[89] By the end of the year, 33 new schools had been built and 4,453 new classrooms.

Second, the need to install televisions, video players and computers in every classroom, requiring huge imports of equipment: 45,000 computers were installed in school computer labs in every primary school and nursery to teach computer skills. In 2002 alone, 1,250 15-year-olds were trained in Havana to work as computer instructors in these labs, while intensive computer training was provided to 15,000 primary school teachers and twelfth grade students. In December 2000, the 'Ernesto Che Guevara' electronics factory in Pinar del Rio began manufacturing solar panels. By June 2001, 2,000 schools in the mountains and other areas outside the reach of the national grid were provided with solar energy for televisions and videos. Even the handful of schools with just one student benefited. From 2002, solar-panelled computers were installed and teachers were trained to run them. Serrano recalls joining Comandante José Ramón Machado in a mountain community in Guantanamo to inaugurate solar panels. 'It was an emotional experience, in a remote community, a hamlet with 10 or 12 families. Thanks to the solar panels, they now had a school, with teachers, computers, a television, a video. Another solar panel supplied a video room so the adults could watch the television, watch the news, the soap operas, whatever they liked!'[90]

Third, the need to create the 'audiovisual programmes' to provide every school in the country with televised classes. By 2002, there were three education programmes for different age groups: My TV to Grow, for primary school level; My TV to Learn, for secondary basic; and My TV to Know, for higher secondary. Broadcasting these via the national network took the programmes into every home with a television. In October 2000, 'University for All' courses began, which enabled all Cubans to study and learn from televised classes, raising the population's general level of knowledge and culture 'in an easy, pleasant and economical manner', in the words of an information leaflet.[91] Two separate education channels were broadcast nationally.

In late 2007, a nationwide debate about Cuba's socioeconomic problems took place, sparked by a critical speech on the island's problems by Raúl Castro on 26 July 2007. The professional adequacy of the young teachers was among the principal concerns expressed. Gómez recognises that the Emergent Teacher programme had deficiencies. It required too many hours of watching video classes in succession, inadequate even after new televisions with larger screens were installed, with the teacher reduced to keeping order and answering questions.[92] There was also concern about their young teachers' lack of knowledge, professionalism and maturity. Children had served as educators previously under the Cuban Revolution, not just during the literacy campaign in the early 1960s but also in the 1980s when, as scholar Rosi Smith wrote, 'Young people had stepped into the breach when educational expansion outstripped the availability of trained adult teachers. Many well-respected older teachers working at the turn of the century had begun their professional life that way.' Almost every conversation with Cubans about the emergent teachers, 'begins with the disclaimer that this was not the first time that children had been used for this function', said Smith.[93] However, by the late 1980s, over 94 per cent of Cuban teachers held degrees in education so the employment of teenagers who had not even finished high school post-2000 was a step backwards.[94]

While Gómez insisted that 'the idea was good, especially the value of having a teacher for every 15 to 20 children', he conceded that 'maybe more time was required to develop the programme. But there was also the social demand.' Here he was referring back to Fidel Castro's concern for 'student number 40' in the classroom. Recalling that Fidel Castro once described himself as 'an activist in the band of the impatient,' Gómez reflected:

> All his revolutionary practice is proof of that; he was impatient to solve problems. But impatience, without a doubt, sometimes leads to new problems that have to be addressed. I think the urgency, the emergency, the impatience to solve this problem, how to look after student number 40 in that classroom, prevailed over the question of training that teacher to a level where they met all requirements, before they could take charge of a group of 20 students.[95]

It was a deeply social concept of education.

After eight years of full-time teaching and university study, regardless of their starting age, those emergent teachers were experienced professionals. Many remained as teachers, others pursued careers shaped by their university degrees. But even those who left had been irrevocably shaped by their experience as professionals, as role models and mentors to younger children.[96]

ART INSTRUCTORS

New schools for training art instructors were set up in every province to provide four years of training to teenagers as young as 15 years old as art instructors, to work in primary and secondary schools, universities and cultural institutions. By 2005, there were 16,000 students enrolled in these schools. Fidel Castro described their social and racial mix as 'more satisfactory than the historical average'.[97] A Cuban information leaflet stated that: 'Every year, 4,000 new students enrol, hailing from the smallest, most isolated towns to the largest, to the most densely populated cities ... They are receiving comprehensive training in the fields of visual arts, music, dance and theatre. They will have the opportunity to continue with university studies in their field of specialisation. These young people will play a crucial role in raising the general, comprehensive cultural level of the Cuban people, fulfilling the principle of promoting education, culture and social development in order to be the most cultured country in the world.'[98] Art instructors were under contract to work professionally for eight years, but the scheme did not give them access to study art at the university, nor to a state salary as professional artists.[99]

BATTLING ON OTHER FRONTS

Having identified the link between criminality and lack of education, there was a huge expansion of educational provision within Cuba's prisons, including university-level courses. Sentencing policy leaned towards community punishments or part-time prison which enabled offenders to maintain family relations and community integration.[100]

Throughout the island, hundreds of video clubs and youth computer clubs were set up, free and accessible to everyone regardless of age. By January 2002, there were 350 video clubs, where films were discussed, as well as watched, raising attendees 'cultural awareness and knowledge of the world through cinematic works', and 300 computer clubs with 3,491 computers. Courses were taught at different levels and included website design and computer sciences.[101] In 2002, 50,000 students were studying computing at university and polytechnic levels, working to provide software and computing services.[102] That year, a new University of Information Science (UCI) was opened to contribute to the island's computerisation and to foster a software industry for domestic application. By 2007, the first group of 1,300 students graduated.

In 2003, the momentous decision was taken, for economic reasons, to close half of Cuba's sugar mills, 'creating thousands of unemployed sugar workers in the Revolution's traditional rural heartland', as historian of Cuba Antoni Kapcia put it.[103] International sugar prices were low and the cost of producing and exporting sugar was greater than that of importing it. Tens of thousands of sugar industry workers were offered further education and retraining.[104] University centres were set up in all 84 closed sugar mills, and many sugar industry officials began to give classes as assistant professors.[105] Besides soaking up otherwise potentially dangerous unemployment, said Kapcia, 'the purpose was to make up for lost schooling earlier in the workers' careers ... Again, higher education was going beyond the previous limits.'[106]

In the process of guaranteeing university education to social workers, emergent teachers and other members of the Citizens' Army in the Battle of Ideas, a new system of university organisation was established, known as 'municipaliation' or 'universalization'. This saw the establishment of a 'satellite' site of the nearest university established in every one of the island's 168 municipalities. Evening or weekend classes took place in local schools or other public buildings. The teachers were local practitioners. Degrees were overseen by the traditional universities to ensure quality. Eventually these municipal universities were opened to all Cubans, especially workers and carers who could study part-time. Consequently, the number of students exploded from 2,000 in the first year to 700,000 at its peak.[107] Many of these young students were the first in their families to enter university. Raising the average educational standard to graduate level within a decade became the aim.

By 2005, there were 600,000 students in Cuban universities, of whom 90,000, or 15%, were 'disconnected' youth before enrolling. There were 958 university centres, including 169 municipal campuses, 84 centres at former sugar refineries and 18 in prisons. Over a thousand centres for public health studies had also been set up in municipalities and healthcare institutions. There were close to 100,000 higher education teachers, including assistant staff. Fidel Castro told Ignacio Ramonet, 'We're now waging a profound educational revolution.' It was not about removing opportunities from the historically privileged who get into the best schools, he explained, but about extending higher education to every Cuban, 'a formidable instrument of social levelling'. The disconnected youth given the chance to study, he asserted, 'are going to be among the most revolutionary of our citizens, because these programmes represent a rebirth for them'.[108]

FIDEL CASTRO'S LAST GREAT BATTLE

Conceptually, the Battle of Ideas addressed many issues still to be resolved under socialism: the balance of responsibility for provision between the individual and the state; how such class antagonisms as remain under socialism should be mediated; ensuring discipline with resources and at work; how the wealth of socialist society should be distributed; and how much control and centralisation is appropriate. These issues were addressed by Fidel Castro in a seminal speech to students at the University of Havana on 17 November 2005. His words sparked a national debate, in workplaces, in homes, in the streets and in the National Assembly. He publicly questioned the survival of the socialist Revolution:

> I ask you all, without exception, to reflect on it: can the revolutionary process be irreversible, or not? Which are the ideas or the degree of consciousness that would make the reversal of the revolutionary process impossible? When those who were the forerunners, the veterans, start disappearing and making room for the new generations of leaders, what will be done and how will it be accomplished? After all, we have been witnesses to many errors, and we didn't notice them.[109]

While the Revolution could not be overthrown by imperialism, he said, 'This country can self-destruct; this Revolution can destroy itself . . . and it would be our fault.'

These questions were being addressed in the face of the unrelenting US blockade and, with the new US administration of George W. Bush from January 2001, a hardening line against Cuba. The invasions of Afghanistan (2001) and Iraq (2003) showed Bush's willingness to ignore both the United Nations and international opinion. Accused of being a 'state sponsor of terrorism', Cuba was added to the 'Axis of Evil' in 2002 (see Chapter 7). So, while the Revolution had survived the threat of economic collapse during the Special Period, by the early 2000s the island faced a renewed political and military threat from the United States.

Against the immense, sophisticated machinery of US imperialism, Fidel Castro pitted his 'Citizens' Army' of social workers, emergent teachers, art instructors, reintegrated youth: 'An entire nation which, in spite of our errors, holds such a high degree of culture, education and consciousness that it will never allow this country to become their colony again.' Dressed in fatigues, Castro declared war on 'parasites', 'the dirty little crooks selling gasoline to the new rich', and on the Bush administration, a 'gang of shit-eaters who don't deserve any respect'.[110]

Then suddenly, Fidel Castro was struck down; it was not a bullet but biology that struck him.[111] I was in Cuba when, five days after his annual speech on 26 July 2006 in Granma province, where the Rebel Army began, the Cuban people were informed that their Commander in Chief was sick and had transferred his numerous responsibilities to Vice President Raúl Castro and four other government leaders. While there were celebrations in Cuban parts of Miami, in Havana most Cubans sighed with concern and carried on as usual. The uncertainty continued throughout 2007: would Fidel Castro die or recover, would he retire or return? In February 2008, his retirement was confirmed and Raúl Castro was formally elected in his place.

What happened to the Battle of Ideas? Many of the programmes had run their course, the social workers continued until 2011, and other projects have carried on until today. But the 'Battle of Ideas' label was dropped and the protagonism of the Citizens' Army petered out. Some external commentators depicted Raúl Castro as sweeping away his brother's programme in favour of a renewed institutionalisation and efficiency cuts. While it is clear that a new stage was introduced by Raúl Castro, this juxtaposition is too stylised, implying a false dichotomy between the brothers. In fact, Raúl Castro's watershed speech of 26 July 2007 expanded on themes raised by Fidel Castro in November 2005, with a view of Cubans as citizens, not consumers, with responsibility to society: 'We need to bring everyone into the daily battle against the very errors which aggravate objective difficulties from external causes.'[112]

Raúl Castro initiated a process of popular consultation in which all Cubans debated Cuba's socioeconomic problems. The government could risk such a public airing of grievances precisely because the Battle of Ideas had alleviated the most acute socioeconomic suffering, raised political consciousness and renewed commitment to the socialist project, and because Cuba had entered a period of economic growth and expanding international relations. The new head of state initiated a drive for efficiency within the socialist framework, to tackle the structural imbalances and economic inefficiencies which had long hindered it. By 2008, when the global economic crisis struck, Cuba confronted the new challenge with a generation of young adults who had been shaped, consciously or not, by Fidel Castro's last great battle.

4

★ ★ ★

POWER TO THE PEOPLE
THE ENERGY REVOLUTION

Standing on the roof of a tall building on a hilltop at the back of the Diez de Octubre neighbourhood in Havana on a hot day in early July, I am acutely aware of the solar energy beating down on my shoulders. The view is spectacular: green tree tops rise between small red-roofed houses, a jigsaw of mismatched and ornate buildings, with, in the distance, the high rise of government ministry buildings, the José Martí monument and a cluster of tall hotels. One thick black plume of smoke rises from the Regla oil refinery in Havana Bay – a warning against complacency. I am not here to admire the Havana cityscape but to appreciate the set of four solar panels and two water heaters that adorn the flat concrete roof.

The home, which doubles as an office, belongs to Luis Bérriz, a scientist and President of the Cuban Society for the Promotion of Renewable Energy Sources and Environmental Respect, known as Cubasolar. We are accompanied by Vice President Eliseo Galván, who talks me through the technical details, enthusing about the equipment's potential contribution to national development. Made in a Cuban factory in Pinar del Rio, western Cuba, the solar panels produce 200 times the electricity Bérriz's household consumes and the surplus is fed into the national grid. The Cuban government has begun to roll out residential solar panels to every home in Cuba. Under a new law approved in March 2017, residents will be nominally allocated bank credit to purchase the equipment and the loan will be repaid over five years by discounting the value of surplus electricity contributed to the national grid by each household.[1] An editorial in the Cuban Workers' Confederation newspaper, *Trabajadores*, states that 'the energy strategy launched is aimed at clean, safe and sustainable energy or, what is the same thing, renewable energy sources'.[2]

Cubasolar was set in up 1994 in the midst of Cuba's acute energy crises during the Special Period when, as Bérriz explains, 'we were obliged to develop a new energy policy, based on our own resources'.[3] Cuban scientists were already working on the development of renewable energies in research institutes and universities around the country. Cubasolar was established to bring together engineers, scientists and planners in an organisation to forge the new energy culture necessary to accompany the policy changes required. Officially, Cubasolar is a non-government organisation; with no state budget it is funded on a project-by-project basis by the Cuban government and foreign partners. It has over 1,000 members and branches in every province installing new technologies and implementing projects.

However, its main function, according to Bérriz, is 'education, new consciousness, discussion and culture', and to these ends it publishes books and two regular magazines which are sent to every Cuban school and to every member of the Central Committee of the Cuban Communist Party (CCP): *Energía y Tu* is for a general readership and *EcoSolar* for scientific readers. It has helped establish study centres, specialised classrooms and scientific circles in universities. In Granma province, in the east of the island, it set up both the Educator's Villa, which hosts national events, and the Solar Study Centre, where hundreds of students and teachers train each year.

Cubasolar has trained technical brigades to install hybrid wind–diesel systems, hybrid photovoltaic (solar) wind technologies, wind farms, firewood kitchens, hydropower plants and drinking water in remote and inaccessible communities.[4] The schemes it has contributed to have taken solar-panelled electricity to over 500 family doctors' clinics, rural hospitals and farmers' homes and over 1,800 television and video rooms for people in remote regions.[5] Cubasolar has also aided projects to mitigate desertification and the effects of drought on the coast and contributed to the domestic manufacture of renewable energies equipment.[6] It has even assisted the transfer of technologies to Bolivia, Chile, Ecuador, Guatemala, Guinea Bissau, Haiti, Honduras, Mali, Mexico, Nicaragua, Peru, South Africa and Venezuela through collaborative missions.[7] This range of activities is an indication of the kind of experimentation with renewable energies underway in Cuba, and Cubasolar is just one of several institutions spearheading developments in this field.

As we sip tea made from Bérriz's moringa tree, he shows me potato chips and spices dried with the solar equipment on the roof.[8] 'We are trying to teach people not to keep speaking about electricity as the universal carrier of energy,' he says. He is beaming about the potential for renewable energies and believes the effects of climate change can be halted. 'Trump is a stupid man,' proclaims Bérriz, referring to the US president's announcement just five weeks earlier that he would withdraw the United States from the Paris Climate Agreement and renegotiate 'a deal that's fair' for US interests. Motivated by greed, Trump's agenda is to enrich the powerful, counters Bérriz. 'But this is my world as well, and what right does he have to contaminate it, to get more money and power!?'[9]

Bérriz is opposed to the two dominant international approaches to climate change: *adaptation* and *mitigation*. 'If climate change was natural I would adapt,' he explains. Since the beginning of the universe, he clarifies, 'natural climate change has been accompanied by a process of adaptation. We are the result of an adaptation over thousands of years.' However, he compares man-made climate change to military aggression, pointing out that people under bombardment do not adapt to being bombed, they prepare: 'So the concept of adaptation is not correct. The concept should be *preparation* for climate change.' He also rejects the notion of mitigation which he caricatures as: 'Don't kill me in 50 years, kill me in 100. Go slower. Don't raise the water level to five metres, raise it only to four metres. Why? Get it back to where it should be! Human beings are at fault!' Logically he condemns the commercialisation of climate change through international carbon trading schemes. 'If you adapt, I will give you money . . . Not only are you telling me to adapt, when I should be preparing, what's more you are buying me.'[10]

As a small island nation in the tropics, Cuba is particularly vulnerable to climate change: extreme weather events, heat waves, drought, torrential rain, hurricanes and rising sea levels.[11] Cuban scientists estimate that sea levels could rise by three feet by the end of the century, wiping out 122 coastal towns, polluting water supplies and destroying agricultural lands.[12] Without preventative action taken to protect the coast by 2050, 2.3 per cent of Cuba could become submerged.[13] However, action *is* being taken. In spring 2017, Cuba's Council of Ministers approved Tarea Vida (Project Life), a 100-year plan to prepare for climate change.[14] Bérriz is among thousands of Cuban scientists and environmentalists preparing for climate change and a more sustainable future in which renewable energies will play a major role.

SUSTAINABLE DEVELOPMENT

The term 'sustainable development' appeared in the World Conservation Strategy report published in 1980.[15] In 1983, the United Nations (UN) founded the World Commission on Environment and Development, known as the Brundtland Commission, to investigate the deterioration of the human environment and natural resources.[16] Four years later, the Commission's main report, *Our Common Future*, defined sustainable development as 'development that meets the needs of the present without compromising the ability of future generations to meet their own needs', thus locating the economy, society and the environment as keys to sustainable development.[17] In 1992, the UN's Conference on Environment and Development, or 'Earth Summit', took place in Rio de Janeiro, Brazil.[18] Agenda 21, a comprehensive plan of action for making the world more sustainable, was agreed at the Summit but there was no enforcement mechanism for countries that signed up.

'An important biological species – humankind – is at risk of disappearing due to the rapid and progressive elimination of its natural habitat,' announced Cuban president Fidel Castro in his uncharacteristically short and appropriately alarming speech to the Earth Summit in 1992. He blamed consumer societies that 'were spawned by the former colonial metropolis. They are the offspring of imperial policies which, in turn, brought forth the backwardness and poverty that have become the scourge for the great majority of humankind.' These societies held one-fifth of the world's population but consumed two-thirds of the metals and three-fourths of the energy produced in the world. 'They have poisoned the seas and the rivers. They have polluted the air. They have weakened and perforated the ozone layer. They have saturated the atmosphere with gases, altering climatic conditions with the catastrophic effects we are already beginning to suffer. The forests are disappearing. The deserts are expanding. Billions of tons of fertile soil are washed every year into the sea. Numerous species are becoming extinct. Population pressures and poverty lead to desperate efforts to survive, even at the expense of nature.'

Third World countries cannot be blamed for this, Fidel Castro insisted. Nor should they be denied the right to develop, as everything that generates underdevelopment and poverty violates the environment. 'Tens of millions of men, women and children die every year in the Third World more than in each of the two world wars. Unequal trade, protectionism and the foreign debt assault the ecological balance and promote the destruction of the environment.' A better distribution of global wealth and technologies was necessary, he insisted, to save mankind from self-destruction. 'Less luxury and less waste in a few countries would mean less poverty and hunger in much of the world.' Environmentally ruinous lifestyles and consumption habits must stop being transferred to the Third World.

'Make human life more rational. Adopt a just international economic order. Use science to achieve sustainable development without pollution. Pay the ecological debt. Eradicate hunger and not humanity.' Now that the demise of communism had eliminated the excuse for cold wars, arms races, and military spending, why were resources not being used to develop the Third World and combat the threat of the ecological destruction of the planet, he asked, calling for an end to selfishness, hegemonies, insensitivity, irresponsibility and deceit, concluding: 'Tomorrow will be too late to do what we should have done a long time ago.'[19]

That same year, the Cuban government added commitment to sustainable development to the nation's constitution and initiated measures to redress past environmental harm and minimise future degradation of air, water and land resources.[20] It was not until 2006 that Cuba's contribution to sustainable development was noted globally. That year, the World Wildlife Fund's (WWF) *Living Planet Report* identified Cuba as the only country in the world achieving sustainable development – improving the quality of human life while living within the carrying capacity of its ecosystem.[21] Meanwhile, *National Geographic* magazine described Cuba's environment as 'largely pristine', pointing to state conservation and reforestation programmes as evidence of its environmental commitments.[22] And the documentary *The Power of Community: How Cuba Survived Peak Oil* celebrated Cuba's embrace of organic farming, agricultural cooperatives and biofuels during the economic crisis of the 1990s, concluding that: 'Cuba has a lot to show the world about a crisis we will all be facing.'[23] 2006 was also the Year of the Energy Revolution in Cuba.

Necessity is the mother of invention, they say. Indeed, the standard explanation for Cuba's turn to organic farming and renewable energies is that its hand was forced by the post-Soviet economic crises. To an extent, that is true. However, the 'simple expediency' explanation overlooks the Revolution's historical record and its socialist development framework. Neglecting these factors could lead to the erroneous assumption that if the Cuban economy booms those commitments will end. The idea that Cuba's environmental success was due to economic underdevelopment was rejected by Jim Barbourak of Conservation International: 'If this were true, then Haiti could be expected to be a verdant ecological paradise, instead of being the most environmentally devastated country in the region.'[24]

Under capitalism, private businesses regard the Earth's natural resources as a 'free gift' to capital.[25] Driven by the profit motive, capitalist businesses are only interested in natural resources such as land, water, raw materials and hydrocarbons in so far as they can be turned into profit. It is the logic of the system of capitalist production, not specific policy decisions, which makes capitalism unsustainable. How can sustainable development be achieved under capitalism if doing so obstructs the capital accumulation process that drives capitalist production? Carbon trading and similar schemes attempt to impose a 'cost' on companies for using or damaging the environment, obliging them to incorporate that cost into their business decisions. However, the lack of political will, legal enforcement mechanisms or method for calculating 'cost' inevitably limits success.[26]

In Cuba's socialist centrally planned economy the profit motive does not determine production and reproduction, meaning that environmental as well as social costs can be factored into economic decisions. It is not enough, for example, for electricity to be within physical reach: it must also be affordable for all Cubans.[27] That does not mean, however, that socialism is synonymous with environmental respect; environmental disasters occurred in the socialist bloc.[28] A leading environmental policy-maker in Cuba pointed out that the process 'is not automatic, you have to try to create a socialist system where the environmental agenda is driven well, otherwise you will still have environmental problems. Nothing is given, it has to be achieved.'[29]

ENERGY INEQUALITY IN PRE-REVOLUTIONARY CUBA

In 1950s Cuba, 56 per cent of the population had access to electricity. Nearly half the population was rural, but only 9 per cent of Cuba's rural dwellings had electric light, compared to 87 per cent of urban homes.[30] US investors controlled 90 per cent of the island's electric services.[31] In his famous 1953 trial defence speech *History Will Absolve Me*, Fidel Castro articulated both the notion of access to electricity as a right, and the commitment to develop renewable energy: 'Two million eight hundred thousand of our rural and suburban population lack electricity . . . [The electricity monopoly] extends lines as far as it is profitable and beyond that point they don't care if people have to live in darkness for the rest of their lives. The State sits back with its arms crossed and the people have neither homes nor electricity . . . today possibilities of taking electricity to the most isolated areas on the island are greater than ever. The use of nuclear energy in this field is now a reality and will greatly reduce the cost of producing electricity.'[32]

During the guerrilla struggle in rural and mountainous Cuba, the Rebel Army rarely had access to electricity. In February 1958 an electric generator was taken to Che Guevara's command post in Pata de la Mesa to power their clandestine radio station, Radio Rebelde, taking the insurrectionary message into Cuban homes.[33]

REVOLUTIONARY CUBA: EARLY DAYS

'Energy is an instrument of power,' asserts Bérriz. 'What did the United States do when it broke off relations with Cuba? Take away our oil supply. What did the USSR do? Give us oil.'[34]

In 1961, the literacy campaign was launched. Some 300,000 *brigadistas*, including 100,000 students, many in their early teens, travelled across Cuba teaching more than 700,000 people to read and write while learning how the country's poorest lived. Illiteracy was eliminated within one year.[35] An enduring image of the literacy campaign is of urban youth, side-by-side with adult *campesinos*, leaning over notebooks under the flickering flame of a Chinese kerosene lamp – a standard part of *brigadistas* kit. Only the main villages in rural areas had electricity, recalled Esther Armenteros, former Cuban Ambassador to Britain, who participated in the literacy campaign as a young teen: 'I was near a village called Julia, in Bayamo, in what is today Granma province. There was no electricity for kilometres around. In my area there was only one house with an electricity generator. I was very friendly with the lady of the house and I went there from time to time to listen to my favourite radio program. I was 13 at the time. Imagine! My family was very poor but we were from Havana so I grew up with electricity and running water, but I must confess to you that sometimes my mother lacked money to pay the electricity bill and the service was suspended, so I had some experience.'[36]

In August 1959 the revolutionary government ordered a 30 per cent reduction in electricity charges. In 1960, the US-owned Cuban Electric Company was nationalised and placed under the jurisdiction of the Department of Industrialisation, headed by Che Guevara.[37] Extending electricity to the entire population was going to be a huge challenge, but it was imperative to reduce socioeconomic differences, especially between urban and rural Cuba. Referring to Lenin's definition of communism as Soviet power plus the electrification, Che Guevara told the Electrical Energy Forum of 1963 that 'Without electricity, it's impossible to locate new industrial centres and often the preferable location from other standpoints has been affected because electrical provision was insufficient for installing factories.'[38]

In October 1960, two days after the US government introduced a partial blockade of Cuba, Guevara led a trade mission to the socialist bloc. From the USSR he secured Soviet assistance in the electrification of the island and power plants were imported from the Soviet Union, Czechoslovakia, East Germany and France.[39] 'The importance that this had for the economic development of the country and for the survival of the Revolution is difficult to overestimate,' stated Ángel Gómez Trueba, who at that time was the Vice Minister of Industrial Construction in Guevara's Ministry of Industries (MININD).[40] Nonetheless, another Vice Minister in MININD, Tirso Saenz, who headed technical development, told me how this also created problems: 'The Eastern European socialist countries worked with 50 hertz, and Cuba worked with 60 hertz. Their technicians had to adapt the equipment before it was sent to us, because we couldn't change the whole electrical system. Those were big problems', he said, 'but the biggest problem was the lack of technical people.'[41]

The agreement to export Cuban sugar to the USSR and import Soviet oil at below world market prices inevitably perpetuated the island's energy dependence and structural underdevelopment. This relationship also fostered the increasing mechanisation of agriculture, as the USSR supplied the island with diesel-fuelled tractors, petroleum-based pesticides and fertilisers.[42] Inevitably, incentives were lacking for the development of alternative energy sources. Nonetheless, a search for alternatives began as early as the 1960s while energy specialists were trained to replace the technicians leaving the island and to staff the extended electrical provision nationally. Table 1 below tracks the key areas of research and investigation from the 1960s to 1980s.

According to Bérriz, by the late 1980s, 'from the scientific perspective, Cuba came to be a power in the development of renewable energy sources. It had its first building completely supplied with renewable sources of energy . . . and was one of the most advanced in renewable sources in tropical conditions.'[43] Nonetheless, beyond the experimentation underway, the application of these technologies was very limited. This was partly due to the lack of technology and investment, and access to both resulting from the US blockade. However, perhaps more decisive was the lack of commitment or incentive to restructure the energy mix away from hydrocarbon fossil fuels given that the island's industry and agriculture were orientated towards cheap imported oil from the USSR. Indeed, as the *Power of Community* documentary noted, Cuba had committed to the Green Revolution, a system which required the massive use of fossil fuels in the form of natural gas-based fertilizers, oil-based pesticides and diesel fuel for tractors and other farm-based machinery. 'The country's agriculture was more industrialised than any other Latin American country and exceeded the US in its use of fertiliser.'[44] Cuba had 90,000 Soviet tractors in the 1980s.

Table 1: Key areas of research and investigation from the 1960s to the 1980s[45]	
1960s–70s	Energy specialists trained in the universities of Havana, Oriente and Las Villas.
1968	Physics Faculty, University of Havana, set up a course on photovoltaic devices. By 1975, they had produced the first Cuban photovoltaic solar cell made with crystalline silicon, the standard first-generation panel material.
1970	Urban population entirely connected to the National Electroenergetic System (SEN), providing electricity at 110 kV. During the decade 1970–80, the SEN was interconnected at voltages of 220 kV.
1970s	Scientists in the sugar industry worked to develop renewable energy from *bagasse*, the residue from sugar cane once the juice has been squeezed out. Sugar cane is the most efficient living captor of solar energy and their work improved the efficiency of the furnaces and boilers in the sugar centrals, where *bagasse* had long been used as fire fuel.
1975	Headed by Bérriz, the Grupo de Energia Solar (Gensolar) was set up to develop renewable energies. Directed by the new Principal State Programme of Research into Use of Solar Energy in Cuba, approved by the First Congress of the CCP, they developed the first Cuban solar heaters, solar dryers, distillers, sea water purifiers, concentrators and technologies for the use of solar energy in the cultivation of microalgae.
Late 1970s	Group of Technical Assistance on Energy was created within the Ministry of Basic Industry to develop strategies for energy saving and developing renewable energies. In 1981 their *Report on Cogeneration* gave perspectives on the use of renewable energy in the sugar industry and other areas.
Early 1980s	Physics Faculty, University of Havana, improved the Cuban-made solar cells with the use of gallium arsenide, increasing the efficiency of solar panels. First Cuban solar heaters were produced.
1983	Environmental Physics Group was set up in the Ministry of Construction, to promote a culture of 'passive' solar energy use, bioclimatic architecture and regulatory norms for the efficient use of energy in buildings.
1983	National Energy Commission (CNE) created to rationalise energy consumption and increase use of national resources, especially renewable sources. Installed 200 (mini and micro) hydroelectric power stations to supply electricity to 34,000 people in mountainous regions. Groups worked to expand the use of renewable energies, mainly hydroelectricity, thermal solar, wind power and biogas.
1984	Centre for Research into Solar Energy (CIES) set up in Santiago de Cuba, to develop renewable energy sources.

Table 1: Key areas of research and investigation from the 1960s to the 1980s (cont.)	
1986	Ministry of Communications laboratory began assembling photovoltaic solar modules made of monocrystalline silicon, with an annual capacity of 200 kWh.
1988	A Combustion Laboratory was established in Cienfuegos to research the combustion of solid renewable fuels.

Even so, the fact that thousands of scientists had conducted research in multiple institutions, working under government directives to develop renewable energies since the 1960s, facilitated the urgent uptake of new practices and a new culture when the shock of the Soviet collapse made doing so an obligation.

THE EXPEDIENCY OF THE SPECIAL PERIOD: AN ACUTE ENERGY CRISIS

It was the Soviet Union's unilateral decision in 1990 to reduce oil exports to Cuba which presaged the Special Period. From 13 million tons in 1989, Soviet oil exports to Cuba slid to 10 million tons in 1990, then 8.5 million tons in 1991, plummeting to 1 million tons in 1992.[46] Reducing dependence on petroleum was no longer a policy choice, but an imperative. Cuba was crippled by critical scarcities of hydrocarbon energy resources, fertilisers, food, medicines, cement, spare parts, equipment and resources in every sector (Chapter 2). Power outages became a defining feature of the era while the island's transport system ground down, almost to a halt.

In agriculture, tractors were replaced by human and animal labour, and organic fertilisers, crop rotation techniques and urban gardens were developed as people cleaned up vacant plots and began to cultivate fruit and vegetables.[47] The army was sent to farm fallow land to increase agricultural production; nearly 40 per cent of state farms were converted into cooperatives and farmers' markets were reintroduced. In small towns and cities, people turned to horses for transportation. The 1950s Cadillacs and Chevrolets were parked up alongside Russian Moskvitch to rust in garages while 1.2 million bicycles were imported from China, and half a million more produced domestically. New centres, ministries and programmes were established in the 1990s to pursue alternative energies with greater urgency. The main entities are listed in Table 2 below.

Despite these efforts, Bérriz admits that 'the country's energy policy remained basically oil-fuelled, with centralised electricity generation in a few

Table 2: Centres, ministries and programmes established in the 1990s to pursue alternative energies

1992	Centre for the Study of Renewable Energy Resources set up as a university teaching–research centre within the José A. Echeverría Polytechnic Higher Institute (ISPJAE) in Havana.
1992	Centre for the Study of Sugar Thermoenergy founded in the Central University of Las Villas, for experimentation related to sugar mill energy production.
1993	National Energy Sources Development Programme approved by the National Assembly of People's Power to improve energy efficiency and renewable energy use, including by substituting imports with increased production of national crude oil and accompanying gas for electricity generation and improving efficiency in the use of *bagasse*.
1994	New Ministry of Science, Technology and the Environment (CITMA) set up in April 1994 to reorganise work in this area.
1994	Hydroenergy Research and Development Area set up in Villa Clara to coordinate researchers and technicians advising government bodies on hydropower, designing, constructing and assembling hydroenergy facilities, and training specialists and technicians.
1994	Cubasolar established to promote all forms of solar energy (biomass, biogas, hydropower, sea and wind, solar photovoltaic, solar thermal and passive use) 'in solving the economic and social problems of the country'.
Mid-1990s	Integrated Centre for Appropriate Technology set up within the National Institute of Hydraulic Resources to develop technologies to supply water to the population with windmills, hydraulic rams, rope pumps and winches.
1996	Centre for the Study of Efficient Energy founded to develop technologies for the combustion of biogas, mainly with *bagasse*, and the use of biogas in internal combustion engines.
Late 1990s	Solar heaters factor built in Morón City, central Cuba.
1997	CITMA creates the Group of Solar Energy Technological Applications (GATES) in Guantanamo to install photovoltaic systems in areas beyond the national grid.
1997	Ministry of Education launched an Energy Saving Programme, or PAEME, 'to involve citizens in the effort to save energy … to teach students, workers, families and communities about energy-saving measures and renewable sources of energy'. Energy Festivals were held to educate Cubans about energy efficiency and conservation, and in schools the theme was integrated into physics, economics and environmental courses.

Table 2: Centres, ministries and programmes established in the 1990s to pursue alternative energies (cont.)	
1999	Cuba's first wind farm was inaugurated on Turiguanó, with two wind turbines of 225 kW each, doubling as a centre for wind energy studies.
2000 onwards	Cubasolar and Ecosol Solar help form groups of specialists in photovoltaic technologies in every province.

thermoelectric plants'.[48] The principal difference in the post-Soviet 1990s was that, in the absence of imported oil, Cuba was burning domestic crude oil reserves.[49] Many Cuban policy-makers still believed that renewable energy sources were scarce, unstable, expensive, inefficient, inadequate for meeting Cuba's energy needs and would require extensive territorial use.[50] Indeed, the cost to Cuba of importing solar panels from Europe was almost prohibitive, but once China began mass production costs plummeted.[51]

There was, however, commitment to developing renewable energies among Cuba's top leadership, and not just Fidel Castro. In the 1950s, Vilma Espín had been one of the first Cuban women to study chemical engineering on the island, before doing post-graduate work at the Massachusetts Institute of Technology (MIT) in the United States. On return to Cuba, she joined the Rebel Army in the Sierra Maestra, married Raúl Castro in 1959 and became a leading member of the revolutionary government. In 1960 she set up the Cuban Women's Federation and served as its president until her death in 2007. She joined the Central Committee and the Political Bureau of the Cuban Communist Party, as well as the Council of State. In the early 1990s, she sent a message to Bérriz asking to meet him. 'I prepared to convince Vilma of the great importance of using renewable energy sources,' Bérriz recalled, 'but when we sat down to talk, Vilma started to convince me of the great importance of using renewable energy sources! I kept quiet and thought "I don't have to do anything here."'[52] Subsequently, he says, Espín visited him frequently in Santiago de Cuba, sometimes accompanied by Raúl Castro and others. He points to a framed photograph on the wall with himself, Espín, Raúl Castro and Esteban Lazo, who is currently president of the National Assembly of People's Power. It was Espín's project to put solar heaters in every nursery in the country, he tells me.

By 1994, Cuba's electricity crisis was critical. The lack of fuel meant that generation capacity was 40 per cent below its potential. Industries were paralysed while energy shortages were rationed, so that in Havana residents experienced regular rotating blackouts for eight hours. Across the island, these lasted longer. Living in Havana from 1995, my sister and I quickly learned to stock up on candles and matches. Blackouts remove more than just light: no air fans, no television, food perishes without refrigeration. Cubans suffered long waits for the massively depleted fleet of public transport to return from work or college and defied the laws of physics to squeeze into already packed buses heaving with hot, sticky bodies. On alternate days they could arrive home to a darkened neighbourhood, obliged to cook, wash, clean or do homework by candle or kerosene flame.

RENEWABLE ENERGY FUELLING THE BATTLE OF IDEAS

The installation of solar panels in remote areas, facilitating access to televisions, videos and computers, was an essential aspect of the Battle of Ideas launched in the early 2000s and discussed in the previous chapter. In December 2000, the Ernesto Che Guevara electronics factory in Pinar del Rio began to manufacture Cuban solar panels; later it produced solar cells, which are the building blocks of solar panels. Within the year, 2,000 schools beyond the reach of the national grid had been supplied with solar panels, including schools in isolated, mountainous areas with just one student.

In 2002, the Council of Ministers set up the Renewable Energy Front to advocate policies and devise strategies to strengthen the sustainable use of renewable energies in Cuba. The previous year, the Centre for Information Management and Energy Development, known as Cubaenergía, was created through the merging of several research and technology institutes. Its 80 scientists and technicians, including experts in nuclear energy, focused on energy efficiency, renewable energies and providing scientific–technical services to state enterprises and government ministries at a provincial level.[53]

In 2004, Cubaenergía launched a pilot project, with funding from the UN Industrial Development Organization, to increase the contribution of renewable energy sources on the Island of Youth (Isla de Juventud).[54] They began with a two-year study which identified the potential of biomass, produced as a residual from the woodland which covers over 54 per cent of the island, and designed demonstration plants for the use of biomass in electricity generation.[55] They also built a small wind farm with folding towers that can be lowered during a hurricane.

Starting in 2000, the trade and cooperation agreements signed between Cuba and Venezuela saw tens of thousands of Cuban medics and educators pour into Venezuela's poor neighbourhoods, while Cuba received up to 90,000 barrels of Venezuelan crude oil a day. The deal bought Cubans some necessary respite from the blackouts and bus queues of the Special Period and gave many millions of Venezuelans access to quality medical care for the first time. However, the 'oil for doctors' programme did not solve Cuba's energy problems. In 2003, Cuba's aged thermoelectric power stations were converted to burn the low quality, sulphur-heavy oil extracted from the surrounding shallow coastal waters. A Cuban expert lamented: 'Without the embargo this high sulphur content oil would have been used for making asphalt, not for energy production. But after the Soviet support was gone we had to turn to our national oil reserves.'[56] The result was a series of breakdowns, starting in 2004 with the major thermoelectric generator in Matanzas. Effectively this set Cuba back to the acute energy crisis of 1994, with electricity generation falling to 38 per cent of its potential. Having returned to live in Havana at that time, I experienced the increase in blackouts resulting from maintenance work and the withdrawal of the faulty thermoelectric plants in Matanzas and Camaguey.

These problems were compounded by hurricanes knocking out parts of Cuba's electricity supply. Pinar del Rio lost electricity for a fortnight and Trinidad de Cuba for a month after Hurricane Dennis struck as a category 4 storm, unseasonably early in July 2005, with winds of up to 220 kilometres per hour, 6-metre high waves and heavy rains, leaving an unusually high trail of death and destruction in a country famed for its national disaster response. The hurricane left 16 people dead – despite over 1.5 million people being evacuated (nearly 14 per cent of the population), caused USD 1.4 billion of damage and seriously affected 120,000 homes, including 15,000 which were completely destroyed.[57] Power cuts and communication systems broke down as 1,025 electricity posts were felled, 21 municipalities were left without electricity and 2.5 million people without a direct water supply.

'Look how weak we were!' exclaimed Bérriz, 'If anyone had thrown a bomb at Guiteras [power station in Holguin] you would have wiped out half of our electro-energetic system. If they had thrown seven, they would have finished us off!' Essentially, Cuba's electricity supply was generated through seven power stations, and this meant the island was extremely vulnerable to attack. Between the military invasion of Afghanistan in 2001 and Iraq in 2003, the US Undersecretary of State John Bolton had added Cuba to the list of 'rogue states' and 'state sponsors of terrorism'; military aggression certainly seemed possible to the Cubans.[58] 'As you said, it is not just the lights that go off, it wipes out industrial production, the warehouses, food, everything.' Furthermore, added

Bérriz, 'we can no longer live without electricity, we are too accustomed to it.'[59] A solution to Cuba's vulnerability was sought through the Energy Revolution.

2006 YEAR OF THE ENERGY REVOLUTION

The Year of the Energy Revolution dawned with the forty-seventh anniversary of the Revolution on 1 January 2006. The Energy Revolution was a major state initiative to improve both energy security and energy efficiency. It incorporated the installation of efficient new power generators in a 'distributed' system, increased emphasis on renewable energy, a progressive electricity tariff, and replacement of old durable goods with energy-saving equipment. The intention was to increase Cuba's capacity for electricity generation to four times its needs, consigning blackouts to the past and addressing the island's energy dependence.

During a seminal speech to student leaders at the University of Havana on 17 November 2005, Fidel Castro located the question of energy (cost to the state, cost to the consumer, state subsidies, theft and wastage, energy efficiency and conservation) in relation to the Battle of Ideas and to the survival of the Cuban Revolution. The state subsidy for fuel was so high that bills were negligible, he said. 'Simply stated, electricity is a gift, and I can prove it to you,' he announced before proving it with audience participation, statistics and examples. 'No one knows the cost of electricity, no one knows the cost of petrol, no one knows its market value.'[60] This placed an immense burden on the state budget and was a disincentive to individuals and businesses to conserve energy. 'We discovered that a *"paladar"* [private] restaurant consumed 11,000 kilowatts and that this stupid state was subsidizing the owner . . . [with] more than 1,000 dollars a month,' he complained.[61] The Energy Revolution would see the state reduce its energy subsidy, inducing an awareness of consumption and saving in the Cuban people.

Fidel Castro estimated that Cuba's new energy policy could save two-thirds of its existing energy consumption, more than USD 1 billion a year, or CUP 25 billion, nearly double the sum of Cuban wages. The total cost of Cuba's higher education system is just 20 per cent of what can be recouped by the energy revolution underway, he said. With this accumulation of wealth, salaries would rise and prices fall as production increased, to achieve what he called 'the dream of everyone being able to live on their salary or on their adequate pension'.[62]

DECENTRALISED GENERATION

When I met with Alfredo Curbelo Alonso, an engineer at Cubaenergía, he confirmed that a key driver behind the Energy Revolution was the commitment to switch to a decentralised, distributed system of energy generation in order to reduce the country's vulnerability to natural disasters and other so-called extraordinary situations, which, he explains, 'could include a war, blockade, something like that'.[63] Despite the centrality of the national security motivation it has been overlooked in externally published reports about the Energy Revolution that focus instead on three other important drivers: the decline of oil supplies, extreme weather conditions due to climate change and economic crises.[64]

In shifting to a 'distributed' system of power generation, 1,531 small generators with a total output of 3,072 MW were imported from Danish and Spanish companies and installed throughout the island.[65] Fidel Castro was personally involved, Curbelo Alonso said: 'Fidel invited the presidents of those businesses to Cuba and negotiated the price, everything. This was a scenario where you had to combine quantity, and it was a great quantity, with quality, which was also essential. What's more, we wanted maximum efficiency, we sought practically the best companies in the world; obviously they couldn't be American because of the US blockade.'[66]

The distributed system of electricity generation decisively reduced Cuba's vulnerability, agreed Bérriz: 'Now we have thousands of electric plant generators. The more electricity generators we have the stronger we become.'[67] In addition, as Curbelo Alonso pointed out, the distributed system is conceptually closer to the kind of localised generation required for a switch to renewable energies.[68] So, as well as solving the energy crises suffered in the 2003–5 period and improving the island's energy security, the Energy Revolution was a step towards a 'New Energy Paradigm' in which renewable energy sources would play an increasing role.[69]

In 2005 extensive blackouts lasting more than one hour had occurred on at least 224 days, but by 2007 power outages caused by the lack of generation capacity had been eliminated.[70] In the same period, Cuba had reduced its carbon dioxide emissions by some 5 million tons, equivalent to 20 per cent of the island's total emissions in 2002.[71] And Cuba was second in the world, after Denmark, in terms of distributed energy production.[72] In addition, more than 4,000 emergency back-up systems had been installed in hospitals, food production centres, schools and other critical sites, representing 500 MW of emergency back-up power.[73] Upgrades were made to 120,000 electrical posts, nearly 3,000 kilometres of cable and half a million electrical metres, reducing wastage and the amount of oil needed to generate one kWh of electricity from 280 grams in 2005 to 271 in 2007. 'While this might seem like a small saving, it translates into thousands of tonnes of imported oil annually,' wrote Laurie

Guevara-Stone, adding that 'in 2006–2007 Cuba saved over 961,000 tonnes of imported oil through energy-saving measures'.[74]

IMPROVING ENERGY EFFICIENCY AT HOME

For most Cubans the first sign of the Energy Revolution began in July 2005 when teenage social workers knocked at their doors delivering free energy-saving fluorescent bulbs. Within just six months, around 9.4 million incandescent bulbs had been replaced making Cuba the first country in the world to complete the switch. Conservative estimates are that this generated an annual saving of 354 million kWh, 3–4 per cent of total electricity consumption.[75] In state enterprises 800,000 inefficient fluorescent tubes with magnetic ballasts were exchanged for more efficient lamps with electronic ballasts.[76]

During their home visits in summer 2005, the social workers drew up inventories of each household's electrical equipment. This information was then used in the subsequent campaign to replace inefficient and ageing domestic appliances with more efficient substitutes imported from China. A Finnish report on the Energy Revolution noted: 'The biggest "energy monsters" were the old refrigerators from the 50s and the ventilators [air fans] that have been made from old Russian washing machines (a remarkable "grass-roots" innovation in itself of course, but a very energy consuming one).'[77] A similar German report calculated that each new Chinese refrigerator brought an annual saving of about 450 kWh per unit.[78] With over 2.5 million old fridges replaced, this totals 1,148 million kWh, an annual sum of 'about 230 million euros saved in operating costs (mainly fuel costs)'.[79] Also replaced were: over a million air fans; 265,500 air conditioners and ventilators; 230,500 televisions; and over 268,000 water pumps. Simple electric hotplates were distributed, along with 3.5 million rice cookers and 5.5 million pressure cookers.[80] As a result Seifried, author of the German report noted: 'While the vast majority of households cooked with kerosene and LPG [liquid petroleum gas] until early 2006, within a few months some 3 million households were converted almost completely to electric cooking. Gas stoves remained only in areas where there was a gas supply.'[81]

The purchase and replacement of this energy-saving equipment required a huge investment by the state. The energy-saving bulbs and fans were distributed to households free of charge, but Cubans were charged for the other equipment. How could Cuban consumers on low salaries be expected to pay back the cost of all this new equipment? A credit scheme was set up for most Cubans who could not pay upfront.[82] Within two years, Cuban banks financed over 4.5 million household appliances with a value of CUP 9 billion.[83] Repayments were adjusted to household incomes. In 2005, the average individual's monthly salary in Cuba was CUP 330.[84] Cuban households with a monthly income of up to CUP 225 were offered credit at an annual interest rate of 2 per cent and a repayment period of 10 years. The interest rose to 3 per cent for households with incomes between CUP 226 and CUP 450, to 4 per cent for incomes between CUP 451 and CUP 600, and so on. The higher the income, the higher the rate of interest. 'With an income of CUP 1,801 and more, loans were no longer granted,' explained Seifried.[85] Some 92 per cent of Cubans who requested credit paid between CUP 10 and CUP 75 monthly.[86]

How much the equipment cost the Cuban government has not been revealed, but based on his own estimations plus the fuel costs saved, Seifried calculated that 'the devices have been amortized in less than two years', concluding that 'we obtain a benefit–cost ratio for the Cuban economy of about ten [to one]'.[87] The switch to electric cooking alongside increased ownership of consumer durables saw electricity consumption increase by 13 per cent. Despite this, these measures saved Cuba about 250,000 tons of oil equivalents annually.[88] In May 2006, Fidel Castro told the state electric company: 'We are not waiting for fuel to fall from the sky, because we have discovered, fortunately, something much more important – energy conservation, which is like finding a great oil deposit.'[89]

A new progressive electricity tariff was introduced to reduce the state subsidy and encourage saving without hurting the country's poorest people. Households consuming less than 100 kWh per month paid the same low rate, just CUP 0.09 per kWh, but for every 50 kWh increase the rate went up. Consumers using over 300 kWh per month paid CUP 1.30 per kWh.[90] In other words, where consumption tripled, the cost of electricity per unit increased nearly 15 times. Subsequently, in 2011 the top rates were revised upwards from CUP 1.3 per kWh to CUP 5 for consumption above 5,000 kWh per month, so the highest band was over 50 times that of the lowest, with no change for low or medium consumption households.[91]

These energy-efficiency measures were largely directed at the residential sector for two reasons. First, because it accounts for some 45 per cent of Cuba's electricity consumption, an unusually high proportion which reflects low levels of industrial activity. Second, the investment required was less than for replacing capital goods, equipment, machinery, infrastructure and transport. 'The last industrial plants introduced into the country are from the

1980s and they were built to use fossil fuels and without prioritising energy efficiency,' explained Curbelo Alonso. Indeed, modern plants might produce the same product with half the energy consumption. 'The same applies for transport. With so many vehicles produced so many years ago and in such a deteriorated state, the amount of fuel you consume to transport a given quantity of products a certain distance is much greater than in a modern vehicle. But energy efficiency measures in transportation are associated with very high investment costs and we would practically have to renovate the entire automotive fleet.'[92]

EMBEDDING THE ENERGY REVOLUTION

'Educating a population of 11.5 million about energy is a tall order,' pointed out an article on the role of education in the Energy Revolution. 'Cuba's energy education program focused on creating a new energy culture and on achieving sustainable development.'[93]

The Ministry of Education's energy-saving programme, PAEME, took the Energy Revolution into schools and communities. Hundreds of educational festivals were held, and thousands of thematic workshops organised.[94] Between 2006 and 2008, to inform the Cuban people about the measures under way, there were 22,000 television and radio broadcasts, 1,600 newspaper articles and more than 1,100 discussions in communities.[95]

New institutions were set up within the framework of the Energy Revolution including the National Group for Renewable Energy Sources, Energy Efficiency and Co-generation, which had 14 commissions covering different types of renewable sources of energy and efficiency, coordinated by the government, to research and propose ways of developing Cuba's renewable energy potential. A new ministerial department for Renewable Energies was created, attached to the Ministry of Basic Industry.[96] National programmes were launched to generate electricity from wind energy, to provide solar water-heating for domestic, social and industrial purposes, to develop hydro and solid waste energy capacities and to research geothermal, ocean energy and other technologies.[97]

By 2009, between 6 and 7 per cent of the Cuban people were receiving electricity from gensets (equipment which converts heat capacity into mechanical energy and then electrical energy), small hydropower stations or solar panels in off-grid areas. Total installed electricity production capacity was some 6,000 MW while energy demand in Havana was around 500 MW. The distributed systems supplied 42 per cent of electricity production capacity. The contribution of renewable energies to *electricity* production was 4 per cent (in 2011), but 20 per cent in primary *energy* production, given the use of *bagasse*-fired energy in the sugar industry. Hence the Finnish report concluded that: 'The emphasis on increasing the use of renewable energy sources in the overall energy mix has, however, been slow and is not yet clearly visible in the statistics.'[98]

In 2010 Cuba's new National Environment Strategy was launched to solve the island's main environmental challenges: land degradation, forest cover, pollution, loss of biological diversity, water scarcity and climate change impacts.[99] Meanwhile, back on the Island of Youth, Cubaenergía's renewable energies project passed from the experimental to the investment phase and the Ministry of Energy and Mines took control.[100] Between January and September 2014, diesel use on the Island of Youth was down by 329 tons, saving the equivalent of USD 253,000 on the international market.[101] In 2015, two solar parks contributed 1,039 MW to the electro-energetic system, equivalent to some 900 tons of fuel, saving USD 517,621 in oil imports for generating electricity. A third solar park was under construction.

Since 2015, Cubaenergía has coordinated a new project with the European Union, worth over EUR 3 million, to develop 'environmental bases for local food sustainability' and 'contribute to food security based on principles of economic, technological, environmental, organisational and gender equity'.[102] Cubaenergía's contribution was to demonstrate the benefits of biogas, photovoltaic solar panels and solar dryers for agriculture. The organisation is also developing a 'bioenergy technology transfer' project in Matanzas province.[103] Curbelo Alonso explained that by 'bioenergy' they refer to the use of biogas, wood waste, forest biomass, including *Dichrostachys cinerea*, known in Cuba as *marabú*, and the production of biodiesel from a plant with the scientific name *Jatropha curcas*. 'In Cuba it is called *Piñón de botija*. It is a plant that grows well with little need for water,' he told me. The project fosters these technologies and the equipment which uses them. 'Cubaenergía is responsible for showing the country that the potential exists, and what kind of regulatory measures would have to be taken to achieve its potential use.'[104]

A BRIGHT AND RENEWABLE CUBA?

According to Bérriz, today the pioneer in renewable energy use in Cuba is the Revolutionary Armed Forces (FAR), which Raúl Castro led between 1959 and 2008. 'Most military buildings have solar heaters and they have many solar parks. They have worked a lot with wood dryers and solar dryers for their agricultural products.'[105] For the FAR, self-sufficiency is an issue of national security and this motivates the military's engagement in productive and economic activities.[106] Renewable energies and energy efficiency bring Cuba closer to energy sovereignty.

Despite the progress made and the aspirations of those driving it, by mid-2017 Cuba's energy structure remained highly dependent on imported fossil fuels, with the associated economic and strategic risks. Renewable energy sources contributed just 4.5 per cent of electricity production for the national grid, compared to 45 per cent crude oil, 18 per cent motor oil, 15.1 per cent thermal fuel, 14.1 per cent natural gas and 3.3 per cent diesel. The national economic and social development plan through to 2030 (*Plan 2030*) seeks to increase the share of renewable energy sources to 24 per cent by 2030, reducing crude oil to 32 per cent, motor fuel to 9 per cent, thermal fuel to 5 per cent, natural gas to 8 per cent, diesel to 1 per cent and 'other combustible fossil fuels' to 21 per cent.[107]

However, these statistics fail to capture the scope of the commitment to renewable energy use in Cuba, because they refer to the production of electricity in the national grid, not the production of energy per se. This distinction is overlooked even in Cuban reports, which refer to the aim of raising renewable energy sources to 24 per cent of energy production by 2030.[108] 'We already have 30 per cent of the country's energy produced by renewable energy sources!' Bérriz exclaimed. 'All the electricity produced by the sugar refineries for their own consumption is not included in the current statistic citing 4 per cent.' He provided another example: the aqueduct at Baracoa was a huge consumer of electricity until it was reconstructed to use gravity, instead of an electrical pump, to supply water. 'Before, it used so much electricity, and now it doesn't use any, so it no longer appears in the statistics,' he pointed out.[109] Table 3 below shows the existing stock of renewable energy by source.[110]

A second statistical error is not factoring in rising production. Reports often describe the stated aim as a six-fold increase in the contribution of renewable energy sources to electricity production (from 4 per cent to 24 per cent) when in fact it represents a multiplication of ten because electricity production is expected to increase from 18 terawatts (TW) to 30 TW in 2030. Bérriz made the calculation: '4 per cent of 18 is 0.72 and 24 per cent of 30 is 7.2; so the amount of electricity that will be produced for the national grid will be a 10-fold multiplication.'[111]

There had also been progress in energy efficiency. By mid-2017, 2 million fluorescent bulbs had been replaced with LED bulbs in the residential sector, with another 11 million to go, plus another 250,000 public lights. Over half a million induction cookers had been sold to Cuban households, with the goal

Table 3: Stocks of renewable energy in 2017		
Technology	**Installed capacity**	**Installations**
Sugarcane biomass	470 MW	57 sugar mills
Wind	11.1 MW	4 wind parks
Solar photovoltaic	37 MW 5543 MW 467 MW 1882 MW 2500 MW	22 photovoltaic solar parks Rural schools Doctors' surgeries Rural TV centres 149 isolated houses
Hydroenergy	66 MW	149 hydroelectric plants
Biogas	0.82 MW	5 biogas plants
Non-sugar biogas	0.5 MW	4 biogas plants

being to replace 2 million electric resistance cookers.[112] In Cuban homes, 550 square metres of solar heaters had been installed out of the planned 200,000 square metres, reducing the electricity consumed in those homes by an average of 12 per cent. By late 2018, 31,000 facilities in Cuba were using solar heaters, 9,476 had solar panels, 9,343 had windmills, 3,234 had biogas plants, and there were 147 hydroelectric facilities and 22 solar farms.[113]

'Natural resources and the environment' is one of six strategic areas for national development in the national *Plan 2030*.[114] The general objectives are: '1) Guarantee the protection and rational use of natural resources, the conservation of ecosystems, and care of the environment and the natural heritage of the nation for the benefit of society. 2) Improve the quality of the environment. 3) Reduce the country's vulnerability to the effects of climate change through the gradual execution of the State Plan [Tarea Vida] for confronting it.' These are followed by twenty-one specific objectives, one of which is to increase energy efficiency and the development of renewable energy sources, 'which, among other benefits, contributes to reducing the generation of greenhouse gases, reduces climate change and promotes less carbon-intensive economic development.'[115]

More specifically, the goals include the installation of 2144 MW of new electrical power, requiring an expenditure of USD 4 billion. This will augment the existing renewable energy sources stock with 19 bioelectric plants, 14 wind parks, solar parks producing 700 MW and 74 small hydroelectric stations by 2030. It will also see the extension of thermal solar energy, forest biomass, solid urban waste, agricultural and organic industrial waste.[116] Industrial biogas plants are being constructed to treat waste and produce energy: of the 500 planned, 5 were already operating in mid-2017. Similar plants will tackle waste contamination from pig farms, with 7,000 biogas plants to be built for use with pig excrement and another 1,700 for cow excrement. There are also ambitious plans for forest biomass, by converting *marabú*, the leguminous tree with deep roots which spread like a weed over 2 million hectares of uncultivated agricultural land, about 18 per cent of the country's territory, from a curse into a resource. An article in *The Economist* about a British–Cuban joint venture in this area described it as 'Cuba's wonderful weed' explaining that: 'Three tonnes of the stuff can produce as much electricity as a tonne of fuel oil.'[117] Small biomass electricity generators will power 67 saw mills. The first of these are under development.[118]

'How will these objectives be achieved?' I asked Curbelo Alonso. 'You know how this works,' he responded. 'The policy goals are public. Then there are teams in the country's institutions working to implement the policies and devise regulations for achieving them. There are work groups which have prepared a renewable energy law which will be an important step. It's not public yet – they are still working on it because it's a complex problem.'[119]

By 2017, three Cuban factories were manufacturing solar water heaters: in Morón, Ciego de Ávila, Cayo Coco. 'We would like to have a factory in every province. And it is one of the things which we are promoting,' said Bérriz, who is committed to converting Cuban homes from net consumers of energy into net producers, or 'positive energy homes'; he believes it is a possibility, not a utopian ideal, if the installation of solar panels is accompanied by moves to cook with biomass and heat water with solar heaters.[120] In Cuba, residential use accounts for nearly half of total electricity consumption and half of that is for food cooking and heating water for bathing. 'No one believes it, but 90 per cent of the Cuban population heats water to bath themselves. In summer, people heat water to wash!' he exclaimed. 'If we put solar heaters in the houses, this immense quantity of electricity will no longer be consumed. Instead of using petroleum to heat water, we could use the sun. The technologies exist, what we have to do is use them.'[121] In August 2019, a new programme was approved to sell solar heaters to residents in Havana.[122] Lights, televisions and other residential electrical equipment use a much smaller proportion of the electricity consumed. Implementing the new law 'Development of Renewable Sources and Efficient Use of Energy' approved on 23 March 2017 will be an important step in this direction.

THE ROLE OF FOREIGN INVESTMENT

Cuba's ability to achieve its ambitious goals is dependent on the government's capacity to attract foreign investment, including Economic Partnership Agreements. Their 2016/17 *Portfolio of Foreign Investment* included USD 3 billion sought for renewable energy projects, with the projected potential to add 2.1 gigawatts of capacity from wind, solar, biogas and biomass plants.[123] The 2017/18 portfolio listed 13 projects for renewable energy development.[124]

The Cuban government has already contracted Spanish renewable energy corporation Gamesa to build seven wind farms in eastern Cuba with a total generating power of 750 MW. These will be added to four existing wind parks in Ciego de Avila, Holguin and the Island of Youth. Another plan is to generate 440 MW of power from solar energy by 2020. Cuba has received a USD 15 million loan 'under favourable terms' from the Abu Dhabi Development Fund to develop 4 solar power plants each producing 10 MW using photovoltaic silicon panels.[125] Given the urgency in securing foreign investment in these areas, the Cuban government is inviting 100 per cent foreign-owned investments for these projects, an ownership status rarely permitted in revolutionary Cuba.[126]

China has been a key partner, offering training for Cuban technicians, technology and credit to help Cuba augment its domestic production of solar panels. Some 60,000 Cuban panels were manufactured in 2016, all of them with Chinese equipment, and the plan is to increase production three-fold and install more automated machines. Chinese capital stepped in to assist a British company, Havana Energy, which had entered a joint venture with Cuban state company Azcuba in 2010 to develop biomass plants using Cuban *bagasse* and *marabú*. The British partners struggled to access financing from Europe, because of the US blockade, so Shanghai Electric stepped in as the major shareholder.[127] By early 2018, two biomass plants were under construction, which according to a business report, would 'contribute 4 per cent more to Cuba's renewable energy share', and were expected to foster significant future foreign investment.[128]

THE PRINCIPLES OF CUBAN ENERGY POLICY

'The world's energy policy is not right; while we follow this we are lost and that's where the big problem is,' said Bérriz. 'We now have the correct national energy policy, based on energy efficiency and the use of renewable sources of energy. We know where we are going, we just have to see how we get there.'[129] What is the Cuban government's energy policy? It is formally guided by the following principles: human beings are at the centre of all considerations; an efficient, diversified, balanced, independent and sustainable energy mix must be achieved; foreign investment must be fostered; and there must be greater territorial participation.[130] With adequate foreign investment, Cuba can pursue its commitment to renewable energy, energy efficiency and, ultimately, energy security. The Trump administration's aggressive measures to tighten the US blockade, outlined in Chapter 10, make implementing the new energy paradigm both more difficult, by obstructing foreign investment, and more urgent.

Although preceded by decades of technical and scientific experimentation and innovation, the Energy Revolution of 2005–2006 was a turning point in Cuba's commitment to renewable energies and sustainable development. It was motivated by multiple factors: reducing spending and dependence on oil imports, and Cuba's susceptibility to volatile international energy prices; the need for energy security and national defence; combatting the effects of climate change; and improving social and economic justice by raising living standards and universalising access to energy. Creating a new energy paradigm is central to the current process of updating the Cuban economy, as shown by the focus it is given in *Plan 2030* and in terms of the opportunities available for foreign investors. According to Bérriz, the solar radiation that Cuba receives in one day is equivalent to the energy produced by 50 million tonnes of petroleum. It is greater in energy value than the petroleum Cuba consumes in five years. There is great potential for a bright and renewable future for the Cuban revolution.

5

★ ★ ★

THE CURIOUS CASE OF CUBA'S
BIOTECH REVOLUTION

In late September 2018, a United States and Cuban biotech joint venture was established to trial and deliver CIMAvax-EGF, an innovative Cuban lung cancer immunotherapy treatment, to patients in the United States. Innovative Immunotherapy Alliance SA was set up by Buffalo-based Roswell Park Comprehensive Cancer Center and Havana's Centre for Molecular Immunology (CIM), an institutional collaboration which benefited from the tentative rapprochement between the United States and Cuba in 2015 and 2016. The sheer fact that such an entity should exist is scientifically and politically groundbreaking for several reasons.[1]

First, it testifies to the extraordinary development of biotechnology in Cuba, which has been largely overlooked in medical science and business history literature on the field.[2] Second, despite six decades of the United States blockade obstructing Cuba's foreign trade, external financing, technology transfers and scientific exchange, including in the medical field, it is the Cubans who have contributed the innovative science to this joint venture: they have cracked a difficult nut, using immunotherapy to combat cancer. Third, while global biopharma is associated with speculative, mostly private, capital, the Cuban industry is entirely state-owned and financed. The emergence of Havana's Scientific Pole for example, was the result of state planning, not of market forces attracting private interests to a given location. The Cuban state was motivated by socioeconomic and welfare concerns, not simply economic gains.[3] Fourth, while domestic production of medical drugs and supplies was an imperative forced on Cuba by the US blockade, particularly in the post-Soviet era, the historical development of medical science on the island, with its focus on parasitology and immunotherapy, was also decisive. So was the involvement from the outset of researchers in biophysics and nuclear physics with the technological and instrumental knowledge necessary to construct the first Cuban laboratories.

The collaboration between Roswell Park and CIM began when Cuban researcher Gisela González, who was visiting her family in Pittsburgh in 2011, 'cold called' the Roswell Park Cancer Centre in Buffalo, New York, to tell them about a lung cancer vaccine developed by Cuba's CIM. They invited her to give a presentation about the CIMAvax-EGF vaccine. Dr Kelvin Lee, chairman of Roswell's Department of Immunology, told me his reaction: 'Gisela came up and gave a great immunology talk. I'm sitting there thinking "Why would that ever work?" Then she goes on to show it works and that they have done all these clinical trials. My good friend from California sitting next to me said "The Cubans just throw out chapter one of every immunology text book we know." And it's like, that's really clever, we would've never thought to do that.'[4]

Dr Lee admits that this was a revelation; he had an outdated, romantic image of Cuba 'from the "I love Lucy" days, the 1950s, Tropicana, and all that. We really hadn't thought about Cuba progressing forward from that time.' With little contact between Cuba and the United States for nearly 60 years, he says, 'they were really flying under the radar'. Roswell Park took the bait and shortly afterwards Lee attended an international immunology convention in Havana. He was impressed by the number of innovative scientists doing remarkable research at CIM.

'Who would have guessed that there was a medium-sized pharmaceutical company that had integrated its basic research all the way through to commercial production in one plant? They were adapting very sophisticated technologies to their economic constraints. Cuban scientists don't have a lot of resources to burn, so they think very carefully about what they're going to do even before they start. They are very thoughtful, thorough planners . . . It was unexpected. The degree of sophistication, the size of their efforts. The fact that Fidel Castro saw this as something very important, at the dawn of the biotech era, and really pushed it forwards. It was all unexpected and very exciting!'[5]

However, Lee's journey to Havana was not quite breaking new ground. Back in 1980, another Dr Lee had made that journey. The visit to Cuba by US oncologist Dr Randolph Lee Clark, Director of the M.D. Anderson Cancer Center in Houston, is credited for catalysing Fidel Castro's determination to develop what has since become Cuba's world-leading biotechnology sector. The quantity and range of Cuba's products is also significant: CIM's lung cancer vaccine is not an exception. Indeed, as Dr Kelvin Lee himself now recognises Cuba's biotechnology successes build on their 'long history of really good infectious disease vaccination'. That story begins back in the nineteenth century.

THE HISTORICAL TRAJECTORY OF CUBAN MEDICAL SCIENCE

Three private science institutes were set up in nineteenth century Cuba,[6] but the best known medical scientist of that century is Carlos Finlay who was born in colonial Cuba in 1833 to a Scottish father and a French mother. In 1881, Finlay presented a ground-breaking theory that the transmission vector, or carrier, of yellow fever was the mosquito. The following year, Finlay identified the *Aedas aegypti* mosquito as the culprit, and recommended controls to halt the spread of the disease. His finding was described as the greatest advance in medical science since the discovery of the smallpox vaccine in 1796.[7] Following Cuba's formal independence, between 1902 and 1909, Finlay served as Cuba's chief health officer.

There were other outstanding individuals in the decades that followed, but the period between Cuban 'independence' in 1902 and the Revolution of 1959 were austere years for medical science. The country had only three universities: in Havana, Oriente (Santiago) and Villa Clara (set up in 1952), and they conducted little medical research. In 1937, Dr Pedro Kourí privately founded the Institute of Tropical Medicine, which did conduct investigations and earned a good international reputation among parasitologists and other specialists of tropical medicine.

Private medical clinics thrived, largely by offering clients from the United States services at a lower cost than home, or services not available in the United States due to more stringent regulations.[8] There was a tradition of eminence in surgery. The big money spinner was cosmetic surgery, which generated USD 5 million a year between 1948 and 1958. The main causes of childhood death on the island were parasitic infestation, gross malnutrition and enteric infections, leading to diarrhoea and dehydration. But the paediatrics department at the University of Havana Medical School barely addressed these ailments. Instead it specialised in hyperactivity and leukaemia.

There was also a medical focus on the diagnosis and treatment of cancer. Created in 1925, the League against Cancer in Cuba secured private funding to set up the 'Calixto García' hospital, where prestigious Cuban medical practitioners held private clinics. In 1929, the Institute of Cancer was set up, the first to treat malignant growths. Subsequently two more oncology centres were founded, mainly to treat patients in the advanced stages of cancer. Most of the doctors did not receive payment; this was philanthropic work. They did teach, however, and exchanged scientific information and experiences with oncology centres in developed countries.[9]

The 1950 report by the Truslow Commission of the International Bank of Reconstruction and Development declared that 'the Mission could not find any suitable applied research laboratory, public or private, in Cuba'.[10] Three years later, the 1953 census recorded that 60 per cent of the population had had had a maximum of three years of education.[11] Just over 1 per cent of Cubans had university education, and of those only 1.7 per cent were science students who mostly graduated without practical experience. Access to health care was also highly unequal, and public healthcare provision was minimal.

PRE-REVOLUTIONARY CUBA: AN UNHEALTHY PLACE TO BE POOR

In pre-1959 Cuba, healthcare provision was divided into contributory, private and public sectors.[12] The contributory sector, where regular payments were made to mutualist or medical associations, or to trade unions, served the middle classes and sections of the organised working class. The smaller private sector served mainly the rich. The public sector served mainly the poor. It has been estimated that one-fifth of Cubans belonged to mutualist health associations or medical cooperatives by 1958 and private clinics also abounded. In the 1930s, some 200 Cuban doctors were paid by local government authorities, the *municipios*, to attend the 'sick poor' part-time. There were free hospital beds in Havana to serve the urban poor. By the 1950s, relative to the rest of Latin America, Cuba had a high number of doctors – 6,286 physicians – and the island's poor had at least the possibility of receiving medical attention.

However, geography, racism and corruption obstructed medical access. Some 62 per cent of medical practitioners were in Havana. Many mutualist associations banned non-white Cubans, while others were racially segregated. This was not the case in the communist-led trade unions, where contributory healthcare plans were funded by payroll deductions. In the 1950s, the Cuban government allocated around 7.5 per cent of its budget to 'health and welfare', but a large proportion was skimmed off through graft and corruption. For the rural population, medical services were channelled through political party leaders, so those requiring access to clinics or hospital beds had to sell their votes accordingly.[13]

Cuba had one medical school, the best in Latin America, recognised by the American Medical Association as on a par with those in the United States.[14] Tuition was free, but only students from expensive private schools could attain the high entry grades. Medical training relied almost exclusively on text books used in US medical schools, preparing doctors for US medical realities. This was not inconvenient, however, given that many graduates planned to establish lucrative practices in urban areas where wealthy clientele, including US health tourists, could afford to pay.

Meanwhile, Cuba's rural infant and maternal death rates were the second highest in Latin America.[15] Some 80 per cent of children in the countryside suffered intestinal parasites in 1959: it was the number one cause of death. And 60 per cent of the rural population was seriously undernourished. Life expectancy in rural areas was 50 years (60 nationally) and infant mortality was 100 per 1,000 live births (58 per 1,000 nationally). And yet there was only one rural hospital. Unsurprisingly, given massive unemployment, low salaries and little access to land, only 4 per cent of Cubans in the rural areas ate meat, 3 per cent ate bread, 11 per cent had milk after weaning and less than 20 per cent ate eggs.[16] More than 75 per cent of rural dwellings were wooden huts; only 2 per cent of rural Cubans had running water and 9 per cent had electricity.[17] The true enemy of public health, a report noted, was 'economic underdevelopment, feudal exploitation, the *latifundia* [plantation system] and its consequences: illiteracy, the hundreds of thousands of unemployed, the terrible *tiempo muerto* [the 'dead season' between sugar harvests when 400,000 cane cutters were left unemployed] with its inescapable companions: misery, hunger, and death.'[18] What were the revolutionaries going to do about it?

REVOLUTIONARY CHANGE: SOCIALISM IS GOOD FOR YOUR HEALTH

Speaking at the Cuban Academy of Sciences in mid-January 1960, one year after the Rebel Army took power, Fidel Castro declared: 'The future of Cuba will be a future of men of science.' This must have seemed like a pipe dream, given the backward state of Cuban scientific research and generally low level of education. The Revolution, declared Castro, was sowing opportunities for intelligence. It needed thinking men who would put their intelligence to 'good', on the side of 'justice', in the interests of the nation.

Initiated the following January, the literacy campaign of 1961 reduced illiteracy from 23 per cent to 3 per cent in Cubans over ten years old within one year. It was followed by the University Reform Law in January 1962, which removed their traditional autonomy and, by eliminating fees and facilitating access at all levels, opened the universities to the children of workers, peasants and non-white Cubans. Courses were introduced to train the specialists required for the Revolution's economic development plans. In 1962 the Cuban government created the National Commission for the Academy of

Sciences of Cuba. New schools, colleges and universities were built, new teachers trained. Thousands of Cuban students studied in the socialist bloc countries, while others received scholarships from institutions in the west.

As the Rebel Army took over Havana, medical professionals followed the dictator Fulgencio Batista off the island. Only 12 of the 250 Cuban teachers at the University of Havana's Medical School remained.[19] The vacancies were filled by volunteer professors from different countries.[20] Cuba signed medical aid treaties with East Germany and Poland. Fidel Castro later recalled 'we were left almost without doctors, because 3,000 of them left out of the 6,000 that had been in the country.'[21] How could the new revolutionary government introduce free universal access to medical treatment, funded by the state rather than through compulsory insurance, with so few medics and lacking the infrastructure necessary to reach the rural and mountainous areas where those most in need lived? Among the stopgap measures taken was the retraining of prostitutes as paramedical staff to meet the critical staff shortages.[22]

Canadian Professor Theodore MacDonald spoke to some of those nurses in 1961 who: 'had only been given a week's training, and equipped with a St John's Ambulance First Aid book (in English!. . .) before being sent individually and on their own to run rural health clinics where none had existed before. As one of them observed, prostitution had been much easier and more highly paid. All of those women subsequently enrolled for proper nursing training in 1960 because they found the work interesting . . . Other ex-prostitutes found themselves assigned to hospitals where they took a six-month emergency certificate course, involving half a day on the ward directed by a fully qualified nurse and the other half of each day receiving classroom instruction.'[23]

Inevitably, says MacDonald, the academic quality of the Revolution's first cohort of medical students fell. They had been selected on the basis of their answers to 'social issues' questions, not just their grades. Of 63 students who applied in 1959, only 38 were selected and 14 of them soon dropped out as they found the course too strenuous.[24]

Cuba's rural structure began to change with the first Agrarian Reform Law of 1959 which distributed deeds to 150,000 landless farmers. In 1960, the Rural Medical Service (RMS) was established and over the next decade hundreds of newly graduated doctors were posted in remote areas.[25] RMS physicians served as health educators as well as clinicians. National programmes were established for infectious disease control and prevention, targeting malaria and acute diarrhoeal and vaccine-preventable illnesses.[26] From 1962 a national immunisation programme provided all Cubans with eight vaccinations free of charge. Infectious diseases were rapidly reduced, then eliminated, including polio (eliminated 1962), malaria (1968), diphtheria (1971), measles (1993), pertussis (1994) and rubella (1995).[27]

CHE GUEVARA PROMOTES MEDICAL SCIENCE

In 1959, Cuba was dependent on US pharma for medicines. The market was dominated by two firms which made exorbitant profits. The industry was expropriated by revolutionary decree, putting production and distribution of medicines into government hands. It fell under the jurisdiction of Ernesto 'Che' Guevara as Minister of Industries. In his pre-revolutionary life, Guevara had graduated as a medic and researched allergies, asthma, leprosy and nutritive theory.

As Minister, he set up nine research and development institutes, including, in 1963, the Institute for the Development of the Chemical Industry to foster the industrial application of human and animal antibiotics.[28] While progress was limited, the Institute established a research methodology which later became a distinctive feature of Cuban biotechnology. 'The idea was excellent,' Tirso Sáenz, Guevara's Vice Minister of Science and Technology in the early 1960s, told me, 'to make an institution with what they call a complete cycle of innovation. The institute develops products at a scale where it can build pilot plants which, if successful, are turned into production plants.'[29]

Guevara commandeered an abandoned farm, to use for socio-productive and botanical experiments.[30] The personnel were students from the Rebel Army School, and they were joined by Chinese medical scientists, a Cuban post-doctoral researcher and three agronomy engineers. From the farm two dozen varieties of medicinal plants were supplied to 40 scientists conducting laboratory experiments with plants, animals and raw materials on the fourth floor at the Hospital of Oncology under Guevara's directives.[31] In this institution lie the roots of CIM.[32] When Juan Valdés Gravalosa, at the time a leading member of the Ministry of Industries, visited the hospital laboratory he saw research being conducted into antibiotics and use of the native *vicaría* flower for fighting leukaemia. He also told me about an experiment mysteriously labelled '31', involving a flower with strong medicinal qualities taken from burial earth: 'They were secretly going round the cemeteries!' he exclaimed.[33]

Guevara left Cuba in 1965 and the farm was transferred to the newly established National Centre for Scientific Research (CENIC), set up to initiate biological studies and a new scientific infrastructure. The directors in the post-

1980 biotechnology institutes all began as students in CENIC.[34] Throughout the 1960s and 1970s, thousands of Cubans trained as scientists and engineers. Cuba achieved 1.8 researchers per 1,000 inhabitants, well above the mean for Latin America (0.4) and close to that of Europe (2.0).[35] Among the many institutions created was the National Council of Science and Technology, in 1975, the same year that a new national scientific policy was approved at the First Congress of the Cuban Communist Party.

EXTENDING AND IMPROVING HEALTH CARE

By 1970, the number of rural hospitals had risen to 53.[36] Provincial medical and nursing schools were established to decentralise training and encourage professionals to practice where they grew up. Tuition was free, academic achievement being the sole requisite for admission. By the mid-1970s, health services were available across the country and indicators improved significantly. A new model of community-based polyclinics was established in 1974 to deliver comprehensive care to residents in their neighbourhoods. Polyclinics gave Cuban communities local access to primary care specialists such as obstetricians, gynaecologists, paediatricians, internists and dental services. Training and policy emphasised the impact of biological, social, cultural, economic and environmental factors on patients. National programmes focused on maternal and child health, infectious diseases, chronic non-communicable diseases and older adult health.

In 1976 a new Ministry of Public Health was established, and a new Cuban constitution approved. Article 50 stated:

> Everybody has the right to health protection and care. The State guarantees this right: by providing free medical and hospital care, by means of the installations of the rural medical service network, polyclinics, hospitals and preventive and specialized treatment centers; by providing free dental care; by promoting the public health campaigns, health education, regular medical examinations, general vaccinations and other measures to prevent the outbreak of disease. All of the population cooperates in these activities and plans through the social and mass organizations.[37]

By the 1980s, Cuba had the health profile of a highly developed country, having eliminated most infectious and poverty-related diseases, so that ailments such as cancer, diabetes and heart disease became priorities, on a par with the developed capitalist world.[38] These conditions are expensive to treat.

Additionally, a new law passed by US president Ronald Reagan in 1982 prohibited foreign nations from exporting goods and equipment to Cuba if any part or process in its manufacture had been mediated by US companies or individuals. Cuban subscriptions to US science and technology journals could not be honoured.[39]

In Cuba, medical focus was extended to tertiary care (specialised consultative care) facilities and research. In 1983, the Family Doctor and Nurse Plan was introduced nationwide. Local practices were to coordinate medical care and lead health promotion efforts, emphasising prevention and epidemiologic analysis. Primary-care professionals were to rely on medical records and clinical skills, reserving costly high-tech procedures for patients requiring them. Comprehensive General Medicine became a new postgraduate specialisation.

Family physicians and nurse teams lived among their patients. Initially, each team was responsible for 120 to 150 families (600–800 people), holding office hours in the mornings and house calls in the afternoons.[40] Generally, either the doctor or the nurse lived with their family above the medical practice, so medical attention was available 24 hours a day. The teams carried out neighbourhood health diagnosis and continuous assessment and risk evaluation for their patients.[41] Family doctors and nurses were also employed in large workplaces and schools, child day care centres, homes for senior citizens and so on.

SAVING AND EXTENDING LIVES IN THE SPECIAL PERIOD

From 1990, the Special Period of economic crisis wreaked havoc on the Cuban population and economy (see Chapter 2). However, action taken by the Cuban government mitigated the deterioration of health for the revolutionary people. This was driven by ideological commitments to the predominance of state ownership, central planning and free, universal welfare provision, and it was essential to secure the people's commitment to the Revolution in such austere conditions. Despite the severity of the economic collapse, the share of Cuba's GDP spent on social programmes in the 1990s increased by nearly 35 per cent.[42]

Scarce medical equipment and medicines were compensated for by increased personnel. Health spending rose 13 per cent and 15,380 medical professionals joined the service between 1990 and 1994, raising the doctor to patient ratio from 1 to every 276 inhabitants to 1 to 202. Between 1990 and 2003, the number of Cuban doctors increased by 76 per cent, dentists by 46 per cent and nurses by 16 per cent. There was an 86 per cent increase in maternity homes, 107 per cent increase in senior day-care centres and 47 per cent increase in homes for people with disabilities.[43] Remarkably, infant mortality declined from 10.7 per 1,000 in 1990 to 7.2 in 1999, while life expectancy rose from 75 to 75.6 years despite the crisis.[44]

By 1999, family doctors served all Cubans, even the most rural populations. Praising the Cuban system in 2000, a United Nations Development Programme study asserted that: 'Cuba is the country with the best health situation in Latin America and the Caribbean', and UN Secretary General Kofi Annan said the island 'demonstrates how much nations can do with the resources they have if they focus on the right priorities – health, education, and literacy'.[45] Remarkable conclusions given the decade of severe economic crises that preceded it and the fact that the US blockade had been tightened three times during the decade, preventing Cubans from accessing healthcare technologies, medicines and even medical journals. Cuban paediatrician Aleida Guevara, daughter of the Argentinian revolutionary Che Guevara, described how, in her hospital, 'We used an X-ray machine for more than 45 years.' They finally purchased a new one for an extortionate price which involved going through two or three intermediaries to circumvent the US blockade.[46]

By 2012 there were 488 polyclinics throughout Cuba, each serving between 20,000 and 60,000 patients and supporting 20 to 40 family doctors.[47] There were an additional 336 maternity homes for women with high-risk pregnancies and 234 senior day-care centres. All 15 of Cuba's provinces had at least one general, one maternal and one paediatric hospital, and most had more. There were 215 hospitals in Cuba. Cubans continue to be well served in medical terms with 7.5 doctors per 1,000 head of population, nearly three times the density of doctors in the United States or the United Kingdom.[48]

HIGH TECH MEDICINE IN LOW TECH CUBA: THE BIOTECHNOLOGY STORY

'Biotechnology is an industrial process,' explains Dr Agustín Lage Dávila, Director of the Centre for Molecular Immunology (CIM) and a key character in Cuba's biotechnology story. We are sitting around a long conference table in a plain room in the CIM premises. 'People have a hard time distinguishing between biological and biotechnological scientific research,' he went on. Biological research into genomes and cells does not constitute biotechnology unless it involves industrial production. 'When you start talking about productive scaling, it begins to look like any manufacturing process; a transformation industry. You transform cotton into fabric, iron into steel, wood into furniture, oil into plastic. You British invented it with the Industrial Revolution! Biotechnology is the same thing, but the transformation of the raw material into a final product is done inside a living cell; the factory is the cell.'[49]

The world's first biotechnology enterprise was established in the United States in 1976. Just five years later, in 1981, the Biological Front, a professional interdisciplinary forum, was set up to develop the industry in Cuba.[50] This was the first time in its economic history that Cuba had incorporated itself into an emerging industrial sector. How did this happen? While most developing countries had little access to the new technologies (recombinant DNA, human gene therapy, biosafety), Cuban biotechnology expanded and took on an increasingly strategic role in both the public health sector and the national economic development plan.[51] It did so despite the US blockade obstructing access to technologies, equipment, materials and even knowledge exchange.

Cuba's biotechnology sector emerged independently from both the Soviet Union and the corporate capitalist model in the United States and Europe.[52] Driven by public health demand, it has been characterised by the fast track from research and innovation to trials and application. This is illustrated by the development and use of interferons to arrest a deadly outbreak of the dengue virus in 1981.[53]

Interferons are 'signalling' proteins produced and released by host cells in response to pathogens (viruses, bacteria, parasites and tumour cells) which alert nearby cells to heighten their defences. Interferons were first identified in 1957 by Jean Lindenmann and Aleck Isaacs at the National Institute of Medical Research in London during their work on 'viral interference', the process by which a cell that is infected by one virus can produce an immune response which protects it from another virus. Following this breakthrough, in the 1960s Ion Gresser, a US researcher in Paris, showed that interferons stimulate lymphocytes that attack tumours in mice.

In the 1970s, US oncologist Randolph Clark Lee had taken up this research. Catching the tail end of US president Jimmy Carter's improved relations with Cuba, Clark joined a delegation to visit the island's health facilities. During the trip Clark met with Fidel Castro and convinced him that interferon was *the* wonder drug. Clark offered to host a Cuban researcher at his hospital. Castro persuaded him to take two. Shortly afterwards, a Cuban doctor and a haematologist spent time in Clark's laboratory. He gave them the latest research about interferon and put them in contact with the Finnish doctor Kari Cantell, who in the 1970s had isolated interferon from human cells. Cantell's commitment to global health led him to share his breakthrough without patenting his interferon procedure. In March 1981, six Cubans spent twelve days in Finland with Cantell learning to produce large quantities of interferon. They were from the first generation of medical scientists entirely trained under the Revolution since 1959.

In April 1981, the day after returning from Finland, the Cubans moved into 'House 149', a former mansion converted into an interferon laboratory, which became the Centre for Biological Studies. Fidel Castro visited them frequently, securing them the resources they required. Within just 45 days the Cubans had produced their first Cuban batch of interferon. Safety and sterility tests were performed on mice before three of the scientists inoculated themselves. They experienced a slight rise in temperature, nothing worse. Cantell's laboratory in Finland confirmed the quality of the Cuban interferon.

Just in time, it turned out. Weeks later Cuba was struck by an epidemic of dengue, another disease transmitted by mosquitos. Notably, it was the first time this particularly virulent strand, which can trigger life-threatening dengue haemorrhagic fever, had appeared in the Americas. The epidemic affected 340,000 Cubans with 11,000 new cases diagnosed every day at its peak.[54] The death toll rose to 180, including 101 children. The Cubans suspected the CIA of releasing the virus. Castro announced: 'We share the people's convictions and strongly suspect that the plagues that have been punishing our country, especially the hemorrhagic [sic] dengue, could have been introduced into Cuba, into our country, by the CIA.'[55] The US State Department flatly denied it, although a recent Cuban investigation claims to provide evidence that the epidemic was introduced from the United States.[56]

At the height of the epidemic, Cuba's Ministry of Public Health (MINSAP) authorised the scientists in House 149 to use interferon to halt the dengue outbreak. This was done at great speed. They found that in advanced cases of dengue interferon was not useful, but in recent infections in children it cut short cases of haemorrhagic dengue shock. Mortality declined. In their historical account, Cuban medical scientists Caballero Torres and Lopez Matilla wrote that: 'It was the most extensive prevention and therapy event with interferon carried out in the world. Cuba began to hold regular symposia, which quickly drew international attention.'[57] The first international event in 1983 was prestigious: Cantell gave the keynote speech and Clark attended with Albert Bruce Sabin, the Polish-American scientist who developed the oral polio vaccine that has helped to nearly eradicate the disease globally.

Convinced about the contribution and strategic importance of innovative medical science, the Cuban government set up the 'Biological Front' to develop the sector. In January 1982, the Centre for Biological Studies moved from

House 149 into a newly built and better-equipped laboratory, with 80 researchers. Cuban scientists went abroad to study, many in western countries.[58] Their research took on more innovative paths as they experimented with cloning interferon. By the time Cantell returned to Cuba in 1986, the Cubans had developed a second generation interferon cloned in yeast.[59]

Meanwhile, in 1982, the United Nations Industrial Development Organisation (UNIDO) launched a competition for an internationally funded project to foster biotechnology in the Third World. UNIDO's International Centre for Genetic Engineering and Biotechnology was to facilitate North–South knowledge transfer and cooperation in science. Reagan's 1982 measures tightening the US blockade gave Cuba an additional incentive to apply. In 1984, the project funds were awarded to a joint application by India and Italy. However, the Cubans, and Fidel Castro most emphatically, decided to proceed without support. Construction immediately began on Cuba's showpiece Centre for Genetic Engineering and Biotechnology (CIGB), to work in biology, chemical engineering and physics. It opened just two years later in 1986. By then Cuba was submerged in another health crisis, a serious outbreak of meningitis B, which further spurred Cuba's biotechnology sector.

CUBA'S MENINGITIS MIRACLE

In 1976, Cuba was struck by meningitis B and C outbreaks.[60] Since 1916 only a few isolated cases had been seen on the island. At that point, internationally, vaccines existed for meningitis A and C, but not for B. Cuban health authorities secured a vaccine from a French pharmaceutical company to immunise people against type C meningitis. However, in the following years, cases of type B meningitis began to rise. With infections and fatalities on the increase, in 1983 MINSAP established a team of specialists from different medical science centres, led by a woman biochemist, Concepción Campa, to work intensively on finding a vaccine. By 1984 meningitis B had become the main health problem in Cuba. After six years of working around the clock, Campa's team produced the world's first successful meningitis B vaccine in 1988. Again, the scientists tested the vaccine on themselves, and their own children, before beginning clinical trials. Between 1987 and 1989, a randomised, double-blind controlled trial of the vaccine efficacy took place with over 100,000 students aged 10 to 14. The results showed the vaccine to be 83 per cent effective. Another member of Campa's team, Dr Gustavo Sierra, recalled their joy: 'This was the moment when we could say it works, and it works in the worst conditions, under pressure of an epidemic and among people of the most vulnerable age.'[61]

MINSAP decided that more lives would be saved by starting nationwide vaccinations immediately with an 83 per cent effective vaccine rather than delaying until a more effective one was produced (or not). During 1989 and 1990, 3 million Cubans, those most at risk (children and young people), were vaccinated. In the roll-out, the efficacy ranged from 83 per cent to 94 per cent in different provinces. No severe reactions occurred and another severe disease outbreak had been halted. Subsequently, 250,000 young people were vaccinated with the VA-MENGOC-BC vaccine, a combined meningitis B and C vaccination. It recorded 95 per cent efficacy overall, with 97 per cent in the high-risk three months to six years age group. Cuba's meningitis B vaccine was awarded a UN Gold Medal for global innovation. This was Cuba's meningitis miracle.[62]

'I tell colleagues that one can work 30 years, 14 hours a day just to enjoy that graph for 10 minutes,' said Agustín Lage, Director of the Centre for Molecular Immunology (CIM), referring to an illustration of the rise and sudden fall of meningitis B cases in Cuba. 'Biotechnology started for that. But then the possibilities of developing an export industry opened up, and today Cuban biotechnology exports to 50 countries.'[63] This possibility came about after an outbreak of meningitis B in Brazil a few years later. 'The Brazilians bought the Cuban vaccine. It was a huge purchase and that money was invested in expanding the biotechnology industry here,' explained Lage.

By 1986, Cuba had 39,000 scientific workers: 1 for every 282 people; 23,000 were involved in research. Thousands had been trained abroad, mainly in the socialist countries, but also in Western Europe. The revolutionary government's investments in education and public health had created the 'critical mass' necessary for further progress in medical science. The Biological Front invested USD 1 billion to develop a biotechnology industry between 1981 and 1989, including establishing the Western Havana Scientific Pole, known as Science City, between 1986 and 1991.[64]

SCIENCE CITY

Science City is a cluster of biotechnology institutions that coordinate and integrate their work. Centre directors get together monthly to discuss projects and exchange information in meetings attended by top government officials, formerly including Fidel Castro. Thousands of housing units were constructed locally to enable the institution's employees, working daily shifts of 14 hours, to walk to work. At the centre of Science City is the CIGB, which has received the greatest investment of any Cuban science institution. Other institutions followed:

- 1987, the Centre for Immunoassay to manufacture computerised and automated equipment for biochemical tests and screenings to detect pathologies;
- 1989, the National Centre for Meningococcal Vaccines for research and production of the VA-MENGOC-BC vaccine and other human vaccines. It was renamed the Finlay Institute (to honour Carlos Finlay) in 1991;
- 1990, the Cuban Centre for Neuroscience for the diagnosis and treatment of brain diseases;
- 1992, the National Centre for Biopreparations to produce Cuban biologicals; and
- 1994, the Centre of Molecular Immunology (CIM).

Along with the pace of these state investments, the astonishing fact is that they took place in the midst of Cuba's acute economic crisis, as the case of Cuba's Centre for Molecular Immunology shows.

ONCOLOGY MEETS BIOTECHNOLOGY

In the 1980s, biotechnology and oncology began to converge globally. In Cuba's National Institute of Oncology and Radiobiology, which had emerged from the Hospital of Oncology where Guevara had directed research, Agustín Lage was among a group of young scientists working on an experimental project into the role of immunology to fight cancer. In the early 1980s, the National Institute of Oncology and Radiobiology (INOR) developed and trialled the first Cuban monoclonal antibodies (MABs) – clones of single antibody cells – with multiple medical uses.[65] By the late 1980s, MABs were used for detecting malignant tumours and preventing organ rejection in Cuban transplant patients.[66] After a visit to INOR in 1989, Fidel Castro recommended expanding the institution, integrating it into the Scientific Pole, and providing it with the capacity for industrial-scale production and authorisation to export. Construction began in 1991. In December 1991, when the USSR collapsed, only the prefabricated columns of the new CIM had been built. Nonetheless, Fidel Castro would not allow the project to be halted. Lage describes this as: 'a very audacious decision, when the country had no financial resources to say "this centre has to be completed". It was Fidel's decision, a kind of offensive defence.'[67] The fact that the sector was entirely state-owned and controlled made that decision possible, and necessary, if CIM was to continue.

THE SPECIAL PERIOD: MEDICAL SCIENCE EXEMPT!

The collapse of the USSR and Eastern European socialism had a traumatic economic impact on Cuba. From having over 85 per cent of its trade conducted under planned agreements with socialist countries (unimpeded by the US blockade), Cuba was suddenly dependent on an international capitalist market dominated by the United States, the country pursuing a merciless blockade on the island. One-third of world pharmaceutical production took place in the US. From where could Cuba get medical equipment and medicines?[68]

In 1993, as Cuban socialism struggled to survive in the post-Soviet world after GDP had plummeted 35 per cent in three years, Fidel Castro declared that science and scientific production would have to occupy the first place in national production one day.[69] Elsewhere there were drastic cuts, things fell apart, production and transport halted, belts tightened and scarcity appeared in almost every sector and space. In this context, the inherently high-risk nascent biotechnology sector was selected as one of three strategic economic sectors for investment, along with tourism and food production.

Between 1990 and 1996, another USD 1 billion (1.5 per cent of Cuba's GNP) was invested into the Scientific Pole. It functioned as an incubator of medical science enterprises which were protected directly by the president's office during the Special Period. When the institutions began to export, that money was reinvested into them; a 'closed economic cycle' was created. Thus it was in the most difficult economic period that Cuban biotechnology flourished. The motivation was domestic public health benefits, Lage explained, 'And because of the US blockade. We could not afford expensive drugs, sometimes we could not get them even if we had all the money in the world, because they would not sell them.'[70] Elsewhere in Latin America, neoliberal structural adjustment programmes saw public health provision privatised and rolled back in the 1990s, but the Cuban government held steadfast to its social-welfare oriented, centrally planned economy.[71]

Gradually the dust covering the country's pharmacy shelves was replaced by Cuban manufactured 'biosimilars' – copies of traditional and biotechnological medicines, as Cuba's biopharma sector was channelled to meet this need. Copying biotech products involves high-level science to synthesise genes and introduce them into cells to clone them. Cuba's Interferon, Erythropoietin and the vaccine against hepatitis B have all been 'copy products'.[72] Homeopathic alternatives also claimed shelf space. Among them was another innovative Cuban treatment for cancer patients: Vidatox 30-CH, made from the venom of *Rhopalurus junceus*, a rare blue scorpion endemic to Cuba. It has analgesic, anti-inflammatory and anti-carcinogenic effects in more than 15 different cancer cell lines.[73] Research began in the Special Period and, by October 2010, Cuba's Labiofam laboratory had tested Vidatox on more than 10,000 cancer patients, some 3,500 of them foreigners, with positive results both in improving quality of life and stopping tumour growth.[74] The need for cheap generic drugs was international, so Cuba increased its pharmaceutical exports. By the mid-1990s, they were earning USD 100 million a year.

BIOTECHNOLOGY UNDER CAPITALISM

The biotech industry in the United States was launched with venture capital.[75] In 1971, the first electronic stock exchange, the NASDAQ, was set up in the US specifically for financing high-tech businesses for which risk is intrinsic, and it shaped the emerging biotechnology sector.[76] It took 24 years for a similar exchange, the Alternative Investment Market, to be established in London, then the pattern was repeated around the world. These developments also reflect the twentieth-century phenomena of 'internalisation of science' within businesses. Electronic and chemical companies established scientific laboratories internally, and businesses set up departments for research and development. Biotechnology took this further with the establishment of firms in which the science is the business. Science businesses are founded without products, and so without profits. With scientific–technological innovations, the task is not to conquer a market, but create one: if the product does not exist, neither does the market. Lage argues that the scientific–technological nature of the task is inimical to capitalist short-term profit-seeking. Capitalist businesses responding to 'market signals' struggle to connect science with the economy, manage risky projects, pay attention to 'human capital' and prioritise long-term investment. Their solution to this contradiction is speculative investment to mobilise capital, he points out.[77]

Internationally, the biotech sector did not achieve profits from product sales until 2009. Nonetheless, billions of dollars poured into the industry. Why does money from venture capital and big pharma flow into an industry in which profits are so hard to come by?[78] The answer is the role of financial mechanisms such as Initial Public Offerings (IPOs), Special Purpose Entities (SPEs), Special Purpose Corporations (SPCs) and patents licences in permitting profits to be made from a high-tech sector with low productivity. Start-up firms typically depend on venture capital investment to underwrite their initial costs. Once some promising products are developed, venture capitalists and other early-stage investors seek to recoup their investment (or a portion of it) by having the firm issue stock to the public in an IPO.[79]

However, biotechnology products can take up to 20 years to commercialise, and many will never reach that point. By 2002, only about 100 biotech-related drugs had reached the market in 30 years, with the top 10 accounting for nearly all of the sales.[80] Virtually all biopharma companies that do IPOs are product-less.[81] However, this financial speculation permits stockmarket investors to reap huge rewards by trading biopharma stock even in the absence of a commercial product.

Nonetheless, public investment underlies this private profit. The United States government gives huge financial, legislative and regulatory support to the sector. Two researchers on the topic conclude: 'The biopharmaceutical industry has become big business because of big government [and] remains highly dependent on big government to sustain its commercial success.'[82] Between 1978 and 2004, the US government's National Institutes of Health spent USD 365 billion on life sciences (2004 prices).[83] Commodification of medical research has been legalised.[84] Regulatory assistance is channelled through US patent policy, the Food and Drug Agency (FDA) approval process and decisions concerning what drugs or therapies to include on national healthcare programmes.[85]

Thus, Cuban 'exceptionalism' does not lie in the mere fact of government support and/or public funding for the biotech industry. It lies in the political economy context – its centrally planned, state-controlled economy, and a development strategy which has prioritised health care, education and research into science and technology since the early 1960s.

BIOTECHNOLOGY WITH CUBAN CHARACTERISTICS

The president of a multinational pharmaceutical company once informed Lage that he was bound by his shareholders' interests. Asked how many shareholders his company had, the president answered that it was 300,000. 'Ah', Lage replied, 'well, I have 11 million. Our shareholders are all 11 million Cubans!'[86] Founded solely through state investment, with financing guaranteed through the state budget, the Cuban biopharma sector is state-owned, with no private interests or speculative investments. Profit is not sought domestically, because the sector is completely integrated into the state-funded public health system. National health needs are prioritised. Medicines that Cuba cannot afford, or cannot get access to because of the US blockade, have to be produced domestically. Today, 517 of the 800 or so medicines consumed in Cuba are produced domestically, close to 70 per cent.

Cooperation prevails over competition as research and innovations are shared between institutions. Teams of scientists are established to take a project through from basic science, to product-oriented research, to manufacturing and marketing – activities that are carried out by different businesses in most countries. Dr Kelvin Lee highlights these 'striking' and 'unique' characteristics of the Cuban biotech sector: 'They start with identifying a need, then figure out the science to develop that in the lab, manufacture their agent, test it in the Cuban medical system and then commercialise it and sell it overseas. Their system is particularly nimble in that ability.'[87] The disadvantage the Cubans face, he added, is that they can't pursue thousands of good ideas and write off those which don't work as sunk costs. 'They don't have the resources to do that.'[88] Their access to capital is extremely limited. So what, then, have been the fruits of this distinctive Cuban system?

THE CUBAN CURE

In 2015, the World Health Organization announced that Cuba was first in the world to eliminate mother-to-child HIV transmission. Cuba has prevented an AIDS epidemic with domestically produced antiretroviral medicine that halts patient transmission, as if it were a vaccine. In 2019, pre-exposure prophylaxis pills were being distributed to prevent the spread of HIV in healthy people.[89] The island's mortality curve for AIDS continues to fall. The universal use of the CIGB's hepatitis B vaccine on newborns means Cuba should be among the first countries free from hepatitis B. This is one of the 8 vaccines (out of 11 vaccines for 13 diseases) administered to Cuban children which are produced in Science City. Within 10 years, 100 million doses of Cuba's hepatitis B vaccine had been used around the world.

By 2017, CIGB employed 1,600 people and sold 21 products internationally. CIGB's portfolio of innovations with major public health implications includes Heberprot-P for diabetic foot ulcers, affecting some 422 million people worldwide, which reduces the need for amputations by 71 per cent.[90] In 10 years, 71,000 patients in Cuba were treated with Heberprot-P plus 130,000 people in 26 other countries.

Cuba was second in the Americas to achieve a complete congenital hypothyroidism screening programme, after Canada and before the United States. Cuba's Immunoassay Centre developed its own Ultramicroanalytic System (SUMA) equipment for prenatal diagnosis for congenital anomalies. In addition to other checks, nearly 4 million babies have been tested for congenital hypothyroidism, which effects the production of thyroxine, a hormone needed for normal growth and development.[91] Treatment is easy and cheap. 'Since this system was introduced some children who would have had problems with their mental development are in universities,' Lage stated.[92] In 2017, the Immunoassay Centre had 418 workers producing 57 million tests per year for 19 different conditions, including hepatitis B and C, dengue fever, cystic fibrosis, Chagas disease, leprosy and HIV.

Cuba's Centre for Neuroscience is developing cognitive and biomarker tests for early screening of Alzheimer's disease. They have developed a hearing aid for children that costs just USD 2, a fraction of the cost in the US and Europe, made to individual specification using a 3D printer.[93]

Cuban professionals have received ten gold medals from the World Intellectual Property Organization (WIPO) over 26 years. The first was in 1989 for the meningitis B vaccine, followed by awards for the *Haemophilus influenza* type b (Hib) vaccine,[94] the result of a collaboration with the University of Ottawa; Heberprot-P; and Itolizumab for treating psoriasis.[95] By summer 2017, the Cuban biotech sector boasted 182 inventions with 543 patents granted in Cuba, 1,816 patents abroad and 2,336 patent applications.[96] Its products were marketed in 49 countries and it had partnerships with 9 countries in the global south. Cuba's pharmaceutical industry has the capacity for large-scale production of Cuban and generic drugs for export cheaply to developing countries.

CIM's focus is on biotechnology of mammalian cells, monoclonal antibodies and cancer vaccines. Cancer is the biggest cause of death for under-65 year olds in Cuba, and second only to heart disease for over-65s. By summer 2017 CIM had 1,100 employees, 4 manufacturing facilities, 25 products in the pipeline, 6 registered products, exported to 30 countries, 5 joint-venture companies abroad, 45 patented inventions and 750 patents abroad. Over 90,000 Cubans had been treated by CIM products. Among CIM's most exciting innovations is CIMAvax-EGF the lung cancer immunotherapy, for which the US–Cuban biotech joint venture mentioned at the start of this chapter was set up.

The term 'cancer' refers to a group of diseases involving abnormal cell growth with the potential to invade or spread to other parts of the body. Epidermal growth factor, or EGF, is a cellular protein that stimulates cell growth by binding to cells via epidermal growth factor receptors (EGFRs) on the cell surface. In 1984, Lage and the scientists at INOR were first in the world to describe the role of EGFRs in breast cancer: EGFRs were over-expressed in 60 per cent of human breast tumours. They discovered that EGF was rapidly distributed, reached tumour cells and recognised specific cell membrane receptors. Lage reported: 'These results suggest that high doses of EGF could eventually be used for inhibition of the cell proliferation in some tumours.' Up until that point, EGF had been seen as part of the cancer problem; it nourishes tumours yet is natural to the body so it does not trigger the immune system. The Cubans were proposing to use human EGF as part of the solution: as an active agent that could be used to interfere with the normal, cancer-producing binding of EGF to its receptor – the EGFR.[97]

It is because the immune system struggles to recognise cancer as foreign to the body that immunology therapy to combat it had proven so difficult. CIM wanted to use EGF to 'train' the body to respond to EGF and so produce cancer-specific antibodies. No other cancer researchers had managed it. This therapy would require one or two doses of a vaccine which would be cheap to develop and could be delivered through primary health care, well-suited to Cuba's public healthcare system. CIMAvax built on the Cuban therapeutic expertise of the vaccinologists at the Finlay Institute (meningitis B) and the CIGB's work on recombinant protein from *Neisseria meningitidis* bacteria P64 K. By using P64 K as a carrier protein with which to introduce EGF into the patient's body, the researchers at CIM broke the body's tolerance to its own EGF.[98] The results are a vaccine that helps the body to help itself. Dr Kelvin Lee pointed out that the Cubans 'designed their lung cancer vaccine to actually be useful in things like colon cancer, head and neck cancer, breast cancer, pancreatic cancer. It has broad applicability,' he told me.[99] The Roswell Park/CIM joint venture, Innovative Immunotherapy Alliance, intends to investigate these additional potentials.

These biotech achievements are accompanied by demographic ones. Most employees in Cuba's medical science centres are the children and grandchildren of workers and peasants, beneficiaries of Cuba's free education system. In 2016, almost half of Cuba's science and technology personnel were women.[100] The inordinate additional burdens imposed on the sector by the unrelenting and extensive US blockade has undoubtedly impoverished Cuba, denying the island access to resources, markets and knowledge transfers. But it has also fostered resilience and creativity in Cuban scientists.[101]

BIOCUBAFARMA

In 2012, BioCubaFarma was created as a kind of 'holding company' for the pharmaceutical and biotechnology sectors. It integrates 38 companies, 60 manufacturing facilities and 22,000 workers, almost one-third of them scientists and engineers. By 2017, BioCubaFarma was exporting to nearly 50 countries with over 2,000 patents granted abroad. This reorganisation of Cuban medical science is integral to the broader restructuring of the Cuban economy under the 'guidelines for updating the economic and social model' and *Plan 2030* discussed in Chapters 8 and 9. The economic reforms, which were initially introduced in 2011, confirm a key role for the biopharma sector in the national development plan. But only 1 per cent of the nearly 3,000 Cuban state enterprises export innovative scientific products. How can this sector expand without the kind of speculative private investment and profit-motivated competition which characterises the capitalist biotech industry?

Lage argues that Cuba's 'high-tech socialist state enterprises' require a regulatory framework that is distinct from Cuba's 'budgeted sector' (health, education and other social provisions funded entirely by state budget) and the state enterprise sector (state-owned and expected to contribute towards the national coffers).[102] Biotechnology institutions should remain under state control, with state investment for scientific research, and the sector must convert 'human capital' into economic growth via the export of high value-added products. This requires strengthening of the integration between science and production, research institutions and universities and the promotion of the closed-cycle of production.

CUBA'S MEDICAL SCIENCE 'DIPLOMACY'

Since the 1960s, many US scientists have forged scientific links with revolutionary Cuba. Albert Bruce Sabin, inventor of the oral polio vaccine unsuccessfully sought an agreement between the Academies of Sciences of both countries in 1967; US oncologist Randolph Lee Clark shared his interferon research; and Ernesto Bravo set up the North American Scientific Exchange Programme in 1983, taking dozens of top US scientists to Cuba.[103] Formal institutions and commercial links were prevented by the US blockade, but thousands of US scientists continued to engage with their Cuban counterparts on an individual basis. 'Even in the Bush era, American scientists still came to Cuba,' said Lage. 'They had to hide, change their visas and travel through third countries, but relations between our scientific communities always existed, though not at the business level, because that is blocked by the Americans.'[104]

By the 1990s, some major western biopharma corporations sought access to Cuba's innovative medical science, including US Merck and British SmithKline Beecham. In 1995, US authorities caught Merck executives returning from Havana with biological samples of the CIGB's hepatitis B vaccine for testing in the United States. The company was fined USD 217,000.[105] In 1999, SmithKline received a licence from the US Treasury's Office of Foreign Asset Control (OFAC) to develop the Finlay Institute's meningitis B vaccine. Although a British company, SmithKline Beecham's research and development took place at a partly US-owned subsidiary in Belgium. Under the licence terms, SmithKline Beecham was to pay the Cubans with food and medicines until they started to sell the vaccine, when the Finlay could be paid in cash.[106]

CIM received the first foreign investment in Cuba's biotech industry from a Canadian venture capital firm, York Medical, which focused on cancer, but did no science research. The company 'in-licensed' promising drugs from small biotech companies and took them through the stages of development (clinical trials, regulatory approvals, partnering relevant companies) into marketable drugs. If successful, these were 'out-licensed' to larger pharmaceutical companies for production and marketing.[107] CIM's Pharmacy Director, Idania Caballero, gave the Cuban perspective: 'When we started in 1994 we did not have money. A Canadian company told us, "We're going to give you money for your innovative head and neck cancer product [TheraCIM], which is unique in the world and has a WIPO award. You can develop the product and we will take it to the market."'[108] This coincided with Cuba's 1995 foreign investment law which facilitated joint-ventures with foreign companies in the context of the Special Period. The Cuban government approved the creation of a joint venture, CIMYM BioSciences.

However, with investors fearful of US regulations and fines, it took York Medical longer than expected to raise the funds the Cubans required. By 1999, the business plan was two years behind.[109] When the product was finally marketed, the CIM scientists were dissatisfied because, as Caballero explained, 'We had committed so much of our profit to paying those Canadians.' CIM had originally offered York Medical first refusal on all their new products, but the Cubans pulled back realising that the benefits of negotiating with foreign investors so early in drug development severely limited the financial returns to Cuba. Caballero told me, 'We explained to Fidel, and to the country, that we have more innovative products and that we face this dilemma, either we continue negotiating under those conditions or the country puts up the money.' Since then, Cuban institutions have developed their products to advanced stages prior to negotiating with foreign companies. A much lower investment is needed in the early stages. The first clinical trials are small scale. 'In the final stage you have to show that the product is better than any other treatment in the market, and that needs statistics and many more patients, which is very expensive. The costs goes up exponentially.'[110]

In the 1980s, Cuba had vociferously opposed the World Trade Organization's proposed Trade-Related Aspects of Intellectual Property Rights (TRIPS). By 1994, however, when TRIPS was agreed at the General Agreement on Tariffs and Trade conference in Uruguay, the socialist bloc had disintegrated and Cuba was forced to play by international market rules. Cubans went overseas to learn about international property rights and patents, business and marketing, and a commercial wing was set up for each of the biotech institutions. The Cubans were ready for business, but political antagonism from the United States intervened once again.

On 6 May 2002, eight months after the 9/11 terrorist attack on the United States led President George W. Bush to split the world into hostile camps, his Undersecretary of State John Bolton made a menacing claim: 'The United States believes that Cuba has at least a limited offensive biological warfare research and development effort. Cuba has provided dual-use biotechnology to other rogue states.'[111] Fidel Castro retorted, 'The only thing true in Bolton's lies is the geographical fact that Cuba is situated 90 miles from the continental territory of the United States.'[112] One week later, former US president Jimmy Carter arrived in Cuba for a prescheduled visit and Cuban television broadcast him visiting the CIGB. Carter refuted Bolton's claims, revealing that US intelligence experts told him they had no such information.[113] The US Secretary of State Colin Powell, backtracked, claiming, 'We didn't say it actually had some weapons, but it has the capacity and capability to conduct such research.' The situation was obviously not conducive to fostering collaboration.[114]

Cuban medical cooperation with the global south has been far more successful. Between 2008 and 2013, Cuban biotech sales earned the state some USD 2.5 billion.[115] In 2015 and 2016, 'medicinal and pharmaceutical products' earned over USD 1 billion, with exports to 49 countries. As a small island nation, domestic demand in Cuba is insufficient to foster the industry, so the establishment of joint ventures with foreign companies providing access to export markets is one solution. By 2019, Cuba had biotech joint ventures in Algeria, Brazil, China, India, Iran, Singapore, South Africa, Thailand, Venezuela and Vietnam.[116]

The CIGB has two joint ventures with China, while CIM has three, manufacturing, variously, monoclonal antibodies and therapeutic cancer vaccines, recombinant proteins and biotech products for agriculture.[117] That China, a country with 1 billion people, capable of manufacturing aeroplanes and heavy industries, made their first monoclonal antibodies with Cuban technology, is a source of pride for Lage. By 2019, CIM had more than 45 partners in 100 countries and was exporting to 30 nations. It had (marketing) joint ventures with Singapore (InnoCIMAB), Thailand (ABINIS) and Spain, for therapeutic cancer vaccines, and consolidated partnerships in emerging countries: Brazil, China and India and Malaysia, where the company Bioven had the rights to CIMAvax for South-East Asia and other territories.[118] A joint enterprise was being set up in Russia.

The low cost of Cuba's biopharma exports encourages collaboration with the developing world. CIMAvax-EGF costs USD 1 per shot to manufacture, much cheaper than alternative lung cancer treatments. Paradoxically, however, because it does not involve a lengthy course of expensive therapy in high-tech institutions, it is arguably antithetical to the profit-motivated interests of the global biopharma corporations and the healthcare insurance industry. Dr Lee points out that, unlike the single payer or nationalised health system, the economic structure of the US medical system does not seek to lower costs.

CANCER DIPLOMACY

CIMAvax-EGF's collaboration with Roswell Park has faced numerous regulatory, political and economic obstacles. 'Our legal consultants say nobody understands the embargo anymore, it's so many regulations accrued over so much time,' said Lee. 'We were sailing into unchartered waters both on the basic science side and the whole question of whether we could do clinical trials of a human biologic, of a Cuban vaccine, in the United States.' They met with many federal authorities and state authorities to discuss feasibility, 'given the myriad laws bound up in the embargo', explains Lee.[119] One official agreed it was a great thing to try because nobody votes for cancer.

First, after a long wait, Roswell Park's application to collaborate with a Cuban institution was approved by OFAC in 2013. In late summer 2016, after the restoration of diplomatic relations between the United States and Cuba, they secured FDA approval to conduct clinical trials in the US.[120] The next hurdle was getting the vaccine from Havana to Buffalo in New York State, in the absence of a direct mail delivery service. On the Monday, the sample was flown from Havana to Toronto, Canada, in a temperature-controlled box, passed Canadian customs and transferred to US customs. On Tuesday, US customs demanded an additional document to permit entry from an embargoed country and the box was returned to Canadian customs to await the paperwork. By the time this was submitted and the box got through US customs it was 5 p.m. on Friday and the sample sat there all weekend, arriving at Roswell Park the following week. 'The box is designed to maintain four degrees for three days, so when we get the box our experimental pharmacist said, "No, that didn't work."'

The whole process had to be repeated. 'It took this huge team of people just to get a shipment from Cuba into the United States,' said Lee. When the Cubans requested the return of the biologic delivery boxes, Roswell Park had to apply for a new export licence. 'That's just one example of the level of complexity; two countries that have not had normal relations for 60 years.'

In October 2017, Lee told me that phase 1 clinical trials were producing 'very interesting, early findings'.[121] Hypothetically, FDA could fast-track the path to CIMAvax commercialisation, given existing data from over 5,000 patients in Cuba, Bosnia and Herzegovina, Colombia, Kazakhstan, Paraguay and Peru, demonstrating that the vaccine is safe and effective.[122] However, this was unlikely, said Lee, simply because they were dealing with a Cuban biologic. Roswell Park's clinical innovation is to test CIMAvax alongside a second line therapy, Opdivo (Nivolumab), which enhances the immune response to CIMAvax.[123] The US blockade and the drug's cost mean Cubans do not have access to Opdivo.[124] In general, Lee explains, the Cubans are extraordinarily limited in the amount of therapeutics they have. 'They don't have the ability to do personalised medicine, which is why they moved into immunotherapy. They are really good at it from their infectious disease experiments; essentially they can actually get the patient to make their own drug, and it is relatively inexpensive because with a little bit of vaccine you get a big immune response.'[125]

In November 2017, the Trump administration published a list of Cuban entities with which US interests were prohibited from engaging. However, a so-called 'grandfather clause' exempted those with existing licences, so Roswell Park's collaboration could continue, and in September 2018 the new joint venture, Innovative Immunotherapy Alliance SA, was set up. Unfortunately, this is not beating a path for others to follow. US medical scientists have pulled out of Cuban conferences, and plans to send Cuban researchers to the United States have been scuppered. Four grants worth USD 50,000 each awarded to IPK by the US National Institutes of Health were put on hold. Initiatives to collaborate on arboviruses, mosquito-borne pathogens (including Zika, Chikungunya and dengue viruses) are under threat.[126] For now, cancer diplomacy is unlikely to have broader implications for US–Cuba relations.

FUTURE CHALLENGES

Reporting on Cuba's biotech sector for the influential Brookings Institute, trustee Bill Haseltine asked: 'How can such a poor, communist system produce such a success?' His answer: 'From the earliest days the government placed health and health technology, along with education, at the center of its efforts.' Haseltine concluded ruefully that Cuba's success 'does make the point that some state-run enterprises can be successful and meet demanding goals'.[127] While acknowledging Cuban medical science achievements, many external commentators default to the argument that only by opening the sector up to private capital and international market forces can its full growth potential be reached. This is clearly an ideological position and quite contrary to the evidence. Nonetheless, the global commodification of biotechnology is a challenge for Cuba.

The first Cuban patents are expiring, and the race is on to produce new innovative products. Globally, the average annual costs of research and development for new drugs are increasing.[128] A 2014 report calculated the cost of developing a prescription drug that gains market approval at USD 2.6 billion, a 145 per cent increase over their previous estimate in 2003.[129] Cuba is seeking substantial foreign investment, not to fund innovations but augment their capacity for industrial production. It also needs international partners to help insert Cuban products into the global market.[130] In the 2017/18 portfolio of investment opportunities the total capital sought for biopharma projects amounted to at least USD 850 million of the USD 9 billion total sought – nearly 9.4 per cent. Of the 14 investment opportunities included in the 2017/18 portfolio, 13 were based at Mariel Special Development Zone, a site included in the Trump administration's November 2017 'list of restricted entities' for Cuba. Then in May 2019, Title III of the Helms–Burton Act, which strengthens and continues the United States embargo, was enacted after 23 years. Will these moves scupper Cuba's plans to expand the sector? There are ways and means around these regulations, even for US businesses, if they are determined. And, given Cuban medical science breakthroughs on some key global health issues, such as cancer, HIV and AIDs, hepatitis and infectious diseases, there are increasing incentives to do so.

6

★ ★ ★

CUBAN MEDICAL INTERNATIONALISM
AN ARMY OF WHITE COATS

The lashing summer rainstorm seems an appropriate backdrop for my interview with Jorge Pérez Ávila, until recently the director of Havana's hospital of tropical diseases, the Instituto Pedro Kourí, known as IPK. We pause to remove a pile of books in danger from an encroaching puddle forming in his office at the Institute.[1] We have been talking about Cuba's medical internationalism and Pérez's role in training the Cubans who went to West Africa to combat the lethal outbreak of Ebola in late 2014.

As the son of a bus driver who became the head of a world-renowned medical institution, Pérez's story exemplifies the Revolution's commitment to universal public health domestically and internationally. Pérez has provided medical services in difficult to access areas, 'in so many countries, from Angola to Nicaragua, to Tanzania, Uganda and the Congo'. He has studied in esteemed institutions of higher learning in Britain and North America.[2] In 2014, when news of the Ebola outbreak in West Africa spread generating panic, Pérez accompanied Cuba's Minister of Public Health to Geneva to offer the island's assistance to the World Health Organization (WHO) in combatting the epidemic. At the IPK, Pérez had been studying Ebola since the 1980s, but he had never actually seen a case.

Ebola was first identified in 1976. It is a viral haemorrhagic infection which causes fever, vomiting, diarrhoea and rashes, affects multiple organs and leads to internal and external bleeding in some victims.[3] On average, 50 per cent of those infected die, but this can rise to 90 per cent under poor conditions. Ebola spreads via body fluids.[4] The WHO reported a major Ebola outbreak in Guinea in March 2014, which rapidly spread to Liberia and Sierra Leone. Little attention was paid in the United States and Western Europe, however, until a handful of their own citizens were infected and alarm bells rang that this highly contagious disease could be introduced into their own populations.

Also alarming was the high proportion of healthcare workers among Ebola fatalities. The lack of public health facilities or programmes in West Africa exacerbated the problem. Thus, when the WHO called for international assistance, rich countries threw them finances, supplies and military personnel, but not the urgently needed medics.[5] In September 2014, WHO director Margaret Chan said: 'Money and materials are important but those two things alone cannot stop Ebola virus transmission . . . Human resources are clearly our most important need. We need most especially compassionate doctors and nurses, who will know how to comfort patients despite the barriers of wearing PPE [personal protective equipment] and working under very demanding conditions.'[6]

Cuba was the first country to respond to the WHO appeal, sending the largest medical contingent – to Guinea, Sierra Leone and Liberia – where they already had medical personnel.[7] When Pérez told WHO officials that the Cubans would stay for at least six months, they replied, 'you are crazy, no one can be there six months, it's too high risk! After three or four weeks the medics will get ill.' Pérez ruled that out, confident that thorough preparation would prevent infection. That training was his responsibility.[8]

Back in Cuba, the Ministry of Public Health (MINSAP) called for medical volunteers. Nothing was said about remuneration, but the risks were made clear. Incredibly, within two weeks more than 10,000 people had volunteered, as Pérez says, 'to gamble with their lives'. Interviewed in Monrovia, the capital of Liberia, Cuban volunteer Dr Leonardo Fernández explained: 'At my hospital they arrived and asked who was willing to go, and told us that we might not return . . . I had treated haemorrhagic fevers in Mozambique, and I raised my hand, and here I am . . . While I have strength and they accept me, I will go where I am needed.'[9]

Pérez had a field hospital set up on the IPK grounds. The Cuban climate created similar conditions to those in West Africa. Over 400 Cuban volunteers were picked for 4 weeks of intensive training in Cuba, and the 256 who were subsequently selected for the mission in West Africa received another 4 weeks training there. Those Cubans had an average age of 47, and 15 years of professional experience.[10] All had faced natural disasters and disease outbreaks in other developing countries as members of Cuba's International Henry Reeve Contingent, which is discussed below.

Arriving in early October 2014, they worked in groups of three doctors and six nurses in six-hour shifts, seven days a week. The 23 Cuban medical professionals *already* working in Sierra Leone were joined by 165 volunteers;

53 went to Liberia and 35 to Guinea where 16 Cuban medical professionals were *already* stationed. The Cubans confronted immense physical, medical and psychological challenges: sweltering in their protective gear, coping with dehydration, patients often reaching them once the disease had caused serious damage. Initially they faced mortality rates of 50 per cent, traumatic even for experienced professionals. Dr Fernández reported: 'We saw entire families die, children left alone . . . But we also saw others who survived Ebola, who after recovering . . . adopted orphaned children.'[11] The Cubans stayed two or three in a room in budget hotels, paid for out of the daily stipend of between USD 220 and USD 250 received from the United Nations to cover food and lodgings.

Cuban medics quickly reduced the morality rates of their patients to 20 per cent and introduced a preventative education programme to stop the disease spreading. Over 400 lives were saved in Sierra Leone and Guinea alone. The Cubans treated hundreds of other patients infected, not by Ebola, but by similar pathologies, such as malaria, a far bigger killer than Ebola, responsible for over 400,000 African deaths every year. Two Cuban doctors died after getting malaria. Just one Cuban doctor, Felix Baez, contracted Ebola. He was transferred to the Geneva University Hospital to be treated at the UN. Pérez rushed from Havana to Geneva to join the medical team treating him. He recalled that Baez arrived 'in critical condition, not always lucid'. However, 'On day two, he recognised me. He told me, "I'm going to be okay, and I'm going back to Sierra Leone" . . . I have to admit, I was very moved.'[12] That is exactly what Baez did.

By January 2015, Cuba had trained over 13,000 people to deal with Ebola in 28 African countries, plus 68,000 people in Latin America and 628 in the Caribbean.[13] A training programme in Havana was attended by 278 specialists in infectious diseases from 34 countries, including the United States. Within Cuba, nearly 324,000 people received Ebola training. By March 2015, the situation in West Africa was under control. The Cuban medics had a staggered return, followed by 21 days in quarantine at the IPK hospital to safeguard against introducing the virus to the island.[14] Three weeks is the maximum incubation period for Ebola. By May 2015, over 26,500 cases of Ebola had been reported, resulting in over 11,000 deaths, one-fifth of them children, and including 507 medical personnel.[15]

Dr Fernández pointed out that the media impact of Cuba's Ebola mission, 'made some believe that we have done something extraordinary, which makes us heroes'.[16] Indeed, Cuba's contribution was lauded internationally. A *New York*

Times editorial exclaimed: 'The work of these Cuban medics benefits the entire global effort and should be recognized for that.'[17] In mid-October 2014, both the US Secretary of State, John Kerry, and US Ambassador to the United Nations, Samantha Power, praised the Cuban role in West Africa. Announcing rapprochement between the United States and Cuba on 17 December 2014, President Obama referred to Cuba's Ebola campaign as an example of the benefits of collaboration: 'American and Cuban health care workers should work side by side to stop the spread of this deadly disease.'[18]

Dr Fernández, however, shied away from special praise. He asked: 'How is it different from those [Cubans] working in the Brazilian jungle? How is it different from those in the Venezuelan jungle, working alone in indigenous communities for months? How is it different from those serving in African villages? [Or] in the jungle, in temperatures reaching 48 degrees . . . The difference is that this was a high-profile international mission.' His point is that the contribution of Cuban healthcare workers elsewhere, and over decades, has been largely ignored. The Cubans combatting Ebola were but a drop in the ocean compared to the 400,000 Cuban medical professionals who have worked overseas in 164 countries since 1960 and about whom politicians and the mainstream media have said almost nothing.[19]

And what an impact they have had! Literally, millions of lives have been saved and hundreds of millions of lives improved. By the Ebola outbreak in 2014, Cuban medical professionals had performed 1.2 billion consultations overseas, attended 2.2 million births and performed over 8 million surgeries.[20] More than 4,000 Cuban medical personnel, over half of them doctors, were *already* working in 32 African countries at that time. Some 76,000 Cuban medical personnel had *already* worked in 39 African countries since the early 1960s. Meanwhile, Cuba had sustained more than 20,000 healthcare workers in Venezuela for a decade, with thousands more in neighbouring countries. Add to their numbers the Cuban soldiers, educators, constructors, technicians and other specialists sent overseas by the government and you get to the astonishing fact that in revolutionary Cuba around one in ten Cubans have been on an internationalist mission![21]

Why does Cuba do it? Cynical, pragmatist or 'realist' explanations focus on geopolitical and financial gains to Cuba: the revolutionary government seeks political allies and advantages in world forums – soft power; it forces healthcare workers into foreign-service contracts to earn the country export revenues; or Cuban professionals are simply motivated by the higher earnings they receive working overseas. More serious commentators observe that Cuban 'medical diplomacy' has been a cornerstone of Cuban foreign policy since 1960, before the *realpolitik* and economic imperatives of the post-Soviet era.[22] Researchers have emphasised how it differs from most global health security responses anchored in military and defence programmes and motivated by a desire to protect domestic populations from external threats of disease.[23] Others recognise that Cuban medical internationalism is rooted in the 'principle of solidarity' with the global population, and that this solidarity differs from notions of responsibility, charity and altruism common in aid frameworks.[24] But what motivates the Cuban approach to solidarity? What are its political and ideological foundations?

First, the Revolution of 1959 combined the values of Cuban national independence hero José Martí with the principles of Marxism–Leninism. Second, the post-1959 public healthcare system was constructed on those values: free, universal, state provision was endorsed as a human and constitutional right. And, third, Cuban medical internationalism is an extension of those principles beyond the island's shores.

Even while galvanising Cuban forces to fight for independence from Spain in the late nineteenth century, Martí warned against the threat of US expansionism, calling for regional unity to block this tendency. This was seen as a precondition to sovereignty and self-determination; thus, anti-imperialism was part of Martí's project for an independent Cuba.[25] The Revolution of 1959 was conceived as a project that had to go beyond the island's shores to include a broad regional alliance of people and political forces to withstand the United States and other imperialist powers. Meanwhile, drawing from Marx's analysis of capitalism, Cuban revolutionaries committed to the decommodification of labour power, to eliminate exploitative social relations in the construction of socialism and put the working class in power.

Taking up battle cries from both Marx ('workers of the world unite, you have nothing to lose but your chains') and Martí ('homeland is humanity'), Cuba's revolutionary leaders saw that liberating the people from exploitation and underdevelopment was a global endeavour. They made the internationalist tradition an explicit sphere of state activity.[26] Cuban foreign policy and anti-imperialist class-conscious solidarity was not to be limited to the confrontation with the United States, but to include an international revolutionary project to promote a global struggle against diverse forms of underdevelopment, imperialism, colonialism and neo-colonialism.[27] Cuban revolutionaries view global poverty and poor health as a result of those exploitative structural conditions. Thus, until the end of the Cold War, the revolutionary government was as ready to send soldiers as doctors, and usually sent both on the same missions. In the post-Soviet period, medical assistance has dominated Cuban internationalism and has been an essential component of the island's foreign policy.

In 1997, Fidel Castro said: 'Our Revolution is not a revolution of millionaires. Instead, it is one carried out by the poor, and is one which dreams of ensuring the well-being not only of our own poor, but rather of all the poor in this world. And that is why we talk of internationalism.'[28] Medical internationalism, then, is simultaneously an integral aspect of Cuba's socialist development path, an expression of the Revolution's deep, historically rooted anti-imperialism, and a big part of the story about how the revolutionary people have survived into the post-Soviet era. It has enabled the revolutionary people to reap the economic and political benefits of the socialist state's investments in health and education. Whereas the US blockade is an economic punishment for Cuba having a socialist system, medical services exports have been an economic benefit.[29] Since 2004, the export of 'professional services' has been the principle source of revenue for Cuba, and the lion's share of that has come from healthcare provision.

At times, Cuban medical assistance overseas has been followed by the restoration of diplomatic relations with the host country; this is less remarkable than the fact that Cuban professionals worked in countries, often in the most impoverished and dangerous regions, with which their government did not have diplomatic relations in the first place.[30] Cuban medical and educational aid has been pivotal to post-2000 regional integration movements in Latin America and the Caribbean, facilitating the adoption of more welfare-focused national development strategies. By 2009, when Barak Obama became president of the United States, regional governments from across the political spectrum were demanding a change in the US's Cuba policy, even threatening to withdraw from the Summit of the Americas unless Cuba were reincorporated. Rapprochement with Cuba came at a lower political cost to Obama than keeping the status quo, as discussed in the following chapter.

In 1965, Cubans had 1 physician for every 1,200 people. In 1975, the ratio was 1:1,000; in 1985 it was 1:500; in 2005, 1:167, the highest ratio in the world.[31] By 2017, the Caribbean island of 11.2 million people had 85,000 doctors and 21 medical faculties graduating thousands of new professionals every year. The island's infant mortality rate in 2017 and 2018 was a record 4 per 1,000 live births, compared to 5.9 per 1,000 in the United States and 10 times lower than its close Caribbean neighbour, Haiti.[32] A US medical journal observed, 'The Cuban healthcare system seems unreal. There are too many doctors. Everybody has a family physician. Everything is free, totally free.'[33]

However, revolutionary Cuba was never just concerned about meeting its own needs. In 1984, when 1,800 students from 75 developing countries were *already* receiving medical training in Cuba, Fidel Castro announced plans to have 75,000 doctors by the year 2000, sufficient for 10,000 to serve overseas at any time.[34] In 1999, the Cubans established the Latin American School of Medicine (ELAM), probably the world's largest medical school, to train foreign students. In the mid-2000s an additional programme was set up to train 60,000 Venezuelans in their own country and Cuba has 25,000 medical personnel available for World Health Organization programmes. It is a mantra of the revolutionary people that they share what they have, not just what is surplus. And the story about the origins of Cuban medical internationalism, at a time when half the doctors on the island had left, certainly vindicates that.

1960s: A BEGGAR'S HELP[35]

Four prevailing approaches to Cuban medical internationalism were initiated early in the 1960s: emergency response medical brigades sent overseas; the establishment abroad of public health apparatus to provide free health care for local residents; foreign patients brought to Cuba for free medical treatment on the island; and medical training for foreigners, both in Cuba and overseas.

In May 1960, Valdivia in Chile was struck by the most powerful earthquake ever recorded. Thousands were killed. Despite the exodus of Cuban doctors and strained diplomatic relations with the right-wing government of Chile, the Cubans sent an emergency medical brigade with six rural field hospitals. In the following two years, when Cuban ships took weapons to the FLN guerrilla movement in Algeria fighting for independence from France, they returned with wounded fighters and orphaned children who received medical attention on the island.[36] Following independence in 1962, Algeria faced challenges similar to those of Cuba, including the exodus of (French) physicians. Despite the lack of medics on the island, in May 1963, 55 Cuban healthcare professionals set sail for Algeria. Head of the mission, José Ramón Ventura, subsequently Minister of Health, said: 'Really what we were offering was so little – just like a beggar who offers help. But we knew that the people of Algeria needed the assistance even more than we did, and we also knew that they deserved it.'[37] A year later a group of 61 Cuban healthcare professionals arrived to help establish Algeria's national health system. The Cubans charged nothing.

Later in the 1960s, Cuba sent medical specialists to North Vietnam.[38] In 1965, 400 Cuban soldiers went to central Africa. Under Che Guevara's command in Zaire (now Democratic Republic of Congo) they supported the struggle against a corrupt US-backed regime. In neighbouring Congo-Brazzaville (now Republic of Congo), they were invited to defend the newly independent government, which feared attack by CIA-backed mercenaries. They were accompanied by Cuban doctors, who organised a mass vaccination campaign, the first in Africa, benefiting 61,000 Congolese children to combat an outbreak of polio in Congo-Brazzaville in 1966. A total of 254 young Congolese went to study in Cuba for free. From 1966, Cuban military advisers assisted another movement for independence from Portugal, led by Amilcar Cabral in Guinea Bissau. A group of Cuban medics went to work in guerrilla-controlled territory where one foreign doctor served 540,000 people. The Cubans trained Guineans in basic nursing and some went to Havana to study. By the end of the 1960s, Cuban physicians were working in dozens of countries, largely in rural areas.

1970s: STEPPING UP MEDICAL AND MILITARY ASSISTANCE

It was not until 1976 that the pre-revolutionary ratio of doctors to citizens was restored on the island, although health indices improved disproportionately.[39] Nonetheless, Cuba shared its medics with others in need, even in countries with politically hostile governments which had broken off diplomatic relations. In 1970, up to 70,000 people were killed in an earthquake in Peru. Cuba sent a 40-strong medical brigade with 10 tons of supplies, while over 100,000 Cubans donated blood for the victims.[40] The next year, Cuban medics returned to Chile following another earthquake. In 1972, the Nicaraguan capital, Managua, was flattened by an earthquake. Although the country was ruled by the repressive dictatorship of the Somoza family, sworn enemies of Cuban socialism, and close allies of the United States, a Cuban disaster relief team rushed to the scene to assist.[41] After the Sandinista Revolution overthrew the Somoza dictatorship in 1979, Cuban healthcare workers helped establish rural and urban clinics to serve Nicaragua's poor and medical training centres to train Nicaraguans.[42] A Cuban medical brigade went to Honduras following an earthquake in 1974.

Meanwhile, throughout the decade, Cuban healthcare professionals set up and staffed comprehensive health programmes in several countries, mainly in Africa. Thousands of young people from those countries went to Havana for medical training. By 1977, Cuba was providing between 45 per cent and 84 per cent of the physicians working in 6 African countries.[43]

In 1975, Angola won independence from Portugal after a long struggle led by the MPLA (Movimento Popular de Liberatção de Angola), headed by

António Agostinho Neto, who became the country's first African president. The subsequent mass exodus of Portuguese professionals left 14 doctors in Angola.[44] Neto's government was attacked by two western-backed parties, UNITA (União Nacional para a Independência Total de Angola) and FNLA (Frente Nacional de Libertação de Angola) and invaded by the army of apartheid South Africa in October 1975. At Neto's request, some 36,000 Cuban soldiers went to Angola between November 1975 and March 1976 to defend the country's independence, accompanied initially by 200 Cuban healthcare workers. Cuba had medical personnel alongside military advisers elsewhere in Africa, including in Ethiopia from 1977.[45]

1980s: MORE MILITARY AND MEDICS

Emergency medical brigades responded to natural disasters which struck Cuba's neighbours: earthquakes in Mexico (1985), El Salvador (1986) and Ecuador (1987), and a hurricane in Nicaragua (1988).[46] Meanwhile, Cuban soldiers and civilians poured back into Angola to support the MPLA forces fighting back South African army incursions from occupied Namibia in 1987–8. At Cuito Cuanavale, the Cubans and Angolans finally pushed South African forces back, ultimately securing independence for Angola and Namibia, which had been occupied by South Africa since 1915. By 1991, over a 16-year period, some 300,000 Cuban soldiers had fought in Angola, sustaining more than 10,000 casualties and 2,077 fatalities.[47] Some 50,000 civilians had accompanied them, including healthcare professionals, educators and construction workers.[48] By 1988, over 30 countries in Africa were in receipt of Cuban medical support. Cuban medical faculties were established to train locals in 11 countries between 1976 and 2010.[49]

TRAINING FOREIGN STUDENTS FOR SUSTAINABLE HEALTHCARE PROVISION

Cuban medical internationalism never intended to foster dependency on Cuban professionals. After witnessing the urgent need for healthcare workers while on tour in Africa in the 1970s, Fidel Castro committed to train the local personnel necessary to build sustainable healthcare systems. However, as those countries lacked educational infrastructure, schools and universities, he concluded that, initially, Cuba would have to train people on the island. 'So they began to bring over the poorest people,' explained Pérez. 'The poorest people had local diseases. We had eradicated most of them here, like malaria, filariasis, schistosomiasis, and poliomyelitis. It was risky, bringing people here, *and* sending Cubans there. Fidel said let's strengthen the IPK [hospital for tropical diseases] and he got Professor Gustavo Kourí to direct it. They began to train medical scientists here to confront these diseases.'[50]

Gustavo Kourí, the IPK's new director, was the son of Pedro Kourí, who had founded the hospital of tropical diseases in 1937 as an annex to the School of Medicine at the University of Havana. Medical science had stagnated in the six decades of the Cuban Republic prior to the Revolution of 1959, but Kourí's hospital was an exception, establishing a good reputation among international specialists of tropical medicine. A communist sympathiser of Lebanese descent, Kourí did not join the exodus of professionals leaving Cuba. Rather, as his son explained, 'He decided to turn his laboratories over to the Revolution and stayed as an adviser to the new pharmaceutical industry.'[51] Aged 23 in 1959, Gustavo Kourí had specialised in microbiology and virology, going on to work as the assistant director of Cuba's National Science Research Centre, set up in 1965, and as Assistant Dean of the School of Medicine and Vice Rector of research and postgraduate studies at the University of Havana. At the revamped IPK, Gustavo invited student doctors to train in tropical diseases. Pérez answered the call in 1979, becoming IPK director shortly before Gustavo's death in May 2011.[52] Inaugurating the new IPK premises in 1993, Fidel Castro described it as a centre for all humanity. A grandiose claim indeed, but one justified by its role in Cuba's medical internationalism.

Foreign students passed through the IPK for medical checks as they arrived in Cuba. If unwell, they were treated at the IPK, or another hospital, before beginning their studies. Some people said they should be sent home but, according to Pérez, Fidel Castro said: 'We cannot lose those people, they are the best, the poorest, who have suffered most, who most deserve to overcome.' Some of the students had to complete primary, secondary or pre-university level training before entering the universities. Their treatment, education, board and subsistence, were provided free. Pérez explained that 'many of those students spent years here without returning to their homes, because there was no money to finance that', unless their own governments paid.[53]

In the 1980s, at least 10,000 foreign students, mostly Africans, were being educated at different levels on Cuba's Island of Youth. These students paid nothing. In 1984, 1,800 students from 75 developing nations were training as physicians, medical technicians or medical specialists. Of over 3,500 foreign medical graduates in 1991, 500 were from North Africa and the rest were split between the Americas and sub-Saharan Africa.[54] Thousands more received training in other professions.[55]

Despite the economic crisis of the post-Soviet era, the Cubans continued to respond to emergencies around the world, in most cases by sending medical brigades: Iran (1990 earthquake), Brazil (1990 radiation poisoning, 52 patients were treated in Cuba), Nicaragua (1991 flooding and 1992 volcanic eruption), Honduras, Guatemala and Nicaragua (1998 Hurricane Mitch), Colombia (1999 earthquake), Honduras (1999 dengue epidemic), Venezuela (1999 floods).[56] In addition, the island continued to receive patients from overseas, but the first large-scale project of this kind was the Children of Chernobyl programme which began in 1990, on the eve of the collapse of the Soviet bloc.

CHILDREN OF CHERNOBYL

'These are children, extremely sick children. How could we *not* treat them?' exclaims Dr Carlos Dotres, Director of the Children of Chernobyl programme. 'Until the Comandante en Jefe [Fidel Castro] tells me otherwise, the doors will not be shut to sick children, wherever they come from.'[57]

In late April 1986, an explosion and fire at the nuclear power plant in Chernobyl, Ukraine, caused a reactor to melt down, generating radioactive pollution 500 times that caused by the atomic bomb in Hiroshima. Almost 8.4 million people were exposed to dangerous levels of radiation. They received assistance from the USSR, of which Ukraine was then part, and the other socialist countries. The nearest town was quickly evacuated, its inhabitants relocated. However, the so-called international community threw exponentially more money at the task of containing the reactor than to assisting the victims.[58]

In the following years, death rates, cancer rates and health problems soared and life expectancy plunged. Alarming numbers of children got sick with thyroid cancer after drinking contaminated water. In winter 1989, Cuba's new Ambassador to the Ukraine, Sergio López Briel, was informed by Ukrainian authorities about their child health concerns. On a Thursday, López relayed the information to Cuba. By the Saturday a reply from Cuba's 'top leadership' informed him that the island's three leading specialists in childhood diseases were to travel there. Early the following week the specialists from Cuba visited towns and cities close to the nuclear plant which had been abandoned by local medical staff, and nearby cities in Russia and Belarus.[59] In late March 1990 they returned with 139 very sick children, accompanied by parents or guardians, for medical treatment in Havana. Fidel Castro promised the children 'the best doctors, the best medical care, the best hospitals, the best medicines that exist in the world'.[60] Documentary footage shows him welcoming them with a pat on the head as they disembark in the airport. 'How many need medical treatment?' he asks a Ukrainian woman. 'One-hundred thousand,' she replies through translation. His eyebrows rise momentarily, then he reassures her: 'We can do something here for a good number of children.'[61]

Not five months later, the Special Period began in Cuba. Eastern Europe abandoned socialism, the socialist bloc collapsed and the USSR disintegrated taking much of its infrastructure, institutions and welfare provision with it. In Cuba, the loss of trade partners sent the economy into freefall, with GDP plummeting one-third by 1993. The population suffered terrible shortages of food, fuel and medicines. And yet, even while Cuban children went to bed hungry, the revolutionary government continued to welcome thousands of Chernobyl victims.

The Children of Chernobyl camp was set up at a polyclinic in Tarará, ten miles outside Havana.[62] Over the next 21 years, over 26,000 people, nearly 22,000 of them children, received free medical care, accommodation, food and other facilities in Cuba.[63] Simultaneously a Cuban medical team worked in a Ukrainian sanatorium. At the height of the programme, with 2,000 patients arriving annually, there were 50 doctors and 80 nurses working at Tarará.[64] Most of the children were between 9 and 14 years old. They stayed for six to seven weeks undergoing extensive tests, and were attended by dentists, paediatricians, psychologists, hygienists, epidemiologists and nurses. They enjoyed visits to the aquarium, Lenin Park and the beach; recreational trips and relaxation in an uncontaminated environment were part of the programme. Those on prolonged stays received schooling from Ukrainian teachers. Fidel Castro visited the children at Tarará and followed their progress.

Cuba has not provided data on the expenses incurred through this programme. In 2010, the Ukrainian-based NGO, International Fund for Chernobyl, estimated the cost in medications alone at USD 350 million. One Ukrainian mother claimed that at home medical care for her son would have cost over USD 105,000.[65] In 2010, Ukrainian president Leonid Kuchma said his country would contribute to the Children of Chernobyl programme and his successor, President Viktor Yanukovych, echoed this in 2011.[66] But Cuba never received Ukrainian government support and the last patients finally left Tarará in 2013.

THE LATIN AMERICAN SCHOOL OF MEDICINE: WORLD 'CLASS' EDUCATION

'Hundreds of Cuban doctors volunteered for disaster response,' said Gail Reed, founder of the US non-profit organization Medical Education

Cooperation with Cuba (MEDICC). She was referring to the Cuban response in autumn 1998 to Hurricanes Georges in Haiti and Mitch in Central America, which left a combined death toll of up to 30,000 and some 2.5 million people homeless. 'But when they got there they found a bigger disaster. Whole communities with no health care. Doors bolted shut on rural hospitals for lack of staff and just too many babies dying before their first birthday. What would happen when the Cuban doctors left? New doctors were needed to make care sustainable, but where would they come from, where would they train?'[67]

Despite not having diplomatic relations with those Central American countries, the host governments asked the Cubans to stay on to establish comprehensive health programmes.[68] Within weeks, Fidel Castro announced plans to open the Latin American School of Medicine (ELAM) to train urgently needed medical personnel for the region. The doctors graduating there, he said, would save more lives every year than those lost in the hurricanes: 'Twenty years can pass without a Mitch and a million people will silently die in Central America without anyone taking notice.'[69]

ELAM was set up on the former premises of a navy training school in Havana.[70] By its formal inauguration in November 1999 there were already nearly 2,000 students from 18 countries receiving free tuition, board, food and a living allowance. They graduated in 2005. By 2019, 29,000 doctors from 105 countries had graduated. Half of them were young women, 75 per cent the children of workers or *campesinos* (peasants or farmers), representing 100 ethnic groups. At the request of the United States' Black Congressional Caucus, students from impoverished areas in the United States began studying at ELAM with scholarships. By 2017, 170 students from the United States had graduated.[71] In 2009, WHO director, Dr Chan, declared:

I know of no other medical school that offers students so much, at no charge. I know of no other medical school with an admission policy that gives first priority to candidates who come from poor communities and know, first-hand, what it means to live without access to essential medical care. For once, if you are poor, female, or from an indigenous population, you have a distinct advantage. This is an institutional ethic that makes this medical school unique.[72]

Since 2012, governments that can afford it have been asked to pay towards their students' tuition. The South African government paid for 1,200 students to study at ELAM for six years at a total cost of USD 60,000 each.[73] However, most students continue to be subsidised by the Cuban state.

ELAM is a huge site, occupying 120 hectares, with 28 buildings housing 130 classrooms, plus laboratories, dormitories, cafeterias and a small hospital. The training endorses the principles of Cuban public health, emphasising preventative hands-on primary and public healthcare, equality of access and environmental factors. In monetary terms, ELAM students graduate debt-free, but they are expected to repay their 'social debt' by working in their own or other poor communities. There is no mechanism, however, to enforce or even audit this stipulation.

Following an intensive Spanish language course, where necessary, and a six-month pre-medical foundation course, students spend two years on campus at ELAM before being allocated to medical facilities throughout the island to learn through experience alongside study.[74] Like Cuban doctors, they are trained to work in austere conditions, without access to sophisticated diagnostic equipment. Cuban professors challenge students to show how they would proceed in the middle of the Amazon.[75] They are taught to work with, not against, alternative and local healers, respecting local customs, using local medicinal herbs. Living among their patients they are expected to advance the community's health and treat patients as equals.

Some critics have dismissed ELAM as 'communist indoctrination'. Defenders have pointed to the lack of ideology or politics in the curriculum to deny the charge.[76] However, if communist indoctrination means fostering a 'class conscious' commitment to serve the poor, then that is what ELAM delivers, and, indeed, what the world needs. This is, in fact, no less politicised than the predominant global approach which inculcates students with the belief that health care is an expensive resource, or commodity, that must be rationed through the market mechanism. This is not about individual medics being greedy or corrupt. The issue is the systemic commodification of health care through capitalist social relations. Medical students 'invest' in their education, paying high tuition fees and graduating with huge debts. They seek well-paid jobs to repay those debts and pursue a privileged standard of living. To ensure medics are well remunerated, demand must be kept above supply. Today the world has a deficit of between 4 and 7 million healthcare workers just to meet basic needs.[77] In addition, increasing dependence on sophisticated medical technology helps keep the cost of medical services high, and is contrary to the preventative, primary care approach adopted in Cuba.[78]

The huge Cuban investment in medical education raises the supply of professionals globally, thus threatening the status of physicians elsewhere operating under a market system. Critically, the Cuban approach removes financial, class, race, gender, religious and any other barriers to joining the medical profession. However, while in revolutionary Cuba the public healthcare system supplanted the private sector, this has not happened even in those Latin American countries which declared they were building socialism for the twenty-first century. Private sector professionals have maintained a powerbase from which to attack the Cubans, Venezuelans and other ELAM graduates whose deployment to poor regions exposes their own neglect of underserved areas where patients cannot pay. The largest contingents of Cuban healthcare workers in the post-Soviet era have been to where government public health programmes for impoverished communities were jeopardised by the refusal of domestic, private-sector physicians to staff them: Venezuela and Brazil. In Honduras and Paraguay, medical associations demanded that the Cuban healthcare workers leave, but popular protests to prevent their withdrawal succeeded in keeping them there.

The return home by Cuban-trained medics has often been problematic.[79] Some have been left frustrated by their inability to fulfil their commitment to public health due to the lack of government investment, and consequently employment, in that sector in their home countries. Some remain unemployed while others enter the private sector despite it being antithetical to their training. There are also inspirational stories about the impact of ELAM alumnae. One example is the story of 69 graduates from the black Garifuna people who make up 20 per cent of the Honduran population and live in deprived, hard-to-access villages lacking water and electricity. The young Cuban-trained doctors mobilised their community to build its own first hospital. Opened in 2007, by 2014 it had provided nearly 1 million consultations to patients who would not otherwise have received medical care. By 2014, nearly 40 healthcare centres around the world were headed by ELAM graduates.[80] Whatever path has been beaten by the ELAM alumnae, as beneficiaries of Cuba's socialist education, they represent an international block of solidarity with the revolutionary people of Cuba.[81]

VENEZUELA AND CUBA: A HEALTHY EMBRACE

'What Cuba has given us is priceless,' declared Venezuelan president Hugo Chávez in 2010. 'If we start to add up, cent by cent, Cuba's contribution, it is clear that this is worth ten times the value of the petroleum that we have sold to Cuba . . . How much would a capitalist country charge us to bring that size of an army of doctors and that sea of medicines for our people, and be on call 24 hours a day?'[82]

Flooding and landslides in Venezuela's Vargas state in December 1999 killed up to 30,000 people. Just ten months into his first term in office, President Hugo Chávez launched a major rescue effort. Cuba sent a 450-strong medical brigade, including 250 doctors, to assist. At the Venezuelans' request, they remained after the emergency. In October 2000, Chávez and Fidel Castro signed their first cooperation agreement, which included Cuban assistance in improving the Venezuelan healthcare system. Cuban doctors would be sent where needed in Venezuela and deliver public health education. Venezuelans would train in Cuba as doctors, nurses and medical technicians and Venezuelan patients would receive medical treatment free of charge in Cuba.[83] Cuba would sell its medical products and equipment to Venezuela.

By 1998, when Chávez was first elected president, 17 million Venezuelans out of a population of 24 million, that is 70 per cent, lacked regular access to medical care, and over 4 million children and adolescents suffered from malnutrition, 1.2 million of them with severe malnutrition. The situation did not sufficiently improve during the early years of Chávez's presidency. In 2004, Héctor Navarro, then the Venezuelan Minister of Higher Education, described the situation as 'a humanitarian crisis' and estimated that 20,000 physicians were required to tackle it.[84]

In 2003, a pro-Chávez mayor in Caracas proposed the Barrio Adentro (into the neighbourhood) health programme to introduce free local health provision to slums in Libertador municipality. The Venezuelan Medical Federation instructed its members to boycott the initiative, so the mayor appealed directly to the Cuban embassy for help. The programme was subsequently launched in April 2003 with 58 Cuban doctors. In May, another 100 arrived and were spread throughout Caracas. Following the programme's success and popularity, it was extended nationwide. Cuban healthcare workers poured into Venezuela to staff it. By December 2003 over 10,000 Cuban medical professionals, half of them women, were in Venezuela and had conducted 9 million patient consultations and 4 million health interventions. They set up local practices in poor neighbourhoods, with one doctor for 250 families, living on the premises, as in Cuba.[85]

Inevitably, the new system had teething problems and living conditions were tough for the Cubans, with several adults sharing one room or sleeping in the homes of local residents. Most Cuban medics proved resilient; they came from humble origins and often overcrowded conditions. The Cubans had survived the deprivations of the Special Period and many had experience of working in poor regions in underdeveloped countries. But in Venezuela they also lived among violent crime and with threats of violence from an ardent opposition movement.

The Chávez government paid the costs of Cuban medical services with Venezuelan oil sold to Cuba at below world market prices. This was the mutually beneficial 'oil for doctors' barter exchange programme based on the resource strengths and socioeconomic needs of each country. The exchange catalysed Cuba's recovery from the Special Period, launched medical services as the island's main source of revenues, and bought Cubans much needed respite from the blackouts and bus queues resulting from oil shortages. These tangible benefits, in addition to the ideological commitment to proletarian internationalism, garnered support from Cuba's revolutionary people.[86] Likewise, the programme enabled Chávez to deliver the social benefits he had promised to Venezuela's impoverished and marginalised majority, the backbone of support for his Bolivarian Revolution.[87]

Significantly, the transaction removed from Cuba the obligation to completely insert itself into the capitalist world market by providing the Revolution with an alternative export strategy that was consistent with its socialist principles, reaped the benefits of the Revolution's investments in health and education and was not obstructed by the US blockade. By undermining capitalist market prices, the exchange with Venezuela limited the reintroduction of capitalist social relations and mechanisms which were gradually being imposed via private, capitalist foreign direct investments and increasing reliance on free enterprise.[88] For Cuba, which had sent doctors abroad since 1960 and engaged in barter exchange within the socialist bloc, the novel feature about this exchange was the scale of personnel.

The Cuba–Venezuela embrace catalysed other regional trade and development cooperation projects, such as the Bolivarian Alliance for the Americas (ALBA), set up in December 2004, opening a space for welfare-focused approaches to development within countries, and 'fair exchange' between countries wracked by neoliberalism. This process facilitated Cuba's full reintegration into regional forums and saw Cuban medical internationalism become inextricably entwined with Cuba's diplomatic and international relations and with its economic development strategy.

By 2010, Cuba's 'army of white coats' as it was called in Venezuela, reached 14,000 Cuban physicians, 15,000 nurses, dentists, physical therapists, optometrists and technicians, providing medical care through 7,000 doctors' offices and 500 larger diagnostic clinics.[89] Barrio Adentro II was launched with the establishment of hundreds of Comprehensive Diagnostic Centres, Comprehensive Rehabilitation Centres and Advanced Technology Centres for more specialised care. Barrio Adentro III saw the modernisation and integration of 300 Venezuelan hospitals and Barrio Adentro IV built new specialist hospitals.

Meanwhile, Cuba–Venezuela medical cooperation intensified through Operación Milagro (Operation Miracle), set up in 2004, under which the Chávez government began paying for Venezuelans with reversible blindness to travel to Cuba for free eye operations to restore their sight. The project emerged when Cuban educators, who had also poured into Venezuelan barrios, found that sight problems were obstructing their literacy efforts. Over 200,000 Venezuelans travelled to Cuba with a family member, staying for one week after surgery in a Cuban hotel, receiving follow-up care, without charge. From October 2005, Venezuelans were treated in a new ophthalmology centre set up in Venezuela as part of Operación Milagro. This was extended to 30 hospitals in 15 Venezuelan states. The programme was also exported so that, by 2017, Cuba had 69 ophthalmology clinics in 15 countries operating under Operación Milagro. By early 2019, over 4 million people in 34 countries had benefited.[90] And yet, beyond solidarity activists, few people in the west had even heard of the programme.

The third project between Cuba and Venezuela is the Comprehensive Community Medicine (Medicina Integral Comunitaria) programme to graduate 60,000 Venezuelan physicians, at home, with Cuban teaching staff. The six-year course is similar to those at ELAM. Following graduation, doctors must serve in public hospitals and clinics for two years.[91] By early 2019, more than 25,000 doctors had graduated.[92] With combined populations of around 40 million, Cuba and Venezuela are now training more doctors than the United States, with its population of nearly 330 million. By 2013, Cuba's medical intervention was estimated to have saved the lives of 1,746,417 Venezuelans.[93] Infant mortality had fallen from 25 per 1,000 live births to 13 by 2010.[94]

HENRY REEVE CONTINGENT: COMBATING DISASTERS AND EPIDEMICS

'On this day a so far unprecedented organization will be formed,' announced Fidel Castro on 19 September 2005, ten months before he was struck down by illness, 'the International Contingent of Doctors Specialized in Disaster Situations and Serious Epidemics . . . to give immediate assistance, with its specially trained staff, to any country that suffers a catastrophe, particularly those that are hit by hurricanes, floods or other natural phenomena of this severity.'[95]

In late August 2005, Hurricane Katrina had struck Louisiana, Mississippi and Alabama like a bomb. Three levees in New Orleans were breached and 80 per cent of the city was submerged in water. Within hours, Fidel Castro offered to send three Cuban field hospitals and the medical personnel to staff them.[96] By 4 September there were 1,586 Cuban volunteer medics, including 86 recent ELAM graduates, loaded with medical backpacks ready to leave for Louisiana. The brigade was named the Henry Reeve Contingent, in honour of a US citizen who fought with Cuban independence forces in the Ten Years War (1868–1878) against Spain.

The Cubans were ideal candidates to provide emergency assistance in those conditions – without clean water, electricity or sophisticated diagnostic equipment. Between them they had worked in 43 countries. President George W. Bush's administration never replied and even omitted Cuba from a list of countries who had offered help. Two weeks later, Fidel Castro said: 'It was as if a big American cruise ship with thousands of passengers aboard were sinking in waters close to our coast . . . It hurts to think that maybe some of those desperate people, trapped by the water and at death's door could have been saved.'[97] An estimated 1,800 people died as a result of Hurricane Katrina; the great majority were poor, black residents of Louisiana.

One month after its formation, the Henry Reeve Contingent was put to the test in Guatemala where, on 4 October 2005, Hurricane Stan had wreaked havoc on poor, mainly indigenous, communities in mountainous areas: 1,482 people were killed, thousands of homes destroyed and 1.5 million people affected. By 9 October the Guatemalan authorities had abandoned communities buried in mud and landslides. The Henry Reeve Contingent arrived with 600 members to work alongside 233 Cuban medical staff *already* stationed in the region. Up in the cold mountains, the Caribbean healthcare workers assisted 442,618 Guatemalans, saving 1,360 lives within two months. Living with their patients, most of whom had never seen a doctor, the Cubans witnessed the poverty and alienation which mark their daily lives.[98] Four days after Hurricane Stan, disaster struck on the other side of the world.

IN THE MOUNTAINS OF KASHMIR

'It has made me more revolutionary,' a young Cuban doctor, tearful with emotion, told reporters at the airport in Havana in mid-March 2006. A member of the Henry Reeve Contingent, she was returning from a five-month medical mission to the Pakistan-administered area of Kashmir, where a devastating earthquake had killed 80,000, left 120,000 injured and made 3.3 million people homeless. With the approaching winter threatening to kill thousands more and while the international media blamed 'compassion fatigue' for the lack of material aid and financial donations from the west, Cuba sent medics.[99] Cuba did not have diplomatic relations with Pakistan, whose president, Pervez Musharraf, was a close ally of US president George W. Bush.

The Henry Reeve Contingent stayed for seven months, with 2,400 healthcare workers treating 1,743,000 patients, three-quarters of all those treated following the earthquake. Half of the Cubans were women, which was necessary to be able to treat the local women. They trekked into mountainous areas, inaccessible by road, lugging backpacks with medical supplies, and making half a million home visits in mountainous communities, including one region where one doctor was serving 25,000 people.[100] They established 32 field hospitals, which were subsequently donated to Pakistan and 450 army physicians were trained to use them. Cuba provided 234.5 tons of medicines and supplies, as well as 275.5 tons of equipment. Complicated amputee cases were flown to Havana for treatment. Cuba also offered 1,000 medical scholarships for students in rural areas to study medicine in Cuba. Within a decade, 900 Pakistani medical students had graduated from ELAM.[101] These missions have hardly been mentioned in the international press.

On 2 February 2006, another 140 doctors of the Henry Reeve Contingent rushed to Bolivia with 20 mobile hospitals to assist the 50,000 rural families affected by heavy flooding at the end of January. Within 3 weeks, nearly 600 Cuban doctors in 9 provinces had treated 56,011 Bolivians.[102] As the disasters continued, so did the Henry Reeve Contingent.

DISASTER HITS HAITI . . . AGAIN

Jean Víctor Généus, Haitian Ambassador to Cuba recognised that, 'Every time a disaster has hit Haiti, Cuba's response has been immediate and altruistic, despite its own scant resources and the unjust, illegal, and inhumane blockade imposed by the United States over the last 50 years.'[103]

Haiti is the poorest country in the western hemisphere, with health indictors similar to or worse than Cuba's in the 1950s. Prior to the devastating earthquake which hit Haiti on 12 January 2010, 86 per cent of the capital's inhabitants lived in slum conditions, 50 per cent lacked access to latrines, and only one-third had access to potable water.[104] Poor infrastructure and living conditions exacerbate the impact of frequent natural disasters. The earthquake killed 230,000 Haitians, injuring another quarter of a million and leaving 1.5 million people homeless – 15 per cent of the population.

International reaction was fast and seemingly 'generous', with 10,000 NGOs elbowing for room on the scene.[105] The US government sent 22,000 armed military personnel, 17 ships and more than 100 aircraft. The USNS *Comfort* (a 1,000-bed hospital ship) attended 8,600 patients over 7 weeks – and then sailed away. Whilst celebrating their own country's reaction, worldwide media practically ignored Cuba's contribution despite the island, once again, being first to respond.[106]

'We send doctors, not soldiers,' announced Fidel Castro 11 days after the disaster.[107] Cuba *already* had 344 medical personnel in Haiti, alongside hundreds of Haitian physicians trained in Cuba. This medical aid had been initiated 11 years earlier following Hurricane Georges in 1998. After 36 years without diplomatic relations, the cooperation agreement signed between Cuba and Haiti in late 1998 committed Cuba to maintaining 300 to 500 medical professionals in Haiti as long as they were needed *and* to training hundreds of Haitians as physicians who could gradually replace them.[108] Cuba set up a comprehensive health programme and Cuban medics were allocated on two-year contracts to the poorest and most deprived areas, including city slums and marginalised rural regions. Many of the Cuban physicians are black and from poor origins, like the Haitians they serve. They live in Haitian communities, sharing their poverty and gaining their trust.

By 2004, 579 Cubans were responsible for the health care of 75 per cent of the Haitian population.[109] Where the Cubans were stationed, infant mortality had fallen from 80 per 1,000 live births in 1998 to 33 in 2003.[110] By 2007, 1 million vaccines had been administered by the Cubans and two ophthalmology centres had been set up in Haiti as part of Operación Milagro. With Venezuelan assistance, the Cubans were building ten comprehensive diagnostic centres (small hospitals). As the numbers of Haitian students at ELAM grew, a second faculty was opened in Santiago de Cuba to train them alongside francophone West African students.[111] By 2011, 625 Haitians had graduated as doctors in Cuba and 430 of them were working in Haiti, mostly in the public health care sector and alongside Cuban medics.[112]

The Henry Reeve Contingent began to arrive in Haiti within 24 hours of the January 2010 earthquake. They were followed by Cuban psychologists, psychiatrists and paediatric psychiatrists and even artists and child entertainers to assist traumatised children. By 1 April 2010, 748 additional Cuban healthcare professionals had arrived, along with 481 Haitian graduates from ELAM and another 278 graduates from 28 other countries. To compound Haiti's woes, in October 2010 an outbreak of cholera began. For a century cholera had disappeared from Haiti, but it was introduced via UN peacekeepers and spread due to the unsanitary conditions in temporary camps lacking safe drinking water or sewage facilities. The Cubans established cholera treatment centres and oral rehydration posts, set up tent-by-tent examinations and launched a public health campaign distributing information in Creole. By August 2013, nearly 700,000 cases of cholera had resulted in over 8,200 deaths.[113] Those numbers would have been far higher without Cuban assistance.

In July 2012, Haitian government minister Marie Carmelle Rose-Anne Auguste revealed that, since late 1998, Cuban healthcare workers in Haiti had performed 331,724 surgeries, attended 140,589 births and saved 312,584 lives (over 80,000 more than those lost in the earthquake).[114] Over 60,000 Haitians had had their eyesight restored through Operación Milagro and 878 Haitians had graduated as physicians under Cuban instruction. Cubans were working in 96 healthcare centres in Haiti.

In May 2017, when Cuba's Henry Reeve Contingent received the WHO Public Health Prize, its 7,254 participants had worked in 19 countries. By early 2019, recipient countries had risen to 45. Many books have and still could be written to record those contributions, to discuss the motivations, experiences and impact of Cuban medical personnel abroad, and the foreign students trained in Cuba.[115] This chapter has not even mentioned the extraordinary role of Cuban medical internationalism in the South Pacific, particularly East Timor, or Cuban-led missions in Venezuela, Ecuador and Bolivia to identify, assist and socially integrate people with physical and psychological disabilities.[116]

THE ECONOMICS OF MEDICAL INTERNATIONALISM

In 2005, Fidel Castro recognised that 'The healthcare system has become the most important sector in the exchange of goods and services between our country and the rest of the world in economic terms,' but pointed out that 'despite this, Cuba has not failed to offer its medical assistance completely free of charge to more than 60 Third World countries lacking economic resources'.[117]

In 2017, Cuban medics were in 62 countries; in 27 of those (44 per cent) the host government paid nothing, the remaining 35 paid according to a sliding scale.[118] For some countries, Cuba covers most of the costs, with others it shares costs. With a third group the host government pays all costs, but at a lower rate than that charged internationally. These agreements are managed by the Cuban corporation Servicios Médicos Cubanos, S.A. Differential payments are used to balance the books, so medical services charged to wealthy Qatar or Saudi Arabia help to subsidise medical assistance to developing countries, such as Burundi or Niger.[119] Where host governments pay, the money goes directly to the Cuban government, which passes a small proportion on to the medics. This is usually higher than (and additional to) their Cuban salary. '[T]he Cuban state keeps the lion's share of the difference, which represents an important source of foreign exchange for the government', explained the Economic Intelligence Unit.[120]

Post-2000, some developed countries, including Britain and France, contributed indirectly towards the costs of Cuban health care personnel working overseas.[121] However, within a few years, 'the help disappeared', laments Dr Aleida Guevara, Cuban medical internationalist and daughter of Che Guevara, 'but the need for help remains'.[122] Cuba could not carry the financial burden, so the system of payments was introduced. This dovetailed with the drive for efficiency within a socialist framework initiated under Raúl Castro.

Earnings from Cuban medical exports have been the largest source of foreign exchange for many years. By way of comparison, in 2018 tourism generated nearly USD 3 billion, while 'health services' earned USD 6.4 billion, according to Cuba's Office of National Statistics, which published the data for the first time in 2018.[123] Prior to 2018, government data combined health care with other 'professional services' including educators, engineers, sports trainers and military personnel working abroad. The annual average export earnings from all 'professional services' (not just medical) between 2011 and 2015 was USD 11.5 billion.[124] In that period, Venezuela and Brazil were the greatest recipients of Cuba's medical service exports. However, Cuban doctors working in China, Saudi Arabia and South Africa also earn important revenues. Meanwhile, state-run health tourism to Cuba is growing: 16 hospitals now provide services to foreigners, from cancer treatments to drug addiction programmes, with an estimated number of patients between 20,000 and 25,000 a year, yielding revenues of USD 30 to 40 million annually.[125]

In discussing Cuban medical exports, few commentators consider the costs to Cuba of resources spent, and revenue lost through not charging or charging below international market rates. In 2010, Mexican journalist José Steinsleger calculated the cost to Cuba of its medical assistance to Haiti between 1998 and 2010. Based on extremely low estimates he calculated a total cost of USD 215 million, asking 'Does Cuba have 215 million dollars left over, or is the idea to share what you have? In 2008 the island was devastated by three consecutive hurricanes and world nickel prices (one of its main revenues) plummeted. I am not going to mention the Yankee blockade . . . a scourge that represented losses of USD 100 billion since 1962.'[126]

· During the first ELAM graduation ceremony in August 2005, Fidel Castro said that an analysis of international data for medical education put the cost of training the 12,000 doctors then at ELAM around USD 3 billion. Cuba's plan to train 100,000 doctors from developing nations, he said, was a contribution to poor countries worth USD 30 billion.[127] Generally, however, the Cuban government says little about the monetary value of its medical internationalism programmes.

INSTABILITY IN VENEZUELA

In 2017, 28,000 Cuban healthcare workers remained in Venezuela but, due to the host country's economic crisis, oil shipments to Cuba had fallen substantially, bringing down the island's export earnings for professional services by 11.8 per cent in 2016 and a further 8.5 per cent 2017.[128] Venezuela was trapped in a spiral of economic and political crises as the US administration attacked the Maduro government, implementing devastating sanctions on Venezuela's vulnerable oil-dependent economy, and generating misery and unrest. Threatening direct military intervention, the Trump administration supported Juan Guaidó's self-proclamation as president and endorsed his military coup attempt in spring 2019, commanding the international community to follow suit.[129]

Whether it arrives violently or via the ballot box, an end of the Maduro United Socialist Party government in Venezuela would produce a major economic and political shock for Cuba, particularly if its medical exports were terminated. However, the proportion of Cuba's trade with Venezuela has never been as high as it was with the USSR and the socialist bloc and the consequent impact of a rupture in trade would be less traumatic. Furthermore, while likely, it is not inevitable that a change in government in Venezuela would mean an end to Cuban medical exports. Cuban medical programmes were not terminated following the ousting of President Aristides in Haiti (2004), President Zelaya in Honduras (2009), President Lugo in Paraguay (2012), nor for two years following the impeachment of President Dilma Rouseff in Brazil (2016).

NO MAIS MEDICOS IN BRAZIL

In 2013, the Brazilian doctors' professional organisation boycotted President Dilma Rouseff's Mais Médicos (More Doctors) programme to extend health care to the Brazilian Amazon and *favelas* (urban slums). After some vacillation due to internal opposition, the government contracted some 11,400 Cuban doctors, via the Pan American Health Organization (PAHO), instead. The Cuban medics in Brazil all had at least ten years' experience, 62 per cent were women, most were family doctors.[130] The Brazilian government paid USD 3,620 a month, USD 43,440 annually, for the Cuban doctors on three-year contracts starting from 2013.

Michel Temer took over as Brazil's interim president in 2016 following Rouseff's suspension and impeachment. 'He hasn't dared to break the contract [with Cuba], but he is not renewing it either,' said Aleida Guevara in late 2017, as the numbers of Cuban medics in Brazil were falling.[131] In late October 2018, Jair Bolsonaro won the presidential election, a man with jaw-dropping far-right views and pride in Brazil's brutal 21-year military dictatorship. Even prior to his mandate, Bolsonaro took aim at the Mais Medicos programme calling the Cubans 'slaves of a dictatorship' and 'not real doctors'. Paradoxically he also suggested he would let them stay, paying a salary direct to them, bypassing the PAHO and the Cuban government. In November 2018, before Bolsonaro could be sworn in, the Cuban government withdrew its remaining 8,400 Cuban medics from Brazil. Up to 2,000 Cuban healthcare professionals fell for Bolsonaro's offer and stayed on but then found they were barred from continuing on the Mais Medicos programme and were required to undertake further training.

As a consequence, 30 million Brazilians have been left without medical attention, and PAHO has warned that 42,000 children under five years old could die by 2030 if the programme is fully closed.[132] Bolsonaro found 7,000 Brazilian physicians to replace the Cubans, but within three months 15 per cent had abandoned the scheme and another nearly 20 per cent were expected to leave. It was suggested that the programme was being shut down.[133]

ORGANISED DEFECTION

In 2006, 11 Cuban healthcare professionals were admitted to the United States after abandoning overseas missions. This figure started to climb, however, when the US administration of George W. Bush launched the Medical Parole Programme.[134] It sought to sabotage Cuban medical export earnings by inducing Cuban medics to defect in return for US citizenship. An annual average of 713 Cubans joined the programme in the following six years (2007 to 2012), rising to 995 in 2013 and 1,278 in 2014.[135] These were medics who had paid no tuition costs, graduated debt free and had voluntarily signed contracts to work abroad assisting underserved populations. The Medical Parole Programme portrayed them as victims of state-sponsored human trafficking.[136] It was clearly designed for propaganda and demoralisation. Cuban medical qualifications are not recognised in the United States.[137] Cuban physicians who defect have had to invest in expensive new qualifications or leave the profession.

Even the *New York Times* called the programme 'particularly hard to justify'. An editorial in 2014 pointed to the hypocrisy of the US administration in praising Cuban medics combatting Ebola in West Africa while the Medical Parole Programme encouraged them to:

abandon their posts, take a taxi to the nearest American Embassy and apply for a little-known immigration program that has allowed thousands of them to defect. Those who are accepted can be on American soil within weeks, on track to becoming United States citizens . . . It is incongruous for the United States to value the contributions of Cuban doctors who are sent by their government to assist in international crises like the 2010 Haiti earthquake while working to subvert that government by making defection so easy.[138]

Despite these inducements, most estimates are that up to 2 per cent of Cuban medics defect. President Obama did not end the Medical Parole Programme until his final days in office in January 2017.[139] The reprieve did not last long: in June 2019, the Trump administration added Cuba to its Tier 3 list of countries failing to combat 'human trafficking' on the basis of its medical cooperation overseas, and USAID established a programme to discredit and sabotage Cuban healthcare programmes.

Back in Cuba, healthcare professionals had two- to three-fold pay increases, prior to salary rises awarded in July 2019 (see Chapter 10). Their salaries remain low compared to counterparts in other countries, but monetary incomes alone do not determine the standard of living in socialist Cuba, where the social wage and state subsidies are very high. Undoubtedly, Cuban internationalists make a huge personal sacrifice regardless of what motivates their decision to volunteer overseas. They leave behind children, partners, parents, homes, their culture and communities to work in challenging and often risky conditions for months or even years. Within Cuba, the dual economy and more recent expansion of private enterprise has encouraged healthcare professionals to shift into lower-skilled, but higher-paid work in other fields. Every year, however, thousands of new medics graduate and there is no private health sector to speak of in Cuba.[140]

THE FIDEL CASTRO EFFECT

In a poor rural area in Ghana in the 1980s, Pérez met a local man who was surprised to learn that he was Cuban because of his white skin. The man was even more astonished to hear that Fidel Castro was white. He had assumed that the Cuban leader was black because, he said, 'Fidel helps black people and does so much for the people of Africa. I cannot believe that Fidel is white.' Pérez pointed out that experience had led the man to associate white people with exploitation. 'For me it was a shock,' said Pérez, 'This poor man had not even seen a photograph of Fidel. Nevertheless, he was talking about what Fidel does for Africa. It really motivates you. I was really moved to see how far the significance of Fidel had reached.' He concluded, 'It's because of that spirit that we follow Fidel's ideas.'[141]

Fidel Castro is clearly the leading protagonist in the history of Cuban medical internationalism. Deeply committed to the ideas of Martí and Marx, he saw proletarian internationalism as a duty for the Cuban people. In the post-Soviet period, international development aid, predominantly health care, replaced the focus on military aid of the Cold War era. Medical aid was to be the main vehicle for combating imperialist oppression and exploitation in the underdeveloped world. It also served to showcase the advantages of state planning and a welfare-based socialist development path. This dovetailed with the Venezuelan embrace, converting it into a significant source of income for the country. The surge in paid medical exports from the mid-2000s enabled the revolutionary government to manage the island's reintegration into the capitalist global economy in a way compatible with its socialist development, reaping the benefits of the Revolution's investments in education and health care. The earnings were ploughed back in to safeguard the socialist system which had facilitated them, securing its survival into the post-Soviet world.

The island's healthcare missions have benefited millions of people around the world; they owe their health, if not their lives, to Cuban professionals and the government which trained and sent them. Medical internationalism has in turn nourished Cuba's international relations: the island has earned gratitude and respect, particularly from the developing world, which has become increasingly vociferous in opposition to the US hostility towards Cuba. In the post-Soviet period, growing numbers of the world's nations defied US pressure to condemn the US blockade at the UN General Assembly; today condemnation is almost unanimous. Within Latin America a groundswell of support for Cuba became a tangible factor pushing the Obama administration towards rapprochement in 2014, as discussed in the next chapter.

The 'guidelines for updating the Cuban economy', approved in 2011 and revised for the period 2016–2021, confirm the government's commitment to universal, free healthcare, to improving the quality and efficiency of provision, and to Cuban medical internationalism, which is perceived to be both a source of revenue and a form of international solidarity: Guideline 70 states that Cuba will 'accelerate the development of Cuban medical and health services and continue expanding markets for their exportation'.[142] Guideline 84 commits the island to continue developing international solidarity by offering cooperation, and adds that it will 'consider, to the extent possible, compensation, at least, of its costs'.[143]

In 2019, 13 years after Fidel Castro retired and 3 years since his death, Cuban medical internationalism remained an indelible feature of Cuba Socialista. Cuban medical graduates continue to pledge an oath: 'to serve the revolution unconditionally wherever we are needed, with the premise that true medicine is not that which cures but that which prevents, whether in an isolated community on our island or in any sister country in the world, where we will always be the standard bearers of solidarity and internationalism'.[144] In early April 2019, the 28th brigade of the Henry Reeve Contingent arrived in flood-devastated Mozambique with 40 professionals and a field hospital. Within one week, 4,000 patients had been treated.[145] Meanwhile, Cuba retained some 20,000 professionals in Venezuela; around 95 per cent of them were medics, of whom 64 per cent were women.[146]

To offset the recent setbacks, particularly the withdrawal of Cuban healthcare services in Brazil, the Cuban government is actively seeking to diversify medical exports, including to oil-rich Arab countries such as Qatar. Cuban medical assistance is still available free in emergencies, and a sliding scale has been introduced for its comprehensive healthcare programmes according to each country's ability to pay. This increasing shift from free to charged provision is driven by necessity and can be seen as 'principled pragmatism', according to John Kirk, a scholar who has researched Cuban medical internationalism extensively.[147] Trump's tightened sanctions are unlikely to drive a significant wedge between the Caribbean island that graduates thousands of new medical professionals every year, and the urgent need for health care around the globe.

7

★ ★ ★

CUBA AND THE UNITED STATES
PLUS ÇA CHANGE, PLUS C'EST LA MÊME CHOSE?

In spring 2019, US president Donald Trump threatened to impose a 'full embargo' on Cuba unless it withdrew support for the Maduro government in Venezuela. Asked about this threat by US television network MSNBC, Carlos Fernández de Cossío, Cuba's General Director of US Affairs, pointed out: 'There is already a practically total embargo of Cuba. We've had it for over 60 years and its been rejected, condemned by the UN almost unanimously for many years. What else can he do?' In 2018, the Cuban government's annual report to the United Nations put the cost of the US blockade over 6 decades as USD 134 billion dollars at today's prices;[1] Cuban economists break this down to USD 12 million every day. 'The whole aim of the policy already is to cause as much economic harm to Cuba, as much damage, and to harm the living standards of the population of Cuba,' pointed out de Cossío, adding 'but what it will not do is to extract concessions from the government of Cuba.'[2]

Trump's threat was some rewind from the discourse of 'engagement' and 'putting the past behind us' delivered by President Obama in his second term. While his penchant for announcing policy via Twitter might be new, Trump's Cuba policy is far from innovative: gifting control over his administration's approach to powerful right-wing Cuban-Americans, defaulting to hostility and strengthening the US blockade of the island. The more things change, the more they stay the same! Even the rhetoric has gone back to the Cold War era. His fanatical anti-communist National Security Advisor John Bolton attacked Cuba in ideological terms as 'the sordid cradle of communism in the western Hemisphere,' warning of the 'perils of poisonous ideologies'.[3] Trump officials have even resurrected the early nineteenth-century Monroe Doctrine to assert the United States' right to reign over the Americas at the exclusion of outside powers; in the case of Cuba this means the socialist Revolution has to go. 'The idea that Cuba belongs to them, that they have special rights of providence over Cuba is older than the existence of the United States as an independent nation state,' said former president of Cuba's National Assembly Ricardo Alarcón.[4] 'That notion remains even though the project to formally annex Cuba to the United States does not,' he told me, despite rapprochement being in full swing when we met. The annexationist tendency has its counterpart among Cubans, he added: 'The idea that the island's incorporation into the United States is in the best interests of a section of Cubans is older than the Republic of Cuba.'

Over six decades, an immense legal, economic and political apparatus of hostility has been built up, almost exclusively on the US side, benefiting many vested interests, including Cuban-American exiles, who obstruct improvements in bilateral relations. Although the balance of power has lain with the United States, Cuba has not been a 'respectable' or subservient neighbour. It has supported attempts to overthrow and undermine US-friendly and client states, punched well above its weight in geopolitical terms and consistently contested US hegemony in the region, and imperialism internationally, contributing military and medical personnel to what President George W. Bush once called 'any dark corner of the world'.[5]

Ultimately, it is *because* the Cuban Revolution has survived that the *real* motivation for opposition to the Cuban Revolution has remained: the intolerable example of a socialist alternative in the United States' backyard. Essentially, then, Cuba *has* to endure US aggression or give up the socialist character of the state. This reality was grasped early on by Cuba's revolutionary leaders. On 16 April 1961, on the eve of the US-backed Bay of Pigs invasions by Cuban exiles, Fidel Castro announced the socialist character of the Cuban Revolution publicly for the first time, stating: 'This is what they cannot forgive . . . that we have carried out a socialist revolution right under the nose of the United States!'[6] In 1964, when Che Guevara was asked by US journalist and former actor Lisa Howard what he wanted from the United States, he replied: 'Perhaps the most frank and objective response would be: Nothing. Nothing for or against us. Just leave us alone.'[7] Over half a century later, Raúl Castro said Cuba aspired to 'civilised co-existence'.

What have Cuba's revolutionary people survived? For six decades, the Caribbean island has withstood manifold and unrelenting aggression from the world's dominant economic and political power: overt and covert military actions; sabotage and terrorism by US authorities and allied exiles; imposition of the blockade to asphyxiate the Cuban economy and its people; obstruction of third parties' trade with Cuba; pressure on regional and international governments to isolate and ostracise Cuba; encouragement of illegal and dangerous emigration, including of unaccompanied Cuban children (Operation Peter Pan, 1960–1962) and Cuban doctors (Cuban Medical Parole Programme, 2006–2017); the obstruction of remittances and family visits and refusal to issue visas to Cubans; and lucrative funding for regime change programmes.[8] Most aspects of this wretched history are well documented.

THE CENTRAL INTELLIGENCE AGENCY SOWS THE SEEDS

The first Central Intelligence Agency (CIA) plan for paramilitary action in Cuba was developed in December 1959, less than a year after Batista fled the island and well before the US blockade was imposed. The CIA recruited operatives inside Cuba to carry out terrorism and sabotage, killing civilians and causing economic damage. Along with Cuban exiles and the Mafia, these recruits were commissioned to assassinate Fidel Castro and other leaders in an avalanche of plots involving everything from snipers to exploding cigars.[9] The April 1961 landing at the 'Bay of Pigs' (Playa Giron) by a CIA-trained force of Cuban exiles was the third and most substantial invasion of Cuba's coasts; it was swiftly trounced by the Revolutionary Armed Forces (FAR) under Fidel Castro's command.

In the aftermath, US president Kennedy instructed the CIA to initiate Operation Mongoose, training thousands of exiles in the Florida Keys in paramilitary exercises and sabotage. Miami soon had the largest CIA substation in its history. In 1962 the US Department of Defense and the Joint Chiefs of Staff concocted Operation Northwood, 'the most corrupt plan ever created by the US government' according to James Bamford, the former National Security Agency (NSA) official who exposed its existence nearly 40 years later in 2001. The Operation was approved by the Pentagon but apparently not by Kennedy. Bamford explained: 'The plan called for innocent people to be shot on American streets; for boats fleeing Cuba to be sunk on the high seas; for a wave of violent terrorism to be launched in Washington DC, Miami and elsewhere. People would be framed for bombings they did not commit, planes would be hijacked. Using phoney evidence, all of it would be blamed on Fidel Castro, thus giving Lemnitzer [Joint Chiefs of Staff Chairman] and his cabal the excuse to launch their war.'[10] You couldn't make it up!

Events bypassed the CIA as the Cuban Missile Crisis brought the world to the brink of nuclear war in October 1962. Both the United States and the Soviets claimed victory, and the US agreed not to invade the island. However,

Fidel Castro was furious that Cuba's five preconditions for the removal of Soviet missiles from the island were not part of the negotiation: an end to the US blockade and other trade and economic pressures; US withdrawal from Guantanamo Naval Base and the return of Cuban territory occupied by the United States; the end to subversive activities; an end to piratical attacks; and an end to violations of air and naval space by US aircraft and warships.[11] The first three remain key issues obstructing normalisation today.

THE CIA'S 'SONS OF BITCHES'[12]

From 1963, at the Fort Benning US army post, Cuban exiles were trained in intelligence, clandestine operations and propaganda. Among the recruits were Félix Rodríguez, Luis Posada Carriles, Orlando Bosch and Jorge Mas Canosa, who became lifelong collaborators epitomising the unrelenting and unrepentant violence of the exile extremists, as well as their hold on US domestic politics. Among other deeds, Rodríguez was the CIA operative who executed Che Guevara in Bolivia in 1967 and ran supplies for the CIA's Contra operations in Nicaragua in the 1980s. He enjoyed close ties to former CIA director George Bush senior, who was then vice president to Reagan. Carriles's terrorist activities earned him a reputation as the 'Osama Bin Laden of the Americas'. He collaborated with Bosch, a convicted terrorist released from prison in 1990 by then president George H. W. Bush and granted US citizenship two years later. Mas Canosa became the intimidating leader of the Cuban exile community in Miami, a powerful businessman personally worth over USD 400 million, who 'controlled access to the White House on Cuban issues, ensuring that only hard-liners participated in policy-making'.[13] All four were venerable members of the Cuban exile community.[14]

By 1967, as US foreign policy was overwhelmed by the Vietnam War, the CIA decided to close its outpost in Miami; the heyday of CIA-sponsored exile operations against Cuba were over, although programmes continued in collaboration with militant exiles who refused to relinquish their war on Fidel Castro and revolutionary Cuba.[15] Miami became the émigrés base of operations where violence, corruption and intimidation reigned. One FBI veteran concluded that 'the *gangsterismo* of Havana was transported to Miami by a handful of early *batistiano* arrivals'.[16] US authorities did not shut down these operations: having been nurtured and trained by US agencies the exiles effectively enjoyed immunity from prosecution by US authorities, lest they reveal that sordid history. Carriles told US journalist Ann Louise Bardach: 'The

CIA taught us everything – everything. They taught us explosives, how to kill, bomb, trained us in acts of sabotage.'[17]

Furthermore, their rabid anti-communism and proclivity for violence was put at the service of the US establishment, to police covert operations throughout the region and further afield. In 1964, Carriles was assigned to run Venezuela's repressive intelligence service.[18] In the 1970s Bosch led a coalition of death squads closely linked to Operation Condor, under which right-wing military regimes in Argentina, Bolivia, Brazil, Chile, Ecuador, Paraguay, Peru and Uruguay colluded to arrest, detain, torture and 'disappear' hundreds of thousands of Latin Americans.[19] In the 1980s, Rodríguez recruited Carriles to help run clandestine operations to support the Contras in Nicaragua. These exiles were deeply involved in repressive 'counter-insurgency' programmes throughout Central America. The activities listed are the tip of the iceberg.[20]

Bardach asserts that: 'No anti-communist opposition in the world has been more fervent or well financed than the Cuban exiles living in the States. And yet . . . they have little to show for their efforts.'[21] This is not entirely true. While they failed to assassinate the Revolution's leaders and return to Havana as conquering heroes, they succeeded in converting Cuba into a US domestic policy issue, turning themselves into presidential kingmakers, obstructing improvements in bilateral relations, furnishing their careers and fortunes, and spilling a great deal of blood on both sides of the Florida Straits and far beyond, as Bardach herself shows. A 2006 Cuban government report detailed acts of sabotage and terrorism on the island launched by or from the United States and responsible for 3,478 Cuban deaths, with another 2,099 Cubans left permanently maimed.[22]

In Miami, the exiles created a fiefdom in which subterfuge, intimidation and violence reigned and where dissent against their hard line on Cuba was punished brutally.[23] Exile politics became mixed up with the drug money that flooded Miami in the 1970s; generalised corruption was widespread and protection rackets forced businesses to contribute to 'the cause' of overthrowing Fidel Castro.[24] In 1974, Bosch warned: 'We will invade the Cuban embassies and will murder the Cuban diplomats and will hijack the Cuban planes until Castro releases some of the political prisoners and begins to deal with us.'[25] Over 150 attacks on Cuban diplomatic missions in the Americas and Europe were recorded. George Bush senior was head of the CIA from November 1975 to January 1977, arguably the most violent years of exile activity according to Bardach.[26]

Some brave Cuban-Americans defied the exile chiefs. In 1977, the Antonio Maceo Brigade was formed in Miami, 'born of ground made fertile by the

Civil Rights and anti-war movements', to visit and learn about the island first-hand.[27] This was possible after US president Jimmy Carter lifted the ban on travel to Cambodia, Cuba, North Korea and Vietnam. The Brigade consisted of 55 participants, all of whom had been children when they left the island and, being mostly based outside Miami, had been exposed to more progressive politics. The *Washington Post* reported: 'Counterrevolutionary extremists issued death threats against some of the founders and were not averse to using bombs as a means to intimidate those believed to be Castro agents or allies.'[28]

Carter reached out to the Democratic Party in Florida to initiate the 'Dialogue' in 1978: it provided political cover for his administration to negotiate with Havana on improving relations. The initiative was handled by Bernardo Benes, a powerful Cuban-American businessman who had financed violent exile operations in the mid–1960s before relinquishing such methods.[29] The Dialogue produced two exile conferences in Havana. Cuban-American scholar Nelson Valdés participated in the first in November 1978. 'Cuba wanted us to go to our own communities and get the names of people who were in prison in Cuba and submit those names during the second meeting,' he explained.[30] During the second meeting, the Cuban government agreed to free some 3,900 prisoners. However, instead of being lauded in Miami, Benes was denounced as a traitor and a communist; the bank he owned was bombed and picketed for three weeks. Even some of the prisoners whose release he had secured criticised him. Within the year, two conference participants had been murdered.[31]

In 1980 Miami was transformed following the influx of 125,000 Cuban migrants with the Mariel boatlift.[32] Never part of the old regime's elite, their arrival altered the demographic of the exile community. Meanwhile, Mas Canosa had concluded that paramilitarism alone could not topple Fidel Castro and, coinciding with the start of the Reagan presidency in 1981, he co-founded the Cuban American National Foundation (CANF) modelled on the powerful Israeli lobby. It became the dominant Cuban-American institution and anyone or anything that stood in its path was dealt with ruthlessly. During the Reagan years of the 1980s the violence in Miami peaked. In 1985, the FBI labelled Miami as the murder capital of America.[33]

Meanwhile in 1987, with evidence supplied by 27 of its own state security agents, the Cuban government publicly exposed CIA operations underway on the island since the late 1960s. Over the decade since Carter opened the US Interest Section in Havana in 1977 as a substitute for an embassy, 38 of the 79 permanent diplomatic posts had been occupied by CIA agents and another 113 CIA agents had operated under the guise of civil servants.[34] Instead of expelling the US representatives the Cubans left them in post, given that their exposure had effectively neutralised them as agents. Over several weeks, Cuban national television broadcast images of those US officials engaged in espionage activities with footage from state security cameras.[35]

'NICE WORK IF YOU CAN GET IT . . .'

Opposition to the Cuba Revolution has been a lucrative business. Bardach records that, from 1981 until his death in 1997, Mas Canosa's crusade to topple Fidel Castro was financed by more than USD 200 million of taxpayer's money and virtually every Florida politician since CANF's inception was enriched by hefty contributions from CANF. Until 2000, CANF enjoyed non-profit, tax-exempt status while securing vast sums of fungible government grants. CANF's various umbrellas and Political Action Committees (PACs), like the Free Cuba Committee, contributed generously to politicians who would back 'the cause'.[36] Ultimately, these exiles sought to make the cost of improving bilateral relations between the US and Cuban governments too high to pursue.

While one hand was buying influence with campaign contributions to politicians, the other was financing terrorist operations. Carriles estimated that Mas Canosa had sent him more than USD 200,000 by 1998. Did Carriles operate as CANF's military wing, Bardach asked him? 'It looks like that,' he replied, and laughed.[37] Most notorious among Carriles's and Bosch's numerous crimes was masterminding the bombing of a Cuban civilian aeroplane in 1976, killing all 73 people on board, including 24 members of Cuba's national fencing team returning victorious from the Central American and Caribbean Championships.[38]

The Reagan administration obliged CANF and Mas Canosa whenever possible. On 20 May 1985, Cuban Independence Day, Radio Martí began broadcasting illegally into Cuba from Miami, in flagrant violation of the International Telecommunications Union procedures. This was a pet project of Mas Canosa. Five years later, TV Martí was added to this propaganda offensive. These broadcasts, to which few Cubans on the island ever paid attention, received USD 700 million of US Congress-approved funds between just 1996 and 2015.[39]

BACKCHANNEL TALKS

'Under this administration,' announced Bolton in November 2018, 'there will no longer be secret channels of communication between Cuba and United

States.'[40] It was a dig at Obama, whose administration held 18 months of secret talks with Havana, facilitated by the Vatican and Canada, prior to announcing rapprochement on 17 December 2014. But, in fact, the three previous Republican administrations Bolton had served also held backchannel in talks with Cuba.[41]

The history of negotiations between the United States and Cuba over the last 60 years reveals five salient points.[42] First, that the United States' pretext for aggression against Cuba keeps changing. Initially it was retaliation for government expropriations and nationalisations of US properties in Cuba, next the adoption of socialism and the alliance with the Soviet Union, then Cuba's anti-imperialist foreign policy more broadly; later the excuse was human rights and the demand for a transition to capitalist democracy was added. In 2019, it became support for President Maduro and the PSUV government in Venezuela.

Second, despite all of this, bilateral talks began just eight months after diplomatic relations were broken on 3 January 1961 and have taken place under every US administration since then. In August 1961, as Cuba's representative to the Inter-American Conference, Che Guevara sent a box of Cuban cigars to White House representative Richard Goodwin before orchestrating a secret dawn meeting with him.[43] Even the most hostile US administrations have entered talks, either about a single issue of mutual interest, or concerning broader relations.[44]

I heard first-hand about the negotiations from Alarcón, who spent decades leading the Cuban side in official and backchannel talks, and at times both simultaneously, having been Cuba's Permanent Representative to the United Nations in New York on and off over 30 years, then Minister of Foreign Relations (1992 to 1993) and President of the National Assembly (1993 to 2013).[45] He recounted how in the 1990s during official migration talks with Dennis Hays, the US government's Coordinator for Cuba Affairs, he was also secretly meeting with Peter Tarnoff, Under Secretary of State for Political Affairs, who pleaded: 'For God's sake don't let these people find out that we are seeing each other!' 'How absurd is that!?' he exclaimed laughing. Alarcón's movements were restricted and under surveillance. 'How do you have a secret meeting in New York with all this paraphernalia?' he asked rhetorically, before explaining how he slipped out of Cuba's UN Mission undetected. The secret talks with Tarnoff produced an agreement that was made public; Hays resigned from government in protest and went to work for CANF. 'The guy was completely linked to those people, and the State Department knew it, which is why Hays couldn't know that we were meeting.'[46]

Third, Fidel Castro was both prepared to talk to the United States and 'involved personally in every aspect of those talks or negotiations', according to Alarcón. 'When I returned to Havana after secret talks, I always met him personally and we talked about everything, including the description of the lunch.' In contrast, he says, 'No American president was ever involved 10 per cent on Cuba or the secret talks with Cuba.' For Cuba, relations with the United States have been a priority issue; for the United States, they have been a minor topic, says Alarcón. Thus, US presidents have been prepared to outsource their Cuba policy to Miami exile power-brokers.

Alarcón described a deterioration he had observed in the 'intellectual and cultural level' of his US counterparts over the decades. He regarded some as 'really serious individuals' with whom, despite disagreements, 'the dialogue enriched both sides'. But as the personnel changed over the years, the knowledge and skill of his counterparts diminished. They arrived at talks with a big book, like an instruction manual, which they constantly consulted. 'Suppose I talked about the weather,' explained Alarcón, you would see this guy moving rapidly through the book to find the section on the weather. That was during the meeting, but afterwards we would go to lunch in a restaurant and they would bring the book! We had to clear space, move the glasses out the way, for that huge book. I recall a series of bureaucrats – really! I don't know whether it was ignorance, or cowardice, not wanting to deviate from strict instructions.'

Cuba's negotiating team hardly changed throughout this period, except for the translator, while on the US side only the translator, Stephanie Van Reigersberg, was consistently present throughout those years.[47] Alarcón describes Reigersberg as 'really the most knowledgeable on the North American side'. Once, when a new State Department official began talks by suggesting that they start with a historical overview of relations, instead of translating his words Reigersberg cried out: 'Oh my God! Again! I know that story. I know what you are going to say now, that in 1959 when Batista left . . .' Alarcón chuckled, 'The poor thing just could not bear to go over it again. She had been in those conversations over the decades and then some new idiot comes along and says, "Why don't we start at the beginning?"'[48]

Fourth, for over five decades, US officials prefaced talks on the basis of a quid pro quo, a trade off. To earn improvements in relations, Cuba was variously to: break with the Soviet Union; stop fomenting guerrilla movements in Latin America; end military intervention in Africa and withdraw Cuban troops from Angola where they were holding back apartheid South African forces; silence their support for Puerto Rican independence; stop assisting armed struggles in

Central America; release political prisoners; and introduce a market economy and multiparty elections. But the Cubans rejected preconditions and ultimatums. During the Carter administration, Fidel Castro told US negotiators that Cuba would not negotiate its support for Angola, nor betray that country's trust. 'We have never discussed with you the activities of the United State throughout the entire world,' he told US officials. 'I never accepted the universal prerogatives of the United States . . . the existence of a different law and different rules.'[49] Mostly, these were preconditions just to *begin* talks about 'normalising' relations. 'I don't remember them ever saying "if you do this we will lift the embargo",' Alarcón stated. The Cubans imposed their own conditions: that the US blockade must be lifted for Cuba and the United States to negotiate as equals. Only once both sides had dropped their preconditions could the restoration of diplomatic relations finally take place during Obama's second term.[50]

Fifth, the ultimate goal of the United States' Cuba policy, the elimination of Cuba's socialist system, has never changed. The United States has never accepted Cuba's right to self-determination.

CUBA'S SHIFTING INTERNATIONAL RELATIONS

The break in diplomatic relations with the United States in 1961 engendered the first of two crises of international relations for the revolutionary government in three decades. The following year, the United States had Cuba expelled from the Organization of American States (OAS) and in 1964 the OAS voted to terminate all diplomatic and commercial relations with Cuba. All except Mexico complied.[51] Canada was not a member of OAS and did not break off diplomatic relations with Cuba despite US pressure. Ostracised by its neighbours, Cuba increasingly aligned to the socialist countries. The island's integration into the socialist trading bloc, the Council for Mutual Economic Assistance, cushioned the impact of the US blockade until 1990.[52]

Before the Soviet embrace was consolidated, however, Cuba's young revolutionaries demonstrated the kind of radical, independent foreign policy they intended to pursue, one that is focused on the developing ('Third') world and support for national liberation struggles and new post-colonial governments. The USSR's disregard for Cuban demands in settling the Cuban Missile Crisis in October 1962 reinforced the island's determination to pursue an independent foreign policy. In 1961, the revolutionaries had initiated their first civic–military internationalist mission, to Algeria. Over the next three decades, civic–military internationalist missions sent thousands of Cubans throughout Africa and the Middle East, sometimes with support from the USSR, but not at their behest.[53] The Cubans changed the course of history in Angola, ensuring the defeat of apartheid South Africa's armed forces. As scholar Piero Gleijeses has pointed out: 'No other Third World country had ever projected its power beyond its immediate neighbourhood.'[54]

Also in 1961 Cuba participated in the founding conference of the Non-Aligned Movement (NAM) in Yugoslavia.[55] In 1966, Havana hosted the Tricontinental Conference of anti-imperialist movements from Asia, Africa and Latin America, and promoted solidarity with the National Liberation Front in Vietnam.[56] From 1972, diplomatic relations were re-established with four English-speaking Caribbean countries, leading the way for other Caribbean Community members.[57] In 1975, the OAS removed the prohibition on member states' relations with Cuba, paving the way for closer regional ties. The European Economic Community established diplomatic relations with Cuba in 1988.

Meanwhile, in the mid-1980s, the Soviet buffer began to weaken as the new Soviet Premier Gorbachev reneged on long-standing economic and military agreements with Cuba. By the end of the decade the socialist regimes of Eastern Europe were collapsing and in December 1991 the USSR disintegrated, eliminating most of Cuba's trade and investments. The Cuban Revolution faced its second crisis of international relations, but now with no alternative world power to turn to. The Cold War was won, capitalism returned to Eastern Europe and Russia, neoliberalism reigned and Latin America was structurally adjusted under the banner of the Washington Consensus.

CUBA–US RELATIONS IN THE POST-SOVIET ERA

To survive in the post-Soviet world, the Cuban government pursued a multi-pronged strategy. First, a managed insertion into the international capitalist economy facilitated by a structural transformation of the island's economy and an almost complete shift in trade partners, as discussed in Chapter 2. Second, investing scarce resources on diversifying international relations; anti-imperialism and solidarity with the underdeveloped world remained central, but the emphasis was on peaceful cooperation with all governments, focusing on Latin America. According to Isabel Allende, Director of the Higher Institute of International Relations (ISRI), which trains diplomats and academics in Havana: 'Cuba developed the scope of foreign relations like never before. In the 1990s, when mere mortals were saying "there is no money to maintain an Embassy", that great genius, the architect of our policy, Fidel Castro said: "No, no, it's now that we have to open, because now we have to counteract immense aggression from the United States.'"[58] The political processes underway in Latin America, from the election of Hugo Chávez in Venezuela in 1998, forged a space for Cuba's participation in projects of regional integration, creating new networks and strategic alliances.

Third, Cuba significantly expanded international development aid, particularly in health care and education, which strengthened direct ties with beneficiary communities globally and catalysed improvements in government-to-government relations. It also led to professional services exports, which became the island's main source of revenue by 2004. The fourth strategy was to nurture the Revolution's global solidarity networks. With groups now active in two-thirds of all world's nations, the solidarity movement became 'a safeguard of the Revolution; an element of our peoples' national security', according to Kenia Serrano, President of the Cuban Institute of Friendships with the Peoples (ICAP) between 2009 and 2017.[59] 'The solidarity movement is autonomous, genuine and authentic,' inspired by Cuba, but not built or led by Cubans, Serrano said. Active solidarity from within the United States has been strategically important.[60] Neither the Cuban people nor the government express animosity towards the US population; on the contrary, they have sought to strengthen ties between them in multiple fields. The solidarity movement was facilitated by Cuba opening up to the world, through tourism, trade and by hosting international events.

Meanwhile, Cuba's enemies in the United States acted fast to hasten the Revolution's downfall. The government tightened the US blockade, while exiles renewed their terrorist campaigns. Both targeted Cuba's nascent tourism industry in the 1990s. More sophisticated and multifaceted 'regime change' programmes were developed, from Clinton's 'People to People' programmes, to President Bush's Plan for a Free Cuba, and Obama's 'civil society engagement'.

BLOCKADE INTENSIFIED

Seeking to exploit Cuba's vulnerability, and despite being 'a devout Republican', Mas Canosa switched his political allegiance to US Democrat Bill Clinton in the 1990s, winning Clinton's support on issues that Reagan and Bush senior had rebuffed him on, Bardach explained. 'The savy exile impresario had quickly sized up Clinton's willingness to trade Cuba policy for immediate political gains and adroitly played him off against Republicans.'[61] The issue at stake was the extra-territorial reach of the US blockade.

In 1988, New Jersey Democrat Congressman Robert Torricelli praised Cuba after visiting the island: 'Living standards are not high, but the homelessness, hunger and disease that is witnessed in much of Latin America does not appear evident.'[62] However, after receiving generous campaign contributions from CANF, he was soon sponsoring the Cuban Democracy Act, subsequently dubbed the Torricelli Act. It prohibited the foreign-based subsidiaries of US companies in third countries from trading with Cuba, banned ships docking in Cuba from entering US ports for six months, barred travel to Cuba by US citizens, and forbade family remittances to the island.[63] In Torricelli's own words, the legislation was intended to 'wreak havoc on that island'. President Bush senior intended to veto the Torricelli Bill, concerned about US allies opposing its extra-territorial reach. Then in April 1992 his rival, presidential candidate Clinton, told an audience of wealthy exiles, 'I have read the Torricelli-Graham Bill and I like it.' He was rewarded with USD 275,000 in campaign contributions at two CANF-sponsored events in one day. Bush reversed his own position and the Bill was approved by Congress in October 1992.[64] The following month, Clinton won the US presidency.

Clinton's first term coincided with Cuba's 1994 rafters' crisis, discussed in Chapter 2, forcing his administration into talks that produced two major migration accords. However, his determination to hold on to the decisive electoral state of Florida overrode his concerns about improving bilateral relations with Cuba.[65] Clinton's second term was won in 1996 with 70 per cent of the Florida exile vote. 'The price, to a large extent,' explained Bardach 'was the passage of the Helms–Burton Bill, officially known as the Cuban Liberty and Democratic Solidarity Act, which demonstrably tightened the Embargo and codified it into law. No longer would an American president simply be able to dispense with the Embargo by the stroke of a pen ... After Helms–Burton, the Embargo can only be terminated by the agreement of the US Congress.'[66]

Title III of the Helms–Burton Act authorises US nationals with claims to nationalised property in Cuba to file suit in US courts against persons 'trafficking' in that property. However, from the outset Title III was suspended for six months at a time by the US president.[67] In protest at the extraterritorial character of this legislation, Canada and the European Union (EU) adopted blocking and 'claw-back' legislation and threatened legal action within the North American Free Trade Agreement and the World Trade Organization (WTO) respectively.[68] On paper, EU and UK citizens and businesses complying with the 1996 Helms–Burton Act can be fined. But in April 1997 the EU and the US made a deal: the US would limit the impact of certain provisions on European companies and citizens and in return the EU agreed to freeze legal action in the WTO. The US would continue suspending Title III every six months, 'so long as the EU and other allies continue their stepped up efforts to promote democracy in Cuba'.[69] In 1996, the EU had adopted the Common Position on Cuba, 'to encourage a process of transition to a pluralist democracy and respect for human rights and fundamental freedoms'.[70]

Even with Title III suspended, the US Treasury's Office of Foreign Asset Control (OFAC) has issued multi-million and -billion dollar fines on banks and companies in third countries for dealings with Cuba, while in the EU and UK anti-US blockade legislation was not enforced.[71] The United Nations advised member states to legislate against the US blockade's extraterritorial reach, but no legal action was taken so international trade with Cuba was severely restricted.

TERRORISM AND COUNTER-TERRORISM

Clinton signed Helms–Burton after the deaths of four Cuban exiles whose planes were shot down by the Cuban Air Force. The Miami-based exile group Brothers to the Rescue had been violating Cuban airspace between late 1995 and early 1996, even dropping agitational leaflets over Havana. Cuban authorities issued warnings and asked the Clinton administration to halt the flights. Finally, in February 1996, the Cubans shot down two planes. José Basulto, another former CIA operative and the groups' leader, escaped in a third plane. The claim that the planes were in international airspace when downed is refuted by the Cubans. Either way, a similar provocation from Cuban shores would never have been tolerated by US authorities. Furthermore, according to Juan Pablo Roque, a Cuban government agent who was working undercover inside the organisation, the Brothers were training its pilots in paramilitary operations and weaponry as part of a larger plan to attack Cuba and its leaders.[72] In December 1997, a US court awarded the families of the dead USD 187 million compensation and, in 2001, USD 58 million was taken from Cuban government bank accounts long since frozen in the United States as part of that award.[73]

In summer 1997, 18 months after the shoot down, Carriles orchestrated a bombing campaign to target Cuba's burgeoning tourist industry.[74] Incredibly, the terror campaign caused just one fatality: a 32-year-old Italian, Fabio di Celmo, killed in a hotel bomb. In September 1997, Cuban authorities arrested and charged a young Salvadoran man who had been paid USD 4,500 per bomb by Carriles. Cuban agents uncovered and prevented other terrorist plots during the decade. The need to keep abreast of these plans, and the abject failure of US authorities to prevent or punish the perpetrators, led Cuban intelligence to create the Wasp Network (La Red Avispa) to infiltrate Miami exile groups and gather information.

In Havana in June 1998 an unprecedented meeting took place between Cuba's Interior Ministry, the FBI and other US agencies, convened after Fidel Castro warned Clinton, in a message carried by Colombian author Gabriel García Márquez, of CANF plans to carry out airborne terrorism. Canadian author Stephen Kimber records that: 'The Cubans presented the Americans with a blizzard of material: photos, audio and video tapes, confessions, wiretap transcripts, bomb-making paraphernalia . . .' The FBI took the evidence away to 'evaluate'. The Cubans were unaware that their agents, including Gerardo Hernández, Rene González, Fernando González, Ramón Labañino and Antonio Guerrero, were already under FBI surveillance. Shortly afterwards, in September 1998, the Wasp Network agents were rounded up.[75] After their arrest they became known as the Cuban Five.

The Cuban Five's court case took place in Miami where a fair trial was impossible. The hearing began five months after hard-line Miami exiles had lost the battle for Elián González described in Chapter 3. Journalists in the pay of the US government whipped up public hostility to demand harsh sentences, which ranged from 15 years to double life.[76] In 2005, a US court ordered a retrial at a new location, but at the government's request the decision was reviewed and reversed the following year. For international solidarity activists the case of the Cuban Five symbolised the resilience and sacrifice of Cuba's revolutionary people, and the hypocrisy of the War on Terrorism launched by President Bush junior in the new millennium.

POST-2000: NEW FRIENDS AND ALLIES IN THE NEW MILLENNIUM

Having survived into the post-Soviet era, socialist Cuba found new allies in the so-called Pink Tide, the wave of left and progressive governments and movements that swept the region. Latin American populations were increasingly the beneficiaries of Cuban development aid, expanded first as emergency assistance and then as a service export. Cuba reaped the benefits of this as diplomatic relations were restored with Guatemala in 1998, Honduras in 2002, Nicaragua in 2007 and El Salvador and Costa Rica in 2009, leaving the United States as the only country in the Americas without diplomatic relations with Cuba.

Hugo Chávez's election as president of Venezuela in late 1998 on an overtly anti-neoliberal and anti-imperialist platform brought Cuba a much-needed political ally and trade partner. The Cuba–Venezuela embrace fostered a form of barter trade based on the resource strengths and socio-economic needs of those countries, the famous 'oil for doctors' programme discussed in Chapter 4. This became the modus operandi for the Bolivarian Alliance for the Americas (Alianza Bolivariana de la Americas), known as ALBA (which means 'dawn' in Spanish) a trade and development cooperation agreement set up between them and subsequently extended to incorporate 11 regional states.[77] Evo Morales and his Movement to Socialism in Bolivia, and Rafael Correa and his Citizen Revolution in Ecuador, became key players within ALBA and important allies of Cuba.[78]

Despite the insignificance of the ALBA bloc in terms of world trade, production, population or land mass, the process alarmed the US administration. Already by October 2005, Daniel Fisk, National Security Advisor for the Western Hemisphere, was reporting on the political threat represented by 'Cuban and Venezuelan attempts to drive a wedge between the US and its Caribbean partners'.[79] When I interviewed the then Ecuadorian President Rafael Correa in October 2009, shortly after Ecuador joined ALBA, he emphasised the centrality of Cuba to the new wave of regional integration. 'ALBA is very inspired by the successes of the Cuban model,' he affirmed, referencing Cuba's long history of basing international trade on solidarity, not economic gain, and the island's unrivalled international development aid. 'Cuba's great example is that despite its poverty, it knows how to share, through all its international programmes. Cuba is the country with the greatest cooperation in terms of its gross domestic product. It is an example for all of us,' he concluded.[80]

Cuba was active in Latin American forums, without reducing its close ties with Africa and Asia, gaining leverage in international affairs and serving as an example of an alternative development path. Most of the regional institutions articulated a pan-Latin Americanism which repelled US interference.[81] The growing complexity of the international system generated by the emergence of global players such as China and Russia, countries with which Cuba had historically close and contemporaneously improving relations, amplified the significance of the regional changes.[82]

THE IRRESISTIBLE RETURN OF POSADA CARRILES

Across the Florida Straits, Carriles sought to turn Cuba's new dawn into an old nightmare. Aged 72 in November 2000, he was arrested with three other exiled terrorists, Gaspar Jimenez Escobedo, Guillermo Novo Sampoll and Pedro Remón Rodríguez, armed with 200 pounds of explosives conspiring to bomb an auditorium in the University of Panama where Fidel Castro was addressing the Ibero-American Summit. Over three years later in April 2004 a Panamanian court finally sentenced the four to between seven and eight years in prison each for endangering public safety and falsifying documents, but not for attempted murder. The president of Panama, Mireya Moscoso, ignored Cuban and Venezuelan extradition requests and then pardoned the terrorists on 'humanitarian grounds' in the last days of her presidency in August 2004.[83] Cuba and Venezuela immediately broke off diplomatic relations with Panama.[84]

After his release Carriles melted away, while Escobedo, Sampoll and Rodríguez were flown back to a hero's welcome in Miami on a private plane provided by exile Santiago Álvarez, who had raised USD 400,000 in Miami towards their legal costs in Panama. In May 2005, Carriles was arrested in Miami after giving a press conference. He was held for illegal entry into the United States and released on bail in 2007, against the advice of the US Justice Department, which described him as 'an admitted mastermind of terrorist plots and attacks', a flight risk and a danger to the community.[85] The US government refused Venezuelan and Cuban extradition requests.

In summer 2003, while Carriles was detained in Panama, the FBI had closed its case against him and shredded five boxes of evidence they held on him. Bardach has recorded that 'Agents who worked on it were staggered. It took them 20 years to put this stuff together.' The FBI had to appeal to her and other journalists to submit evidence for Carriles's new trial, which took place in Texas in 2010, not on terrorism charges but for lying to US authorities about his entry into the country and about his involvement in the 1997 bombing campaign in Cuba.[86] Seemingly inevitably, in 2011 Carriles was acquitted, and enjoyed his final years at full liberty in Miami. In May 2018 he died, aged 90, at a government home for veterans.

THE UNITED STATES WAR ON TERRORISM AND ITS COUNTERPART IN CUBA

The backdrop to these deplorable events was the War on Terrorism launched following the 11 September 2001 terrorist attacks on the United States with President George W. Bush's statement to the world: 'Either you are with us, or you are with the terrorists. From this day forward, any nation that continues to harbor or support terrorism will be regarded by the United States as a hostile regime.'[87]

In October 2001, the United States and Britain invaded Afghanistan and, in March 2003, the US-led 'coalition of the willing' invaded Iraq. Cuba was effectively threatened in the interim by Bolton's announcement in May 2002 that: 'The United States believes that Cuba has at least a limited offensive biological warfare research and development effort. Cuba has provided dual-use biotechnology to other rogue states.'[88] The claim was refuted by former president Carter, who visited Cuba several days later and revealed that US intelligence experts told him they had no such information.[89]

Meanwhile, US diplomats in the US Interest Section (USIS) in Havana, headed by James Cason from 2002 to 2005 and Michael Parmly from 2005 to 2008, flagrantly violated diplomatic norms by attempting to foster an internal opposition.[90] Cason hosted meetings at his home for the leaders of Cuba's many small opposition groups, travelled around the island delivering 'packages' to government opponents, organised workshops at the USIS and so on. Effectively, Cason was exposing his network of contacts to Cuban intelligence, who clearly gained inside knowledge of these activities.[91]

On 18 March, on the eve of the 2003 invasion of Iraq, the arrests began of Cuban opposition activists. Outside Cuba, there was robust condemnation of what was described as a clampdown on journalists, writers and the intelligentsia.[92] Within three weeks, 75 defendants had been tried and sentenced to prison for between 6 and 28 years under Article 91 of the Cuban Penal Code for 'actions against the independence or territorial integrity of the State', a provision introduced to Cuba under the Spanish Penal Code. Internationally, the 75 were portrayed as being persecuted for dissenting ideas or ideologies and the events became known as Cuba's Black Spring. Those with better insight, however, such as former CIA agent Philip Agee, described them as 'central to current US government efforts to overthrow the Cuban government and destroy the work of the revolution'.[93] US Marxist scholar James Petras pointed out that: 'No country in the world tolerates or labels domestic citizens paid by and working for a foreign power to act for its imperial interests as "dissidents".'[94]

On 9 April, Cuba's Foreign Minister, Felipe Pérez Roque, presented part of the evidence used to convict the 75 'dissidents' to journalists at an international press conference: photographs, videos, notes of payment, publications, receipts of money transactions and testimony of several Cuban security agents working inside these groups. The 37 defendants claiming to be 'independent journalists', he said, published in outlets printed in, or distributed by, the USIS. Only four of them had studied journalism or worked professionally as journalists.[95] He presented evidence of payments they received from US agencies distributing

US Congress-approved funds. During the trial, which was open to the public, eight 'dissidents' had revealed that they worked undercover for Cuban state security and the press conference was shown video footage of their testimonies.[96]

Witness Néstor Baguer Sánchez Galarraga had worked for Cuban state security for 42 years, since 1960, unbeknownst to USIS, which, he claimed, recruited him as Chairman of the Cuban Independent Press Association granting him a privileged 'open pass' to enter USIS. He described that Association's members as 'mercenaries paid to slander . . . not journalists', and explained how cash and other material benefits were distributed. He claimed that 'independent journalists' booked two-hour slots in the USIS internet room to write stories on themes dictated to them by USIS staff, which were sent to Miami-based website CubaNet, a recipient of USD 343,000 in USAID funds in 2001 and over USD 800,000 in 2002.[97] Next up was Odilia Collazo, President of the Pro Human Rights Party of Cuba, and author of regular reports on human rights violations in Cuba, which were sent to the US State Department, foreign embassies, the United Nations, Amnesty International and Americas Watch among other organisations. The press conference witnessed her declare: 'I have the privilege of telling you . . . I am an agent.'[98]

Cubans are not fools, Roque told the press conference, 'we have only revealed a small part of what we know . . . our people have learned to defend themselves and depend on the people because we have, more than anything, the support of the people . . . while he [Cason] got here only a short time ago, he has to consider the task he has undertaken; or we will have to continue organizing his meetings and attending the cocktail parties he throws.'[99] Roque condemned as hypocritical the outcry about the arrests, pointing to 'more than 600 prisoners who are still locked up at the [US] Guantánamo Naval Base, in a juridical limbo, who are not treated as persons and will be presented in secret US military courts'.[100] While criticising Cuba, he said, the EU has shown no concern for the over 2,000 prisoners detained by US occupation forces in Iraq whose names were not even known.[101]

Other incidents between the arrest and trial of the 75 'dissidents' reveal additional pressures facing Cuba in this period. On 6 April, a Florida newspaper, the *Sun Sentinel*, had profiled a violent terrorist group, Commandos F–4, which was training with heavy weapons for an armed action, possibly an invasion of Cuba. On 2 April, a Cuban ferry was hijacked by 11 Cubans armed with knives who threatened to throw civilian hostages overboard as they headed for the United States. Exceptionally, the US coast guard turned them back to Cuban authorities, who captured them. This was the seventh violent hijacking of sea and aircraft by Cubans between August 2002 and April 2003. However, on every previous occasion the perpetrators had been received with impunity in the United States; US authorities had even sold off the stolen Cuban aircraft. This last group of hijackers were tried in Cuba and 3 of the 11 were sentenced to death. It was the first use of the death penalty in Cuba for many years – and the last. That these trials coincided enabled Cuba's critics to conflate the cases, implying that the death sentence was given to opposition journalists and human rights activists, which it was not.

The link between the two cases, Roque told the press conference, was the US's Cuba policy. Under the Migration Accord of 1994, the United States had agreed to issue at least 20,000 visas a year for Cubans to enter the country legally, while Cuban emigrants intercepted at sea were to be turned back. However, the US consulate had issued half that minimum of visas in 2000: 8,300 in 2001 and 7,237 in 2002. During Cason's mandate, in the five months from October 2002 to March 2003, only 505 visas were granted, 2.5 per cent of the quota agreed. 'We are witnessing the implementation of a premeditated plan to encourage illegal emigration, to leave those who want to emigrate from Cuba no other option than to hijack boats, planes,' declared Roque.[102]

Following their sentencing, female relatives and supporters of the 75 'dissidents' created a new organisation, the Ladies in White, to demand their release. The Ladies held short parades after Sunday Mass through Miramar, an area in Havana where foreign embassies are concentrated.[103] These proceeded regularly and mostly without incident despite the group's spokeswoman, Laura Pollan, admitting on camera that the Ladies received payment for each march from the Rescate Juridico, a US-based opposition group headed by Carriles's ally and fellow terrorist Santiago Álvarez.[104] In 2005, the Ladies were awarded the European Parliament's EUR 50,000 Sakharov Prize for Freedom of Thought.

In October 2003, President Bush junior announced a set of measures to redouble pressure on the Cuban government: increasing restrictions (and prosecutions) on US citizens, including Cuban-Americans, travelling to Cuba; promoting Cuban emigration to the US; expanding internet and radio transmissions; and establishing a Commission for Assistance to a Free Cuba, 'to explore ways we can help hasten and ease Cuba's democratic transition'.[105]

The Commission's first report was published in May 2004, with over 450 pages of demonising propaganda, plans for destabilisation, regime change and a tightly US-controlled transition to a 'democratic' capitalist Cuba. This required dismantling the socialist state apparatus, reorganising the economy and education system and introducing 'multiparty' elections from which

Cuban communists and officials would be excluded. The report recommended drawing on the experience of transitions to capitalism in the Czech Republic, Hungary and Poland and targeting Cuban youth.[106] The report's flagrant violations of national sovereignty and international law sparked outrage, not least from within Cuba.

The Commission's second report was published in July 2006, by which time the United States was bogged down in Afghanistan and Iraq. The tone is less confident about regime change, highlighting the challenges of population displacement, property claims and the return of Cuban exiles, and there is greater emphasis on change coming from 'within Cuba'. The Commission recommended USD 80 million be channelled into US programmes over the following two years to boost Cuban 'civil society' and plan for a post-Castro transition to capitalism, followed by USD 20 million to be spent annually 'until the dictatorship ceases to exist'.[107] The report contained a 'secret annex' classified for security reasons. Alarcón asked reporters: 'What on earth could the secret part say when the public part violates all kinds of international law?'[108]

On 31 July 2006, just three weeks after the second report was published, Cuban television announced that Fidel Castro was seriously ill and had delegated his responsibilities to Raúl Castro and other leaders. US authorities had always expected Fidel Castro's demise to spark a civil uprising, a leadership power struggle or a military rebellion serving as a pretext for US intervention.[109] However, as I saw at first-hand, in Havana the overwhelming response was calm concern.

SUBVERSION FROM WITHIN

Raúl Capote was a double agent – Pablo for the CIA and Daniel for Cuban intelligence. His autobiographical account claims the following: immediately after the announcement that Fidel Castro was sick he was contacted by CIA agent René Greenwald, then on 13 August 2006 he was summoned to USIS and told that a 'popular uprising' had been prepared for Central Havana. USIS spokesman Drew Blackeney told him: 'We don't need Central Havana to rise up, it's enough to have a group who goes out to protest. They will have the main media outlets covering the news.' Capote would then read a proclamation in the name of the Cuban people, requesting US Army intervention to guarantee a transition without chaos. Blackeney outlined US plans: US forces would police the coastlines and control the entry of exiles, they would occupy Cuba for three years establishing a provisional government in Havana with

Cuban-Americans and the internal opposition. Washington would create a Commission to restructure the Cuban economy, redraft the Constitution, establish new military forces and bring to trial members of Cuba's Revolutionary Armed Forces, the Ministry of the Interior, the Cuban Communist Party, revolutionary leaders and militants in general. In the event, the protest saw one opposition activist sheepishly shout a slogan, throw a handful of leaflets in an isolated spot, then leave.[110]

The new head of USIS from 2005, Michael Parmly, had continued efforts to foster and unite the small, fractured and infiltrated opposition. More sophisticated programmes were developed to target discontented youth: to use hip-hop, Afro-Cuban groups, artists, foreign students and social media to engage young Cubans in opposition activities. The celebrity 'dissident' of this era was Yoani Sánchez, who had emigrated to wealthy Switzerland in 2002, where she studied computer science, before returning to Cuba two years later and setting up the blog Generation Y in 2007. One year later she was awarded over USD 320,000 (equivalent to 1,488 years of Cuba's minimum salary) in international journalism prizes and human rights awards, despite having no track record and no following in Cuba. *Time* magazine listed her among its top 100 most influential people in 2008.[111]

In an April 2009 cable leaked by Wikileaks, Jonathan Farrar, head of USIS from 2008 to 2011, noted that Sánchez's 'international fame . . . fuels further jealousy among the traditional dissident organizations' and that there is no effective civil society opposition. The main dissident organisations had little resonance among ordinary Cubans, were unlikely to supplant the Cuban government, had been infiltrated by government agents, were consumed by internal conflict and preoccupied with obtaining resources and salaries.[112] Indeed, in November 2006, a US Government Accountability Office report revealing how USAID (taxpayers') money was being spent, recorded expenditure on computer gaming equipment and software, leather coats, cashmere sweaters, crab meat and Godiva chocolates.[113]

While investing heavily on putative 'democracy programmes', the Bush administration further squeezed the Cuban economy. In May 2004 the US Federal Reserve imposed a fine of USD 100,000 on USB, Switzerland's largest bank, for transferring US dollar notes to Cuba.[114] In October 2004, Daniel Fisk explained the administration's strategy 'to identify long-ignored revenue streams for the Castro regime and then move to degrade them. For example, tourism . . . When factoring in the decline in all revenue flows, we estimate we will have denied the regime at least half a billion dollars [over a calendar year].'[115] A Cuban Assets Targeting Group was established to investigate and stop hard currency flows into and out of Cuba.[116] The Cuban government responded by removing US dollars from domestic commerce, substituting it with the Cuban Convertible Peso (CUC), which was printed in Cuba.[117] A tax of 10 per cent was levied on transactions to exchange US dollars into CUC on the island, to compensate Cuba for the risks incurred when using the dollar in international transactions.

However, in 2008, the capitalist system entered the most severe structural crisis for 80 years, following the global financial collapse and subsequent international recession. In late September 2008, President Bush junior professed: 'The market is not functioning properly' and oversaw unprecedented government bailouts for private financial institutions, undermining faith in the curative power of market forces. This compounded the challenges facing the Bush administration, whose 'shock and awe' strategy had entangled the US military in bloody occupations in Afghanistan and Iraq.

Meanwhile, the rise of the BRICs (Brazil, Russia, India and China) and other emerging economies revived the state-led development path. With Latin American swept along by the Pink Tide and ALBA membership expanding, Brazil hosted a Summit for Latin American and Caribbean Integration and Development in December 2008; it was the first time in nearly 200 years of independence that the region's heads of states had met without representatives from the US or Europe. The Summit led to the foundation of the Community of Latin American and Caribbean States (CELAC) in 2011 and Havana hosted its second summit. In this complex context, in January 2009, coinciding with the fiftieth anniversary of the Cuban Revolution, the Oval Office opened its doors to Barak Obama, whose campaign pledges included closing its prison camps in Guantanamo Bay and resetting US relations with Latin America.

PRESIDENT OBAMA: NEW DOG, OLD TRICKS?

Obama's first term in office brought few changes in the United States' Cuba policy. In April 2009, prior to attending the Fifth Summit of the Americas in Trinidad, his first regional forum, he reversed Bush's 2004 restrictions on Cuban–American visits and remittances to the island. The move did little to assuage regional leaders' vociferous demands for an end to the US blockade, normalisation of relations with Cuba and the island's reincorporation into the summits. In a complete reversal of the 1960s, the United States was now isolated by virtue of its policy towards Cuba. 'The United States seeks a new beginning with Cuba,' Obama reassured the Summit of the Americas, but by the end of the year little change was evident.

Then, on 4 December 2009, US private contractor Alan Gross was arrested in Havana on a half-a-million-dollar mission to take satellite and internet equipment into Cuba to facilitate subversion. His case became a major obstacle to the improving US–Cuba relations. Given the inefficiency and corruption of Cuba's domestic opposition, USAID had turned to professional contractors. Gross was recruited by the private US company Development Alternatives Inc., which held a USD 6 million contract with USAID to 'advance democracy' in Cuba; he had worked under similar contracts with USAID in Afghanistan and Iraq. He travelled to Cuba as a tourist five times in nine months, targeting the island's tiny Jewish community, which had good relations with the government.[118] It is illegal under Cuban law to give or receive goods under US regime change programmes or to bring satellite equipment into Cuba without a permit. In 2011 Gross was sentenced to 15 years' incarceration.[119]

Also in December 2009, having failed to galvanise public support, the Ladies in White left the beaten track to parade through a residential area of Havana, accompanied by diplomats from USIS and the German embassy. Video footage shows how local residents, mainly women, surrounded them, singing and chanting their rejection.[120] In March 2010, the Ladies launched a month of action to raise their profile outside Cuba, again entering residential neighbourhoods. International media filmed them being herded onto buses by Cuban authorities, apparently to protect them from angry locals. Again, the Ladies were accompanied by US, British and European diplomats.

In February 2010, 42-year-old Cuban Orlando Zapata Tamayo died in hospital after a hunger strike, the first such incident in nearly four decades. Coincidentally Zapata had been arrested in March 2003, but he had never engaged in anti-government activities prior to his incarceration. Western politicians and press erroneously referred to Zapata as one of the 75 'dissidents' arrested that month, a 'prisoner of conscience' and political activist, ignoring his long, violent criminal record and the demands of his hunger strike – a television and separate kitchen in his cell and a mobile phone to call his family.[121] After being put forward as a 'dissident' by his mother in 2004, Amnesty International adopted him on a list of 55 'prisoners of conscience' in Cuba.[122] Cuban doctors fought hard to save Zapata's life, without resorting to forced feeding.[123] The day he died another Cuban with a long record of non-political violent crimes, Guillermo Fariñas Hernández, initiated his latest hunger strike.[124] In late 2010, the European Parliament awarded Fariñas its Sakharov Prize.

Among the more innovative covert programmes funded through USAID during Obama's first term was the establishment of a Twitter-style programme, called ZunZuneo (Cuban slang for a hummingbird's tweet), to be used to foment political opposition amongst Cuba's youth. There was also a programme to send young Latin Americans to Cuba to identify 'potential social change actors', under the pretext of organising workshops on issues such as HIV prevention.[125] These programmes reflected the belief that social media and youth activism were behind the Arab Spring protests from late 2010.

At the Sixth Summit of the Americas in Colombia in 2012, the ALBA countries, backed by Argentina, Brazil, Colombia and Uruguay, threatened to boycott future Summits if Cuba were not invited. The following year, in summer 2013, Obama authorised secret talks to be initiated with the Cuban government. The result was the astonishing simultaneous, live, televised announcements by the two heads of state on 17 December 2014 of the decision to re-establish diplomatic relations after more than half a century. That same day, high-profile prisoner releases took place: three of the Cuban Five remaining in US prisons were swapped for Rolando Sarraff Trujillo, a Cuban intelligence agent who provided information for the CIA and Alan Gross.[126] A series of Bilateral Commissions began negotiations about multiple issues of conflict and mutual interest, working towards the far more complex matter of 'normalisation'. In summer 2015, embassies were reopened after 54 years and in March 2016, Obama became the first US president since 1929 to visit the island.

RAPPROCHEMENT AT LAST?

As head of the United States Department at Cuba's Ministry of Foreign Relations, Josefina Vidal led the Cuban team in those secret talks. We met in late December 2016, three weeks before Obama handed over to Trump. 'There are many factors,' Vidal responded when I asked what had motivated the Obama rapprochement. 'Cuba's resistance and determination were key elements, number one. History had shown that pressure, preconditions and aggression do not work with Cuba.'[127]

Internationally, 'the loss of US prestige resulting from the failed policy maintained towards Cuba provoked an unbearable isolation for the United States government', explained Vidal, pointing to the increasing number of countries at the United Nations General Assembly voting in favour of the Cuban resolution to condemn the US blockade.[128] 'It was also seen very clearly when all of Latin America and the Caribbean told the United States: "no more Summit of the Americas without Cuba, no more regional meetings without Cuba. Cuba must participate".' This support was 'recognition of what Cuba, with its modest resources, has done in favour of those countries, not only in material support but also in defence of regional interests.' With rapprochement, Washington moved to eliminate an irritant in US relations with Latin America as a necessary step in the process of regaining and reinforcing US control over the region.

Despite the extraterritorial imposition of the US blockade, since the 1990s the revolutionary government had diversified trade and secured international investment partners. The pace of these collaborations sped up with the economic reforms introduced from 2011. In 2013, the Mariel Special Development Zone and super-port were opened with Brazil as a major partner, and in 2014 a new international investment law was approved. US business interests watched with frustration from the sidelines as their rivals moved into 'the Cuban market'.[129]

In summer 2014 the presidents of Russia and China visited Havana. During Putin's trip, USD 32 billion of Cuba's Soviet-era debt was written off, leaving just USD 3 billion to be paid over 10 years in joint projects. 'We will provide support to our Cuban friends to overcome the illegal blockade of Cuba,' Putin said.[130] Two weeks later, Chinese president Xi Jinping signed 29 trade, debt, credit and other agreements in Havana and thanked Cuba for advancing cooperation between China and Latin America.[131] Meanwhile, the European Union had become Cuba's biggest external investor, accounting for 20 per cent of total Cuban trade. 'Very pragmatically,' said Vidal, 'the United States realised that the only country left out, by its own choice not because of Cuba, is the United States.'

Domestically, a shift in the balance of forces managing Washington's Cuba policy meant a policy change on Cuba might at last be possible, enabling Obama to leave a legacy in an area that most presidents had steered clear of. His administration calculated that there was more to gain through 'engaging' Cuba than there was to lose in a conflict with a political elite that was losing its leverage. US policy was considered a failure, said Vidal, 'in public opinion, by business sectors, religious sectors, academics, people visiting Cuba, in the US Congress itself'. In autumn 2014, the *New York Times* ran a series of editorials criticising US policy towards Cuba and arguing for the restoration of diplomatic relations. This was probably contrived to generate support for Obama's pending announcement. Pointing to the economic reforms underway inside Cuba, US commentators could claim that Cuba was making the liberalising reforms stipulated as prerequisites for an improvement in relations.

Migration and generational changes had significantly altered the Cuban-American community, especially in Miami, generating increased support for engagement with Cuba. 'More than 50 per cent of Cubans living in the United States emigrated after 1990,' explained Vidal. Being mostly economic emigrants, 'they do not want to cut ties with their country or families. They want to live and work in the US, but visit Cuba, or maintain a double citizenship, a double residence.' On the other hand and given demographic changes, the US administration sought greater influence on the island in anticipation of the departure of the 'historic generation': the leaders and veterans of the Cuban Revolution.

Along with every Cuban with whom I discussed US–Cuba relations, Vidal did not believe that 'rapprochement' equated to a change in the United States' strategic objectives, nor that Obama accepted Cuba's right to self-determination. Obama himself was clear about that. '[W]e will end an outdated approach that, for decades, has failed to advance our interests . . . these 50 years have shown that isolation has not worked. It's time for a new approach . . . through a policy of engagement, we can more effectively stand up for our values.'[132] Instead of isolation and aggression, Obama sought to erode Cuban socialism by persuasion, seduction and bribery, through 'engagement': foisting the logic of the capitalist market, social relations and cultural values on the revolutionary people. This was part of Obama's 'smart diplomacy' approach to foreign relations.

The notion of 'normalisation' itself was contentious. Historically the United States had never respected Cuban sovereignty, implying that the US definition of 'normal' would be Cuba's reintegration into the US-centred power structure – a situation which Cuba's revolutionary government could not accept. On the Cuban side, President Raúl Castro stated that normalisation was not possible, 'as long as the blockade exists, or as long as the territory illegally occupied by the Guantanamo Naval Base is not returned, or radio and television broadcasts which violate international norms continue, or just compensation is not provided to our people for the human and economic damage they have suffered . . . If these problems are not resolved, this diplomatic rapprochement between Cuba and the United States makes no sense.'[133] During our interview at ISRI, Isabel Allende reiterated the point: 'You cannot have normal relations when you have a military base in a country, against their wishes . . . when you are constantly trying to overthrow that country's government, when you want to impose your ways on others. There can't be normal relations, but there may be a certain relationship of coexistence.'[134] That was what Cuba sought from rapprochement.

CASTLES MADE OF SAND

With the restoration of diplomatic relations, embassies were opened; the US removed Cuba from its list of states supporting terrorism; the Havana Club rum label was finally registered in the United States, resolving a 20-year-long ownership dispute instigated by the Bacardi Corporation; coastguard cooperation issues were resolved; regular flights and postal services were restored after decades. Obama eased restrictions on US citizens' travel to the island, although visits still required a license. In 2016, over half a million US citizens travelled to Cuba from the US, around half of whom were Cuban-Americans. In his final days as president, Obama eliminated the 'wet foot, dry foot' policy which encouraged illegal and dangerous emigration from Cuba.[135]

However, commercial and economic progress was minimal. While a Congressional vote is required to end the US blockade, Obama could have dismantled it much further with decisive use of executive powers. On the contrary, in September 2015 and 2016, he signed annual extensions on the Trading with the Enemy Act against Cuba, one of the laws which sustains the US blockade. Obama took only small, strategic steps to 'engage' Cuba by signing executive orders to bypass Congress. His administration introduced five packets of measures and granted licences to a handful of US companies to trade with and/or operate in Cuba: six telecoms firms, four cruise companies, one hotel chain, eight airlines, two small banks. In mid-December 2016, Google signed a deal with the Cuban government to install servers on the island to speed up internet access.[136]

Regulations issued under Obama authorised financial institutions to provide Cuba with finance and credit. However, US banks were not willing to test this. International banks remained terrified of fines being imposed while Cuba remains on the list of countries under US sanctions. And for good reason: under Obama a record-breaking 49 entities were fined for transactions with Cuba – more than under the previous Bush administration. Effectively, Cuba still could not use the dollar in the international economy, nor make deposits in international banks. Cuban goods still could not be exported to the United States.[137]

THE DEMONSTRATION EFFECT

For Cuba, the greatest benefit of rapprochement came from the so-called 'demonstration effect'. It served as a green light to third parties to increase engagement with Cuba. 'American policy vis a vis Cuba has a big impact on us and any other actor,' Alberto Navarro, the EU's High Representative in Cuba told me at the EU mission in Havana in March 2018.[138] The EU opened an office in Havana in 2003 and initiated projects of cooperation from 2008. Following rapprochement, EU engagement with Cuba accelerated. In May 2015 French president François Hollande became the first French head of state to visit Cuba, and other European heads of state and ministers followed suit. In 2016, the EU and Cuba signed a non-preferential Political Dialogue and Cooperation Agreement (PDCA), which entered into force on 1 November 2017, formally replacing its 1996 Common Position. In May 2018, the first EU–Cuba Council meeting took place to discuss implementation of the PDCA. The EU has allocated EUR 50 million to projects in Cuba in the 2014–2020 period, Navarro told me.[139]

In June 2015, the Paris Club of debtors agreed to cancel 70 per cent of Cuba's historic debt, and, after a long negotiation, in early 2018, the London Club also presented Cuba with a debt relief offer.[140] Hundreds of companies from dozens of countries have applied to the Cuban government to commence investments in the Mariel Special Development Zone and, by late 2018, some 43 applications had been approved and 17 projects were already operating.[141]

Reporting on the restoration of diplomatic relations between Cuba and the United States, most commentators described the move as ending the island's international isolation. This was wrong and disingenuous, and was premised on an assumption that rapprochement would facilitate Cuba's reintegration into the capitalist 'global community'. In fact, with or without relations with the United States, Cuba is far from isolated. The revolutionary government today has diplomatic relations with 195 countries, up from 50 in 1958.[142] This testifies to the abject failure of the US policy of isolation. 'We have diplomatic relations with more countries than have membership of the UN,' explained Cuban Ambassador Eduardo Delgado Bermudez, a diplomat for nearly 60 years, 'because we also have relations with Palestine and Western Sahara.'[143]

While Obama's rapprochement sought to end the United States isolation resulting from its hostile Cuba policy, in reversing that rapprochement, the Trump administration has resorted to threats and intimidation to drive a wedge between revolutionary Cuba and the rest of the world. In the process they have marginalised the United States once again, as discussed in Chapter 10 on the post-rapprochement period.

8

★ ★ ★

RAÚL CASTRO'S REFORMS
SOCIALIST EFFICIENCY OR CAPITALIST OPENING?

We are sauntering along the hot and dusty central highway in our swim wear, myself and a group of Cuban adults and children, returning from the nearby river on the outskirts of Florida, a town 40 kilometres from the city of Camaguey in the east of the island. We stop at the tall obelisk statue, known locally as the 'Machete of Maceo', outside the Maceo Park, to take a photograph. It is named in honour of General José Antonio Maceo, a hero of Cuba's independence wars who died fighting Spanish colonists in 1896. Suddenly a military jeep pulls up and, with authority but without menace, army personnel instruct us to delete the photo and move on. It is an issue of national security, we are told. The park had just been taken over for military manoeuvres. Our reservist friends had been summoned to participate in the exercises while we were enjoying our swim.

This is 6 August 2006, one week after the announcement that Fidel Castro had fallen sick and passed his numerous responsibilities over to his deputy and younger brother, Raúl Castro, and four other government leaders.[1] In the United States, President George W. Bush had stepped up his hostile rhetoric and senior US officials made statements about exploiting the situation. It was a little over three years since Bush had stood under a triumphant banner emblazoned with the words 'Mission Accomplished' in Iraq. Cuba was on the alert, launching Operation Caguairán to mobilise hundreds of thousands of Cuban militia and reservists to join the regulars of the Revolutionary Armed Forces in military preparations.

Almost a year later, on 26 July 2007, and not far from the Machete of Maceo, in Camaguey's Agramonte Square, acting president of Cuba's Council of State, Raúl Castro took the podium for the annual Moncada Day event. It was exactly one year since Fidel Castro's last public appearance and 18 years since, from the same spot, he had anticipated both the collapse of the USSR and that against the odds the Cuban Revolution would survive into a post-Soviet world. Just as Fidel Castro's speech in 1989 foretold of a new chapter in the Cuban Revolution, Raúl Castro's speech in 2007 ushered in a new stage of development in Cuba, a period of restructuring and reform.

In Fidel Castro's absence, commentators outside Cuba had been searching for signs of change in Cuba's revolutionary government. Critics had eagerly anticipated an Eastern European style transition to capitalism with the Commander in Chief's exit. But there had been no power vacuum and no counter-revolution rising to reject everything he stood for. Fidel Castro had withdrawn, recuperated and then resumed with his published 'reflections' as the government and the Cuban Communist Party (CCP) sped up the process of transition to a generation of younger leaders at the local and national levels. The enemies of Cuban socialism were frustrated: transition had taken place but not in the direction desired. That frustration obstructed their ability to analyse or understand new developments.

Outside Cuba, 'Raúl's reforms' were portrayed as a faltering march towards economic liberalisation in which 'progress' was measured in steps taken towards a capitalist democracy. Every shift towards commercialisation and the expansion of a private sector was applauded, while every retreat was lambasted as reflecting the grip on power of an orthodox old guard in the CCP. However, the apparent hesitancy was not clumsiness or lethargy from Cubans who don't understand how to 'do' capitalism. It reflects the tension between political preference and economic necessity: the attempt to balance equity, social property, central planning and socialist consciousness with the urgent need to increase productivity and economic efficiency.

Cuba needs capital to foster economic development, rebuild infrastructure and productive capacity, and raise the standard of living. Government policy-makers estimate that a minimum annual growth rate of 5 per cent is required to see significant socioeconomic improvements and the kind of infrastructural developments necessary to benefit the entire population. To achieve the 5 per cent goal, an investment rate of 20 per cent of GDP is required. But the rate of Cuban savings is half that. Thus, the government cannot find sufficient capital domestically; the internal market is too small and domestic savings too low. Capital must come from abroad. With no socialist bloc to turn to, and without membership of international financial institutions which provide access to loans, Cuba has to turn to foreign direct investment (FDI) and remittances, channelled through self-employment and small private businesses. Doing so is a 'concession' that introduces serious contradictions into the process of socialist development. It means legalising a social relationship of exploitation (in Marxist terms) and necessitates simultaneously permitting and restricting the accumulation of private capital.

The revolutionary leadership does not portray the reforms as theoretical advances or political improvements. The measures reflect the Revolution's flexibility in devising policies to deal with urgent problems without straying from the paradigm of Cuba Socialista. State ownership, central planning and state sector employment continue to predominate, socialist welfare and internationalism are prioritised, and private accumulation is restricted, all of which undermine the reign of market forces. The Cuban government's flexibility has in turn reflected the lack of consensus about the best strategies for building socialism in a blockaded and trade-dependent island. The Great Debate of the 1960s about which economic management system was appropriate for Cuba was never resolved.[2]

Hence the debate initiated under Raúl Castro's presidency about 'updating' the Cuban economy and 'conceptualising' Cuban socialism has been referred to as a 'new great debate'. It returns to many of the same themes addressed in the earlier period: how can production and productivity be stimulated in a welfare-based socialist development process? How can growth be obtained alongside equity and social justice? Who should own and who should control production and distribution? What should be the balance between private and social accumulation, the plan versus the market? What democratic structures should exist? This explains the pendulum, the to and fro, which so frustrates external commentators who only see 'contradictory policies [which] mean one step forward and one step back for Cuba's ailing economy', concluding that 'Cuba's economic leaders are going around in circles'.[3]

Raúl's reforms were introduced to deal with Cuba's liquidity and balance of payments crises, low productivity and investment rate, and dependence on international trade under deteriorating conditions and with the unrelenting United States blockade. These are historical problems of the Cuban political economy, which must be understood with reference to three phenomena. First, the challenge of (under)development in broad terms, which is introduced in Chapter 1. Second, the deep scars left on Cuba after the collapse of the USSR and the socialist bloc, and the impact of measures implemented to survive the crisis, as discussed in Chapter 2. Third, the impact of the global financial crisis and economic recession of 2008, which underscored the need for the structural reforms which are the focus of this chapter.

While external commentators sought discrepancy between the Castro brothers, the principal difference turned out to be in management style. And, while changing circumstances imposed new imperatives in the context of the global capitalist crisis, the 'reformer' Raúl Castro was as committed to Cuban socialism as his elder brother. Raúl Castro described his 'principal mission and purpose in life' as defending, preserving and continuing to improve socialism and never allowing the return of the capitalist regime.[4] There is little evidence to doubt it. While his reforms evoked anticipation from market advocates, they proceeded at a measured pace according to objectives that had been thrashed out and approved by the Cuban people, *including* by Cuba's communists.

This chapter provides the chronology of those reforms, highlighting the motivations and the democratic component of the measures introduced. Raúl Castro's mandate was characterised by broad popular consultations and countrywide debates; half a dozen national consultations took place over ten years. These were no mere public relations exercises: the Cuban population shaped the laws, policies and development plans generated over the decade. This process bestowed those measures with the legitimacy necessary for their acceptance and institutionalisation, in order to endure once the 'veteran generation' has handed over to new leaders.

RAÚL CASTRO TAKES THE PODIUM

Underlying Raúl Castro's reforms was the drive to improve efficiency and productivity within the socialist framework. This echoed the concerns of Che Guevara in the early 1960s, and it picked up on more recent statements by Fidel Castro during a speech in November 2005 criticising excessive state subsidies which allowed a parasitic layer to avoid contributing to Cuban society. Emphasising the need for energy efficiency, he spoke of 'the dream of everyone being able to live on their salary or on their adequate pension', facilitating the removal of the ration book.[5] 'Subsidies and free services will be considered only in essentials. Medical services will be free, so will education and the like. Housing will not be free. Maybe there will be some subsidy,' he announced.[6]

Deepening the analysis in a concrete way, Raúl Castro initiated a new stage in the Cuban Revolution. In his first public speech as Cuba's stand-in president in Camaguey on 26 July 2007, he recognised: 'Wages today are clearly insufficient to satisfy all needs and have thus ceased to play a role in ensuring the socialist principle that each should contribute according to their capacity and receive according to their work. This has bred forms of social indiscipline and tolerance which, having taken root, prove difficult to eradicate, even after the objective causes behind them are eradicated.'[7] Prices cannot go down, Raúl Castro pointed out, until production and productivity go up: 'Any increase in wages or decrease in prices, to be real, can only stem from greater and more efficient production and services offered, which will increase the country's incomes . . . To have more, we have to begin by producing more, with a sense of rationality and efficiency.'

Cuba must reduce imports, he stated, explaining that the cost of importing oil, milk and frozen chicken had increased 200 to 300 per cent in four years, sapping Cuban hard currency reserves. 'In these four years, nearly 500 million dollars have been spent on these purchases.' Meanwhile, the cost to Cuban consumers, highly subsidised by the state, had barely changed: 'I am talking of products that I think can be grown here,' he said, lamenting the abundance of *marabú*, a thorny bush invading productive land left fallow throughout the island particularly since half of Cuba's sugar mills had been closed in 2003. Production must be rationalised, he said, using the example of milk which 'travelled hundreds of miles [to pasteurisation plants] before reaching a consumer who, quite often, lived a few hundred metres away from the livestock farm'. Rationalisation would reduce both product losses and fuel expenses.

The US blockade remained a real and severe obstacle to development he stated, influencing all major economic decisions and impacting on each Cuban's most basic needs. 'Directly and on a daily basis, it weighs heavily on our food supply, transportation, housing and even on the fact that we cannot rely on the necessary raw materials and equipment to work with.' Cuba needed foreign investment, he said, to 'provide us with capital, technology or markets . . . upon well-defined legal bases which preserve the role of the state and the predominance of socialist property'. He revealed that 'the Party and the government have been studying these and other complex and difficult problems in depth'. Underlying Raúl Castro's speech was the concept of Cubans as citizens, not consumers, a revolutionary people with responsibility for social development: 'We need to bring everyone into the daily battle against the very errors which aggravate objective difficulties from external causes . . . All of us, from the leaders to the rank-and-file workers, are duty-bound to accurately identify and analyse every problem in depth . . . to combat the problem with the most convenient methods.' He emphasised the leading role of the CCP in this process.

Raúl Castro's speech stirred such debate among the Cuban people that the CCP decided to initiate a nationwide popular consultation, creating forums for Cubans to thrash out the island's socioeconomic problems in every branch of the CCP, trade unions, street committees, women's federation, the Union of

Young Communists and in every workplace. Raúl Castro invited the people to speak with frankness and realism. Cubans committed whole-heartedly, not just complaining, but suggesting improvements. Every intervention was anonymously recorded and collated for analysis.[8] Some 1.3 million proposals were logged, which facilitated a comprehensive assessment of the state of the country and the consciousness of its people. Many of the grievances reflected a search for individualistic solutions to material scarcity, proposals to increase private interests and capitalist mechanisms. The desire to remove state control was the result of the state's inability to resolve production and distribution problems, attributable to both domestic inefficiencies and the 'very trying international economic situation' identified by Raúl Castro.[9]

'PERFECT STORM' COMPELS STRUCTURAL REFORMS

As the debate was underway, the external situation deteriorated with the global financial crisis and recession, calling a halt to the robust economic growth of the mid-2000s. 2008 was something of a perfect storm for Cuba. With the rise in international prices, in 2008 it cost Cuba an extra USD 1.1 billion to import the same volume of food as the previous year. The highly subsidised state 'ration' shielded the Cuban population from the dramatic global rise in food prices, but not the government, which was importing 84 per cent of the basic food basket. Cubans augment their ration with domestically grown and imported foodstuffs. The high price for domestic produce reflected low productivity. And while import costs soared, export earnings plummeted. The international price for nickel, a key Cuban export, fell from USD 50,000 per tonne in late 2007 to just USD 9,000 in 2008, while tourist spending on the island decreased as cash-strapped holidaymakers spent less.[10] Productivity also declined. To add to Cuba's woes, the island was hit by the worst hurricane season on record, with Hurricanes Ike and Paloma causing some USD 10 billion of damage, around 20 per cent of GDP, and piling on the costs of emergency imports and repairs.

Exacerbating the structural imbalances inherent in the Cuban economy and the incomplete recovery from the Special Period, these circumstances conspired to produce serious fiscal and trade deficits and a liquidity crisis in 2008–09.[11] The Cuban government temporarily froze foreign businesses' bank accounts in Cuba and stopped paying foreign suppliers, which further reduced its access to external financing. The measures described below were taken to reduce Cuba's vulnerability to volatile international markets and the global rise in food and fuel prices, by increasing domestic production and reducing imports.

In summer 2008, the wage cap on bonuses for workers who meet or exceed production targets was lifted, thus standardising salary policy across the economy as the Enterprise Perfection System of economic management, which had been operating in military enterprises since 1987, was rolled out to all state enterprises.[12] Bonus payments remained capped at 30 per cent for various bureaucrats, technicians and economists to prevent the emergence of a technocratic elite.

Under a new law, from November 2008 the state began distributing land in 'usufruct', a conditional rent-free loan for between 10 and 25 years, to Cuban individuals and groups who wished to work it. This approach had been applied during the Special Period, when 43,000 Cubans had received land in 'usufruct'. With the closure of the sugar mills, the amount of cultivated land had fallen by 33 per cent between 1998 and 2007, leaving up to 50 per cent of arable land idle or under-used, some 2 million hectares (nearly 5 million acres). The measure aimed to augment agricultural and food production, without permanently changing property relations. Usufruct farmers cannot buy nor sell the land, nor transfer it to third parties; they pay taxes and sell an agreed proportion to the state at fixed prices. Introducing the legislation in July 2008, Raúl Castro told the National Assembly of People's Power, 'I am a firm admirer and defender of large socialist state enterprises, be they agricultural, industrial, or otherwise.'[13] Within one week over 34,600 individuals and entities, most of whom had never owned land, had applied for close to half a million hectares of land to exploit free of charge: up to 13.42 hectares (33 acres), each with the prospect of subsequently expanding to 40 hectares (99 acres).[14]

Over two months in autumn 2008, 3.4 million workers (70 per cent of the workforce) met in 80,000 workplace assemblies to debate the proposal to raise the retirement age from 60 to 65 years for men, and from 55 to 60 years for women. The new law was approved by the National Assembly in December. Additionally, retired school and university teachers were authorised to return to work with a full salary on top of their pension, a measure to bridge the gap until the new retirement ages were implemented and pension increases were introduced.[15] Cuba has the oldest population in the Americas thanks to high life expectancy and low birth rates and the ratio of active workers to retirees had fallen from 7 to 1 in 1970 to less than half that by 2007, making the challenge of sustaining high social expenditures even greater.

DEEPENING DEBATE AND STRUCTURAL CHANGES

In September 2009, the CCP once again created forums for national debate about the island's socioeconomic situation in every community and workplace.

Two key recurrent complaints were the dual currency and low wages in national currency. *Granma*, the daily newspaper of the CCP, began publishing four pages of public letters and articles about these and other problems, including corruption, every Friday. The Ministry of Auditing and Control was replaced by a Comptroller's Office, supervised directly from the Council of State, to root out corruption. Raúl Castro claimed to 'personally check its everyday performance'.[16] Meanwhile, monthly salaries were increased by an average of nearly 3 per cent.

In 2009 import spending fell by 37 per cent, following reductions in volume and international prices, particularly of fuel and food.[17] Raúl Castro described the development of Cuban agriculture as an issue of national security, as reliance on imports undermined the country's independence.[18] Nearly 1 million hectares of arable land had been distributed in usufruct and the state increased payments to farmers to stimulate production. The fiscal deficit was reduced from 6.7 per cent of GDP in 2008 to 4.8 per cent in 2009.[19] However, the goods deficit was 67 per cent in 2009, underscoring the urgent need to raise domestic production, reduce imports and increase goods exports.

In September 2010, the Cuban Workers' Confederation (CTC) announced the state's plans to transfer 1 million unproductive state sector workers into alternative employment between 2011 and 2015 – half of them within six months. A *Financial Times* editorial described it as a 'reform that makes Margaret Thatcher look like a leftist radical'.[20] Raúl Castro, meanwhile, reassured the Cuban people that 'No one will be abandoned to their fate. The socialist state will offer the support necessary for a dignified life through a system of social assistance to those who really are not able to work.'[21]

In 2010, Cuba's workforce was 5.2 million, of whom 800,000, or 15.4 per cent, already worked in the non-state sector, mostly in agricultural cooperatives whose production features in the central plan and a proportion of which is sold to the state. Just 140,000 Cubans or 2.7 per cent of the total workforce were self-employed. Official unemployment was low at 1.7 per cent, but this figure excluded workers in the informal economy, where earnings are often higher and no tax is paid, those not seeking employment and those who have no work to do but who remain on payrolls, receiving a reduced salary.[22] Announcing the decision to restructure employment, the CTC statement said: 'Our state cannot and should not continue maintaining enterprises, productive, service and budgeted entities, with inflated payrolls, and losses that hurt the economy.' The first workers dismissed were from within government ministries.

Trade union representatives met with management in every state entity to determine which posts were expendable. The 'surplus' workers could take up employment in understaffed areas of the state sector (agriculture, construction or industry), join (and, from December 2012, create) cooperatives or become self-employed in any of the 178 activities authorised at that time – mainly services and artisan trades. In 83 of these occupations existing regulations specifying that only family members or cohabitants could be employed by the licence holder were removed. The self-employed category of 'contracted worker' was introduced, which allowed non-family members to be taken on as 'assistants' to other self-employed people.[23] Self-employed workers remained a minority of Cuban workers, their incomes progressively taxed, and they were prohibited from strategic sectors, healthcare, education, the armed forces and domestic security. Alongside the employment changes the education system was adjusted to give greater emphasis to technical training and manual skills. This halted the massive extension of (free) access to university education which was part of the Battle of Ideas but had failed to address shortages in skilled and semi-skilled trades.

When Raúl Castro insisted on the need to end the 'paternalistic' state he was not referring to welfare provision, such as health and education services, but to the notion that in Cuba 'you can live without working'.[24] This was not a new concern from Cuba's revolutionary leaders. In 1962 Che Guevara had pointed out that 'every excess worker in a factory means social unemployment . . . the worker stuck in a job where he has to divide his work with another worker adds nothing to society', and in 1986 Fidel Castro warned against 'speaking about the standard of living as if it was divorced from productivity, from economic and social development, as if it was divorced from the development needs of a country in the Third World, even a socialist one'.[25] The employment reforms were intended to create the structure under which all Cubans could contribute towards social development.

Within a year, however, it was clear that the CTC itself had put the brakes on the process, evidence of their leverage over government policy. In September 2011, at the headquarters of the CTC, I asked Ernesto Freire Cazañas, head of the Confederation's International Relations department why. 'This is a gradual process that cannot be hurried,' he told me. 'The objective of restructuring the workforce is the rational use of human and material resources. We must ensure that no worker is left helpless through a policy of "shock therapy". Rather, we want to use their work skills, knowledge and technical–professional training in the areas where we have a deficit in the country's labour force.' The role of the CTC and Cuba's 19 national trade unions, he said, was to 'guard against violations of the procedures established for the restructuring of the workforce'. He explained the process of consultation behind each decision to redeploy a worker and the multiple levels of appeal available to each state employee (Labour Justice Committees, municipal labour courts, trade union workplace branches or municipal and provincial offices). 'We are representing people who do not agree with the decisions made. Many workers come here for clarification or to complain about measures taken.'[26] Workers unhappy with their proposed redeployment had a period of salary guaranteed and could register with the municipal work organisation to see what alternative employment was available.

'Under socialism the trade union has two main functions,' Freire Cazañas said. 'The first is universal for any trade union, the representation and defence of workers' rights. In the case of socialist Cuba, we have another mission – to actively participate in the effort to develop the economy of the country, which is the economy of the people.' However, this process must be understood in the broader context of Cuba's dependence on foreign trade, the need to substitute imports, the global economic and financial crisis and the US blockade and hostility, he added.[27]

By late December 2011, some 357,000 individuals, less than 7 per cent of the total workforce, were self-employed, mostly occupied in goods and people transportation, food preparation and sale, renting out rooms, selling agricultural products – including from roadside carts (*carretilleros*) – making household items, as couriers and carpenters, or as 'contracted workers'.[28] Two-thirds of them had been officially unemployed beforehand, 16 per cent were retirees and 18 per cent had left the state sector. The process was pulling workers from the informal sector, and the unemployed, into formal work where they contribute to the social product, pay taxes and receive the protection afforded to all workers.[29]

THE GENIUS IS IN THE PEOPLE: GUIDELINES FOR UPDATING THE CUBAN ECONOMY

In April 2011, on the fiftieth anniversary of the defeat of the Bay of Pigs invasion, the CCP held its long-overdue Sixth Congress, the first for nearly 14 years.[30] For three months prior to the Congress, the Cuban people had debated a document written and distributed by the CCP called the *Draft Guidelines of the Economic and Social Policy of the Party and the Revolution* (referred to as the *Guidelines*). Informed by the national public consultations of 2007 and 2009, this document contained 291 'guidelines' for consolidating or amending social and economic policy in 12 broad categories.[31] The introduction to the *Guidelines* affirmed 'the principle that only socialism is capable of overcoming the difficulties and preserving the conquests of the Revolution, and that in the updating of the economic model, planning will be supreme, not the market'.

'Socialism,' it stated, means 'equality of rights and opportunities for the citizens, not egalitarianism. Work is both a right and a duty, the personal responsibility of every citizen, and must be remunerated according to its quantity and quality.'[32] The short-term aim was to eliminate the balance of payments deficit, increase national income, substitute imports with internal production, improve economic efficiency, work motivation and income distribution, 'and create the necessary infrastructural and productive conditions to permit transition to a higher stage of development', the document stated. The long-term aim was 'food and energy self-sufficiency, an efficient use of human potential, a higher level of competitiveness in traditional production areas, and the development of new forms of the production of goods and services of higher added value'.[33]

CCP membership was around 800,000 but every single Cuban, regardless of political or organisational affiliation, could obtain the guidelines and participate once again in open debates about their contents. Work and study centres, political and residential groups organised 163,000 meetings. Out of a total population of 11.2 million, almost 9 million people participated (it was possible to participate more than once) and over 3 million opinions were registered, analysed and organised into 780,000 distinct recommendations. Proving that this was no mere public relations exercise, 68 per cent of the guidelines were subsequently modified following consultation with the Cuban people.[34] Raúl Castro announced that 45 proposals advocating the concentration of property were not included because they 'openly contradicted the essence of socialism'.[35] Over half of all proposals, Raúl Castro reported, concerned the *Guideline*'s chapters on social and macroeconomic policies; most related to the removal of the ration book, pricing policy, passenger transport, education, the establishment of a single currency and the quality of health care services. The essence of these details is what they reveal about a revolutionary leadership with its finger on the pulse of the people.

The CCP Congress in April 2011 was attended by nearly 1,000 delegates, who split into five commissions to discuss the guidelines and the population's recommendations. As a result, a further 86 guidelines were modified and 2 added before the document was approved. In summer 2011, the now 313 guidelines were submitted to the National Assembly of People's Power for legislative ratification. A Permanent Commission for the Implementation and Development of the Guidelines was set up and the Central Committee began to analyse progress in implementing the guidelines in plenary meetings twice a year. Raúl Castro counselled against 'haste or improvisation' and warned that the Cuban people must be kept on board with the 'updating' process.

The Congress also resolved to strengthen the institutions of the People's Power and their system of participatory democracy, devolving control to the local assemblies.[36] Raúl Castro's 'Central Report' was approved, with proposals to limit leadership roles to two terms of five years and to increase the proportion of women and non-white Cubans in leadership positions.[37] It also emphasised the need for greater separation between the CCP (which should provide political and ideological leadership) and the government (which is concerned with management, administrative and legislative functions).[38] In this report, Raúl Castro slated the Cuban media for 'describing the national reality in pretentious high-flown language or with excessive formality' and for 'boring, improvised or superficial reports'. The media's role, he insisted, was to stimulate public debate and produce 'objective, continuous and critical reports on the progress of the updating of the economic model'.

Raúl Castro reassured the people that the ration book would not be eliminated 'before creating the proper conditions to do so . . . which means undertaking other transformations of the economic model with a view to increasing labour efficiency and productivity in order to guarantee stable levels of production and supplies of basic goods and services accessible to all citizens, but no longer subsidised'. Socialism would never use the 'shock therapy' of neoliberalism, he said. 'The social welfare system is being reorganised to ensure a rational and differential support to those who really need it. Instead of massively subsidising products as we do now, we shall gradually provide for those people lacking other support.'[39]

In November 2011, new regulations were introduced to permit the direct purchase/sale of privately owned houses and cars (by Cuban citizens only); to authorise agricultural producers to sell direct to state-owned tourist entities (regulated under the national plan); to provide loans from the state to non-state workers, farmers and people who need to repair their homes (previously only farming cooperatives had access to loans); to permit trade between state enterprises and workers in the non-state sector (using bank transfers, not cash payments); and to authorise Cubans emigrating to transfer ownership of their homes to relatives or co-habitants. While foreign commentators portrayed these as new steps towards a free market, in some cases they were a return to Soviet-era regulations, for example the public sale of privately owned homes and of agricultural products by farmers were both permitted in the 1980s.[40] These measures aimed to cut bureaucracy and improve efficiency without fundamentally changing social relations in Cuba. Although direct sales were permitted, the concentration of property remained prohibited.[41]

While 96 per cent of Cubans own their own homes, the housing stock is in poor condition. In January 2012, the government began to grant subsidies of up to CUP 80,000 for home repairs to those in need. Previously the government had paid for maintenance regardless of the recipient's economic situation, but, this was inefficient and contributed to the housing shortage, waste and corruption. Subsidies would be provided only to families affected by catastrophes or natural disasters, or those in 'vulnerable conditions' or lacking funds for construction materials or labour.[42]

NON-AGRICULTURAL COOPERATIVES

As part of the process of reducing the state payroll, from December 2012 new non-agricultural cooperatives (*cooperativa no agrícola*, or CNA) were authorised with an 'experimental' status. Employees in some state entities, for example cafes or hairdressers, were invited to lease the properties to form a CNA; these were known as 'conversion' cooperatives.[43] 'Self-effort' CNAs were formed from scratch at the initiative of three or more people. Funded by employee contributions, bank loans and a Ministry of Finance fund, CNAs were authorised to conduct business with government entities, state enterprises and private enterprises. They set their own prices except in specific state-regulated markets, pay 10 per cent tax on sales (lower than for self-employed workers), 20 per cent tax on non-member labour contracts, and must make social security contributions for each worker and set aside contingency reserves.

Cooperatives were permitted to hire self-employed workers for up to 90 days, after which that worker either must move on or join the cooperative.[44] Once credits are paid off, CNAs decide how to distribute their surplus. By the end of 2014, there were 498 CNAs: 384 'conversions' and 114 'self-effort'; 43 per cent were in the gastronomy sector, 14 per cent in construction and 6.5 per cent in personal and technical services. In 2017, the process of issuing licences for the non-state sector, both CNAs and self-employment, was suspended while 'irregularities' were investigated, and new regulations and better auditing systems were implemented. It was not until December 2018 that the process resumed in both sectors.

THE REVOLUTION DIGS DEEP

In May 2012, the island's economic prospects faced another setback, when the Spanish company Repsol gave up drilling for oil in Cuban waters. In 2008, the government had announced that 20 billion barrels of offshore oil were estimated to exist in the island's 'exclusive economic zone' around the Gulf of Mexico, an amount significantly higher than the 5 to 7 billion estimated by the US Geological Survey. If true, this would place Cuba among the world's top 20 nations in terms of oil reserves.[45] What a prospect for a country made vulnerable by its dependence on oil imports! Some 120,000 barrels per day (bpd) were being imported, mainly from Venezuela, with another 50,000 bpd supplied domestically.

Accessing deep water oil reserves requires highly specialised technology; agreements to dig exploratory wells had been reached with state oil companies and conglomerates from Angola, Canada, China, India, Malaysia, Norway, Russia, Spain, Venezuela and Vietnam. The first dig was carried out with the Scarabeo 9, one of the world's largest semi-submersible oil drilling rigs, a USD 750 million investment, especially designed and constructed to avoid violating US sanctions which prohibit non-US owned or controlled companies in third countries providing Cuba with foreign-made products containing 20 per cent or more US-origin parts, components or materials.[46] Scarabeo 9 was owned by Italian oil giant Saipem, designed with the aid of Norwegian engineers, built in the shipyards of Yantai, China, fitted with advanced technology in Singapore and initially contracted by the Spanish company Repsol.

Powerful Cuban-American politicians in Miami were enraged at the prospect of Cuba striking 'black gold', and demanded that President Obama 'prevent a State Sponsor of Terrorism, just 90 miles from our shores, from engaging in risky deep-sea oil drilling projects that will harm US interests'.[47] Congresswoman Illena Ros-Lehtinen introduced three 'no-drill bills' in 2011 to impose punitive measures against Cuba's foreign oil partners.[48] The threat of fines from the US Office of Foreign Asset Control (OFAC) had already risen in general. In less than four years of Obama's first administration, USD 2.26 billion in fines had been levied on foreign companies dealing with Cuba. Respol's chairman faced legal threats.[49] However, the US establishment was split over the issue. Between April and July 2010, the BP Deepwater Horizon disaster saw nearly 5 million barrels of oil gush into the Gulf of Mexico and the National Commission on the Deepwater Horizon spill called for negotiations between the US and Cuba on regulatory oversight, containment and response strategies in the case of another spill.

Ros-Lehtinen and her associates must have been pleased after Repsol drilled three wells and found them all dry. By 2015, a dozen foreign firms had explored for Cuba's offshore oil without success, but new survey data confirmed billions of barrels of oil lay beneath Cuba's Gulf of Mexico waters and new deals with foreign partners were underway.[50] Nonetheless, energy supply continues to be an issue of national security for Cuba.

WELCOME HOME

New Cuban migration laws enacted in January 2013 removed the requirement for an exit visa and letter of invitation for Cubans travelling overseas, extended the period for which Cubans could stay abroad without losing citizenship rights and facilitated the return to Cuba, either permanently or for visits, of the diaspora, including Cubans who left illegally or abandoned internationalist missions. Reporting the news, the *New York Times* blamed the exit visa for 'discouraging all but the favored or fortunate from leaving the island', and the *Washington Post* said 'many Cubans are simply denied the visa'.[51] In fact, between 2000 and 31 August 2012, 99.4 per cent of the 941,953 exit visa applications were successful; Cubans were internationally mobile, and not just on internationalist missions, but also visiting families overseas, working and studying abroad. Almost 1 million Cubans travelled abroad in this 12-year period (nearly 1 in 11 people) and of those only 12.8 per cent settled abroad, while the rest returned. In 2011 alone, 250,000 Cubans went overseas legally.[52]

In 2009, President Obama had revoked the Bush-era restrictions on Cuban-Americans visiting and sending money to Cuba.[53] However, once again, the US Interest Section in Cuba was issuing far fewer visas annually than the quota of 20,000 agreed in 1994. Cuba's new migration law presented a challenge to the US administration as, regardless of their initial destination, many new Cuban emigrants would head for the United States claiming the right to citizenship within one year of arrival granted under US law. Indeed, four years later, President Obama would end the 'wet foot, dry foot' policy, which allowed Cubans entering the United States, illegally or not, to settle there but turned back Cubans intercepted at sea.[54]

MONETARY UNIFICATION: UNATTAINABLE IMPERATIVE?

In October 2013 the revolutionary government announced that the process of reunifying Cuba's two currencies, the Cuban peso (CUP) and the Cuban convertible peso (CUC), was underway. Eliminating the dual currency had been a major priority highlighted during the national consultations held over the previous years and in the *Guidelines* for updating the economy. The government statement advised that 'monetary and currency exchange unification is not a measure which will, in itself, resolve all of the economy's current problems, but its implementation is indispensable to re-establishing the value of the Cuban peso and its function as money; that is to say, as a unit of accounting, payment and savings'.[55] This was necessary, the statement said, for 'developing the conditions which will lead to increased efficiency, more accurate measurement of economic activity and incentives for those sectors which produce goods and services for export and to replace imports'.[56]

At that time the exchange rate for individuals was CUP 25 to CUC 1, but it was one dollar to one peso in state-owned companies.[57] The first stage of unification involved devaluation of the official exchange rate in the state sector (1:1), which 'everybody knows is not real', as former Economy Minister José Luis Rodríguez told me.[58] In December 2011, a special exchange rate of CUP 7 to USD 1 had been established for direct transactions between state hotels and restaurants, and agricultural cooperatives. In 2013 this exchange rate was raised to CUP 10 to USD 1, effectively a 900 per cent devaluation of the Cuban peso value in state entities. This meant that, in the internal economy, 'costs will immediately increase, because something that cost you one dollar, or one peso in the near past, now will cost you ten peso', explained Rodríguez.

The October 2013 announcement reassured Cubans that the value of CUCs legally held by the general population would not fall in the process of monetary unification. This required raising the value of the CUP against the CUC. To prevent the population from suffering, Rodriguez explained, 'you have to put more purchasing power in that peso; it is equal to reducing prices, and to do that you need the means – you have to put money in. How much money will be necessary? Well, it is billions of pesos.'[59]

In Cuba the announcement was greeted positively. Rodríguez recognises that most Cubans 'identify income inequality with the dual monetary system, because the inequality appears to be between those that have and those who do not have convertible pesos', so they assume that monetary unification will automatically see inequalities disappear. However, if monetary unification is not accompanied by an increase in production and goods available, consumption problems will remain unsolved. Cubans with greater purchasing power will be competing for insufficient goods, resulting in inflation and not tackling inequality.[60]

The process was flagged to take three years, but that deadline had come and gone when I met with Rodríguez in late 2016. 'It has been three years and we have done practically nothing because we don't have the money to do it,' he admitted. He estimated that monetary unification would take another five years. In part, the effort to seek foreign direct investment took precedence and the precondition for that was the renegotiation of Cuba's massive, historical debts. Financial reserves were then dedicated to paying some of these off.

SETTLING CUBA'S DEBTS

Because of the US policy of persecuting Cuban financial and economic links around the world, the Cuban government stopped publishing information about its debt and financial reserves.[61] However, debt resettlement deals made between 2013 and 2016, on extremely favourable terms, reveal the historic burden of Cuba's international debt. Russia amortised 90 per cent of the (disputed) Soviet-era debt (USD 35 billion) giving Cuba 10 years to pay the rest on favourable terms; Mexico wrote off 70 per cent of the 1980s-era debt (USD 487 million), with the rest to be paid over 10 years; and the Paris Club cancelled 70 per cent of its debt (USD 11.1 billion) from the same era, with the remainder to be paid over 18 years.[62] Cuba has also restructured its USD 6 billion debt with China.

To meet its development plans, the Cuban government needs between USD 2 and 2.5 billion in foreign capital, mainly foreign investment, annually. International investors are keen despite the disincentives of the US blockade. On the Cuban side, as Raúl Castro repeatedly complained, ideological resistance, a cautious approach and lack of experience have slowed the process of approving investment proposals. Only USD 1.3 billion-worth of projects were approved within two years of the 2014 Investment Law, discussed below. Between 2016 and 2018, the Cuban government signed USD 3.5 billion-worth of investment deals, but little of that has entered Cuba.[63] The Trump administration's tightening of the US blockade has multiplied the obstacles faced since 2017.

MARIEL PORT AND SPECIAL DEVELOPMENT ZONE

A key axis in the policy of attracting foreign business to Cuba has been the huge investment in the Mariel Port and Special Development Zone (SDZ), a deep-water sea port and a 465km² special development zone. In January 2014, Dilma Rousseff, president of Brazil at the time, accompanied Raúl Castro to inaugurate the first 700 metre section of the new container terminal at the port of Mariel, in Artemisa Province, 45 kilometres west of Havana. The ceremony was attended by the presidents of Bolivia, Guyana, Haiti and Venezuela and the prime minister of Jamaica who were in Havana for a summit of the Community of Latin American and Caribbean States, known as CELAC.

After Venezuela, Brazil was Cuba's second largest trading partner in Latin America and the Mariel port was being built by the Brazilian engineering group Odebrecht in partnership with the Cuban state and subsidised with USD 682 million from the Brazilian government's Development Bank (BNDES).[64] The project involved 400 Brazilian companies, generating some 156,000 jobs in Brazil and earning USD 802 million for construction businesses. In Cuba, more than 2,000 workers from nearby towns were employed; 99 per cent of the port workers are Cubans.

A long-term contract for managing the Mariel TC, the Cuban company which owns the port, went to Singapore's PSA International, which runs several of the world's largest ports. Given its depth and the installation of world-leading technology, Mariel can accommodate huge post-Panamax vessels, giving it the potential to serve as a transhipment hub for the region, particularly following the expansion of the Panama Canal completed in June 2016.[65] The port will have an annual capacity of up to 1 million containers, replacing Havana Port as Cuba's main harbour.[66]

In 2018, in the plush settings of the Meliá Habana hotel, I met up with a non-Cuban general manager of TC Mariel, an employee of PSA who relocated to Cuba in 2011 when the project started.[67] 'Mariel is a huge site,' he said, 'approximately half the land mass of Singapore,' but virgin territory. 'The Cuban state has invested about USD 300 million a year for the last five or six years, in infrastructure – taking out water, electricity, building roads and railways, things like that, so that foreign investors who want to put a factory there have all the amenities they need. And that's starting from nothing, I mean there was literally nothing out there. Not even *marabú* had reached Mariel!' he joked. While the Cuban people think it's not moving very fast, he says, 'actually it's not moving very slowly either. There's a lot of activity out there.'[68]

PSA is owned by the sovereign wealth fund of Singapore and it is not listed on any stock exchange. 'So that gives you a government-to-government element, which the Cubans love,' the manager explained. 'They've had so many bad experiences with large corporations and suddenly an American influence comes in and that piece of software or hardware gets shutdown, taken away and it messes them up.' Normally, PSA invest in the large ports they manage but in Mariel, he said, 'the Cubans did not want an investor because [Brazilian president] Lula had given them a loan of more than USD 600 million dollars through BNDES, so they didn't need the cash. But they did need the expertise.' PSA brought in equipment from China. Their host computer systems run on

IBM servers, but, because of the US blockade, IBM would not guarantee support, so they had to adopt a Chinese software system.

The new port infrastructure means that investors in Mariel SDZ need not transport products 60 kilometres back to the congested port in Havana. 'In the longer term, Mariel is well positioned geographically to serve as a hub particularly for South Atlantic US ports and the US Gulf and northern Caribbean and Central Mexico.' Its big Achilles heel is US legislation, the manager continued, which prohibits the handling of US origin or destination containers. 'The ship could stop here but we couldn't touch any containers that were destined for Houston or Miami.'

Long-standing US legislation prohibits ships from any country that dock in Cuba from entering US ports for six months. Does this apply to Mariel given measures taken under the Obama-era rapprochement? 'If you can find the answer to that question, I will buy your book', he laughed. 'In theory, Obama's last changes in 2016 allowed all non-US shipping lines to stop in Mariel or another Cuban port, discharge whatever containers were destined for Cuba and then go to Miami, Norfolk and New York. In practice nobody has done it.' Why? 'Because the election of Trump means that everybody is more cautious. Like the stock market, it functions on confidence and commentary.'[69]

Mariel is the first and largest of several SDZs planned in Cuba. In Santiago de Cuba, in the east, work began in 2015 on upgrading the port and introducing another SDZ. These are not, however, the 'free-trade zones' associated with exploitative foreign-owned factories and sweatshops. 'The Cubans are not interested in that,' explains the Mariel general manager. 'They don't have a surplus of unskilled workers.' On the contrary, the 7,000 Cubans employed in Mariel are young and skilled, he said. 'We have lots of people with university degrees, good technicians. They learn very fast, so you could do "advance manufacturing", or what they call "injection moulding" here, you could put together iPhones.'[70] Cuban workers are recruited via a state-run employment agency, which imposes strict conditions on foreign investors. The Cuban state receives payment for their labour in hard currency and converts a proportion of this into Cuban currency for the payment of salaries.

The inauguration at Mariel was followed by two major new laws: one regulating foreign investments, replacing legislation introduced during the Special Period in 1995; and the other a new labour code, updating legislation from 1985. The new Investment Law approved by the National Assembly in March 2014 allows 100 per cent foreign-owned companies to operate in Cuba in 'special cases', usually with a higher tax burden than for joint state–foreign enterprises, speeds up official responses to foreign investment proposals, and reduces some taxes and provides exemptions on others.[71] Foreign investment is prohibited in the armed forces and security, education, health care and legal services, preserving Cuba's sovereignty and protecting 'los logros', the social welfare achievements of the Revolution.

The introduction of the new Labour Code in June 2014 followed five months of debate involving 2.8 million workers in nearly 70,000 workplace assemblies and in the CTC, the Ministry of Labour and the National Assembly. The process led to over 100 amendments to the draft Code. Among the substantial changes was the removal of a new workplace grievance and disciplinary procedure which would have given powers to management that previously were exercised by panels dominated by elected workers.[72] The fundamental laws enshrined, as before, the rights to equal pay, minimum salary and non-discrimination, while reference to sexual orientation was added for the first time and others, such as maternity rights, were enhanced. The rights of Cuba's self-employed workers and the new non-agricultural cooperative members were incorporated. The Code gives contracted workers the right to written contracts, minimum salaries, maximum hours, rest periods, paid holidays, and health and safety at work.[73]

Repeating a historical pattern, Cuban efforts to access foreign capital were countered by increased US hostility. In May 2014, French Bank BNP Paribas pleaded guilty to two 'criminal' charges and agreed to pay nearly USD 9 billion to US authorities for violating that country's sanctions against Cuba, Iran and Sudan. The fine was a warning to financial institutions around the world. BNP Paribas was just one of the record-breaking 49 entities fined for transactions with Cuba under the two Obama terms; the fine was issued even while the United States and Cuba engaged in backchannel talks about improving relations. With rapprochement announced on 14 December 2014, the US administration's strategy appeared to be to fend off international rivals from Cuba, while facilitating greater engagement with the island in the interests of US capital. Nonetheless, rapprochement served as a green light for international investors.

UPDATING THE GUIDELINES FOR UPDATING THE ECONOMY

In April 2016, the CCP held its Seventh Congress; it focused on updating the *Guidelines* approved five years earlier. Of the original 313 guidelines,

21 per cent had been fully implemented and 77 per cent were underway, a process generating 130 new policies and 344 new legal regulations. In the intervening period, 2011–2016, GDP growth had averaged 2.7 per cent (just over half the 5 per cent aspired to) but Cuba's macroeconomic situation had improved with the rebalancing of external finances, particularly through the renegotiation of foreign debt and the increase in foreign direct investment. Imports had been reduced, exports increased and diversified, and government spending had been cut. The *Guidelines* were updated during the PCC Congress for the 2016–2021 period.[74]

During his speech to the Congress, Raúl Castro acknowledged that the reform of property relations had generated controversy, 'and logically so, as depending on the predominance of one form of ownership over another, a country's social system is determined'. However, in socialist Cuba, he asserted, the people would retain ownership of the basic means of production, which meant that state ownership would continue to dominate the national economy and the socioeconomic system, serving as the basis of the Cuban workers' power. He continued:

> The recognition of the existence of private property has generated more than a few honest concerns from participants in the discussions prior to the [Seventh] Congress, who expressed concerns that in doing so we would be taking the first steps towards the restoration of capitalism in Cuba . . . I have the duty to assert that this is not, in the least, the purpose of this conceptual idea. The increase in self-employment and the authorisation to contract a workforce has led in practice to the existence of medium, small and micro private enterprises which today operate without proper legal status and are regulated under the law by a regulatory framework designed for individuals engaged in small business conducted by the worker and his/her family.
>
> Guideline number 3 approved by the Sixth Congress and which we intend to maintain and strengthen in the updated draft [*Guidelines*] categorically specifies that "In the forms of non-state management, the concentration of property shall not be allowed" and it is added "nor of wealth"; therefore, the private company will operate within well-defined limits and will constitute a complementary element in the economic framework of the country, all of which should be regulated by law.[75]

The Seventh Congress took place during rapprochement and in reference to Obama's policy of strategic 'engagement' Raúl Castro declared: 'We are not naive nor do we ignore the aspirations of powerful external forces that are committed to what they call the "empowerment" of non-state forms of management, in order to create agents of change in the hope of putting an end to the Revolution and socialism in Cuba by other means.' But, he insisted, 'Cooperatives, self-employment and medium, small and micro private enterprise are not in their essence anti-socialist or counter-revolutionary and the enormous majority of those who work in them are revolutionaries and patriots who defend the principles and benefit from the achievements of this Revolution.'[76]

In the run-up to the Seventh Congress, four documents were discussed by delegates and some 3,500 invited guests representing different sectors of Cuban society: 1) An evaluation of the national economy between 2011 and 2015 and the updated *Guidelines* for 2016 to 2021; 2) A national plan of economic and social development to 2030 [*Plan 2030*]; 3) A 'conceptualisation' of Cuba's social and economic model of socialist development [*Conceptualisation*]; and 4) a report on progress made towards objectives agreed on by the First National Conference of the CCP in January 2012.[77] These documents establish the parameters within which the 'updating' of the economic and social system takes place. As mundane as these events may at first seem, in them lies the key to Cuba's survival as a sovereign socialist state in the post-Soviet world. In form and content, they illustrate the democratic input which underscores the resilience of Cuba's revolutionary process. The documents approved at both Congresses had the participation of millions of Cubans: the population was mobilised through work, study and community structures to participate in decision-making about their own future.

These documents formally confirm the existence of small and medium private businesses in Cuba, a precondition for the introduction of urgently needed legislation to regulate and control what already exists. Cuban economist Juan Alejandro Triana Barros underscored the significance of 'private businesses' being recognised in an official document which 'came out of the most important and highest level of the political power of Cuba: the central committee of the Communist party.'[78]

CONCEPTUALISING CUBAN SOCIALISM: WHERE IS IT GOING AND HOW WILL IT GET THERE?

Rarely do states engage in consultation about their own ideologies, policies, aims and objectives. In Cuba this took place following the Seventh Congress, as the *Conceptualisation* and the *Plan 2030* documents were debated by 1.6 million Cubans in some 47,000 meetings of the CCP and the UJC, and by representatives of 'organisations of the masses' (FMC, CDRs, CTC, ANAP among many) and in other sectors. In May 2017, the documents were approved by the Central Committee of the CCP, then debated again in National Assembly work commissions. A total of 208,161 changes were made in this process. Consequently, 92 per cent of the original *Conceptualisation* document was modified.[79] Raúl Castro described them as 'the most studied, discussed and re-discussed documents in the history of the Revolution', which is indicative of their importance.[80] An extraordinary session of the National Assembly in June 2017 approved the *Conceptualisation* document, the updated *Guidelines*, and the *Plan 2030*.

The three essential pillars of the 'updated' economic model are: the consolidation of the socialist state in its economic (enterprise), political (organs of people's power and workers' representation) and social (socialist welfare and cohesion) aspects; the introduction of a diversity of non-state forms of management and ownership; and the primacy of planning which 'takes into account' the functioning of the market.[81] Given the greater space being opened to market relations through private ownership and business, self-employment and foreign investment, the establishment of social welfare and national development priorities are essential to prevent market forces asserting a capitalist logic over Cuban development. With Raúl Castro retiring as President of the Council of State in February 2018, the Cuban leadership was working to strengthen the institutional basis of socialism to help safeguard its future when Cuba is no longer led by the 'historic generation' who carried out the Revolution.

Cuban academics and government specialists worked on the *Conceptualisation* document for four years prior to the CCP Congress in 2016: this was the first official document to 'conceptualise' Cuba's socialist system. While it 'summarises the essential conceptions to promote socioeconomic development in accordance with the current aspirations and features of the Cuban revolutionary process', it is not concerned with the concrete measures or policies required, but with the main changes necessary in order to consolidate and advance the principles of Cuban socialism and construct an 'independent, sovereign, socialist, democratic, prosperous and sustainable' socialism.[82] The order in which these descriptors appear is no accident: sovereignty and independence are the only viable frameworks within which the other principles are deemed feasible.[83] Real 'sovereignty' means control over national resources and development strategy, but that has to be balanced with the need for foreign capital.

The introduction to the *Conceptualisation* document highlights the Cuban feat of surviving into the post-Soviet era and the gradual recuperation under the difficult conditions imposed by the US blockade, international uncertainty and internal problems that have slowed social and economic development. It recognises Cuba's structural underdevelopment and economic imbalances: the lack of correspondence between work and remuneration; between the availability and need for hard currency; the offer and supply of products and services; low productivity, inefficiency and the technological obsolescence of industry and infrastructure; dependence on hydrocarbons; limited productive chains; weak organisation, work discipline and management, including in the investment process; and the negative impact of the dual currency. It flags up economic and social differences between Cubans not based on their labour and acknowledges behaviour contrary to the Revolution's principles and values, manifestations of individualism, bureaucracy, corruption, crime, indiscipline and other forms of social marginalisation. It goes on to underscore the strengths and opportunities which will facilitate progress: unity and resilience; the legacy of Fidel Castro; majority support; essential values, such as patriotism and anti-imperialism and the vocation for international solidarity; the youth; universal social provision; effective armed institutions; civil defence system; diverse and active civil society; potential capacity and natural advantages; human potential with high values and levels of education.[84]

The first chapter concerns 'the principles of our socialism that sustain the Model and their main transformations'.[85] Chapter 2, on 'ownership of the means of production', notes that: 'Relations of ownership over the means of production define the nature of any socioeconomic system, since the dominant form of ownership determines the relations of production, distribution, exchange and consumption in society.'[86] Property ownership is not a merely 'economic' fact but shapes the reproduction of social relations, consciousness, class and ideology.

Chapter 3, on 'planned management of the economy', asserts that: 'The system of planned management of economic and social development takes into account the presence of market relations and regulates their action according to socialist development,' explaining that: 'The objective existence of market laws is fundamentally explained by the level of development of productive forces, the social division of labour and the coexistence of different forms of ownership and management.'[87] Chapter 4, on 'social policy', lists economic and social rights but also underscores the importance of work as the source of welfare and prosperity. The 'final considerations' stress the importance of debate, the exchange of ideas, communication strategies and 'other actions that contribute to modifying obsolete conceptions and practices that constitute the main obstacle to updating the Model.'[88] It asserts the role of the CCP in driving and controlling the process of updating.

Framed as the principal tool to achieve the approach set out in the *Conceptualisation* document, the *Plan 2030* incorporates 24 'guiding principles and themes for elaborating the national development plan'. The six 'strategic areas' outlined are: effective, efficient socialist government and social integration; productive transformation and international insertion; infrastructure; human potential, science, technology and innovation; natural resources and the environment; and human development, justice and equity. Each of these is divided into lists of general and specific objectives.

Again, there are no details about what policies will be formulated to achieve these objectives and how they may be implemented. The final section defines the 'strategic economic sectors' as those which: represent a significant proportion of economic activity; produce and export value added; positively affect the balance of payments; facilitate development of the productive sector and productive chains; promote the internal market; generate productive employment; connect with new international technology paradigms; remove logistical and infrastructural restraints; contribute to sovereignty and national security; and do not negatively impact environmental sustainability.[89]

While the participative process behind the compilation of these documents promotes consensus and commitment to the collective project, the real test will emerge in the practice of formulating, implementing and enforcing the policies required to achieve their aims. In practice, how can market forces be both encouraged, as a means of increasing employment and enterprise, and simultaneously constrained, which is imperative if the dominance of non-exploitative social relations is to be maintained? These are the difficult challenges facing Cuban socialism.

In April 2018, Raúl Castro told the National Assembly that in 2011, when the *Guidelines* were introduced, he expected that, by the present date, 'we would have advanced more'. He added:

> We never had any illusions that it would be a short and easy path. We knew that we were beginning a process of enormous complexity, due to its scope, which encompassed all elements of society, which required overcoming the colossal obstacle of a mentality based on decades of paternalism and egalitarianism, with significant consequences for the functioning of the economy.[90]

Cuba still confronted enormous and growing economic difficulties with budget deficits, hard currency scarcity, low salaries and productivity, difficulty accessing foreign capital, the distortions to accounting and incentives resulting from the dual economy. While many of these are historic difficulties associated with the challenge of (under) development, clearly the US blockade generates multiple problems. The principal social problems included the slow pace of housing construction, despite CUP 6 billion distributed to Cubans to build homes via their own efforts, the exodus of qualified professionals from the state sector, especially in education and science, and the emigration of Cuban youth.[91]

Nonetheless, Cuban GDP grew on average 2.3 per cent from 2009 to 2015.[92] In 2016, the island's economy went into recession for the first time since 1993, with a contraction of 0.9 per cent, largely reflecting circumstances outside the Cuban government's control: powerful and destructive hurricanes (Hurricane Irma caused losses estimated above USD 13 billion), and political and economic instability in Venezuela which hit Cuban oil imports and their revenues for professional services exports. From late 2017, the Trump administration began incrementally tightening the US blockade, undermining the 'demonstration effect' of rapprochement with Obama. According to Rodríguez:

> The best results were achieved in the process of restructuring the balance of payments through renegotiation processes and payment of foreign debt, an essential prerequisite for obtaining external financing and direct foreign investment. However, on several occasions it was assumed that once the situation with the creditors was normalised, new loans would be received in a similar proportion to what was paid, something that did not happen. On the other hand, the normalisation of the country's external debt had a high cost, since its servicing during the period 2009–2017 reached an estimated figure close to USD 23 billion, which objectively limited the possibility of raising the amount of investments or consumption with our own resources.[93]

Furthermore, in Rodríguez's analysis, regulations introduced to address monetary–mercantile relations 'failed to prevent the expansion of the informal economy, tax evasion and the breakdown of the state monopoly of financial and commercial flows through various channels, in many cases impossible to control, to which have been added criminal practices that need to be repressed more quickly'.[94]

In the social sphere, indicators continued to improve: despite the recession of 2016, in 2017 infant mortality dropped to a record low of 4 per 1,000 live births, and stayed there in 2018, with decreases in under-five and maternal mortality rates also. Human welfare remains at the heart of the revolutionary process in Cuba, and the concern extends outwards as Cuban medical internationalism continues to save and improve lives around the world.

Raúl Castro's reforms went some way to getting the Cuban house in order. Viewing them through the narrow lens of economic efficiency, productivity and growth, their success was limited. Those who saw them as a base from which to launch Cuba back towards capitalism were disappointed. For Cuban revolutionaries, however, the efficiency and growth which the reforms hoped to promote was not the end but the means – to improving the prospects for the human-centred, socialist development project. The following chapter discusses the role of Cuban thinkers, policy-makers and activists in keeping the reform process on that track, resisting its derailment by purely economic concerns.

In January 2012, Raúl Castro declared:

A revolution without errors has never existed and never will because they are the result of the actions of imperfect human beings and peoples, faced moreover with new and colossal challenges. For that reason, I believe that we need not be ashamed of errors; it is more serious and shameful not to have the courage to delve more profoundly into them and analyse them in order to extract the lessons from each one and correct them in time.[95]

How 'errors' are defined and by whom, the way they are addressed and in whose interests, is the essence to understanding the revolutionary process in Cuba.

9

THE CUBAN TIGHTROPE
BETWEEN THE PLAN AND THE MARKET

In a tidy, sunlit, apartment on the third-floor of an old colonial residence in Havana in December 2016, Geidys Fundora Nevot tells me about the 'strong debate' which followed the National Assembly's approval of the *Guidelines for Updating the Economic and Social Model* in 2011. Fundora was then a young doctoral student concerned to promote equity through local and community development and had investigated the situation of self-employed workers in Cuba. This new 'great debate' was initiated when a group of economic sociologists, social psychologists, social scientists and philosophers criticised the narrow focus on economic efficiency in the *Guidelines* which, they argued, left aside the issue of social equity. Not all Cubans, they warned, enjoyed the same starting point to be able to take advantage of the 'new opportunities' generated by the changes being introduced.[1] She acknowledged that most of this critique was not aired outside Cuba and is barely detectable on the internet. Fundora herself allied with critics of the *Guidelines* after encountering investigations and analysis which referred to the 'winners and losers of the reforms'.[2]

Fifteen months after my conversation with Fundora, I shared a sofa at the office of the Centre for Research on the World Economy (Centro de Investigaciones de la Economía Mundial, or CIEM) with economist Blanca Munster, a specialist in 'women's economy'. Discussing the work which produced that debate, she told me: 'These investigations flashed a red light to say "stop, stop", don't just focus on how much we export, how much investment there is – look at the people who are lagging behind.'[3] She was referring to Cubans still suffering in socioeconomic terms from problems accumulated since the Special Period: the unresolved issue of housing, where deteriorating conditions increase vulnerability to hurricanes; the growing gap between incomes, wages and fixed pensions, and prices; and the removal of social assistance as part of the effort to reduce the 'paternalistic state' under Raúl Castro's mandate.

At the outset of the reform process, Raúl Castro complained that many Cubans have come to confuse social equality and justice with 'egalitarianism'. 'Socialism means social justice and equality, but equal rights, opportunities, not income. Equality is not egalitarianism. This, in the final analysis, is also a form of exploitation: of the worker who is good by those who are not, or worse yet, by the lazy.'[4] Raúl Castro asserted that confusion over these principles had undermined the socialist concept of work: from each according to their ability, to each according to their labour.[5] He criticised policies of egalitarianism, the 'excess of subsidies' and public services, and undue gratuities – essentially freebies. Provision via the ration book (*libreta*) was cut. Since 1962, the *libreta* has provided every person in Cuba with a basic basket of foods, and some hygiene products at highly subsidised prices, regardless of their income or wealth. Free lunches in state-run workplaces were eliminated, mostly compensated by a rise in salaries so workers could buy lunch from local outlets.

Between 2009 and 2014 spending on social assistance was reduced dramatically by 60 per cent, and the number of recipients plummeted from 426,000 to 169,778 people in the same period.[6] In the view of another young Cuban doctoral researcher, Jenny Morín, this was injurious even within the framework of the drive for economic efficiency. 'The reduction of social expenditures does not contribute to economic growth; on the contrary, it is counterproductive, since it strips the Revolution and, therefore, the Cuban government of its legitimising base.'[7]

Blanca Munster said that 'The emphasis on economic issues hides the process of differentiation and poverty affecting segments of the population.' Inequality, measured by the GINI coefficient, is increasing in Cuba, she revealed: 'it is known, but it is not published officially'. Munster described this as 'unjust' inequality because it is not linked to work contribution or qualifications. 'Most painful is that many of our youth have plans to study and work outside Cuba. Their individual project is linked to going abroad.'[8]

Thus, these Cuban critics pushed back against what they identified as a market liberalising notion of 'sacrificing today to reap benefits tomorrow'. For them, this approach echoed neoliberal theories about how economic growth will 'spill over' to the rest of society, dragging it towards progress. 'Anyone on the left in Latin America knew this neoliberal thesis was a total lie,' said Fundora. Latin America had been through it and come out the other end.

Underlying this debate, Fundora believes, are different concepts of development. 'What is our development paradigm for moving forward with our project?' she asked. This question can be approached through the lens of forms of 'socialist' economic organisation and/or the lens of developed versus developing countries. Should Cuba follow the development path of the advanced capitalist countries, the less developed countries, the 'emerging economies' or the former socialist countries? In 2011, Cuban planning economist, Oscar Fernández asked: 'From the traditional state socialism that characterises present-day Cuba will it move towards a more decentralised state socialism? An Asian-style market socialism? A self-managed socialism of the Yugoslav variety? To the so-called participatory socialism of the twenty-first century?'[9] But are these the right questions? Each one of those 'socialist' alternatives reverted to capitalism or has otherwise floundered. Others see the options as between the present state socialism, market socialism or 'socialisation', with a greater role for cooperative and other forms of so-called social ownership.[10]

'Many economists', complains Fundora, 'take China and Vietnam as reference countries, despite knowing that, although they have improved a little economically, social inequality has also increased.' An alternative, she argues, is to examine new forms of economic organisation developed by social movements independently of the nation state, such as the Zapatistas in Mexico, the Landless Movement in Brazil, or the movement by workers to recover factories in Argentina. Fundora continued:

> If in a socialist economy, social property should prevail, why don't we diversify the forms of social property, instead of promoting private property so much more? Why do we bet more on small private property, which has increased by half a million people whilst cooperative property has grown by a much lower percentage? According to socialist theory, because of the type of values it produces, the cooperative form of production and distribution is more attuned to that new man and woman needed in a socialist society.

She pointed out that under socialism 'the social objective of the economy is not growth for the sake of growth, but for the social implication of that growth'.

So, what was the result of this critique? A change in both narrative and policy around 2016, it is said. Fundora indicates the shift in Raúl Castro's speeches to the National Assembly: between 2010 and 2012 he focused on economic efficiency, but by 2016 he spoke about equity and distribution as priorities to be addressed. 'That tells me that, yes, what is happening in terms of distribution is being fed back,' she concluded.[11] She even referred to a 'small rectification' in 2016, with the reopening of some local health and education centres which had recently been absorbed into larger centres in the drive for economic efficiency.[12] The reversal followed investigations by the Cuban Communist Party (CCP), which were never made public, about the impact the closure of these municipal facilities was having on local residents.

Ricardo Torres, an economist at the Centre for the Study of the Cuban Economy (Centro de Estudios de la Economía Cubana, or CEEC) also identified a change around 2016; he called it a 'backward step'. The impetus to this, he said, were the December 2015 discussions in the National Assembly about rising food prices exacerbating inequality, a sense that rapprochement with the United States was proceeding too fast and concerns about the 'growing clout of the private sector', which was believed to be draining labour from state companies, competing in key industries, essentially tourism, and generating 'informality and individual trading'. 2016 was also the year of US president Barack Obama's historic visit to Cuba in March, the CCP's Seventh Congress in April, and in November both the election of Donald Trump as US president and the death of Fidel Castro.[13] As the economic situation in Venezuela deteriorated, Cuba entered its first recession for 23 years.

Evidence of changing priorities is contained in two documents with long titles which were debated in the National Assembly of People's Power in summer 2017: *Conceptualisation of the Economic and Social Model of Cuban Socialist Development (Conceptualisation)* and *Basis for the Plan of Economic and Social Development up to 2030: Vision of the Nation, Axes and Strategic Sectors* (*Plan 2030*) (see Chapter 8). One of the *Conceptualisation* document's four chapters is dedicated to social policy. 'This is a novel element,' explained Fundora, 'not because Cuba doesn't work on this, but because it wasn't previously so explicitly a theme of public debate. Here a section appears on economic, social and political rights.' Following an intense debate involving 1.6 million Cubans, 92 per cent of the original draft was modified. One out of six strategic areas outlined in the *Plan 2030* is dedicated to 'human development, equity and social justice'. It does indeed appear that these Cuban researchers, and the debates they stirred up, have rescued Cuba's development policy from the economistic clutches of those who view progress from a technical, narrowly economic perspective.

Among those economists are Cubans who trust in the efficacy of market mechanisms and want to give them space to operate within the centrally planned economy. They do not consider the market to be in conflict with the socialist plan, as Che Guevara did, and argue that it can be harnessed to foster national development.[14] Some believe that after 60 years of socialism, Cuba is well placed to develop 'social entrepreneurship', an abstract model defying the logic of both capitalism and socialism, under which private interests mould their profit-seeking around social, cultural or environmental well-being. Cuban economist Juan Alejandro Triana Barros regards it as 'very controversial' that 'there is no word, no sign of social entrepreneurship in the Constitution nor in the national development plan'.[15] 'Social entrepreneurship' implies a kind of pre-monopoly capitalism, without the cut-throat competition in which the fiercest profit-makers devour the rest. There is also a group of Cuban economists who effectively argue for a transition to capitalism, although some are more overt than others.

In late March 2018, a fortnight before Cuba's new president was named, I attended a talk in Havana by Torres to students from a British university.[16] After he gave an overview of economic developments on the island, a student asked the economist what changes he would make to the Cuban economy were he to become Cuba's new president. His response encapsulated the approach of many Cuban economists on the island and abroad:

> I would engage with the currency unification and an exchange rate reform, economically speaking that would be the first measure. Second, I would start gradually lifting most of the restrictions that are in place for the domestic private sector, because I think that the most valuable asset Cuba has is its people, so we need to give them full opportunities to take advantage of what they've got, and we are not doing that right now. So that will certainly be a priority. I think definitely that foreign investment has to be a component of Cuba's economic strategy for many years to come. But I would try to be more strategic in terms of foreign investment. I think we are wasting time and energy on projects that are not very impactful. I would try to join as many development institutions as possible, multilateral and development institutions, probably the IMF and the World Bank will be the last two in that list for obvious reasons, but I would pursue that.[17]

Cuba's participation in such international financial institutions would de facto imply conditions that impact upon its domestic economy. In theory, Cuba could join the IMF without restructuring its domestic economy. This would give it access to technical assistance, 'free' advice by experts in areas such as fiscal policy, financial policy, statistics and so on, but these would be experts in capitalist economics. What is more, Cuba would have to pay its annual 'quota' for membership, so the advice is not actually free. The IMF would produce an annual report on the Cuban economy. It is difficult to imagine why a 'socialist' Cuba would wish to join the IMF, with its experts in capitalist economics, other than for the ability to access an emergency loan. An IMF economist told me that: 'As an IMF member, this loan would be provided but against the agreement that some reforms would take place in due course to put the economy back on track. These reforms, agreed with the Cuban government, should tackle the causes of the crisis to make sure that no similar crisis would happen in the future.'[18] If these reforms were not implemented in the agreed time, the disbursement could be withheld or cancelled. She admitted that 'it is not clear how much a government can negotiate in times of crisis, so the economic measures can feel more "imposed" than negotiated'.

The United States is the major shareholder and dominant player in the IMF, so Cuba could not join without that country's approval and thus, the IMF economist explained, 'the conditionality coming with emergency lending would also be shaped by the United States and other members. Would this be acceptable for the Cuban government? I guess not, as it would be considered as America meddling in their domestic policies. So all in all, I understand that you don't join a club if you don't trust the other members, even if it could be beneficial for the various resources it could give you.' What kind of structural reforms would the IMF impose on Cuba? Neoliberal ones ceding state control to private interests and rolling back spending on social welfare.

Torres's final 'presidential priority' is: 'I would try to get a better deal with the United States . . . Having said that, if the Americans are not interested, I would look to other countries: Russia, China, the European Union, and I would try to get a better deal with them.'[19] It is difficult to imagine better deals than those struck with the island's Russian, Chinese and European creditors between 2013 and 2015 (see Chapter 8, p. 220). When I had interviewed Torres's colleague, Humberto Blanco, who was Director of CEEC in late 2016, he had a more positive view of Cuban dealings with its debtor countries. 'The renegotiation of the debt has been a big success,' Blanco told me. 'I think one of the reasons absolutely has to do with the renegotiating team. [Cuban Economy Minister Ricardo] Cabrisas is on this very effective renegotiation team.'[20]

Back at the talk with Torres, I asked him for clarification on his second point about removing restrictions on the private sector in Cuba. 'As you know,'

I began, 'the logic of capital accumulation would imply . . .' Torres interjects: 'inequality . . .', as if the answer was obvious. '. . . a transition to capitalism,' I finish. 'State capitalism,' he replies. 'In countries like Cuba you cannot have free markets. That's an illusion. No country in the world has free markets. I mean central planning did not solve Cuba's problems, but I do believe that in countries such as Cuba if you want to break the inertia that underdevelopment and periphery have brought to us you need a powerful central government that is able to run the country. Americans believe so as well. Does he mean like the Chinese model? 'Well, a variation probably, but yes, I think the state has to be there. It doesn't mean that it has to be big, but it has to be powerful and it has to be smart, that is a different thing.' For Torres, Cuba's big state is weak. 'I believe more in a state such as Singapore or such as Sweden or, I don't know, Norway without the oil and the coal. It's a big difference.' This aspiration is surprising; the Kingdoms of Norway and Sweden prospered from long imperial histories, so the comparison is completely abstract.[21]

Blanco rejects China as a model because of the two countries' concrete differences: the geographical size and population, natural resources and culture, habits, values, ways of living, behaviours, 'these are good reasons to say we should not copy-paste what China did. It doesn't mean we should not consider experiences such as, for example, the Development Zones etc.'[22] Despite these disparities between the countries, according to Jesús García Brigos Pastor, political scientist and philosopher at the Institute of Philosophy: 'Agreements have even been signed for the exchange of experiences and the formation of [Cuban] business cadres and managers in China, where management is characterised by technocratic approaches.' He added that, in China, 'decisions are not discussed and relations of boss-subordinate prevail, requiring loyalty and obedience, far from a participatory or cooperative management', which is the objective of the process of updating the economic and social model in Cuba.[23]

Hence the Cuban government has set out to find its own solution to the problems the island faces: structural trade dependence, balance of payments deficits, hard currency shortages, technological obsolescence and the under-use and inefficiency of the productive base, infrastructure and the investment process – all in the context of the punishing US blockade. The question is whether it can find solutions within the socialist planned economy framework whilst having to operate within the global capitalist economy. The question, as formulated in the previous chapter, is how can market forces be both encouraged, as a means of increasing employment and enterprise, and simultaneously constrained, which is imperative to maintain the dominance of non-exploitative social relations? These are the difficult challenges facing Cuban socialism under the presidency of Miguel Díaz-Canel.

WHO ARE THE SELF-EMPLOYED AND WHO DO THEY WORK FOR?

Behind many grandiose, ageing facades of tall, high-ceiled mansions in Havana are hosted private restaurants and bars. Some owners have cultivated the edifices' ageing elegance, with ornate dark wood furniture, thick with history and warped by humidity. Others offer modernist simplicity, with decor and furniture liberated from custom and culture. Escaping a rainstorm between meetings in Havana in 2017, I slipped under the shelter of a private restaurant, a *paladar*, in the sleek, modern style. There were two entrance facades and a service counter on each floor. Most of those serving were young women with short brightly coloured skirts. This is clearly not a family business and the workers rushed about joylessly to meet orders and serve customers. One young waitress told me there are three shifts of eight hours with eight employees each: this is a 24-hour a day establishment. Set-ups like this are emerging across Cuban cities and everybody knows it. Triana Barros claimed there are private restaurants in Cuba that make more than USD 3 million a year, with over 80 direct employees, and mechanical workshops making over USD 1 million a year.[24]

Self-employment is a big feature of the economic reforms, promoted since 2010 to provide employment, to meet the demand for goods and services the state cannot produce, to attract foreign capital (through remittances), and to raise incomes for participants and tax revenues for the state. There are now over 200 officially recognised categories for self-employment, extending to some 900 activities in 'non-strategic' areas of economic activity: one in five are occupied in the production and sale of food or transportation, mainly of passengers.[25]

However, the status of 'self-employed' applies to a range of workers in disparate employment situations. The traditional 'self-employed' are independent workers, sometimes supported by families, who pay no one and receive no salary. The employment changes of 2010 introduced the new status of the 'contracted worker', who is formally self-employed but contracted as an 'assistant' to another self-employed person.[26] After an intense debate, however, the Cuban Supreme Court recognised them as employees subordinated to an employer, and the new Labour Code of 2014 afforded them workers' protections.[27] The legalisation of 'contracted workers' facilitated the emergence of small and medium private businesses that hire those employees. Prior to that, the self-employed were restricted to employing family members only. So the third category of formally self-employed workers are actually private business owners. To further complicate the issue, workers can exist in any of these categories informally, that is illegally, as their activity is not registered, and they do not pay tax nor receive protection. Like anywhere in the world, employees without contracts are in a precarious situation.

The private sector does not have material or commercial autonomy from the state. Most self-employed workers have higher incomes than state sector employees and seemingly contradictory state policies simultaneously encourage and restrict the growth of self-employment. This is because the sector is considered necessary for the reasons outlined above, but at the same time it clearly has the potential to threaten the socialist system, by changing the predominant social relations in Cuba, facilitating the emergence of a pro-market political class, and through its links to foreign capital, especially from the United States.

By 2016, around one in five self-employed Cubans were employees (contracted workers). Technically this was in contravention of the 1976 Constitution which prohibits Cubans from obtaining income from the exploitation of the work of others.[28] In Marxist terms, contracted workers *are* in a relationship of exploitation because the surplus they produce is expropriated by the private owner. Nonetheless, the fact that they receive a larger share of that surplus, via higher salaries, means that they are less likely to recognise their position as exploited workers.[29] They feel privileged in comparison to state employees and this has negative implications for class consciousness. It also serves to draw state workers into the private sector.

Irrespective of their salaries, contracted workers increasingly complain about exploitative conditions: bad treatment from 'bosses', long hours, poor conditions, lack of employment rights. This is occurring in a country where workers' rights have been primary. Based on her own investigations, Fundora described small rebellions among contracted workers to undermine their bosses. Previously, private business owners identified their biggest problem as the lack of a wholesale market, whereas more recently, she has been told, 'My biggest problem is that my workers rob me and sabotage my business, my own workers!' Fundora regards this as a small form of resistance against the perception of exploitation and job instability. However, contracted workers have also consciously decided to endure bad conditions because their wages are substantially higher than alternative employment in the state sector. 'People are not blind, they recognize that they are being exploited and they tell you, "I am going to keep going for another three months and then I'll leave." They don't think about taking legal action against their employer.'[30] This creates major challenges for the work of Cuban trade unions.

In September 2011, when I met with Ernesto Freire Cazañas, head of the International Relations Department at the Cuban Workers Confederations (CTC), in Havana, it was a year since the CTC had announced plans to transfer 1 million unproductive state workers to alternative employment.[31] Already, the proportion of Cuba's workforce in self-employment had shot up from 2.7 per cent of the total workforce in 2010 to 7 per cent, from 140,000 to 357,000 individuals, but it was still early days in the process of the employment restructuring process.

I asked him how the CTC was ensuring that non-state sector workers join trade unions. Cuban trade unions are organised according to branch or sector, he pointed out, so self-employed or cooperative workers would continue in the same trade unions as when they were state employees: 'It will be those who had no formal employment that the CTC will work with to encourage to join the trade unions.'[32] That constitutes two-thirds of the newly self-employed. The challenge, he explained, was in the form and method of representing and defending workers' rights:

> With workers in a social entity or in a closed centre we can call a meeting or an assembly for everyone to attend. But we cannot tell non-state workers to leave their business, or stop working, to come to the trade union. We are studying ways to address their problems and to represent them . . . we are aware of non-state workers' concerns, about taxes, inspections and fines. We have been transmitting these concerns to the government. Our experience and that of those other institutions has led to the decision to introduce greater flexibility in self-employment legislation.

He is referring to modifications announced a few days earlier permitting the hiring of 'contracted workers' in all authorised self-employment activities, limited and specific tax exemptions, and the exemption from social security payments for those of pension age.

But how can the trade unions ensure that contracted workers have fair representation and protection when they are in the same trade unions as their employers? I asked. 'Contracted workers have an employment licence, have the right to join a union, social security, and the right to a salary as a contracted worker that cannot be less than double the minimum state salary for this employment,' he told me. Freire Cazañas contended that: 'They cannot be exploited or made to work 14 or 15 hours. The trade union is here to prevent violations of their rights. All Cuban workers are protected by collective bargaining agreements.'

Four years down the line, when I discussed the trade unions' work in the self-employed sector with Fundora, it is clear that Freire Cazañas was overly optimistic. Fundora certainly regards it as a 'contradiction' for contracted workers and their employers to be in the same trade union and, while she recognises that theoretically, under socialism, contradictions should be resolvable through dialogue and consensus, in reality 'there is a conflict of interests and a conflict of class there'.[33] This is qualitatively different from a worker participating in a trade union with a director or line manager in a state entity: both are employees of the state. In the self-employed sector, the boss profits personally from the contracted workers' labour, and the disparities between them in terms of income and hierarchy means that they are unlikely to share interests, except in the broadest sense.

With time it has become clear that many self-employed workers are not unionised, either because they were previously in the informal sector or because they have not maintained their membership. A study of private sector shoemakers by Cuban economist Yailenis Mulet Concepción, for example, found that only 25 per cent of workers were unionised and another 29 per cent said they wanted to join a union.[34] Even where workers are in trade unions, said Fundora, there is a failure to appreciate that workers' rights are the product of historical struggles, not 'natural rights' to be taken for granted. The strength of workers' rights guaranteed by the socialist revolution over 60 years has meant the loss of a culture of fighting for labour rights, she explained.

'As a Cuban, I feel that my way of living with rights is passive because I was born with them . . . I have never had to fight, almost never, for rights. The culture of fighting for rights is created in practice and there are many Cubans who don't have this practice.' Many Cuban trade union activists know the law and receive training, she said, but when they need to take action they are unsure how to defend their case. 'We have been protected by the state for so long, with such strong guarantees, that we are disconnected, unable to exercise rights we had taken for granted. This is also why many Cubans get a big shock in terms of labour relations when they go to other countries.'

She went on to ask: 'What role can the trade union have when many workers are willing to put up with anything, to go home with back pain, aching bones, because they want more money?' If the trade union says they must not work more than eight hours, they will respond that they want to – whether this is done through excessive hours in one job, or two employments, which is also permitted. What is more, that exploited worker can retort: 'I would not be prepared to work so many hours if I did not have to pay so much for food.' This reflects a larger structural problem, Fundora explained, as people work more to have more money to cover needs that cost more each day. However, this is not just about subsistence, she added, it also reflects Cubans' rising expectations in terms of consumption.

THE 'BUSINESS' OF SELF-EMPLOYMENT

Indignation from private business owners about their resources being pilfered is, in some cases, ironic, given the sourcing of their own resources. The Cuban government retains centralised control over foreign trade, essentially a monopoly, and, despite the stated intention to establish a wholesale market for self-employed workers, provision has been insufficient.[35] This creates a problem. The self-employed sectors' inputs are often derived from either state supplies or contraband. State resources are habitually stolen by state employees who sell them directly to the private sector, or they are secured through non-legal bulk buying in Cuban retail stores, including products sold at subsidised prices by the Cuban state, leading to shortages and frustration for normal Cuban consumers.[36]

Cuban self-employment, explained Concepción, 'is centred on the circulation and recirculation of goods and services, with a strong tendency towards non-legal growth and very strong links with the so-called submerged [that is, illegal] economy'. It is difficult, therefore, to separate the formal and informal economies in Cuba. Many activities which are legal in terms of the final product are actually illegal from the perspective of the production process: because they involve illegally obtained state materials, and consequently real incomes are not reported. 'This is similar to what occurred in the former USSR and other Eastern European nations,' warned Concepción. Furthermore, 'Self-employment units have developed bogus comparative advantages, whether through price regulations, benefits offered by the informal or submerged economy, or because the needs of a scarcity-afflicted population generate a demand that does not seek quality but only immediate satisfaction.'[37]

Concepción's research led her to conclude that private sector shoemakers 'mistakenly believe that the gains generated through the informal and submerged economy can also be achieved in conditions of free competition and formal institutionalisation.' This is no doubt relevant to most activities in Cuba's private sector.

As long as the so-called entrepreneurs benefit from private accumulation, they will push for greater freedoms for market forces; they do not perceive the accumulation of private wealth as jeopardising the public wealth which funds the welfare provision that many take for granted as a right. 'This is a sector that doesn't pay for their hospital treatment, that doesn't pay for the education of their children, they have the best of both worlds, of both systems,' Ricardo Alarcón, former president of Cuba's National Assembly, pointed out.[38]

Concepción's study of private shoemakers illustrates the tendencies inherent in the self-employed sector. Private shoemakers meet 70 per cent of domestic demand, producing 8 million pairs of shoes a year to the state's 5.3 million.[39] Excluding producers affiliated to the Cuban Association of Artists and Craftsmen, there are 2,065 shoe manufacturers and sellers registered as self-employed, plus 5,226 cobblers and 175 tanners. Over 12,000 people in the private sector are associated with the shoe production chain but only 60 per cent of them are officially registered. Of those, 40 per cent are small to medium businesses, 15 per cent are owners of the business and the rest are individual workers.[40]

While the tax office calculates tax dues on the assumption that one pair of shoes is sold every day, established manufacturers knock out up to 160 pairs a day. Business owners employ an average of ten to fifteen workers a day but declare one or two. Most of those are young people between 17 and 30 years old, with no training as shoemakers and no legal contract with the shoemaker. The businesses were started with an average initial investment of around USD 16,000 and 80 per cent of the raw materials have to be imported and include contraband. Altogether 90 per cent of Concepción's interviewees said there were no opportunities to obtain qualifications, apparently unaware of state-run trade schools for shoemakers. Most of the shoes retail for between USD 6 and USD 16 a pair, high quality shoes for up to USD 50; 70 per cent were sold wholesale, showing the prevalence of intermediaries. The basic cost of production was roughly 50 per cent of the sale price. But none of the interviewees kept balance sheets or financial status records for their business. 'We shadowed some businesses, estimating that the minimum net monthly income was USD 452 – 10 times the average Cuban salary.'[41] A lucrative business by Cuban standards.

Interestingly, only 15 per cent of the shoemakers interviewed said they wanted to access foreign investment. More significantly, however, given the government's objective of limiting the concentration of wealth and property, 85 per cent of interviewees said they had investments in other businesses and 40 per cent considered state control over their business to be excessive.[42] In other words, the innate tendency to expand and demand more 'freedom' for market forces is clearly evident.

Concepción divided the earning capacity of Cuba's self-employed workers into three groups according to size. The first and smallest group enjoyed an average income 17 times the average salary in Cuba (which was then CUP 600). The income of the second group was 2.7 times the average. The third and largest group earned 6 times the average.[43] Some have other incomes; in 2016, 17 per cent of licence holders for self-employment were salaried workers augmenting their incomes.[44]

The simplified view is that self-employment in Cuba provides an impetus for an emerging private enterprise. Advocates of market reforms in Cuba refer to all self-employed Cubans as 'entrepreneurs' regardless of their status, occupation or revenues. However, researcher Jenny Morín points out that most are not successful entrepreneurs. Indeed, she insists, there are self-employed workers who struggle to subsist. During the Special Period, as part of the 'lucha' (struggle) to get by, many Cubans sought 'inventos' (invented solutions) to 'resolver' (resolve problems); they sought and invented various endeavours to earn additional incomes to maintain their families, with or without licences. Self-employment continues to be a subsistence strategy today, claims Morín. The success stories are written by those who receive financial help from outside Cuba through remittances, those who integrate into informal networks of entrepreneurs and 'suppliers', and those with links to the tourism sector.[45]

In 2016 women were hugely under-represented in the self-employed sector making up just 30 per cent.[46] Only 8 per cent of self-employed women were business owners and there was a gender divide according to occupation. 'The best paid activities – plumbers, bricklayers, carpenters – are almost always done by men and paid more,' Blanca Munster pointed out. 'Women you mainly see in sales or cleaning – selling DVDs or working in a restaurant, and that is as salaried employees, hired, not owners.'[47] In the non-agricultural cooperatives women made up 22 per cent of members and just 13.6 per cent in agricultural cooperatives in 2015.[48] This is a huge step backward in a country where women make up 66 per cent of the labour force, including more than 60 per cent of all professionals, and over half of all scientists.[49]

KEEPING THE GENIE IN THE BOTTLE

The rules and regulations which hold back the development of the non-state sector in Cuba are not 'mistakes' or arbitrary. They are measures designed precisely to restrict the growth of private businesses, the concentration of capital and the inevitable growth of inequality. For example, there are no inheritance rights associated with these private businesses, licences are personal and non-transferable. Specialisation within an activity – such as shoemaking – is not permitted, which restricts the division of labour; licenses are only granted for 'producer–vendors' and each licence holder must partake in the whole process, from design to commercialisation.[50]

Another Cuban economist, Saira Pons explained that the tax on the use of a labour force reflects 'the need to establish mechanisms to discourage the growth of microenterprises . . . a progressive tax base has been implemented, such that more taxes are paid as more workers are hired'.[51] However, there was also a schedule in place to reduce this tax significantly between 2015 and 2017. Pons points to the high risk 'that tax liabilities can exceed the net profit', incentivising businesses to raise sales prices or evade taxes. In 2014, 60 per cent of audited taxpayers had underpaid. There is also a high tax rate for personal income tax, and surveys confirm that a 'significant portion of self-employed workers consider it necessary to evade taxes, even though they recognize it is a felony for which they could be severely punished. That attitude is reinforced by the fact that tax authorities still lack mechanisms to know the actual income of taxpayers.'[52] The need to create a progressive, redistributive and inviolable taxation apparatus has become a priority in Cuba, a country where taxes were all but eliminated for decades.

PUTTING ON THE BRAKES

In August 2017 there was a freeze on the issuing of licences for self-employment and non-agricultural cooperatives (CNAs) while authorities addressed the impact of those sectors and worked to create an adequate legislative framework to enforce taxation, prevent exploitative practices, put limits on private accumulation and strengthen mechanisms to ensure that private profits have social benefits. The issuing of licences was not resumed until December 2018 and it came with new regulations which tightened account-keeping and clamped down on tax avoidance. However, two unpopular measures, that self-employed workers be limited to holding one licence, and that restaurants could not exceed 50 seats, were eliminated following complaints from those sectors.

This reflects the drive from private interests for greater space to be opened up for market forces and their growing clout as an interest group.

Beyond this there are broader, more conceptual challenges to address. In the non-state sector efficiency, competitiveness and results are stimulated by material incentives – essentially the profit motive. At the same time the state affirms that: 'In non-state management forms, the concentration of property and material and financial wealth in non-state natural or legal persons will not be allowed.'[53] In other words, material incentives stimulate production and services in these areas, but the profit motive is constrained by the imperative of maintaining the dominance of non-exploitative social-relations; keeping the market mechanisms within a socialist framework; and restraining inequalities. In his critique of the Soviet political economy, Che Guevara pointed out: 'Individual material interest was the arm of capital par excellence and today it is elevated as a lever of development, but it is limited by the existence of a society where exploitation is not permitted. In these conditions, man neither develops his fabulous productive capacities, nor does he develop himself as the conscious builder of a new society.'[54] Cuba now confronts a similar conundrum.

Significantly, however, unlike the *Soviet Manual of Political Economy*, the Cuban leaders overseeing the reform process, particularly Raúl Castro and Miguel Díaz Canel, have portrayed the space given to the private sector as a necessary concession, not an inherent aspect of socialist society. At the outset, Raúl Castro declared: 'I am a firm admirer and defender of large socialist state enterprises, be they agricultural, industrial, or otherwise.'[55] He made clear that the reforms were understood as measures of expediency, not political preference. Díaz-Canel described the 'very intense debates' following the introduction of the *Guidelines* which concluded with the need to update the economy in the unfavourable circumstances of the US blockade. 'We have conceived and recognised a non-state sector of the economy . . . it is not the private sector, let's say, of neoliberalism. It is a non-state sector, a private sector that complements what is done from the state enterprise, which relates to the state company or to the State, which is in the economic plan and in our planning.'[56]

The imperative of controlling the private sector is also a question of national security for Cuba. Morín points out that Obama's policy of empowering Cuban civil society and private sector actors, 'which include both self-employed workers, NGOs and opponents of the Castro regime', was intended to create a social base economically independent of the Cuban government.[57] She states that microenterprises, not self-employed workers, were the greatest beneficiaries of Obama's new policy, which softened the US blockade in areas that could be key for private sector expansion in Cuba.[58]

García Brigos points out that the concentration of property, as a possession of resources and income, is an inevitable process of accumulation which has external linkages and financing (through remittances) that link this form of ownership to Cubans and other actors abroad. It also fosters marketing chains that recycle production from state sources, generating a process of speculation. It generates the use of imported resources over which the state does not exercise control or effective regulation. It is clear why the Obama administration advocated financial and economic exchange with Cuba's non-state sector.

Trade unions play an especially important role, according to García Brigos, because as well as being directly linked with economic activity they are spaces for social reproduction, linked to the daily life of workers and their families and representing diverse interests. 'It is no coincidence that the US government pays special attention to the work of the unions,' he writes, 'supporting the creation of "free trade unions" in Cuba, the strengthening of "civil society", the development of "democracy", "free elections", "freedom of expression", as Obama clearly expressed in his intervention on December 17, 2014.'[59] In that speech Obama said: 'While Cuba has made reforms to gradually open up its economy, we continue to believe that Cuban workers should be free to form unions, just as their citizens should be free to participate in the political process.'[60] Of course Obama meant trade unions operating outside the socialist state apparatus.

NON-AGRICULTURAL COOPERATIVES

The non-agricultural cooperatives (CNAs) authorised from December 2012 are generally considered to be more compatible than the private sector with the socialist system in Cuba.[61] However, they also present challenges. Most of the nearly 500 cooperatives set up were 'conversions', where the state announced it was shutting down an enterprise and gave workers the option to form a cooperative instead. García Brigos referred to this as 'creating cooperatives that from their own emergence have little to do with the essential principals of this [cooperative] movement'.[62] They have not been raised from the base by an association of free producers. By late 2014, 384 cooperatives had been established through this kind of conversion. Another 114 had been set up through 'self-effort', that is, by the initiative of three of more workers. Nearly half (43 per cent) of the total CNAs were eateries of some sort, 14 per cent were in construction and 6.5 per cent in personal and technical services.

In his report on Cuba's new CNAs, Cliff DuRand from the Center for Global Justice in Mexico pointed out that the socialisation of workers into self-managed cooperatives does not occur automatically. 'It is a gradual process of learning, particularly when a cooperative is converted from a state enterprise previously defined by hierarchical relations between workers and management.' He gives the example of an elected manager in a 'converted' cooperative that makes traditional Cuban guayabera shirts and dresses, who referred to her fellow associates as 'my workers', even though she effectively answers to them in their monthly General Assembly meetings. 'Old habits run deep,' he said, 'and it appeared that the main change for her under the new model was that she no longer had to clear her decisions with higher authorities, and now enjoys some autonomy. For this reason, the country's Institute of Philosophy conducts regular training workshops for new cooperatives, educating members and managers in practices of democratic self-management.'[63]

García Brigos argues that, while under capitalism, cooperatives are only linked to the system through markets, under socialism they must be integrated into state structures. Rather than being viewed as autonomous cells within the system, they must contribute to the political decisions made by the whole of society which guide economic development. They must function genuinely as reproducers of values of social cooperation not just 'groups that get together to do business' or 'to have greater incomes'.[64] García Brigos asks: 'How to deal with cooperative workers who are only concerned with the possibility of earning more?' This takes us back to the question of trade unions: 'How do we deal with union work in a cooperative?'[65] The answers are not yet apparent.

In mid-2015 a set of changes were approved to strengthen CNAs, including the extension of both the grace period of taxes and the maximum contract that could be offered to non-members from three months to one year.[66] Then, as explained above, there was a freeze on new licences from August 2016 while authorities addressed inadequacies in the financial management of the existing CNAs and in anticipation of a new comprehensive Cooperative Law, which still had not been introduced by September 2019, even though the issuing of licenses resumed in December 2018.

In May 2016, the Cuban website CubaDebate published its own study of the country's 69 construction cooperatives, 42 of which were in Havana. Within 2 years the membership of those 69 cooperatives had grown from 518 workers to 3,127 members.[67] Most of the cooperatives worked directly for state entities, so their 'client' could purchase the materials they needed at the subsidised prices accessible to state institutions. Otherwise, the cooperatives had to purchase materials and tools with a 20 per cent discount from the Ministry of Domestic Trade.

Enquiring about the social contribution of those cooperatives, CubaDebate found there was a tendency to put aside social projects in favour of more profitable work. 'The tendency is to search in the market for what generates hard currency in the contract, because the profit is assumed to be significant.'[68] The total income for these cooperatives in 2015 was CUP 1.25 billion, comparable to the income of the Ministry of Construction itself. This is complicated, however, because, while the Ministry's earnings are calculated with an exchange rate of CUP 1 to CUC 1, the cooperatives use an exchange rate of CUP 25 to CUC 1. This means that each CUC they earn counts as CUP 25, whereas each CUC the Ministry earns counts as CUP 1 (or more, where the new exchange rates have been introduced).[69] Cooperatives are not [yet] authorised to purchase equipment or means of transportation, and what adds most to their costs is the need to hire transport.

The average salary for the cooperative members in 2016 was CUP 4,400 per month (over 7 times the average state salary), although in some cooperatives this was as high as CUP 8,000 (13 times higher). With salaries in the cooperative sector substantially higher than for construction workers in the state sector, state employees will inevitably be tempted to shift to cooperatives where the opportunity arises. 'Do cooperatives means the end of corruption?' CubaDebate asked their interviewees. 'Yes', says one, 'there is no stealing.' 'No', says another, explaining that their cooperative had to expel a group who were stealing and selling-on scrap materials. Another says that if a member steals, the value of the good is deducted from their wage and it is explained that they are stealing from themselves and their partners.

At the outset of the process, the formation of CNAs was described as 'experimental', rather than as a form of social production integral to Cuban socialist development. This had not changed by late 2019. However, as the contradictions thrown up by the small business sector grow, many Cubans have complained that more effort has not been made to foster and expand CNAs instead.

THE NEW CONSTITUTION OF 2019

The introduction of the new constitution was deemed necessary to safeguard the legacy of the Revolution of 1959, in the absence of the veteran generation, the historic leaders who made it, to formalise the political-economy changes made since 1976 and to prepare for the new leadership generation. In 2013, Raúl Castro had set up a special commission to draft the new constitution, which he headed, and in April 2016 he told the National Assembly: 'Everything we have been doing must be reflected in the Constitution.'[70] However, to gain legitimacy and acceptance from the Cuban people, the new constitution had to be subject to national debate, like the *Guidelines,* the *Conceptualisation* document and *Plan 2030* before them. This process coincided with the handover to Miguel Díaz-Canel as the new president of Cuba's Council of State from April 2018.[71]

Proposals to incorporate changes came under more than one heading. Some were concerned with the introduction of new forms of ownership and management, including private businesses with employees. The increased space for market exchanges and the effort to foster foreign investment had generated contradictions within the socialist development framework which needed to be addressed in order to be controlled. The ability to do so, however, had been limited not just by the complexity of the challenge, but also because of the lack of a legal framework and fiscal apparatus. The reforms created social relations which technically violated the 1976 Constitution, notwithstanding the constitutional amendments of 1992 which reduced mandatory state ownership to the 'fundamental' means of production. The private businesses which emerged post–2010 were a legal anomaly. Thus, their income was deemed as personal, subject to different liabilities than the profits of state or foreign companies or cooperatives, with no reductions associated with investment, production losses, commercialisation expenses and other circumstances.[72]

Another set of proposals for the 2019 Constitution concerned new age limits and lengths of term for appointments to the top government jobs. An additional matter that needed to be addressed was the move towards decentralising administrative and political structures, which had been the subject of experimentation when Havana Province was split into Artemisa and Mayabeque from 2011.

In July 2018, the National Assembly of People's Power held two days of debate over a draft of the new constitution. Once approved, the document was distributed throughout the island for two months of grassroots debates open to everyone in Cuba. Even Cubans living abroad were invited to comment via a website forum. Halfway through the process, Díaz-Canel told an interviewer that he had participated in six grassroots assemblies and that everyone turned up with annotated hard copies of the draft constitution, evidence that they had studied the text. Some approached the discussion as engineers, he said, 'making block diagrams to look for interrelationships'. Three print editions of the constitution had run out, he explained, and requests for additional copies had been received from the most remote mountainous communities. The population's participation was serious and committed he said, claiming that 'the last word will take into account issues that the people raise'.[73]

The claim was given substance after significant changes were made to the draft document following the nationwide debate. First, and the focus of most international commentary, was the proposal to replace the existing recognition of marriage as a union between a man and a woman with the stipulation that it was the union between two people. In an unprecedented development, the evangelical church in Cuba mobilised quite openly against the proposed revision, and the issue was among the most intensely debated across the country. Subsequently, specification about the character of the marriage union was removed from the document and it was announced that the topic would be debated in the process of constituting a new Family Code.[74] Second, the goal of progressing towards a communist society, which had been omitted in the draft constitution, was reinstated by popular demand.[75] That amendment received little attention from external commentators; it contradicted the narrative of a country gradually 'liberalising'.

Unchanged is the (irrevocable) socialist system, the role of the CCP as the country's ideological leadership and emphasis on national unity. Cuba is committed to 'never returning to capitalism as a regime sustained by the exploitation of man by man.'[76] State enterprises remain the mainstay of the economy, and 'Socialist planning constitutes the central component of the system of governance for economic and social development.'[77] The participation of workers in the economy and of labour collectives in management and administration of state entities is key. Social services and other provisions and benefits remain just and free.[78] International relations continue to be guided by the principles of anti-imperialism, proletarian internationalism, international solidarity, Third World unity, and respect for sovereignty and the right to self-determination.

New to the Constitution, but not to the Cuban political economy, is the promotion of foreign investment ('as an important element for the economic development of the country') and private ownership ('exercised over specific means of production . . . [it has] a complementary role in the economy').[79] However, as stated in the *Guidelines*, the state will restrict the private accumulation process: 'The concentration of property in natural or legal persons is regulated by the State, which also guarantees an increasingly just redistribution of wealth in order to conserve the limits that are compatible with the socialist values of equity and social justice.'[80] How the state will guarantee an *increasingly* just redistribution of wealth whilst embedding private enterprise is not clear.

Also newly incorporated is protection of the environment and response to climate change. There is greater specification of the rights, duties and guarantees of Cuban citizens and foreigners, both individual rights and social, economic, cultural and human rights. The Constitution decrees equality before the law, 'without discrimination for reasons of sex, gender, sexual orientation, gender identity, age, ethnic origin, skin colour, religious belief, disability, national or territorial origin, or any other personal condition or circumstance that implies a distinction injurious to human dignity', plus 'equal salary for equal work'. And it states that: 'Women and men have equal rights and responsibilities in the economic, political, cultural, occupational, social, and familial domains, as well as in any other domain.'[81]

The Constitution also restructures national and local government, decentralising and streamlining authority and resources, improving administrative efficiency and popular participation. The Provincial Assemblies of People's Power are replaced by a Provincial Government composed of a Governor and a Provincial Council, which incorporates the presidents and vice presidents of the corresponding Municipal Assemblies of People's Power and the municipal Mayors.[82] Power and responsibility is more balanced at the top of government. New roles of President and Vice President of the Republic and Prime Minister were created. Until now, there has been a President of the Council of State. Now there will be a President of the Republic who is the Head of State, elected for a five-year term by the National Assembly from among its deputies by an absolute majority. They can serve a maximum of two terms and must be aged between 35 and 60 when first elected. The vice president is elected in the same way. The prime minister is the head of government, designated by the president, elected by the National Assembly and presiding over the Council of Ministers.

The redrafted Constitution was put to a straight yes or no referendum in February 2019, 'a complex moment for Cuba', as David Jessop, editor of *Cuba Briefing*, recognised, 'with the economy in recession, growing concerns about what may happen in Venezuela, increasing US hostility, the use of social media to express alternative opinions and to question government decisions, continuing internal differences over the economy, and the continuing transition to a younger generation of leaders who do not have the same moral authority as the country's historic figures'.[83] It was approved by nearly 87 per cent of voters, with a turnout of over 84 per cent.[84] A flurry of legislation is set to follow as the provisions of the Constitution are codified in law.

CHALLENGES AHEAD

In his famous 1965 letter, 'Socialism and Man in Cuba', Che Guevara warned: 'Pursuing the chimera of achieving socialism with the aid of the blunted weapons left to us by capitalism (the commodity as the economic cell, profitability, and individual material interest as levers, etc.) it is possible to come to a blind alley ... Meanwhile, the adapted economic base has undermined the development of consciousness.'[85] Aware that Cuba's former President of the National Assembly Ricardo Alarcón is well versed in Guevara's writings, when we met in December 2016 I asked him about the relevance of this warning for contemporary Cuba.

'Look from the corner of this house and you will see the blunted weapons of capitalism surround us on every side,' he replied. 'Because inevitably, we have had to make a series of concessions, that is the only word for it.' However, 'Not everything is a concession, because there are things that did not have to be in the way they were.' He is referring to the excessive state control, which was never originally intended but resulted from the Great Revolutionary Offensive of 1968 when the remaining small non-agricultural private sector in Cuba was nationalised. This was presented as a necessary response to actions by private businesses which undermined the state's ability to direct the economy. Acknowledging the 'fairly large and growing sector of workers who are employees of a private employer', Alarcón admitted, 'I am not sure there's an answer for that. Logically, it suits us that it grows, but we have to be careful, because private interests are concentrating. To remain a socialist revolution, it must be of the working class, because there is no other socialism than that. And the Party, as the vanguard of that class, must promote its interests against those who are extracting surplus value from it, which is no longer a foreign company or an ultra-powerful monopoly. There are tens of thousands of private interests that have been created by us. All this is very complicated.'[86] García Brigos points out that Cuba has the objective necessity of producing more, with greater efficiency, quality, efficacy, to compete successfully in the hostile context of neoliberal globalised capital, which will not disappear with the lifting of the US blockade and all the current restrictions by the United States, whilst maintaining its socialist sense of development.[87] Complex indeed;

and history has shown that the socialist apparatus can be dismantled without a shot being fired either to destroy or defend it.

Are new socioeconomic classes emerging in Cuba? 'I think that someone who has a private restaurant, money and employees is in a different class to me,' says Isabel Allende, Director of the Higher Institute of International Relations when we met in Havana. 'But hey, we have to live with it because it is clear that otherwise the State cannot continue doing what it does [social welfare provision and so on]. Maybe if the Soviet Union still existed we could continue as we were, but it does not exist anymore, nor will it return.'[88] While a significant number of Cubans are emerging with higher monetary incomes, and with the means for accumulating wealth, Cuba is nowhere near seeing the kind of class privilege that determines access to services such as health care, education, sport and culture. That will not change as long as the system of universal, free, socialist welfare remains a key tenet of the Revolution and a parallel private system is prohibited.

Allende admits to having been 'extraordinarily worried' about the future of the Cuban Revolution given the ageing population, the emigration of young people, growing discontent among the population, and the complicated process of updating the economic model. But, she explains, following the death of Fidel Castro on 25 November 2016 she stopped worrying. I ask her why. 'Because of the young people,' she says, 'I did not expect the young people to react as they did to the death of Fidel. And it was a spontaneous reaction, they were not mobilised by anyone. The young people felt the death of Fidel and they knew that something very important had gone, but that there is still something to defend. Young people took to the streets and went to pay tribute to Fidel. It was the youth, not the old people. I know young people who are neither members of the Union of Young Communists, nor are they especially concerned about politics, who in the days of mourning asked everyone to show respect. So I'm not so worried because there are still young people who value what we have.'

Evidence that Cuban youth remain engaged was provided by their participation in the constitutional debates and the elections to the National Assembly in spring 2018. The average age of delegates fell from 57 to 49 years old; the youngest was a black woman aged 19. A generational transition is underway. The sense that the Cuban youth retain a collective and revolutionary sensitivity was reinforced by their spontaneous mobilisation following the rare and devastating tornado which struck Havana in January 2019, killing 4 people, injuring nearly 200 and damaging or destroying over 8,300 homes. Young Cubans from across the island mobilised to help those affected and contribute to the recovery and reconstruction. The state, by then presided over by Díaz-Canel, also proved its efficiency in the face of the disaster: within less than five months, 80 per cent of the reconstruction work had been completed.[89]

The Cuban Revolution is cautiously advancing along a tightrope, balancing between the plan and the market. This was symbolised by President Díaz-Canel's September 2018 visit to New York for the UN General Assembly. There he delivered a blistering attack on capitalism and imperialism, later addressing thousands of solidarity activists at an event in Harlem. But he also sat down with corporate executives 'in the belly of the beast' encouraging them to invest in Cuba.

The challenge is exacerbated by multiple economic, social, political and environmental factors: budget deficits, hard currency shortage, low productivity and wages, difficulties in accessing foreign capital, distortions of accounting and incentives derived from the dual currency, inadequate housing provision, the exodus of qualified professionals from the state to the private sector, emigration of young Cubans overseas, and natural and environmental disasters. Ultimately the revolutionary people of Cuba will determine how the contradictions inherent in the process of updating the economy are to be resolved and in whose interests. But there are also extremely adverse external factors beyond their control which limit the room for manoeuvre: the crisis in Venezuela and its impact on the Cuban economy, and the loss of allies and trade partners in Latin America (including the end of the Mais Medicos programme in Brazil) and, most especially, the extra-territorial impact of escalating hostility from the US government.

In early 2019, the Trump administration significantly tightened the US blockade, enacting Title III of the 1996 Helms–Burton Act among other measures. This has intensified both the challenges and restraints the island confronts. These measures are so aggressive that they threaten to push the revolutionary people back into survival mode. The following chapter discusses these developments and their impact.

10

SURVIVING INTO THE POST-RAPPROCHEMENT PERIOD

In spring 2019, sporadic electricity blackouts returned to areas of Cuba and state control over the distribution of basic goods was increased to protect the population against growing scarcities. The talk was of whether the island would see a return to the conditions which characterised the economic crisis of the 1990s. From a political economy perspective, the principal concern is less how socialist Cuba can balance between the plan and the market, and more about how the revolutionary people will survive in the post-rapprochement period, with the inexorable, all-consuming slog towards the United States presidential elections of November 2020 in which attitudes towards Cuba and Venezuela will be a litmus test for candidates in both parties. Under the Trump administration, and particularly from autumn 2018, hostility towards Cuba has been ratcheted up, with rhetoric reminiscent of the Cold War and an injurious tightening of the US blockade. What happened?

In late December 2016, three weeks before Donald Trump entered the Oval Office, lead Cuban negotiator Josefina Vidal told me that it was 'too early' to predict the incoming administration's stance on Cuba. Vidal was head of the United States Department at the Ministry of Foreign Relations and had led Cuba's team in the secret talks which produced the rapprochement under Obama in December 2014.[1] During the US presidential campaign, it emerged that businessman Trump sent corporate representatives to Cuba in 1998, violating the US blockade, and again in the 2000s, to probe for openings. In September 2015 he told an interviewer, 'The concept of opening with Cuba is fine.'[2] The US business sector was keen to trade with and invest in Cuba and the political cost had already been paid by Obama.

A year later, however, by then a serious presidential contender, Trump told an audience of right-wing Cuban exiles in Miami that 'all of the concessions that Obama has granted the Castro regime were done through executive order which means the next president can reverse them and that is exactly what I will do unless the Castro regime meets our demands.'[3] After winning the presidency in November 2016, he insulted millions of Cubans with his tweets following Fidel Castro's death later that month and incorporated three pro-US blockade, anti-rapprochement Cuban-Americans into his transition team. There were mixed messages, however. Vidal pointed out that: 'other functionaries, businessmen, that Trump has named, including in government roles, are in favour of business with Cuba ... so we have to wait for the government to take office, start governing, start making policy decisions. Based on what has been said so far we find it difficult to make an objective assessment.'[4]

The then Secretary of State Rex Tillerson had promised to announce the administration's new Cuba policy, but nothing had happened by 2 May 2017, when right-wing Florida Senator and second-generation Cuban-American Marco Rubio marched into the White House to demand Trump get on with reversing Obama's rapprochement towards Cuba. Trump had a one-seat majority in the Senate and Rubio was an indispensable vote.[5] With little personal interest, Trump had outsourced his Cuba policy to Rubio. 'According to one report when he was elected the only instruction about Cuba [Trump] gave to his senior aides was "make Rubio happy",' explained William LeoGrande a leading scholar on US–Cuba relations.[6] Rubio became a member of the Senate Intelligence Committee's investigation into accusations of Russian meddling in the 2016 election.

In mid-June 2017, Trump went to Miami to announce: 'I am cancelling the last administration's completely one-sided deal with Cuba.' He committed to restricting travel between the US and Cuba, prohibiting commerce with Cuban businesses owned by the military and intelligence services, and to convening an Internet Task Force.[7] In September 2017, 60 per cent of the staff at the US embassy in Havana were withdrawn following the still disputed claim that 24 US officials, and subsequently 14 Canadian diplomats, were subject to some sort of undetectable attack causing brain damage and other symptoms.[8] Initially this was labelled as a 'sonic attack' or 'acoustic attack', then microwaves were blamed, and finally, with no causal explanation available, it was simply referred to as 'Havana Syndrome'. The first people affected, just days after Trump won the presidency in November 2016, were the CIA agents posted under diplomatic cover in the US embassy, but the 'incident' was not exposed until August 2017.[9]

The reduction of US embassy staff was the pretext to effectively close consular services on the island. Cubans applying to travel legally are now obliged to journey overseas to apply for a visa, without any guarantee of acceptance, an additional cost and time burden designed to minimise legal travel.[10] Another result of the 'sonic attacks' allegation, and the mysterious 'Havana Syndrome', was to mute the US business community, who might overwise lobby to keep rapprochement. LeoGrande explained that business people 'were concerned that if they defended the policy of engagement they might end up defending an engagement with a government that had attacked US diplomats. That was just something politically they were not interested in doing.'[11] Thus in November 2017, when the US Department of State published a list of Cuban entities which US businesses were prohibited from dealing with and which US travellers were banned from patronising, there was little kick back from the business community.[12]

A so-called 'grandfather clause' meant that businesses already engaging with Cuba, with licences issued under Obama, were not affected, and that included those with 'contingency contracts', open-ended licences incorporating future projects. Furthermore, the list could be bypassed by changing the company name. US lawyer Robert Muse, an expert in US laws relating to Cuba, concluded in late November 2017 that the Trump administration was leaving in place the possibility of improving relations in the future but, he added, the wild card is Rubio – the administration reacts when he makes a noise.[13]

In February 2018, Trump's new Cuba Internet Task Force, set up to promote 'the free and unregulated flow of information' to the island, met for the first time.[14] The following month, when I asked young Cuban television journalist Cristina Escobar for her view, she described it as 'symbolic', and yet another justification for the money spent on regime change programmes: 'They have tried to use the internet to create social disorder in Cuba, but they haven't achieved it,' she said. 'Actually, the real outcome has been that conservative voices inside the Cuban government have used this as an excuse to stop the opening of the internet in Cuba, pointing out that "the enemy is using the internet against us". And the thing is that they are. It's a fact. But you can't ban the internet because it's a reality and we need to be in that battle.'[15] In summer 2018, US government plans to create 'native' and 'non-branded', apparently Cuban, Facebook accounts propagated with US government-created regime-change content were exposed.[16] Cuban Facebook users will be unaware of their true provenance. Despite this, President Díaz-Canel is pushing for Cuban institutions and officials to embrace the internet and social media and has initiated an 'e-government' implementation programme. In May 2019, it was announced that private Wi-Fi networks, cybercafes and the importation of equipment such as routers would be permitted.[17]

Throughout 2018, the Bilateral Commissions set up during rapprochement to discuss collaboration between the US and Cuba on issues of mutual interest were continuing, as were business relations and other official exchanges. A high-profile meeting took place in Cuba between the Chair of the Senate Foreign Relations Committee, Republican Bob Corker, and President Díaz-Canel in September 2018. Later that month, during his trip to New York for the United Nations General Assembly, Díaz-Canel met top executives from Google, VaynerMedia, Connectify, Mapbox, McKinsey & Company, Virgin Group, AirBnB, Revolution, Twitter, Microsoft, Bloomberg and Cresta to discuss developing IT capacity in Cuba.

However, the April 2018 appointments of neoliberal ideologues Mike Pompeo as Secretary of State and John Bolton as the National Security Advisor presaged a new stage in the Trump Administration.[18] Bolton has a long history of animosity towards Cuba. Previous chapters have mentioned how in 2002, as a member of President George W. Bush's administration, Bolton had accused Cuba of developing biological weapons, despite opposition from the intelligence community, and, as LeoGrande says, 'then tried to have fired the intelligence analysts who had objected to the invention'.[19] The *New York Times* described Bolton's return to government as heralding 'the most radically aggressive foreign policy team around the American president in modern memory'.[20] Bolton appointed Mauricio Claver-Carone, another second-generation Cuban-American opposed to rapprochement who had served in Trump's transition team, as Latin-America Office Director at the National Security Council.[21]

On 1 November 2018, just before the mid-term elections, Bolton was applauded by an audience in Miami as he announced a new wave of sanctions against what he labelled as the 'Troika of Tyranny' – Cuba, Nicaragua and Venezuela.[22] The objective was clear, said LeoGrande, and was even communicated off record to the media by some administration officials: to overthrow the Maduro government in Venezuela, ending oil exports to Cuba, causing economic collapse on the island and enabling the overthrow of the Cuban government, leaving Nicaragua as an easy third target. 'And in this way socialism would be extirpated from the western Hemisphere.'[23] As efforts to overthrow Maduro floundered, the attacks on Cuba became more frenzied.

By mid-January 2019, Pompeo was threatening to enact Title III of the Cuban Liberty and Democratic Solidarity (Libertad) Act of 1996, known as the Helms–Burton Act, which authorises US nationals with claims to property nationalised in Cuba after the Revolution to file suits in US courts against persons 'trafficking' in that property.[24] Title III had been suspended by presidential decree every six months for 23 years, including three times by Trump, but Pompeo announced it would now be held over for 45 days only. This was a threat designed to scare off foreign investors from Cuba at a time when foreign capital has been awarded a pivotal role in the island's development strategy. One week later, US-backed Venezuelan opposition leader Juan Guaidó nominated himself as that country's president, but hopes that he would rally the military and the general public to sweep out the Maduro government were soon dashed. Cuba refused to withdraw support for the Venezuelan government or to enter mediation to resolve the crisis without Maduro's approval. Pompeo squeezed tighter, announcing that Title III would be activated from 19 March, but only in relation to the Cuban companies included on the November 2017 List of Restricted Entities.

On 17 April 2019, the 58th anniversary of the Bay of Pigs invasion in 1961, Bolton and Pompeo announced that Title III would be enacted from 2 May; that 'U-turn financial transactions' (which Cuba uses to circumvent sanctions and access hard currency and the US banking system) would be blocked, cutting off Cuba's access to dollar-denominated transactions; that non-family travel to the island would be limited; that caps would be imposed on the value of personal remittances (at USD 4,000 annually); and that visa restrictions would be enforced on foreigners 'trafficking in confiscated properties' (Title IV of the Helms–Burton Act). Talks under the Bilateral Commissions were finally closed down, against the wishes of officials involved on both sides.[25]

On 30 April 2019, Trump tweeted the warning: 'If Cuban Troops and Militia do not immediately CEASE military and other operations . . .[in]. . . Venezuela, a full and complete embargo, together with the highest-level sanctions, will be placed on the island of Cuba.'[26] The attempted coup earlier that day by Guaidó had fizzled out despite US support. Seeking excuses, Bolton had accused Cuba of propping up the Maduro regime with at least 20,000 Cuban troops. It was another sinister fabrication, depicting Cuban healthcare workers in the country as military personnel.[27] Cuban foreign minister, Bruno Rodríguez tweeted back that Bolton was a 'pathological liar who misinforms Trump'. Those were not Cuban troops in Venezuela, 'only medical staff on humanitarian missions'.[28]

The next day, millions of people took to the streets in Cuba and Venezuela to celebrate International Workers Day and demonstrate defiance. On 2 May, Title III was fully enacted. The first two claims were filed immediately in US courts against Carnival Cruise Lines, an international business with headquarters in Florida. The claimants had not been forcibly removed from their premises in Cuba by the Rebel Army: they were the 'descendants' of dock owners in Havana and Santiago de Cuba.[29] Carnival was being sued, their lawyer stated, for profiting from: 'Property that was confiscated from our clients wrongfully by the communist government of Cuba in 1960.'[30] The term 'confiscated', along with 'expropriated', are applied to delegitimise the nationalisations carried out by the revolutionary government in accordance with international norms, including the offer of compensation which US interests turned down on the advice of their own government. The legal action clarified that even those US businesses exempted from the November 2017 List of Restricted Entities, because of their pre-existing licenses granted under Obama, would be targeted under Title III.

How many further claims can we expect to follow? One source cites 6,000 certified claims for US properties totalling an estimated USD 8 billion in current values.[31] The State Department says the number of lawsuits could soar to 200,000. Claims are limited to properties worth more than USD 50,000 when nationalised (more than USD 427,000 today), in commercial use and which are not used by diplomatic missions.[32] The cost of legal action will rule out smaller claims. What matters, however, is the uncertainty this presents for international businesses. 'Cuba's not an easy place for foreign investors to do business anyway,' said LeoGrande, 'and so adding one more risk on top of the existing ones is going to discourage everyone except the most intrepid investors . . . it's a very serious sanction.'[33]

The Cuban government responded indignantly and within days measures were introduced to control the availability of some basic foodstuffs and other products on the island, to ensure scarce goods were distributed fairly and to prevent hoarding. First, limits were placed on shop purchases per person of some goods and for other foodstuffs Cubans were required to present their ration card before buying.[34] Queues formed outside stores when certain items entered. Second, the government worked hard to source products from origins unaffected by the tightened US sanctions. The official position is that, with broader trade relations and a more diversified economy, Cuba will not return to the traumatic post-Soviet crisis conditions.[35] Third, from 1 July 2019, nearly half of Cuba's state sector employees saw their salaries rise substantially, along with all pensions, directly benefiting over 2.75 million Cubans. Fourth, a broader set of reforms to increase national production was also announced. The latter two measures were announced by President Díaz-Canel on the *Mesa Redonda*, a live televised current affairs programme, and are explained below.

THE TELECOMS EXEMPTION

In mid-May 2019, I asked an employee at Google what the impact of Title III would be on the 'peering agreement' signed six weeks earlier between Google and Cuba's telecoms monopoly ETECSA to build a physical infrastructure connecting their networks and speeding up global internet data flows into and out of Cuba.[36] An initial agreement signed in the last week of the Obama administration, on 12 December 2016, had seen Google install 'edge caching and services nodes' on the island in 2017, enabling Cubans to access Google content cached on local servers.[37] Since then, the employee said, 'We have seen tremendous growth, on YouTube in particular, which bodes well for our products more generally. We are seeing a ground up thirst for a lot of our products. In that way there's certainly a commercial case to be made. If you also look at the infrastructure in the region, and how Google is situated geographically, it's quite strategic from a commercial standpoint to have connections through Cuba.'[38] In December 2018, ETECSA rolled out a 3G service facilitating connection to the internet directly via mobile phones in Cuba, and within three months 2 million Cubans had signed up. Millions more use government-provided Wi-Fi hot spots in hundreds of public areas throughout the island.[39]

Despite Title III, the Google employee informed me that, 'We feel positively about our work going forwards because of the existing carve outs.' He is referring to the exemption written into the Helms–Burtons Act in 1996 permitting US telecommunications firms to do business with Cuba. Jorge Mas Canosa, the notorious Cuban-American leader who drove through the legislation under President Clinton, presided over a large phone cable system and the exemption was introduced to protect his interests.[40] 'The general spirit of the law is that if you are providing information into Cuba, that is seen as "blessed" by the US government, it is not subject to US sanctions. The caveat is that the law was written in 1996 before the internet was really a thing and a company like Google really existed. It will be hard for regulators to try to place some of our initiatives within the scope of the spirit of the law when it was written in 1996.' As a telecommunications company, Google was not required to secure a licence under Obama because of this general authorisation. Nonetheless, some Google apps are unavailable on the island, not because of Cuban government objections, but because of the US blockade.[41]

Pedro Freye, a Cuban-American legal expert, recognised that the Google agreement would create a dilemma for the US administration: 'Free information and greater connectivity with Cuba has been a long-held US objective,' he claimed. 'But how does that square with Washington's new policy to get tough on Cuba? It's a contradiction.'[42] While the Google employee recognises that the Trump administration could attempt to shut down all contact with Cuba, he added: 'Legally I am not sure they are able to do that because there is, specifically, this carve out for telecommunications. I remain quite confident that we can move forward.'[43] For others trying to engage with Cuba, however, he recognises this as a really sour moment. 'It's not just that there's been a reversal from the Obama administration, that is undoubtedly true. I think you could argue that it's worse than it was in decades.' Even Trump's replacement by a new government committed to returning to rapprochement could not put the lid back on the can of worms already opened by Helms–Burton. Once lawsuits have been filed under Title III, they cannot be reversed or stopped.

One month after Title III targeted foreign investment with Cuba, new measures were suddenly introduced to hit Cuba's tourism sector. On 4 June 2019, the 'people-to-people' category for licensed group travel from the US to Cuba was eliminated with almost immediate effect. This is the category most commonly used by US visitors. The new rules also ended recreational and passenger vessels, including cruise ships, yachts and sail boats, and private aircraft travel. Cruise companies with hundreds of thousands of pre-booked customers switched destinations within one day. In 2018, some 638,000 US citizens visited Cuba, around two-thirds of them on cruises.[44] Commercial airline flights remained unaffected by the new measures, as well as group travel under eleven other licence categories, for example university groups, journalists or professionals. Collin Laverty, president of the US-based NGO Cuba Educational Travel, described the move as 'political grandstanding aimed at Florida in the run up to the 2020 elections'. As well as the millions of Cubans who would suffer, he pointed out: 'It's also terrible for US companies that are providing employment and paying taxes in the US and creating an economic footprint on the island.'[45]

INTERNATIONAL REPUDIATION

Title III was also a direct hit against European interests: in 1997 and 1998 the EU had agreed to freeze legal action in the World Trade Organization (WTO) against the extraterritorial application of US domestic laws, while the US agreed to suspend Title III. EU relations with Cuba had improved, particularly since the Obama rapprochement. 'Now we are again number one in terms of trade with Cuba, overtaking China and Venezuela,' stated Alberto Navarro, EU Ambassador in Havana, in March 2018, 14 months prior to the enactment of Title III.[46] Annual trade between the EU and Cuba is worth around EUR 2.5 billion, although Cuba imports far more than it exports. Eighteen European countries have embassies in Havana, the EU is Cuba's largest donor, having allocated EUR 50 million to Cuba in the 2014–2020 period, including EUR 21 million dedicated to agriculture, EUR 18 million to assist rural electrification and EUR 4 million for 'expert exchange' programmes. Cooperation was focused on higher education, assistance with Cuba's taxation apparatus and digitalisation of the civil register and the *Gaceta Oficial*, the law registry. The EU was also offering Havana its expertise on currency unification.

I asked Navarro why, given the EU desire to increase trade and cooperation with Cuba, almost no action had been taken to protect EU interests from US legislation, despite the legal frameworks existing to do so. The US Treasury's Office of Foreign Asset Control had imposed multimillion and multibillion dollar fines on European financial institutions and companies for trading with Cuba (*prior* to the enactment of Title III). 'The EU should be more assertive about the US embargo,' Navarro conceded, recognising that, 'the biggest burden on development in Cuba is the US embargo, no doubt about that.' This was not easy, he explained. Cuba represents 0.1 per cent, or less, of the EU's external trade; miniscule compared to the interests of EU members in the United States, the global superpower. 'So, you understand that member states are very cautious sometimes.'[47] In January 2018, during her visit to Havana, Federica Mogherini, EU High Representative for Foreign Affairs and Security Policy, had publicly described the US blockade as 'illegal'.

Even before the threat of Title III, the uncertainty generated by Trump's Cuba policy meant companies and banks were halting operations with Cuba in fear of fines. Navarro listed European banks which had withdrawn financial services from anything linked to Cuba. 'They should make a statue to the companies that are able to operate in Cuba and the United States at the same time – there are not many. A good example is [Spanish hotel chain] Meliá, the largest operator of hotels in Cuba ... those companies devote a lot of time to separating their businesses to fulfil the American Treasury requirements.'[48] Cuba is among the minority of countries in the world where the European Investment Bank (EIB) is not active. 'So we are starting the process to change that,' said Navarro, 'but it means that 28 member states have to ask the bank to operate in Cuba, because of the embargo.' Furthermore, one-third of the bank's denominations are in dollars, which means proceeding with Cuba could jeopardise the EIB's triple 'A' rating.

In response to the US threat of enacting Title III, the EU and the Canadian government issued a joint statement denouncing the measure as a violation of international law and stating that they would act to protect their own companies within the WTO and by prohibiting the enforcement of US court judgements based on Title III in the EU and Canada. 'Our respective laws allow any US claims to be followed by counter-claims in European and Canadian courts, so the US decision to allow suits against foreign companies can only lead to an unnecessary spiral of legal actions,' their statement concluded.[49] Their condemnation was reiterated on 2 May when the legislation was enacted.[50] Individual EU member states announced that they would work with the EU to defend the interests of their citizens and companies engaging with Cuba.[51] Talks were held in Havana.[52] The condemnation was echoed in declarations from the Caribbean Community (CARICOM), China, Japan, Russia and other countries and multilateral institutions. Cuba's own laws state that any person or entity engaging with Title III now will be excluded from any future agreements on compensation for nationalised properties.[53]

Despite the Trump administration's onslaught, high-profile visits, trade delegations and agreements with international partners continued apace. In late March 2019, Prince Charles and his wife the Duchess of Cornwall became the first members of the British Royal Family to visit Cuba in an official capacity; the trip was intended to promote bilateral trade and the positive media coverage it generated undermined US efforts to portray the island as a dangerous destination. Not long after that, a delegation of British businesses attended a forum in Havana, which was opened by President Díaz-Canel and attended by other Cuban Ministers, to discuss trade and investment in areas that are priorities for the Cuban government, including renewable energies, food production, tourism and increasing Cuban exports.[54] A brief look at Cuban news in May 2019 alone shows multiple collaborations, exchanges and agreements continuing with international partners from Bolivia to the Caribbean, Canada, China, India and Vietnam.[55]

At the United Nation's General Assembly on 1 November 2018, 189 countries voted in favour of Cuba's annual motion condemning the United States blockade, with only the United States and Israel against. That was despite the US introducing seven new amendments condemning Cuba for human rights violations among other issues. Each amendment was roundly defeated. It was the twenty-seventh consecutive year that the General Assembly had repudiated the US blockade. Cuba has 148 diplomatic missions overseas.[56] Isabel Allende, Director of the Higher Institute of International Relations, which trains diplomats, points out that Cuba's diplomatic representation abroad is greater than that of Mexico and Brazil. Cuba has an embassy in Kiribati, she explains, a state constituted by 32 coral atolls and one raised coral island, with a population of 110,000. 'In Kiribati there are only four embassies!'[57]

Clearly the tightening of the US blockade will hurt the Cuban people. How severely will depend on whether the EU, Canada and other countries move from words into action to neutralise its extraterritorial reach. Evidence that they would act came when a Spanish court dismissed a Helms–Burton related case against Meliá Hotels in early September 2019.[58]

The impact of the new sanctions will also depend on the success of internal measures to increase domestic production in Cuba.

DOMESTIC REFORMS: PAYING MORE, PRODUCING MORE

From 1 July 2019, every one of the 1,470,736 employees in Cuba's 'budgeted' state sector received significant salary rises. Employing 48 per cent of all state sector workers, the budgeted sector incorporates organisations and entities which operate with a state budget and mostly provide services free to the population without returning revenue to the state: public health, education, culture and sport, public administration, community services, housing and defence.[59] Simultaneously, 1,281,523 pensions rose, taking the number of direct beneficiaries to over 2.75 million Cubans. The new salary scale raises the incomes of the lowest earners (the minimum monthly salary rises from CUP 225 to CUP 400, up from CUP 125 in 2005) and expands the wage differential between these and the highest earners from between 2.9 to 7.5 times, so jobs demanding greater complexity, responsibility and qualifications receive substantially higher remuneration, serving as an incentive to work towards leadership positions.[60] The average monthly salary in the budgeted sector rose from CUP 634 in June, to CUP 1,065 in July – above the 2018 average salary in state enterprises, which was CUP 871 (up from CUP 600 in 2014).

Speaking on the *Mesa Redonda* on 2 and 3 July, Cuban President Miguel Díaz-Canel framed the pay and pension increases and the new economic measures announced simultaneously in relation to several factors.[61] First, the tightening of the US blockade, particularly with the implementation of Title III. Second, determination not to return to the hardships suffered by the Cuban people during the Special Period. Third, the long-standing demand for a pay rise. Fourth, acknowledgement of the loyalty and commitment of workers who stayed in state employment, often in the lowest-paid jobs, defending the 'conquests' of Cuba's socialist revolution.[62] Lastly, the salary rise is a step towards a broader economic restructuring to come, which will change the way salaries and prices are set, introducing greater flexibility into the planning process with greater initial input from workers, eliminate the dual currency, increase cooperation between state enterprises, non-state entities and foreign investors, and give greater financial autonomy to state enterprises. These measures aim to boost national production and improve Cuba's balance of payments, so as to withstand the onslaught of US imperialism and advance the national development plan.

The salary rise provokes two issues of immediate concern: the danger of inflation, and the need to meet the additional costs to the state without exceeding the previously planned deficit. Inflation would undermine the positive effect of the pay rise, increased purchasing power, to the detriment of all Cubans, not just the beneficiaries.[63] Economy Minister Alejandro Gil claimed that, in Cuba's planned economy, the salary rise should not cause inflation because: (a) the budgeted sector provides free goods and services, so increased salaries cannot push up non-existent sale prices; (b) most retail trade is under state control and subject to administrative controls, including fixed or capped prices; and (c) the state is not raising wholesale or retail prices, taxes or other payments. Consequently, said Gil, the non-state sector had no excuse for raising prices. Prices in all sectors would be capped and closely monitored and the public was urged to report 'irresponsible' and 'opportunistic' price rises to authorities. Subsequently, in late July 2019, a generalised system of price controls was introduced on all goods and services sold or provided by both state and private enterprises.[64]

With inflation 'repressed', the danger is that as beneficiaries buy more they will quickly exhaust the goods currently available, generating greater scarcity. To prevent either inflation or scarcity, the Cuban economy must expand the supply of goods and services available to the general public, a result which the new economic reforms are designed to achieve. While excluded from the salary rise, workers in the state enterprise sector can increase their incomes, said Gil, by producing more, but not by charging more. Local development will be fostered on the basis of local resources to meet demand without increasing imports (which bleeds hard currency). Other measures are being designed to retain the hard currency which Cubans receive as pay or remittances, and which often leaves the country, for example when individuals travel abroad to purchase goods to bring back to Cuba.[65] New financial services products are being created to encourage savings.

The cost of the salary rise to the Cuban state is over CUP 7 billion annually, and the pension increase adds another CUP 838 million to the bill. This is greater than the CUP 6.4 billion social security budget for 2019 and the planned budget deficit at CUP 6.1 billion.[66] How can the state cover the additional cost without increasing the deficit? The ministers talked in general terms about redirecting investment funds from unimplemented projects, while planned budgets to all entities will be reduced by some 10 per cent, obliging them to prioritise their spending. Meanwhile, all social programmes will be preserved.

BROADER ECONOMIC REFORMS

The broader economic strategy seeks to strengthen state enterprises and national production, the diversity and quantity of exports, import substitution, productive linkages, self-sufficiency in the municipalities, local development projects, investments, agricultural production, food sovereignty and housing provision and to keep hard currency in the country. Díaz-Canel talked about overcoming the obstacles and bureaucracy, which Cubans refer to as the 'internal blockade', and breaking the pattern of relying on imports.[67] Cuba's principal imports are food and fuels, which drain billions in hard currency. A critical solution is to increase agricultural production and the use of renewable energies. Moving Cuba towards food and fuel sovereignty is a political necessity given the aggressive, extraterritorial imposition of the US blockade.

To achieve this, state enterprises will be given more independence in planning, financing, investment, collaboration and incentives for workers. In turn they must eliminate budget deficits and stop using budgets without proper cost assessments. Ministers talked about replacing 'administrative controls' with 'financial and economic mechanisms', that is, increasing individual material incentives for workers to expand domestic production, exports and import substitution, essential both to save hard currency and to balance the books. Where surpluses rise, bonuses can increase workers' pay up to five times the average salary (previously capped at three times). 'Anything that increases efficiency must be evaluated for incorporation into the plan,' said Gil. Decentralising the plan implies decentralising access to resources, and so increased autonomy for state enterprises.[68]

FINATUR, an existing financial institution in the tourism sector, will provide investment credit directly to enterprises, outside allocations from the Central Fund, to reduce delays and bureaucracy in funding investments.[69]

Other incentives will foster municipal self-sufficiency and increased agricultural productivity. By introducing more extensive market mechanisms into the Cuban economy, the reforms present risks to Cuba's socialist planned economy, but they are necessary concessions made in the context of renewed US aggression and deteriorating international conditions. Díaz-Canel recognises the challenges and the importance of the population's support. In the most difficult times, he said, Fidel and Raúl Castro always 'went to the people'. This was the essence of the revolution, he added, 'as the people are the source of wisdom and creation'.

Given US actions intended to block Cuba's use of the US dollar, the possibility of adopting a crypto currency for the government's international transactions is under evaluation.[70] In early September 2019 the US Treasury announced that the forewarned prohibition of 'U-turn' financial transactions would be enacted on 9 October.[71] The cap on family remittances would also begin that day.[72] Treasury Secretary Steven Mnuchin said they were 'denying Cuba access to hard currency' to curb the island's 'bad behaviour'.[73]

A few days later, on 11 September, Díaz-Canel 'went to the people', returning to the *Mesa Redonda* to explain the new measures being implemented to mitigate the impact of fuel shortages resulting directly from US sanctions and threats to governments and shipping companies supplying Cuba with oil. This was an externally imposed temporary energy crisis, he said, that would impact on transportation, the distribution of products and the generation of electricity during peak demand periods. Long queues had already formed at bus stops while Cubans squeezed into buses in scenes reminiscent of the Special Period. However, Díaz-Canel reiterated that Cuba would not return to the economic crisis of the 1990s: the island is far less vulnerable than before, today meeting some 40 per cent of its oil needs with domestic production while its international partners and markets are more diversified. Nevertheless, some of the useful and creative measures adopted to pull Cubans through the fuel-scarce 1990s are already being reinstated: organised hitch-hiking and flexible work schedules, for example. The creativity and resilience which got the revolutionary people through the post-Soviet crisis are being channelled today to survive US attempts to cause misery and suffering in the post-rapprochement period.

WILL THE REVOLUTIONARY PEOPLE SURVIVE IN A POST-RAPPROCHEMENT PERIOD?

There is no attempt here to predict the future, a vainglorious habit which historians, of all people, should avoid. Nonetheless, by examining how the revolutionary people have survived into the post-Soviet world, this book has identified the tools, mechanisms and ethos which they will harness to determine their future. By way of a conclusion, I have pulled out the salient themes below, linking them to the preceding chapters.

The commitment to socialism as the solution to the challenge of development. Chapter 1 explains why, for the Cuban revolutionaries of the 1950s, colonialism and imperialism were *the* principle explanations for the island's structural weaknesses. Dependent development had fostered an economy, and a national capitalist class, which was subservient to foreign, mainly US interests. Thus, they perceived two real alternatives: to renounce fundamental change, beyond expelling the dictator Fulgencio Batista, so the new government would be acceptable to Washington; or to pursue the deep structural changes necessary to address the island's socioeconomic ills and dependent development, which would bring hostility from the United States. That is, it could either operate within the limits imposed by Cuba's subordination to United States, at most bolstering Cuban national capital, or break that dependant relationship and build real sovereignty, confronting both US imperialist interests and the Cuban 'bourgeoisie' which was allied to them. Cuban revolutionaries opted for the latter, adopting socialism as the only viable alternative. The post-1959 government chose state action over free market exchange as the lever for development, expropriating the private sector and adopting a centrally planned economy and state ownership because they believed it was the best approach to tackle Cuba's historical development challenges.

As US government machinations effectively blocked Cuba from accessing capital or trade with other capitalist countries, the Cuban state sought socialist allies. Socialist bloc trade and cooperation was established so developing nations could obtain financial and material resources under conditions which did not exploit or undermine sovereignty, and could engage in international exchange without deteriorating terms of trade.[74] However, the Cuban commitment to operate within a socialist paradigm implied additional restraints and complications. The Soviet embrace generated its own problems and failed to solve the island's sugar trade dependence. Indeed, Cuba was particularly vulnerable to the disintegration of the socialist bloc and the USSR between 1989 and 1991. Nonetheless, instead of reversing the commitment to socialist development, the severe economic crisis of the 1990s strengthened the Cuban resolve.

What has fluctuated over six decades, however, are the strategies adopted by the state to build socialism: to increase production and productivity within a welfare-centred development process. The lack of consensus on this issue explains why multiple systems of economic management have been adopted under the Revolution: five different systems in the first three decades and at least three distinct approaches in the post-Soviet period. Each one reframed the relationship between market mechanisms and the state plan in accordance with the economic and political imperatives of the period and international conditions. Cuban revolutionaries have shown great flexibility in devising policies to deal with urgent problems without straying from the paradigm of Cuba Socialista.

The disposition the Cuban leadership to take an independent path, to defend sovereignty and social justice, even at the expense of economic growth, is also illustrated in Chapter 1 with the discussion of the Rectification period, during which the Cubans pulled back from the Soviet model prior to its collapse. Rectification holds clues to the survival of Cuban socialism into the post-Soviet world. During this period, Fidel Castro expressed deep-rooted distrust and indeed disdain for capitalist social relations; his speeches from this period complement the work of Che Guevara in the early 1960s to create a rich archive of arguments against 'liberalising' the economy. Rectification saw efforts to strengthen the link between the CCP and the revolutionary people, with renewed emphasis on political mobilisation and socialism as a conscious process of construction and self-transformation. This approach proved essential in the post-Soviet period and is today being pursued by Díaz-Canel in response to the strains imposed in the post-rapprochement period.

The revolutionary resilience of the Cuban people. In late June 2019, President Miguel Díaz-Canel described the Special Period as 'a great act of collective creation with a strong and creative leadership that never rested'. He revealed that some measures taken during the economic crisis of the 1990s are currently under study.[75] Chapter 2, on the Special Period, demonstrates the revolutionary resilience of the Cuban people: the ability to pull together to get through economic hardship, with creativity and community, despite fragmentation of the socioeconomic structure, and seeking inventive solutions to daily scarcity and suffering. The leadership never wavered in its commitment to socialism, which it saw as tantamount to the survival of the Revolution itself. Against the 'economic rationality' of capitalism, welfare spending was prioritised, for example by subsidising employment despite low productivity and the lack of inputs. The government proved responsive to the new circumstances, restructuring the economy for reintegration into global capitalist markets while maintaining state control over trade and financial institutions, enabling it to harness scarce hard currency and other revenues to direct spending and imports according to its social and political priorities.

The measures taken in the 1990s, and their enduring impact, are key to understanding the subsequent reforms introduced to 'update the Cuban economy' under Raúl Castro's mandate. The ethos and institutions which got Cubans through the crisis will be vital resources to which the government of Díaz-Canel will have recourse in the difficult contemporary period, including the extensive apparatus controlling production, distribution, prices, imports and exports.[76] The ability to control distribution has already proven vital for safeguarding social justice in Cuba's post-rapprochement period. Other legacies of the Special Period that will also prove useful in the newly adverse times are those of community mobilisation, targeted social assistance and decentralised organic and urban farming. While Cubans are dismayed by the prospect of a return to the daily grind of the previous economic crisis there is also an attitude that 'If we could survive the Special Period, we can survive this.' For others, however, particularly young Cubans who lack this point of reference and have rising consumerist expectations, it will be the tipping point. Emigration, which has been high for several years, is likely to rise, depleting the young labour force Cuba needs but also serving as a pressure valve and reducing social tensions.

The importance of education and culture in inculcating a commitment to national sovereignty and social justice and to resist the imperialist offensive. Chapter 3 on the Battle of Ideas demonstrates the propensity of Cuban leaders to take the ideological offensive when under attack from US imperialism. Today that can be seen in the increasingly combative messages emanating from Díaz-Canel and government ministers, these days via social media. In late May 2019 reconstruction work began on the Anti-Imperialist Tribunal, the physical space outside the US embassy (formerly an 'Interest Section') where mass rallies and concerts took place in the early 2000s, first to demand the return of Cuban boy Elián González and subsequently throughout the period of the Battle of Ideas.[77] During the Battle of Ideas Fidel Castro confronted a 'parasitic' layer within Cuba which he identified as endangering the revolutionary process. That approach has shaped Cuba's new leaders, who accept the non-state sector's productive contribution but are less tolerant of freeloading off the state.

The ability of the Revolution to rejuvenate its ranks and the composition of its 'vanguard' was also evident during the Battle of Ideas. The process cultivated new revolutionary protagonists, drawn from the youngest, poorest and most racially diverse sections of Cuban society – a citizens' army of young social workers, emergent teachers and medical internationalists, who mobilised through rallies and marches, armed with energy-saving light bulbs and political T-shirts. The Battle of Ideas also demonstrates the determination of Cuban leaders, thinkers and activists not to leave people behind. This resolve was reasserted to counter the 'economism' implicit in the post-2011 process of updating the Cuban economy.

Energy is an issue of national security for Cuba, a point stressed in Chapter 4 on the Energy Revolution. Measures taken during the Energy Revolution reduced the island's vulnerability through the introduction of the distributed system of energy generation, the focus on energy efficiency and the fostering of renewable energies. These factors will prove increasingly important in the post-rapprochement period as the Trump administration attempts to block the supply of Venezuelan oil to Cuba. However, the government's 2030 renewable energy goals require huge investments, much of which must come from foreign partners, but which Title III has been enacted to block. Fortunately, a major partner in this field is China, which is unlikely to be driven off by the US measures.

The commitment to sustainable development and preparing for climate change, is also discussed in Chapter 4. In the context of a growing and increasingly radical global environmental movement, Cuba's achievements in sustainability and its long-term plan to protect the population from the devastating impact of global warming serve as an inspiration, countering attempts to ostracise the island. The fact that Cuba is socialist introduces to the environmentalist table a discussion about alternative development models. It strengthens the argument that the profit-driven capitalist system is incapable of redressing the environmental damage caused by the process of accumulation (through exploitation) integral to capitalism.

State investments in science and technology to foster endogenous solutions and innovation. Chapter 5 on Cuba's biotech revolution shows the results of the state's commitment to medical science, free from private interests and speculation and directed to meet public health needs. Its achievements in this field have placed it at the fore front of a globally emerging industry, despite six decades of the US blockade. In the post-Soviet period, Cuba bolstered the domestic production of medicines, which now meet close to 70 per cent of the population's needs. This makes Cuba far less susceptible to US pressures today than the Venezuelan people, who in early 2019 were suffering an estimated 85 per cent shortage of medicines because of US sanctions.[78]

Cuba's biotech revolution has brought international prestige and provided strong incentives for global biopharma interests to engage with Cuba, undermining the US blockade. The export of biopharma goods has made a growing contribution to Cuban revenues. Potential earnings from the commercial production in the United States of its lung-cancer vaccine CIMAvax and its treatment for diabetic foot ulcers, hebrobrot-P, could be significant. These innovations, and those in the pipeline, may provide incentives for US biopharma companies to lobby against the US sanctions. However, to fulfil its potential, the biotechnology sector also requires substantial foreign investment, which US sanctions intend to block.

The commitment to internationalism as part of the struggle against capitalism, imperialism and underdevelopment. Chapter 6 on medical internationalism explains how Cuban revolutionaries view global poverty and poor health as the result of structurally exploitative conditions resulting from capitalism and imperialism. While during the Cold War, the principle expression of Cuban internationalism was military assistance for national liberation struggles, in the post-Soviet period, medical assistance prevailed, becoming an essential component of the island's foreign policy. The island's global healthcare missions and the forms that this assistance have taken, have expanded hugely, from emergency response brigades and establishing public healthcare systems overseas, to the training and treatment of foreigners on the island. These programmes have benefited millions of people, who owe their health, and perhaps their lives, to those professionals and the government which trained and sent them. This in turn improved Cuba's international relations and became the principal source of export earnings as the Revolution's investments in health and education were converted into revenues for the state, vital for sustaining the socialist system which produced them.

Cuban development aid was pivotal in the post-2000 regional integration movements and the welfare-focused national development strategies pursued to varying degrees in Latin America and the Caribbean. As the 'Pink Tide' has been turned back, Cuban medical exports have fallen, most injuriously in Brazil. The Trump administration is working furiously to destroy Cuban prestige and revenues, characterising Cuban medical missions as 'human trafficking', while USAID finances actions to, in the words of Cuba's Foreign Ministry, 'discredit and sabotage the international cooperation provided by Cuba in the area of health in dozens of countries and for the benefit of millions of people.'[79] The Cubans, meanwhile, are working to diversify their medical cooperation and exports, securing payment on a sliding scale where possible and maintaining free provision in emergencies and for those too poor to pay.

Principled intransigence in defence of sovereignty and in the face of external (US) pressure. Chapter 7 on Cuba–US relations argues that the real motivation for US hostility towards the Cuban Revolution is the intolerable example of a socialist alternative in the US backyard. As long as Cuba remains socialist, it will face US antagonism. For the revolutionary people, the choice of socialism is a question of national sovereignty and relinquishing that choice due to external pressure would be tantamount to recolonisation. This is not something they will countenance. 'Pressure, preconditions and aggression do not work with Cuba,' affirmed Josefina Vidal.[80]

It is a lesson lost on the Trump administration, whose ultimatum that Cuba withdraw support for the Maduro government in Venezuela or suffer the consequences is simply the latest pretext for US hostility and will not be met regardless of the cost to the island itself. While Trump may have crowned himself as a 'deal-maker', history has shown that US efforts to conduct talks on the basis of a largely one-sided quid pro quo have not been successful. In response to multifaceted aggression from the US establishment and Miami-based exiles, the Cuban state has devised a versatile defence: from undercover agents and denunciations in international forums, to cultivating scientific and cultural links, embracing solidarity and welcoming US visitors.

The drive for productivity and efficiency within a socialist framework. Outside Cuba, 'Raúl's reforms' were portrayed as a faltering march towards economic liberalisation. However, the Cuban state viewed them as part of a drive for productivity and efficiency within a socialist framework. Chapter 8 provides a chronological account of the structural changes undertaken explaining how each measure was designed to rebalance the economy and bolster domestic production. The reforms were driven by expediency: they never represented an embrace of the market or capitalism. Rather they reflect the tension between political preference and economic necessity: the attempt to balance social production and accumulation under central planning with the urgent need to increase productivity and economic efficiency, and the need for foreign investment and trade in order to do so.

While success has been limited, the reforms have gone some way towards getting the Cuban house in order, particularly in terms of debt restructuring and infrastructural investments, both of which increase incentives for foreign investors. That the new private sector has been so hard hit by the Trump administration's sanctions serves to reinforce the importance of the protections offered by the centralised state apparatus and its control over production and distribution. The Trump administration's hostility shatters the illusion, fostered by Obama, that the US establishment is concerned to improve the lives of the Cuban people by promoting the private sector and civil society.

Extensive grassroots participation in nationwide debates shaping policies and legislation. This was also underscored in Chapter 8. The process of national and sectoral consultations was repeated throughout Raúl Castro's decade as president, involving ordinary Cubans in shaping their own futures and securing legitimacy and acceptance for the changes underway. This procedure was reinforced under Díaz-Canel's presidency with the mass participation in debates about the new Constitution which was approved in the referendum of February 2019.

The tendency to reassert the centrality of social justice in the development process. Fidel Castro expressed disdain for market forces, pointing to the human cost of exploitative social relations and the drive for profit. When capitalist mechanisms were increased under his leadership, they were articulated as concessions imposed on Cuba by its underdevelopment and by external factors; the revolutionary people were to be protected from their nefarious impacts. From 2007, even while introducing 'liberalising' reforms, Raúl Castro repeatedly asserted that no one would be abandoned to their fate. The introduction of market mechanisms in the process of 'updating the Cuban economy' has intensified the contradictions between the plan and the market that are inherent to the process of socialist transition; and it requires political action to prevent a capitalist logic being incrementally imposed on society.

Chapter 9 on the tightrope Cuba is walking considers debates which took place in the post-2011 period, as Cuban social scientists and others criticised the economic reforms for their narrow focus on economic efficiency at the cost of social equity. Objecting to market exchanges, private accumulation and the emergence of exploitative social relations, they demanded action to halt growing inequality and marginalisation. Subsequently, licences to the non-state sector were suspended, the institutional apparatus was strengthened to audit, tax, monitor and restrict the private sector and the state reinforced its control over production, distribution and prices to protect the general public.

The socialist state retains the mobilising capacity to support the people through economic crisis. In 2019, the contradictions inherent in the reform process became less of an existential threat to Cuban socialism than belligerence from the Trump administration, as this chapter shows. New US sanctions severely hinder the emerging Cuban private sector, which is dependent on foreign remittances and US tourism, reducing incomes for participants, tax revenues for the state and domestic spending in general. However, private interests were only permitted in non-strategic, marginal areas of the economy. The government is now focused on strengthening the state sector. The Cuban people still rely on the centralised state apparatus for most resources and the state retains the institutional capacity to mobilise those to get the revolutionary people through the current difficulties.

So, the prospects for the revolutionary people of Cuba are deteriorating, at least in the short term. No one, however, should underestimate the resilience of the revolutionary people, as this book makes clear, nor doubt the enduring commitment of the Díaz-Canel government to socialism. The system is neither static nor dogmatic: proceeding cautiously on the Cuban tightrope it can lean further towards the market, making the 'concessions' necessary to bolster production and productivity, without losing the counter-balance of the state plan, production, employment and welfare. The domestic challenge is knowing how far it can lean without passing the tipping point from which the internal logic of the capital accumulation process will, like gravity, bring the socialist system down.

Beyond that, the situation will be shaped by international factors: will Canada, the EU, Britain and other nations actively counter the extra-territorial imposition of the US blockade, so that Cuba can access the finances and resources it needs to invest in its national development? Will the global solidarity movement and the beneficiaries of Cuban development aid push their governments to take that stand? Will China and Russia increase trade and investment to offset losses from the west? Will Latin American governments swing back under control of the left, opening new avenues for trade and cooperation with Cuba? Will those who find hope in Cuba's biotechnology innovations and in its commitment to sustainable development demand that Cuba is given the space to breathe, to fulfil its potential?

Cuba continues to defy expectations and flout the rules; this small Caribbean nation has had the audacity to survive six decades of hostility from the United States and its international allies. The revolutionary people have never been forgiven for dispossessing those who exploited Cuba and intransigently refusing to compromise their principles and objectives. They have paid a high price. No doubt, and inevitably, there have been errors, misjudgements, contestation and hardship. More notable than those, however, has been the ability to redress these issues in each period, making adjustments to realign the process with the project of social transformation under way.

Revolutionary Cuba, it appears, wrote the rule-book on resilience. However, its best form of resistance has been not just the assertion of national sovereignty, but the creation of an alternative model of development that places human welfare and environmental concerns at its core. That this poor, blockaded island has achieved world-leading human development indicators, that it mobilises the world's largest international humanitarian assistance, that it has contributed to global innovations in medical science, that its contributions in culture and the arts are admired throughout the world, is an achievement to be examined and respected. We are left to ask, what could the revolutionary people of Cuba achieve if they were left in peace – if they were finally given the chance to prosper, and not just survive.

INTERVIEWS AND SELECTED TALKS

I have only listed interviews that are cited directly in this book. The list of 'talks' here does not include seminar or conference presentations from which I have drawn. They refer to talks organised for a small group of students from the London School of Economics in March/April 2018 in which I participated and had plenty of opportunity to effectively interview the speaker following the presentation.

Alarcón, Ricardo. Interview in Havana, 27 December 2016.
Alarcón, Ricardo. Talk in Havana, 5 December 2018.
Allende, Isabel. Interview in Havana, 4 January 2017.
Bérriz, Luis. Interview in Havana, 5 July 2017.
Blanco, Humberto. Interview in Havana, 20 December 2016.
Caballero, Idania. Interview in Havana, 7 July 2017.
Chomón Mediavilla, Faure. Interview in Havana, 16 February 2005.
Correa Delgado, Rafael. Interview in London, 28 October 2009.
Coyula, Miguel. Talk in Havana, 29 March 2018.
Curbelo Alonso, Alfredo. Interview in Havana, 5 July 2017.
Escobar, Cristina. Talk in Havana, 28 March 2018.
Freire Cazañas, Ernesto. Interview in Havana, mid-September 2011.
Fundora, Geidys. Interview in Havana, 22 December 2016.
General manager, Mariel TC. Interview in Havana, March 2018.
Gómez Cabezas, Enrique Javier. Interview in Havana, 16 April 2018.
González Gutiérrez, Alfredo. Interview in Havana, 1 February 2006.
Google employee. Interview, 14 May 2019.
Graduates of the Higher Institute of International Relations. Talk in Havana, 2 March 2018.
Hernández, Rafael. Interview in Havana, 4 January 2017.
Lage Dávila, Agustín. Interview in Havana, 7 July 2017.
Lee, Kelvin. Interview, 3 October 2017.
Munster, Blanca. Interview in Havana, 28 March 2018.
Navarro, Alberto. Talk in Havana, March 2018.
Pérez Ávila, Jorge. Interview in Havana, 6 July 2017.
Pérez, Hassan. Interview in Havana, 6 March 2018.
Pérez, Hassan. Interview in Havana, 8 March 2018.
Rodríguez, Anayansi. Interview in New York, 27 March 2017.
Rodríguez, José Luis. Interview in Havana, 20 December 2016.
Rodríguez, José Luis. Interview in Havana, 7 July 2017.
Rodríguez, Raúl. Talk in Havana, 29 March 2018.
Sáenz, Tirso. Interview in Havana, 7 January 2005.
Sáenz, Tirso. Interview in Havana, 20 February 2006.
Serrano, Kenia. Interview in Havana, 4 January 2017.
Serrano, Kenia. Interview in Havana, 4 April 2018.

Torres, Ricardo. Talk in Havana, 30 March 2018.
Velázquez, Edison. Interview in Havana, 21 January 2006.
Valdés Gravalosa, Juan. Interview in Havana, 22 February 2006.
Vidal, Josefina. Interview in Havana, 28 December 2016.

NOTES

INTRODUCTION: '*¡SOMOS CUBA! ¡SOMOS CONTINUIDAD!*'

1. Telesur tv, 'Cubanos reconocen cercanía del pdte. Miguel Díaz-Canel', 14 September 2018. https://www.youtube.com/watch?v=BfslhCNj5Hm.
2. See, for example, the conclusion to Díaz-Canel's speech at the closing session of the Union of Cuban Writers and Artists (UNEAC) IX Congress, in Havana's Convention Center, 30 June 2019. *Granma International*, 1 July 2019. http://en.granma.cu/cuba/2019-07-01/. On Twitter, the hashtags #SomosCuba (We are Cuba) and #SomosContinuidad (We are continuity) have become standard use among revolutionary Cubans, including members of the government.
3. Miguel Díaz-Canel, cited by Telesur, 'Cubanos reconocen'.
4. Che Guevara, speech at the Central University of Las Villas, 28 December 1959. https://blackopinion.co.za/2016/04/22/che-guevara-speaks-decolonising-university/.
5. Díaz-Canel received 603 out of 604 possible votes: 99.83%.
6. However, Raúl Castro remains First Secretary of the Cuban Communist Party, an important position that he is likely to hold until 2021.
7. In 2006, the World Wide Fund for Nature identified Cuba as the only country in the world achieving sustainable development, as discussed in Chapter 5 on the Energy Revolution.
8. Isabel Allende, Interview in Havana, 4 January 2017.
9. Fidel Castro speech in Camaguey on Moncada Day, 26 July 1989. http://lanic.utexas.edu/project/castro/db/1989/19890726-1.html.
10. Helen Yaffe, *Che Guevara: The Economics of Revolution*, Palgrave Macmillan, 2009.
11. Kelvin Lee, Interview via Skype, 3 October 2017.
12. Hal Klepak, *Raúl Castro and Cuba: A Military Story*, Palgrave Macmillan, 2012, 61.
13. Rafael Hernández, 'Looking at Cuba: Notes towards a Discussion', *Boundary 2*, 29:3 2002, 125.
14. For example, Julia Sweig's otherwise useful book *What Everyone Needs to Know about Cuba*, Oxford University Press, 2009, overlooks most of the developments which are the focus of this book.
15. All translations from Spanish to English are my own.
16. Other social scientists interviewed include: Blanca Munster, Ernesto Domínguez López, Geydis Fundora, Humberto Blanco and José Martin. I also recorded talks about Cuban development with Raúl Rodríguez, Miguel Coyula, Ricardo Torres, Ricardo González, Anicia García, Juan Triana Cordoví, Olivia Álvarez Méndez, Lázaro Peña, Luis René Fernández. On the issue of Cuban health internationalism and global health security I benefited from the contributions to an academic seminar by Jorge Pérez Ávila, Jorge Alfredo Carballo Concepción, Alejandro Lage, Luisa Iñiguez Rojas and Olga Rosa González Martín.
17. This clarification is made in response to a comment received from a peer reviewer of the manuscript.

18. For more on the summer 2019 salary rises see Helen Yaffe, 'Cuban Workers Celebrate Salary Rise from New Economic Measures', *Counterpunch*, 19 July 2019. https://www. counterpunch.org/.
19. Allende, Interview in Havana, 4 January 2017.
20. With the exception of Dr Kelvin Lee cited above, they requested anonymity.
21. Many useful insights came from presenters at the Latin American Studies Association (LASA) Annual Congress in Boston in May 2019, as referenced in the text. Unfortunately, most of the Cuban participants at LASA were denied visas to enter the United States so could not present their papers.
22. In addition, Cubanology tends to dismiss sources from Cuba as 'ideological' or unreliable, while dissidents enjoy a special status regardless of their previous ideological or institutional position. For a discussion of the politics of Cuba studies see chapter 2, Helen Yaffe, 'Ernesto 'Che' Guevara: Socialist Political Economy and Economic Management in Cuba 1959–1965', PhD thesis, London: London School of Economics, 2007. http://etheses.lse.ac. uk/2311/1/U615258.pdf.
23. In the fundamental neoclassical paradigm, economies are static, tending towards equilibrium, operated by rational men engaged in a competitive 'game'. There is no explanation of how the economy evolved; no concept of development; no concept of colonialism, neo-colonialism or imperialism; no notion of monopoly, oligarchy or class. Indeed, there is no theory of value (as distinct from price), so the idea of surplus value produced from the exploitation of workers is rejected. These omissions are significant because they are central to the Cuban approach.
24. The Cubans reply, 'lift the blockade then, remove our excuse, and let's see what happens'.
25. Rafael Correa Delgado, Interview in London, 28 October 2009.
26. Nelson P. Valdés, 'Revolution and Paradigms: A Critical Assessment of Cuban Studies', in Andrew Zimbalist (ed.) *Cuban Political Economy: Controversies in Cubanology*, London: Westview Press, 1988, 184.
27. See particularly work by Peter Roman, D.L. Raby and Arnold August.
28. Steve Ludlam, 'Regime Change and Human Rights: A Perspective on the Cuba Polemic', *Bulletin of Latin American Research,* 31:s1, 110–26 2012.
29. Article 1 of the Cuban Constitution of 2019 states that: 'Cuba is a democratic, independent and sovereign socialist State of law and social justice, organized by all and for the good of all, as an indivisible and unitary republic, founded by the labor, dignity, humanism, and ethic of its citizens for the enjoyment of liberty, equity, justice, and equality, solidarity, and individual and collective well-being and prosperity.' Article 18 says, 'The Republic of Cuba is governed by a socialist economic system based on ownership by all people of the fundamental means of production as the primary form of property as well as the planned direction of the economy, which considers, regulates, and monitors the economy according to the interests of the society.' The preamble to the Constitution commits Cuba to 'never returning to capitalism as a regime sustained by the exploitation of man by man. . .'. www. constituteproject.org/constitution/Cuba_2019D?lang=en#1.
30. Geidys Fundora, Interview in Havana, 22 December 2016.
31. José Luis Rodriguez, Interview in Havana, 20 December 2016.
32. Al Campbell, in Al Campbell (ed.) *Cuban Economists on the Cuban Economy*, University Press of Florida, 2013, 2.
33. In fact, when analysts have awarded a monetary value to all those goods and services which the Cuban population receives free or heavily subsidised from the government, it turns out that they are pretty well off compared to many neighbouring populations.
34. In this respect, Cuba is no different with other small trade-dependent nations. That Cuba has sought government-to-government relations from their foreign partners, mainly other 'socialist' or state-dominated economies, reflects the Cuban's aversion to the private/ capitalist market.

1. THE CHALLENGE OF (SOCIALIST) DEVELOPMENT

1. The first industrialised nations also have many labels, including: developed, imperialist, advanced capitalist, First World and Global North.

2. Adam Smith's theory of 'absolute advantage' in international trade was superseded by David Ricardo's theory of 'comparative advantage', and the latter was adopted by neoclassical economists, but detached from the underlying principle, the labour theory of value, which made it work.

3. From their earlier assertions about the revolutionising impact of the capitalist mode of production, Karl Marx and Friedrich Engels moved on to reassess the effect of the international expansion of British capitalism on its colonies. Marx observed that in Ireland, Britain's oldest colony, when the landed aristocracy drove peasants off the land the absence of alternative industrial development meant they were plunged into poverty and famine. Marx and Engels, *Ireland and the Irish Question*, 1978, 93–4. In 1880 Marx described Britain's role in India, Britain's largest colony, as 'an act of English vandalism which pushed the indigenous people not forward but backwards'. Marx, letter to V.I. Zasulich, March 1881, *Selected Works*, 1961, 241. They concluded that capitalist social relations and productive forces will only be developed in those sectors and to the extent that they serve foreign capital in extracting surplus value [profit] and raw materials or creating export markets as required.

4. Building upon Hobson's 1902 *Imperialism: A Study* and applying Marx's analysis described above, Vladimir Ilyich Lenin produced his theory of imperialism as the highest stage of capitalism. He defined five core features which included: concentration of production and capital, generating monopolies; merging bank and industrial capital, creating finance capital and a financial oligarchy; export of capital; formation of capitalist monopolies; world territorial division. Vladimir Ilyich Lenin, *Imperialism, the Highest Stage of Capitalism*, 1917, Marxists Internet Archive. www.marxists.org/archive/lenin/works/1916/imp-hsc/

5. In the 1960s and 1970s Marxists, neo-Marxists and dependency theorists debated how the relationship between the advanced capitalist countries and the so-called Third World impacted on development, focusing on Latin America.

6. That is imperialism in the Leninist sense, as distinct from colonialism and from the region's early integration into world markets.

7. Edward Boorstein, *The Economic Transformation of Cuba*, Modern Reader Paperback, 1969, 1.

8. The structural link between the US domination of the Cuban economy, the corruption and lack of patriotism from Cuban elites, and the island's socioeconomic problems were clearly elucidated by Fidel Castro in his famous court speech of 1953, 'History Will Absolve Me'. Despite this, most Cubanologists have lamely argued that the Revolution's turn to socialism and its integration into the socialist bloc was merely a tactic adopted by Fidel Castro to secure personal power. See, for example, Samuel Farber, *The Origins of the Cuban Revolution Reconsidered*, University of North Carolina Press, 2006, and Luis Martínez-Fernández, *Revolutionary Cuba: A History*, University Press of Florida, 2014.

9. This section draws on my own previously published material, particularly Yaffe, *Che Guevara*, and Ernesto Domínguez López and Helen Yaffe, 'The Deep Historical Roots of Cuban Anti-imperialism' in *Third World Quarterly*, 38:11, 2017, 2517–535.

10. Cited by Philip Foner, *A History of Cuba and its Relations with the United States*, Vol. 1, New York: International Publishers, 1962, 145.

11. Foner, *History of Cuba*, Vol. 2, 20–29.

12. Foner, *History of Cuba*, Vol. 2, 241.

13. William Appleman Williams, *Roots of the Modern American Empire: A Study of the Growth and Shaping of Social Consciousness in a Marketplace Society*, Random House, 1969, 5.

14. Louis A. Pérez, Jr. *Cuba and the United States: Ties of Singular Intimacy*, University of Georgia Press, 2003, 83–84.

15. Cited by Richard Gott, *Cuba: A New History*, Yale University Press, 2004, 111.

16. Steve Cushion, *A Hidden History of the Cuban Revolution: How the Working Class Shaped the Guerrilla Victory*, Monthly Review Press, 2016, 45.

17. US Department of Commerce, 'Investment in Cuba: Information for United States Businessmen', Washington, DC: GPO, July 1956, 9–10.

18. Arturo Guzmán Pascual, 'La Acción del Comandante Ernesto Guevara en el Campo Industrial', *Revista Bimestre Cubana*, 8, 1998, Sociedad Económica Amigos del País, 29.

19. The Jones–Costigan Sugar Act, was passed in May 1934.
20. Manuel Moreno Fraginals, 'Plantation Economies and Societies in the Spanish Caribbean, 1860–1930', in Leslie Bethell (ed.), *The Cambridge History of Latin America*, Vol. 4, 1986, 190.
21. US Department of Commerce, *Investment in Cuba*, 37. Cuban businesses owned three-quarters of the island's sugar mills, producing nearly 60% of its sugar. This figure demonstrates that foreign-owned mills were more productive.
22. US Department of Commerce, *Investment in Cuba*, 103.
23. US Department of Commerce, *Investment in Cuba*, 10.
24. As claimed by Jaime Schulicki, *Cuba: From Columbus to Castro*, Pergamon-Brassey's, 1986, 135. This is a reference to Walt Rostow's theory of development.
25. Boorstein, *Economic Transformation*, 6.
26. Jean-Paul Sartre, *Sartre on Cuba*, Ballantine Books, 1961, 12.
27. Boorstein, *Economic Transformation*, 6–7.
28. Cited by Marifeli Pérez-Stable, *The Cuban Revolution: Origins, Course and Legacy*, Oxford: Oxford University Press, 1999, 31.
29. US Department of Commerce, *Investment in Cuba*, 23–4.
30. Theodore MacDonald, *Hippocrates in Havana: An Analytical and Expository Account of the Development of the Cuban System of Healthcare from the Revolution to the Present Day*, Bolivar Books, 1995, 50.
31. US Department of Commerce, *Investment in Cuba*, 187.
32. US Department of Commerce, *Investment in Cuba*, 181, and MacDonald, *Hippocrates in Havana*, 59.
33. In the post-Soviet era a further three shifts in economic management have taken place: the structural changes and reforms introduced during the Special Period; the financial recentralisation and generalisation of the Enterprise Perfection System in the 2000s and onwards; and the process of updating the economic and social model introduced from 2011. This brings the total to eight.
34. This issue is explained in greater detail in my previous publications. See Yaffe, 'Che Guevara and the Great Debate, Past and Present' in *Science & Society*, 76: 1, 2012, 11–40; Yaffe, *Che Guevara*, 45–69.
35. See Yaffe, *Che Guevara*, for a comprehensive analysis of the Budgetary Finance System.
36. From as early as 1962, Guevara warned that the USSR was on that trajectory, and by 1966 he warned that, without a dramatic policy change, capitalism would return to the Soviet Union.
37. JUCEPLAN worked according to the national development strategy which was formulated by the government's Economic Commission on which sat Guevara (MININD), Rodríguez (INRA) and Osvaldo Dorticos (president of Cuba).
38. See Yaffe, 'Che Guevara and the Great Debate', 11–40 and Yaffe, *Che Guevara*, 45–69.
39. Tirso Sáenz, Interview in Havana, 7 January 2005.
40. Alfredo González Gutiérrez, Interview in Havana, 1 February 2006.
41. Faure Chomón Mediavilla, Interview in Havana, 16 February 2005.
42. Fidel Castro, *Report of the Central Committee of the CPC to the First Congress*, La Habana: Department of Revolutionary Orientation, 1977, 149–51.
43. José Luis Rodríguez, 'Fifty Years of Revolution in the Cuban Economy' in Campbell (ed.) *Cuban Economists*, 30. Guevara had criticised both imperialist and socialist countries for basing trade prices on those set in the international capitalist market, which are determined by the operation of the law of value. Trade between socialist and underdeveloped countries should not perpetuate the structural inequalities between countries resulting from differential levels of development, he argued. See Guevara, 'At the Afro-Asian conference in Algeria', https://www.marxists.org/archive/guevara/1965/02/24.htm.
44. José Luis Rodríguez, Interview in Havana, 20 December 2016.
45. Paul Sweezy, '15th and 20th Anniversaries for Cuba', *Monthly Review*, September 1973, 25:4.
46. Andrew Zimbalist, 'An Overview', in Zimbalist (ed.), *Cuban Political Economy: Controversies in Cubanology*, Westview Press, 1988, 9.
47. José Luis Rodríguez, Interview in Havana, 7 July 2017.

48. Brian H. Pollitt and G.B. Hagelberg, 'The Cuban Sugar Economy in the Soviet Era and After' in *Cambridge Journal of Economics*, 18:6, December 1994, 564; Carmelo Mesa-Lago, 'Cuba's Economic Counter-reform (rectificatión): Causes, Policies and Effects', *Journal of Communist Studies*, 5:4, 1989, 131.
49. Rodríguez, Interview in Havana, 7 July 2017.
50. Mesa-Lago, 'Cuba's Economic Counter-reform', 107.
51. Mesa-Lago, 'Cuba's Economic Counter-reform', 108.
52. Mesa-Lago, 'Cuba's Economic Counter-reform', 118. Between 1980 and 1985, annual growth in Cuba's non-traditional exports reached 18.8%. Zimbalist and Brundenius, *The Cuban Economy*, 147.
53. Allende, Interview in Havana, 4 January 2017.
54. Zimbalist and Brundenius, *The Cuban Economy*, 129.
55. Rodríguez, Interview in Havana, 7 July 2017.
56. Edison Velázquez, Interview in Havana, 21 January 2006. Fidel Castro had received two secret documents from Guevara critiquing Soviet political economy: a letter spelling out his concerns more directly than in his published articles; and his critical notes on the *Soviet Manual of Political Economy*, written between 1965 and 1966 and not made public until 2006.
57. Fidel Castro, 'Main Report to the Second Congress of the Cuban Communist Party', 1980, cited by Thomas Angotti, 'The Cuban Revolution: a new turn' in *Nature, Society, and Thought*, 1, 538. The full speech is available here: http://www1.lanic.utexas.edu/project/castro/db/1980/19801217.html but Angotti's translation is better.
58. Angotti, *A New Turn*, 538.
59. Cited by Mesa-Lago, 'Cuba's Economic Counter-reform', 102.
60. Zimbalist and Brundenius, *The Cuban Economy*, 128. By 1985, 3.2% of the labour force were small private farmers, 2.1% cooperative members, 1.6% were self-employed and the remaining 93.2% were employed in the state sector. Mesa-Lago, 'Cuba's Economic Counter-reform', 105.
61. Cuba is often referred to as a one-party state. Political parties which oppose the socialist character of the Cuban state are not given public space. However, the Cuban Communist Party does not stand candidates in elections, which are non-party elections. There are many different sectoral-based organisations in Cuba which do have representatives in the Organs of People's Power.
62. Money plays no part in Cuban elections, and advertising is confined to a one-page sheet of the candidate's biographical information. Participatory democracy is also practised through mass organisations and through regular, unprecedented public consultations on new legislation and planned reforms.
63. Zimbalist and Brundenius, *The Cuban Economy*, 128.
64. By 1991, 2,077 Cubans had died in Angola.
65. The Central Group was composed of vice-presidents of the Council of Ministers, all ministers, the president of JUCEPLAN, provincial heads of Popular Power, and the heads of departments of the Communist Party. It functioned until 1988.
66. Antoni Kapcia, 'Back to Basics: The Deferred Session of the Third Congress of the Cuban Communist Party', *Journal of Communist Studies*, 3:3, 1987, 311.
67. Fidel Castro, 'Discurso en la Clausura de la Sesión Diferida del Tercer Congreso del Partido Comunista de Cuba, en el Teatro "Carlos Marx",' 2 December 1986.
68. Kapcia, 'Back to Basics', 312.
69. Fidel Castro, 'Discurso pronunciado por el Comandante en Jefe Fidel Castro Ruz, Primer Secretario del Comité Central del Partido Comunista de Cuba y Presidente de los Consejos de Estado y de Ministros, en el acto central por el XX Aniversario de la caída en combate del comandante Ernesto Che Guevara, efectuado en la ciudad de Pinar del Río, el 8 de octubre de 1987, "Año 29 de la Revolución". http://www.cuba.cu/gobierno/discursos/1987/esp/f081087e.html.
70. Fidel Castro, 'Discurso pronunciado', 8 October 1987.
71. Fidel Castro, 'Discurso pronunciado', 8 October 1987.
72. Mesa-Lago, 'Cuba's Economic Counter-reform', 104 and 114.

73. In 1974 over 40% of the revenues of the Organisation of Oil Exporting Countries (OPEC) were deposited in European banks in the form of Eurocurrency deposits, known as petrodollars.
74. Rodríguez, 'Fifty Years', 30.
75. The current account surplus of oil producers soared from USD 3 billion in 1978 to USD 115 billion in 1980, while the current account deficits of non-oil-producing developing economies ballooned from USD 39 billion to USD 100 billion. Deficits were met by more international borrowing, but now under far worse conditions with rising interest rates. The United States had put up its interest rates, from 9.5% in August 1979 to 16% by May 1981. The cost of servicing existing debt was further increased by the appreciation of the US dollar by 25% from 1980 to 1982. In 1981 alone, Mexico's debt had increased from USD 55 billion to USD 80 billion. In August 1982, the Mexican government announced a default on its sovereign debt; Argentina, Brazil and Chile followed suit. Between 1981 and 1984, Latin American GDP fell by almost 10%. In just two years, 1983 and 1984, the net flow of financial resources out of Latin America was a devastating USD 56.7 billion. See Catherine R. Schenk, *International Economic Relations since 1945*, Taylor and Francis, 2011, chapter 4 'Years of Crisis'.
76. Rodríguez, Interview in Havana, 7 July 2017.
77. Rodríguez, 'Fifty Years', 31.
78. Castro Ruz, cited by David Yaffe, 'Is There a Solution to the Debt Crisis?' *Fight Racism! Fight Imperialism!* 59, 15 May–15 June 1986.
79. Gott, *Cuba: A New History*, 273–4. Gott points out that the Soviets continued to sell Cuba conventional weapons between 1983 and 1990. According to some sources, the Soviet defence guarantee ended earlier.
80. Mesa-Lago, 'Cuba's Economic Counter-reform', 128.
81. See Klepak, *Raúl Castro and Cuba*.
82. Rodríguez, Interview in Havana, 7 July 2017. He added that, despite rules about what should happen to shared resources, these were simply appropriated by those who took control. 'The building of CMEA that was in Moscow suddenly became the property of the mayor of Moscow.'
83. Rodríguez, Interview in Havana, 7 July 2017.
84. Gott, *Cuba: A New History*, 274.
85. Kapcia, *Back to Basics,* 312.
86. Zimbalist and Brundenius, *The Cuban Economy*, 129.
87. Zimbalist and Brundenius, *The Cuban Economy*, 187.
88. Mesa-Lago, 'Cuba's Economic Counter-reform', 108–9.
89. Guevara had been involved in a similar task of revising employment categories and pay-scales which, after two years' work, produced a new salary scale in 1964. See Yaffe, *Che Guevara*, 95–8.
90. Mesa-Lago, 'Cuba's Economic Counter-reform', 121.
91. Rodríguez, 'Fifty Years', 33.
92. For an extensive analysis of Guevara's views on these issues see Yaffe, *Che Guevara*.
93. Mesa-Lago, 'Cuba's Economic Counter-reform', 122.
94. Fidel Castro, 8 October 1987.
95. Fidel Castro, 8 October 1987.
96. These figures are disputed by Mesa-Lago in 'Cuba's Economic Counter-reform'.
97. Mesa-Lago, 'Cuba's Economic Counter-reform', 106.
98. Zimbalist and Brundenius, *The Cuban Economy*, 145.
99. Rodríguez, Interview in Havana, 7 July 2016.
100. Mesa-Lago, 'Cuba's Economic Counter-reform', 120.
101. Miren Uriarte, *Cuba: Social Policy at the Crossroads: Maintaining Priorities, Transforming Practice*, An Oxfam America Report, 45.
102. Angotti, 'The Cuban Revolution', 128.
103. Oscar U-Echevarría Vallejo, 'The Evolution of Cuba's Macroeconomy: From the Triumph of the Revolution through the Special Period', in Campbell (ed.) *Cuban Economists*, 76.
104. Angotti, 'The Cuban Revolution', 128.

2. SURVIVING THE CRISIS: THE SPECIAL PERIOD

1. Fidel Castro speech, 26 July 1989. http://lanic.utexas.edu/project/castro/db/1989/19890726-1.html.
2. In 1994, Rodríguez was named Minister of Finances and Prices, then became Minister of the Economy and Planning in 1995, a position he held until 2009. Subsequently he served as Vice President of the Executive Committee of the Council of Ministers and among other posts.
3. Rodríguez, Interview in Havana, 7 July 2017.
4. Rodríguez, 'Fifty Years', 34–5. Initially a short-term economic shock was expected, but by October 1991 the Cuban Communist Party Congress anticipated a deep and prolonged crisis.
5. Susan Yaffe, 'The Gains of the Revolution are Unique', *Fight Racism! Fight Imperialism!* October/November 1994, 5.
6. I have been told that during this period even British Embassy personnel traded the tomatoes grown in their garden for fish at the harbour.
7. Yaffe, 'Gains of the Revolution'.
8. Susan Yaffe and Helen Yaffe, 'Letter from Cuba', *Fight Racism! Fight Imperialism!* December 1995/January 1996, 8.
9. Yaffe and Yaffe, 'Letter from Cuba'
10. Rodríguez, 'Fifty Years', 37–8.
11. Rectification was as much an attempt to arrest the political stagnation of the socialist project as to address economic weaknesses, a process interrupted by the new crisis.
12. Information draws from Emily Morris, 'Cuban Economic Policy and Performance, 1990–2000: A Case Study in Economic "Transition"', PhD thesis, University of London, 2011, 44–50; Mavis Álvarez, Martin Bourque, Fernando Funes et al, 'Surviving the Crisis in Cuba: The Second Agrarian Reform and Sustainable Agriculture', in Peter Rosset, Raj Patel and Michael Courville (eds), *Promised Land: Competing Visions of Agrarian Reform*, 232; Klepak, *Raúl Castro and Cuba*, 57; Uriarte, *Cuba: Social Policy*, 9.
13. Prices were set according to the 5-year average on the world market prior to transactions. The measure protected the least-developed member states from the historical relative deterioration in the terms of trade for primary product exports.
14. Cuban GDP data for this period is problematic and involves conversion from the Material Product System of accounts applied in the socialist countries.
15. The blockade was estimated to cost Cuba USD 30 billion between 1960 and 1990, an average annual cost of USD 3 billion, equivalent to over 20% of GDP in 1993. Rodríguez, 'Fifty Years', 35.
16. The Mack Amendment of October 1990, the Torricelli Act in October 1992 and the Helms–Burton Act of March 1996.
17. Information from Nancy A. Quiñones, 'Cuba's Insertion in the International Economy since 1990', in Campbell (ed.) *Cuban Economists*, 91 and 105; Oscar U-Echevarría Vallejo, 'Cuba's Macroeconomy' in Campbell (ed.) *Cuban Economists*, 71; Morris, 'Cuban Economic Policy', 134; Ángela Ferriol, 'Fighting Poverty: Cuba's Experience' in Campbell (ed.) *Cuban Economists*, 17; Claes Brundenius, 'Whither the Cuban Economy after Recovery?', in *Journal of Latin American Studies*, 2002, 34, 367; Uriarte, *Cuba: Social Policy*, 3. The decrease of real wages was greater than the fall in consumption because a large part of consumption was met by state provision and self-provisioning of food.
18. Vallejo, 'Cuba's Macroeconomy', 76.
19. Morris, 'Cuban Economic Policy', 129–30.
20. Imports were 10 million tons in 1990 and 8 million in 1991.
21. Rodríguez, Interview in Havana, 7 July 2017.
22. A new Unitary Plan of Economic and Social Development was introduced.
23. The Cuban peso (CUP) fell from around CUP 7 to USD 1 in 1990 to over CUP 100 to USD 1 by late 1993. Morris, 'Cuban Economic Policy', 131–3.
24. This and following information from Morris, 'Cuban Economic Policy', 116–17; Rodriguez, 'Fifty Years', 39.
25. Rodríguez, 'Fifty Years', 40.

26. Cited by Morris, 'Cuban Economic Policy', 166.
27. Fidel Castro, cited by Rodríguez, 'Fifty Years', 37.
28. Rodríguez, 'Fifty Years', 36. A minority among Cuban economists did, and still do, advocate an increasing transition to capitalism, as discussed in Chapter 9.
29. See Chapter 3.
30. Pedro Sánchez, *Dual Currency in Cuba*, pamphlet, Agencia de Información Nacional Cuba, 2.
31. Fidel Castro, speech, 26 July 1993. http://www.cuba.cu/gobierno/discursos/1993/esp/f260793e.html.
32. Rodríguez, 'Fifty Years', 41.
33. Susan Eckstein, 'The Immigrant Divide: How Cuban Americans Changed the US and Their Homeland', in Susan Eckstein and Adil Najam (eds.), *How Immigrants Impact their Homeland*, Duke University Press, 2013, 222.
34. Susan Yaffe, 'Gains of the Revolution'.
35. Morris, 'Cuban Economic Policy', 176, 178. Morris points out that no other ex-CMEA country currency rebounded like Cuba's between 1994 and 1996.
36. Rodríguez, 'Fifty Years', 41. Payment in CUC was an award for productivity increases.
37. Net current transfers increased yearly from less than USD 50 million in 1992 to USD 650 million in 1995. Morris, 'Cuban Economic Policy', 156.
38. Uriate, 'Cuba: Social Policy', 28. Due to the US blockade, a large proportion of remittances are transported via visitors to Cuba, so figures are necessarily estimates.
39. Morris, 'Cuban Economic Policy', 223.
40. Information from Álvarez et al., 'Surviving the Crisis', 233–9. The usufruct model was expanded with the 2008 measures introduced by Raúl Castro to transfer idle state land to individuals and families.
41. The First Agrarian Reform Law nationalised 5.5 million hectares and turned 1.1 million hectares over to farmers. Álvarez et al., 'Surviving the Crisis', 230. In 1995, my sister and I visited a newly formed UBPC which had 1,000 hectares of sugarcane plus 50 hectares of land for the workers' individual use. We wrote: 'The bank lends the farm money to buy materials cheaply from the state. After the harvest, the workers sell their produce to the government, pay back the bank and 50 per cent of the profits are shared out among the workers with consideration made for the workers' contribution and efforts. The directors of the farm then discuss with the workers their ideas for social projects using the other 50 per cent of the gains . . . the priority is housing. Social activities are also planned for workers and their families.' Yaffe and Yaffe, 'Letter from Cuba'.
42. Forms of state farms were: 1) animal breeding, large-scale pig and poultry production and other mechanised activities; 2) farms belonging to the Revolutionary Armed Forces and Ministry of the Interior; 3) self-provisioning farms at workplaces and public institutions; and 4) the New-Type State Farms (known as GENT farms), which initiated a more gradual transition from state to cooperative use. Collective non-state farms were: 1) Agricultural Production Cooperatives (CPAs), set up in 1977 by private farmers voluntarily joining individual lands and resources to raise efficiency; and 2) the UBPCs set up from 1993. Individual production was divided between: 1) Credit and Service Cooperatives, in which independent farmers work their own land but cooperate to rent machinery and equipment and receive credit and services from state agencies; 2) individual farmers in usufruct; and 3) private farmers working their own land. The mixed sector involved joint ventures with foreign companies, mainly in citrus exports. See Álvarez et al, 'Surviving the Crisis'.
43. It was perhaps indicative that Raúl Castro made the announcement, not Fidel. There were rumours of a heated debate among the Revolution's leadership in which Fidel had to concede.
44. Rodríguez, 'Fifty Years', 44.
45. Morris, 'Cuban Economic Policy', 172–3. According to Morris, Cuba was the only ex-CMEA country where consumer prices fell.
46. Uriarte, *Cuba: Social Policy*, 15.
47. This and following from Morris, 'Cuban Economic Policy', 163. Competition with state enterprises was not encouraged.
48. Rodríguez, 'Fifty Years', 44.

49. A 2003 survey recorded an average monthly income for the self-employed of CUP 1,326 after taxes, compared to CUP 273 in the state sector. Morris, 'Cuban Economic Policy', 164.
50. Rodríguez, 'Fifty Years', 42.
51. Morris, 'Cuban Economic Policy', 168.
52. Rodríguez, 'Fifty Years', 42. Cuba's fiscal deficit soared again from 2008, as discussed in the chapter on Raúl's reforms.
53. US Department of Commerce, 'Investment in Cuba', 37.
54. Quiñones, 'Cuba's Insertion', 93.
55. Morris, 'Cuban Economic Policy', 191.
56. The island's sovereign risk rating was below junk status. The US blockade was augmented to prevent private capital from other countries investing in, or trading with, Cuba. The European Union introduced its hostile Common Position in 1996, so renegotiation of Cuba's large Paris Club debt was impossible.
57. Quiñones, 'Cuba's Insertion', 94.
58. Uriarte, *Cuba: Social Policy*, 26–7.
59. The contribution to GDP of Cuba's deals with foreign investors rose from 1.1% in 1994 to 14.5% in 2008 and the share of exports increased from 4.5% to 17.6%. Quiñones, 'Cuba's Insertion', 96.
60. Brundenius, 'Whither the Cuban Economy', 374.
61. Quiñones, 'Cuba's Insertion', 104; Morris, 'Cuban Economic Policy', 212.
62. Morris, 'Cuban Economic Policy', 213.
63. Quiñones, 'Cuba's Insertion', 103; Morris, 'Cuban Economic Policy', 213.
64. Many tourists from the United States entered Cuba via third countries.
65. This and following information from Morris, 'Cuban Economic Policy', 216 and 207.
66. Free trade zones are expected to offer a competitive advantage to foreign investors. However, without access to the US market, and with Cuban legislation prohibiting companies from undercutting competitors by reducing wages, the benefits of Cuba's free trade zones were questionable.
67. Quiñones, 'Cuba's Insertion', 105.
68. Quiñones, 'Cuba's Insertion', 104; Morris, 'Cuban Economic Policy', 213. Domestic sugar production fell by more than half in the same period. By 2008, sugar production was down to 1.4 million tons.
69. These three products rose from 11.2% of goods exports in 1990 to 55.5% in 2009. Quiñones, 'Cuba's Insertion', 103.
70. Vallejo, 'Cuba's Macroeconomy', 83.
71. Cuban services exports rose from USD 2.64 billion in 2000 to USD 7.28 billion in 2005. Figures from Elda Molina Díaz, 'Cuba: Economic Restructuring, Recent Trends and Major Challenges', posted 13 April 2009, MR Online: https://mronline.org/2009/04/13/cuba-economic-restructuring-recent-trends-and-major-challenges/.
72. Rodríguez, 'Fifty Years', 45.
73. Morris, 'Cuban Economic Policy', 209.
74. Source: ECLAC: 'Cuba. Evolucion Economica en el 2005 y Perspectivas para el 2006', cited by Molina Díaz, 'Cuba: Economic Restructuring', 7.
75. Thus converting Cuban's CUP wage into dollars for country comparisons reveals very little about comparative living standards, although it is an easy trick for Cuba's critics.
76. To reduce costs, the military turned to food production; by 1991, it was meeting 60% of its needs.
77. Klepak, *Raúl Castro and Cuba*, 59.
78. Rodríguez, 'Fifty Years', 45.
79. Morris, 'Cuban Economic Policy', 119–120.
80. Social distribution policies, such as the ration book, had the same effect as the benefit was attached to residence. In addition, a comprehensive public welfare infrastructure exists throughout the country.
81. Morris, 'Cuban Economic Policy', 217.
82. Uriarte, *Cuba: Social Policy*, 64.

83. Blanca Munster, Interview in Havana, 28 March 2018. The training was extended to women from various Latin American women's organisations, especially from Mexico, Guatemala and Venezuela who sent people to Cuba.

84. Uriarte, *Cuba: Social Policy*, 16. Meanwhile, Uriarte points out that one in ten children in Latin America works for a living before they are 14 years old.

85. Susan Yaffe, 'Gains of the Revolution'. In 1996 we left Cuba for Mexico, Venezuela and Colombia, three far wealthier countries where children beg for food as a matter of survival.

86. Vallejo, 'Cuba's Macroeconomy', 76.

87. Rodríguez, 'Fifty Years', 44. By 1999, productivity had increased 3.3% per year, energy use per unit of national output decreased by 7.7% per year and investment efficiency had improved 74%.

88. Uriarte, *Cuba: Social Policy*, 32.

89. Average calorie intake fell from 2,845 in kilocalories 1989 to 1,863 in 1993. Quiñones, 'Cuba's Insertion', 91. Consumption of the poorest Cubans was estimated to be under 1,500 calories.

90. Morris, 'Cuban Economic Policy', 140–41.

91. As reported by Manuel Franco, Usama Bilal, Pedro Orduñez, Mikhail Benet, Alain Morejón, Benjamín Caballero, Joan F. Kennelly, Richard S. Cooper, 'Population-wide weight loss and regain in relation to diabetes burden and cardiovascular mortality in Cuba 1980–2010: Repeated cross sectional surveys and ecological comparison of secular trends', *British Medical Journal*, 2013, 346, f1515 https://www.bmj.com/content/346/bmj.f1515.

92. Morris, 'Cuban Economic Policy', 140–41.

93. No one died from this and the incidence declined substantially after the Ministry of Public Health issued multivitamin supplements to the population from June 1993.

94. Uriarte, *Cuba: Social Policy*, 29. The divorce rate returned to pre-crisis levels by 1998.

95. Unfortunately, bikes were left to rust as alternative transport improved.

96. Uriarte, *Cuba: Social Policy*, 23.

97. Susan Yaffe, 'Gains of the Revolution'.

98. In a subsequent interview he explained that on hearing about the disturbance: 'I felt that my first duty was to be there where the riots were, with the people. Well, there was not one more stone, not one more shot. I told our escorts not to fire a shot. I told them "frankly I prefer to be shot than to tell you to shoot". Because I have always believed that there are weapons much more powerful than firearms and they are moral weapons.' See 'Fidel Castro sobre los sucesos del 5 de agosto'. https://www.youtube.com/watch?v=pc_zgN-735I

99. See the documentary by Estela Bravo, *Fidel Castro: The Untold Story*, Bravo Films, 2001 https://www.youtube.com/watch?v=P2Obp6YS4SY.

100. Susan Yaffe, 'Gains of the Revolution'.

101. William M. LeoGrande and Peter Kornbluh, *Back Channel to Cuba: The Hidden History of Negotiations between Washington and Havana*, University North Carolina Press, 2014, 281.

102. LeoGrande and Kornbluh, *Back Channel*, 294.

103. Uriarte, *Cuba: Social Policy*, 30.

104. Hal Klepak, *Raúl Castro*, 61.

105. Uriarte, *Cuba: Social Policy*, 3.

106. Uriarte, *Cuba: Social Policy*, 21. The situation had reversed by 1995, and infant mortality declined throughout the decade.

107. Morris, 'Cuban Economic Policy', 118–19.

108. Morris, 'Cuban Economic Policy', 128. Social security showed the sharpest increase in relation to GDP, surpassing education in 1993 as the largest social expenditure. Uriarte, *Cuba: Social Policy*, 36.

109. Susan Yaffe, 'Gains of the Revolution'.

110. Uriarte, *Cuba: Social Policy*, 13 and 33–4. Over 53,000 families received cash payments in 1994.

111. Hannah Caller, 'Socialism is Healthier', *Fight Racism! Fight Imperialism!*, 208, April–May 2009, http://www.ratb.org.uk/frfi/208.html.

112. Uriarte, *Cuba: Social Policy*, 9.

113. Morris, 'Cuban Economic Policy', 128.

114. Uriate, *Cuba: Social Policy*, 12 and 27. The lack of teachers and poor state of education facilities was subsequently addressed during the Battle of Ideas from 2000, discussed in the following chapter.

115. Uriarte, *Cuba: Social Policy*, 27.

116. Vallejo, 'Cuba's Macroeconomy', 77.

117. Ferriol, 'Fighting Poverty', 171.

118. Figures from Morris, 'Cuban Economic Policy', 142.

119. Ferriol, 'Fighting Poverty', 171.

120. Cited by Tania Jackson, 'Defending Socialism: Fighting Prostitution in Cuba', *Fight Racism! Fight Imperialism!* 146, December 1998/January 1999.

121. Jackson, 'Defending Socialism'. While in 1958, for most of the estimated 100,000 prostitutes in Cuba, the trade was a question of survival, in the 1990s many sought access to hard currency.

122. Margaret Randall, *Exporting Revolution: Cuba's Global Solidarity*, 2017, Duke University Press, 26.

123. Cited by Cristina Venegas, 'Filmmaking with Foreigners' in A. Hernández-Reguant (ed.), *Cuba in the Special Period: Culture and Ideology in the 1990s*, Palgrave Macmillan, 2009, 38.

124. Venegas, 'Filmmaking with Foreigners', 41.

125. A. Hernández-Reguant, 'Writing the Special Period: An Introduction', in Hernández-Reguant (ed.), *Cuba in the Special Period: Culture and Ideology in the 1990s*, Palgrave Macmillan, 2009, 5–6.

126. Kevin Delgado, 'Spiritual Capital: Foreign Patronage and the Trafficking of Santería', in Hernández-Reguant, *Cuba in the Special Period*, 52.

127. The 2005 documentary 'Inventos: Hip Hop Cubano', directed by Eli Jacobs-Fantauzzi, explores this movement.

128. 'The Power of Community: How Cuba Survived Peak Oil', documentary film, Arthur Morgan Institute for Community Solutions, 2006.

129. For a historical account of Cuba's structural dependency on food imports, which grew with the expansion of the sugar industry, see Louis A. Pérez Jr, *Rice in a Time of Sugar*, University of North Carolina Press, 2019.

130. Uriarte, *Cuba: Social Policy*, 19.

131. Uriarte, *Cuba: Social Policy*, 15, and 'Power of Community', 2006.

132. Morris, 'Cuban Economic Policy', 118 and 136. Much of this production was formalised with the opening of private farmers' markets in 1994.

133. 'Power of Community', 2006.

134. In addition to biofertilizers, they turned to earthworms, compost, other organic fertilizers, animal and green manures, and the integration of animal grazing. Álvarez, 'Surviving the Crisis in Cuba', 226.

135. Sinan Koont, 'The Urban Agriculture of Havana' in *Monthly Review*, January 2009, 60:8, 45.

136. About this process see Peter Rosset and Benjamin Medea, *The Greening of the Revolution: Cuba's Experiment with Organic Agriculture*, Ocean Press, 1994; Fernando Funes Aguilar and Luis L. Vázquez Moreno (eds), *Avances de la agroecología en Cuba*, Estación Experimental de Pastos y Forrajes Indio Hatuey, 2016; Julia E. Wright, *Sustainable Agriculture and Food Security in an Era of Oil Scarcity: Lessons from Cuba*, Routledge, 2009.

137. While intensive, high-yielding horticulture production systems, such as hydroponics, rely on chemical inputs, Cuban organopónicos use organic materials. *Growing Greener Cities in Latin American and the Caribbean*, An FAO report on urban and peri-urban agriculture in the region, 2014, http://www.fao.org/3/a-i3696e.pdf, 11.

138. *Growing Greener Cities*, 15. By 2015 Havana alone hosted 318 urban gardens, 89,000 productive backyards and 5,100 agricultural plots.

139. *Growing Greener Cities*, 10.

140. *Urban agriculture in Havana*, Centre for Public Impact, 1 March 2014 https://www.centreforpublicimpact.org/

141. Koont, 'Urban Agriculture', 48.

142. Monty Don, 'Around the World in 80 Gardens', Episode 1, BBC 2, 27 January 2008. https://www.bbc.co.uk/iplayer/episode/b008wf8l/
143. This and following information from Koont, 'Urban Agriculture', 47.
144. The fuel cost per tonne of organic vegetables was estimated at USD 0.55 compared to the fertilizer cost of USD 40 per tonne under conventional agriculture. The cost of pest control was reduced from USD 2.8 million to USD 300,000 per tonne. Additional costs were saved through domestic seed production. *Growing Greener Cities*, 17.
145. 'Power of Community'; Koont, 'Urban Agriculture', 44. The WWF's Sustainability Index Report identified Cuba as the only country in the world to have achieved sustainable development.
146. Sinan Knoot, *Sustainable Urban Agriculture in Havana*, Gainesville, Fl: University of Florida Press, 2011.
147. 'Power of Community'.
148. Monty Don, 'Around the World'.
149. Uriarte, *Cuba: Social Policy*, 43 and 46.
150. Uriarte, *Cuba: Social Policy*, 47.
151. According to official claims, only 0.1% of participants questioned whether socialism could get them through the crisis, while just 0.005% specifically proposed a market economy. Rodríguez, 'Fifty Years', 36.
152. From 2007, under Raúl Castro's leadership, popular consultations increased.
153. Rodríguez, 'Fifty Years', 43.
154. Kenia Serrano, Interview in Havana, 4 April 2018.
155. Rita Castiñeiras García, 'Creating a Better Life: The Human Dimensions of the Cuban Economy', in Campbell (ed.), *Cuban Economists*, 144.
156. Cited by LeoGrande and Kornbluh, *Back Channel*, 276–277.
157. Rodríguez, 'Fifty Years', 37.
158. United Nations Human Development Report, 1999, 146.

3. FIDEL CASTRO'S CITIZENS' ARMY: THE BATTLE OF IDEAS

1. See Yaffe, *Che Guevara*.
2. In 1998 Oswaldo Paya set up the Varela Project to seek 10,000 signatories who would endorse political changes to the Cuban constitution, implying the end of the socialist system.
3. They were all friends and family. The five-year-old daughter of one couple was left behind at the last minute. For a disturbing account of the shipwreck and deaths see Ann Louise Bardach, *Cuba Confidential: Love and Vengeance in Miami and Havana*, Vintage Books, 2002, 17.
4. Different sources have slightly different dates for these events.
5. Journalist Tim Golden reported that 'the cause has been dominated by the Cuban American National Foundation, which has sponsored most of the Gonzálezes political activities, advised them on strategy and helped arrange what has thus far been a largely no-show job for Lázaro, who had been unemployed, at the Ford dealership of one of its directors.' Golden, 'Just Another Cuban Family Saga', *New York Times Magazine*, 23 April 2000, https://archive.nytimes.com/www.nytimes.com/library/magazine/home/20000423mag-elian.html
6. Hassan Pérez Casabona, *Palabra en Combate: uno más*, Casa Editora Abril, 2001, 409.
7. Juventud Rebelde, cited by Pérez Casabona, *Palabra en Combate*, 409.
8. The 1966 Cuban Adjustment Act granted Cubans permanent residency in the United States after two years. The 1976 Immigration and Nationality Act Amendments reduced this to one year. In addition, Cubans were exempt from the requirement to enter the United States legally, thus these provisions encourage illegal immigration.
9. 'Following in his father's path, Juan Miguel joined the Union of Young Communists at 15 and threw himself into the duties it presented: attending political rallies, volunteering to work on the agricultural harvest, keeping an eye on the "revolutionary morale" of his comrades. He became a full member of the Cuban Communist Party at the tender age of

24, an achievement he called "the proudest thing that can happen to you".' Golden, *Cuban Family Saga*.

10. Fidel Castro, 'Letter to Hassan, 8 December 1999', cited by Pérez Casabona, *Palabra en Combate*, 29.

11. Hassan Pérez, Interview in Havana, 8 April 2018.

12. Pérez, Interview in Havana, 8 April 2018.

13. The Cuban delegation had been participating in a Summit of the World Health Organization.

14. Subsequently, 5 December 1999 was marked as the official beginning of the Battle of Ideas.

15. Pérez Casabona, *Palabra en Combate*, 412–13.

16. Golden described Elián González as 'the biggest revolutionary symbol since Che'.

17. Enrique Javier Gómez Cabezas, Interview in Havana, 16 April 2018. Some 'repentists' resident overseas actually returned to live in Cuba.

18. As a result of the economic contraction, Cuban television had only two channels both of which broadcast the *Mesa Redonda*, so the Cuban public watched that or nothing. The *Mesa Redonda* programmes have continued until today, but, with more channels available airing alternative programmes, viewing is optional.

19. For his birthday on 6 December, Elián was given a piñata styled like an aeroplane inscribed with 'Brothers to the Rescue', the name of a Cuban exile organisation whose provocations in Cuban airspace had ended with the island's authorities shooting down two planes in February 1996 (see Chapter 7).

20. Serrano, Interview in Havana, 4 April 2018.

21. Members of the Spanish, French and Russian governments publicly called for Elián's return to his father in Cuba.

22. For a detailed account of the ties between the Bush family and the Cuban-American exile elite see Bardach, *Cuba Confidential*.

23. Mariano Faget passed the false information on to a business partner. His father, also Mariano Faget, had been the head of the Bureau for the Repression of Communist Activities (BRAC) under the Batista dictatorship. Described as 'a technician of torture' by Carlos Franqui, one of his victims, according to Don Bohning, 'Faget's father was a brutal Batista official', *Miami Herald*, 19 February 2000. http://www.jonathanpollard.org/2000/021900b.htm. The Cuban diplomat José Imperatori had met with Faget.

24. Letter dated 22 February 2000, cited by Pérez Casabona, *Palabra en Combate*, 434.

25. However, as Richard Gott points out, this may have been a tactical misjudgement, as 63% of Miami voters believed Elián should be sent home. Gott, *Cuba: A New History*, 313.

26. Bardach's book details who was around Elián and their role in the *real politik* of the Miami exile community.

27. According to Pérez, CNN's coverage of the raid had more viewers than the fall of the Berlin Wall or the death of Princess Diana. Pérez, Interview in Havana, 8 April 2018.

28. Julian Borger wrote about the 'Photo War' over Elián in *Guardian*, 26 April 2000. www.theguardian.com/world/2000/apr/26/cuba.usa1.

29. Statement by Rogelio Polanco on the *Mesa Redonda*, 28 June 2000. www.youtube.com/watch?v=UsS9GNeJRB4&feature=share.

30. Fidel Castro's first meeting with Elián is shown in the video *Fidel y Elián, luchando por una causa justa*. www.youtube.com/watch?v=Lfb0rjT1f4E.

31. Bardach, *Cuba Confidential*, 17.

32. Fidel Castro informed Ignacio Ramonet that his books *The Tyranny of Communication* (1999) and *Propagandes Silencie* (2000) about cultural invasion had informed this debate. Ignacio Ramonet, *Cien Horas con Fidel: conversaciones con Ignacio Ramonet*, segunda edición, Oficina de Publicaciones del Consejo del Estado, 2006, 456.

33. Enrique Javier Gómez Cabezas, 'Sistematización de la experiencia del programa de trabajadores sociales' in Caballero Labaut and Ana María (eds.), *Trabajo Social en Cuba: Retos en el siglo XXI*, Editorial Unión, 47. Interviews in Havana with Gómez Cabezas, 16 April 2018, and Pérez, 8 April 2018.

34. Gómez Cabezas, Interview in Havana, 16 April 2018.

35. Fidel Castro to Ramonet, *Cien Horas con Fidel*, 402.

36. Serrano, Interview in Havana, 4 April 2018.

37. Pérez, Interview in Havana, 8 April 2018.
38. Serrano, Interview in Havana, 4 April 2018. Gómez Cabezas, Interview in Havana, 16 April 2018.
39. Gómez Cabezas, Interview in Havana, 16 April 2018.
40. Gómez Cabezas, *Trabajadores Sociales*, footnote 5, 50; Rosi Smith, *Education, Citizenship, and Cuban Identity*, Palgrave Macmillan, 2016, 119.
41. Smith, *Education*, 127.
42. Gómez Cabezas, *Trabajadores Sociales*, 48.
43. Gómez Cabezas, Interview in Havana, 16 April 2018.
44. Smith, *Education*, 138 and 131.
45. Gómez Cabezas, *Trabajadores Sociales*.
46. Gómez Cabezas, *Trabajadores Sociales*, 50. Subsequently this study was extended to all Cubans up to 30 years old.
47. See Yaffe, *Che Guevara*, chapter 4 on 'Education, Training and Salaries', for information about the Peoples' Schools and 'Superacion' (improvement) courses set up in the early 1960s.
48. *Cuba: Batalla de Ideas*, information leaflet, January 2002.
49. *Cuba: Batalla de Ideas*. The oldest of this age-range had completed compulsory schooling as the Special Period began.
50. Gómez Cabezas, *Trabajadores Sociales*, 52.
51. Fidel, cited by Gómez Cabezas, Interview in Havana, 16 April 2018.
52. Gómez Cabezas, Interview in Havana, 16 April 2018.
53. The exact figure was 2,202,068 children.
54. Gómez Cabezas, *Trabajadores Sociales*, 53.
55. Gómez Cabezas, *Trabajadores Sociales*, 54.
56. Gómez Cabezas, *Trabajadores Sociales*, 54–5.
57. Gómez Cabezas, *Trabajadores Sociales*, 55. Fidel Castro, speech 5 December 2004. www.fidelcastro.cu/en/discursos/speech-given-closing-session-young-communists-league–8th-congressheld-havana-convention. This campaign was subsequently adopted in other ALBA countries.
58. Smith refers to this as a 'betrayal' of the social workers' potential. Smith, *Education*, 157.
59. A national group was composed of ministries of Education and Health, the Centre for Youth Studies, the Office of National Statistics, the Institute of Pedagogic Research, the Institute of Nutrition and the social workers. The Programme took months to design and prepare and for social workers to be trained.
60. Mayra Espina discusses the benefits of this approach, in 'Viejas y nuevas desigualdades en Cuba: Ambivalencias y perspectivas de la reestratificación social' in *Nueva Sociedad*, No. 216, julio–agosto, 2008, 133–46.
61. Rodríguez, 'Fifty Years', 46.
62. Rodríguez, 'Fifty Years', 46.
63. Helen Yaffe, 'Cuba reclaims its monetary sovereignty', *Fight Racism! Fight Imperialism!* December 2004–January 2005. See Chapter 3 on the Special Period and the establishment of dollar shops.
64. Angela Ferriol Muruaga, 'La Revolucion Cubana: A 50 Años Del Triunfo: Aspectos Socioeconomicos', presentation, *Conferencia Internacional La Obra De Carlos Marx Y Los Desafíos Del Siglo XXI*, May 2008. Despite the increase, the proportion of Cuba's international trade with Latin America was well below the figure represented by the USSR and the socialist bloc pre-1959, which was 75% to 85%. Cuba's 'dependence' on Venezuela was well below that on its former socialist allies.
65. Living in a Cuban home in this period, I witnessed this process first-hand.
66. The following chapter on the Energy Revolution refers to the impact of this campaign in terms of energy efficiency and economics.
67. As Cuba's Energy Revolution spread to Latin America and the Caribbean through ALBA, Cuban social workers travelled to 11 countries in the region to assist energy efficiency projects.
68. Fidel Castro, 'Speech delivered by Dr. Fidel Castro Ruz, President of the Republic of Cuba, at the Commemoration of the 60th Anniversary of his admission to University of Havana, in the Aula Magna of the University of Havana', 17 November 2005. http://www.cuba.cu/gobierno/discursos/2005/ing/f171105i.html.

69. Gómez Cabezas, Interview in Havana, 16 April 2018.
70. Gómez Cabezas, Interview in Havana, 16 April 2018.
71. 10 October is Cuba's Independence Day.
72. Fidel Castro, 'Speech in the Aula Magna'.
73. Gómez Cabezas, Interview in Havana, 16 April 2018.
74. Gómez Cabezas, Interview in Havana, 16 April 2018.
75. Gómez Cabezas, Interview in Havana, 16 April 2018. The theft of fuel continues to be a perennial problem, however, as digital systems can be tampered with.
76. Gómez Cabezas, *Trabajadores Sociales*, 69. The social worker programme was restructured to meet the requirements of the Energy Revolution. Specialised work fronts were created for: the Energy Revolution; disconnected youth; comprehensive improvement courses; the prison population and social reinsertion; attention to children; the disabled and patients with low prevalence diseases; the elderly; critical social cases; reproduction of audio-visual educational materials; Operation Milagro (ophthalmological programme to correct reversible blindness); and the training of Latin American doctors. The process of professional specialisation was reversed in 2010, after the Secretariat of the Central Committee decided that social workers should prioritise the prevention of criminal activities and promote a comprehensive social work programme, without specialisation.
77. Gómez Cabezas, *Trabajadores Sociales*, 69–70.
78. Gómez Cabezas, Interview in Havana, 16 April 2018. Gómez told me about meeting former social workers now working as everything from taxi drivers to television producers.
79. Gómez Cabezas, Interview in Havana, 16 April 2018.
80. As pointed out by Smith, *Education*, 127.
81. Serrano, Interview in Havana, 4 April 2018.
82. Gómez Cabezas, Interview in Havana, 16 April 2018.
83. There could be 30 secondary school students in one classroom; there must be 2 teachers to attend to them.
84. Smith, *Education*, 127–8. All the participants interviewed by Smith had met their obligations.
85. Smith, *Education*, 138–9.
86. Gómez Cabezas, Interview in Havana, 16 April 2018. Figure cited by Smith, *Education*, 128.
87. Cited by Gómez Cabezas, Interview in Havana, 16 April 2018. The general teacher was exempt from teaching physical education or foreign languages, Smith, *Education*, 128.
88. Gómez Cabezas, Interview in Havana, 16 April 2018.
89. Pérez, Interview in Havana, 8 April 2018.
90. Serrano, Interview in Havana, 4 April 2018.
91. *Cuba: Batalla de Ideas*.
92. Gomez Cabezas, Interview in Havana, 16 April 2018; Smith, *Education*, 128.
93. Smith, *Education*, 128.
94. Lavinia Gasperini, 'The Cuban Education System: Lessons and Dilemmas', in *Country Studies: Education Reform and Management Publication Series* 1:5, 2000, 67.
95. Gómez Cabezas, Interview in Havana, 16 April 2018.
96. Smith, *Education*, discusses the forms this took.
97. Fidel Castro to Ramonet, *Cien Horas con Fidel*, 403.
98. *Cuba: Batalla de Ideas*.
99. Smith, *Eduation*, 150–1.
100. Smith, *Education*, 123–4.
101. *Cuba: Batalla de Ideas*.
102. Speech by Carlos Valenciaga, 'La UCI es fruto de la Batalla de las Ideas', *Granma*, online, 20 July 2007. www.granma.cu/granmad/2007/07/20/nacional/artic05.html.
103. Antoni Kapcia, 'Educational Revolution and Revolutionary Morality in Cuba: The "New Man", Youth and the New "Battle of Ideas" ', *Journal of Moral Education*, 34:4, 2005, 402.
104. I recall an argument between two Cubans about the merits of this decision: a middle-aged metal engineer at a sugar mill dismissed the attempt to retrain workers his age, arguing that the state should have kept them employed on the land, producing food crops for domestic consumption. Against this a smallholder farmer, who was the municipal

representative for the Ministry of Agriculture, insisted that this was not an option as the island lacked, and could not import, the necessary resources (tools and seeds) for alternative crop production on state farms.

105. Fidel Castro to Ramonet, *Cien Horas con Fidel*, 404.
106. Kapcia, 'Educational Revolution', 402.
107. Smith, *Education*, 152.
108. Fidel to Ramonet, *Cien Horas con Fidel*, 403. This claim has not been tested.
109. Fidel Castro, 'Speech in the Aula Magna'.
110. Fidel Castro, 'Speech in the Aula Magna'.
111. According to Ann Louise Bardach, Fidel Castro suffered from malignant diverticulitis. 'Ann Louise Bardach on Cuban Exile Carriles and Her Book "Without Fidel" 2', in Interview with Democracy Now!, 2009 https://www.youtube.com/watch?v=4Hm1rGpV0vg.
112. Raúl Castro, speech in Camaguey 26 July 2007. http://www.granma.cu/granmad/2007/07/27/nacional/artic01.html.

4. POWER TO THE PEOPLE: THE ENERGY REVOLUTION

1. Decree Law 345, *Development of Renewable Sources and Efficient Use of Energy*, was approved on 23 March 2017, regulating the production of self-supply and sale back to Cuba's Electric Union by Cuban residences under individualised contracts. Luis Bérriz, 'La Política Energética Cubana en el Camino del Desarrollo Sostenible', presentación, June 2017.
2. Editorial, *Trabajadores*, 28 May 2017, http://www.trabajadores.cu/20170528/apuesta-necesaria/.
3. Luis Bérriz, Interview in Havana, 5 July 2017.
4. The beneficiaries of these have been thousands of schools and other social facilities.
5. See Chapter 3 on the Battle of Ideas for more about the communal television and video rooms.
6. The equipment manufactured domestically includes solar panels, hydropower turbines, portable photovoltaic lamps, small wind turbines, solar heaters and distillers, solar wood dryers, medicinal plants, fruits and other products with state-of-the-art modular building technologies. Cubasolar have also built greenhouses for research into seed cultivation and *vitroplants* (plants studied in test tubes of glass, outside their normal biological context) and participated in the construction of aqueducts by gravity and hydraulic rams. Cubasolar, presentation: 'Cubasolar: Sociedad Cubana para la Promocion de las Fuentes Renovables de Energia y el respect Ambiental', undated.
7. In homage to Che Guevara, they helped provide solar electricity for the old school in La Higuera, Bolivia, where Guevara was killed, and which now hosts a medical post.
8. Fidel Castro became a champion of moringa while recovering from the serious stomach illness which almost killed him in 2006. In 2012 he wrote: 'It is the only plant that has every kind of amino acid . . . has dozens of medicinal properties . . . [and its] effects on the digestive system are very good as with all plants, apart from its high protein qualities'. He revealed that 'samples of seeds from different varieties have been provided to the agricultural research institutes in our country'. See 'Rare photo of Fidel Castro harvesting Moringa from his personal Moringa Farm' *Moringapowder*, 24 May 2015. https://www.moringapowder.com/news/rare-photo-of-fidel-castro-harvesting-moringa-from-his-personal-moringa-farm/.
9. Bérriz, Interview in Havana, 5 July 2017.
10. Bérriz, Interview in Havana, 5 July 2017.
11. For a full discussion of Cuba's disaster response see Javier Sandoval Guzman, 'Popular Power and Environmental Governance: The Cuban Approach to Natural Hazards and Disaster Risk Reduction', Master Thesis, Norwegian University of Life Sciences, 2014.
12. Lea Terry, 'Cuba Climate Change Impact: How Scientists Say Global Warming Will Hurt', Newsmax. 9 November 2015. www.newsmax.com/FastFeatures/Cuba-climate-change-scientists/2015/11/09/id/701380/.
13. Ivet González, 'Cuba Wakes Up to Costs of Climate Change Effects'. *Inter Press Service News Agency*, 17 June 2013. http://www.ipsnews.net/2013/06/cuba-wakes-up-to-costs-of-climate-change-effects/.

14. Richard Stone, 'Cuba Embarks on a 100-year Plan to Protect Itself from Climate Change', *Science*, 10 January 2018. https://www.sciencemag.org/. The plan will be spearheaded by the Ministry of Science, Technology and the Environment.
15. This was compiled by three environmental organisations: *International Union for Conservation of Nature*, World Widelife Fund and the United Nations Environmental Programme.
16. Named after Chairperson, Gro Harlem Brundtland, former prime minister of Norway.
17. Christopher Amacker, 'The Concept of Sustainable Development', 27 July 2011. http://www.e-ir.info/2011/07/27/the-concept-of-sustainable-development/.
18. Followed up by the UN's World Summit on Sustainable Development, Johannesburg, South Africa in 2002 and the UN's Conference on Sustainable Development in Rio de Janeiro, Brazil in 2012.
19. Fidel Castro, 'Tomorrow Will be Too Late', speech at the Rio Summit, 1992, https://www.greenleft.org.au/content/fidel-castro-earth-summit. He returned to this issue in numerous national and international forums. For examples, see 'Editorial' *Energía y Tú*, No. 77, ene-mar., 2017, 2–3.
20. Daniel Whittle and Orlando Rey Santos, *Protecting Cuba's Environment: Efforts to Design and Implement Effective Environmental Laws and Policies in Cuba*, 2006, University of Pittsburg press, 73.
21. WWF, Living Planet Report, 2006, 19, https://wwf.ru/en/resources/publications/booklets/living-planet-report-2006/. See also research by, Daniel D. Moran, Mathis Wackernagel, Justin A. Kitzes, Steven H. Goldfinger and Aurélien Boutaud, 'Measuring Sustainable Development – Nation by Nation', in *Ecological Economics* 64, 2007, 470–474, which compared changes in both HDI and Ecological Footprint indexes between 1975 and 2003. On presentation of the Living Planet Report 2016, Cuba's leading position in the world was confirmed. See, www.telesurtv.net/english/news/As-World-Burns-Cuba-Number–1-For-Sustainable-Development-WWF–20161027–0018.html.
22. Stefan Lovgren, 'Castro the Conservationist? By Default or Design, Cuba Largely Pristine', 6 August 2006, *National Geographic*, http://news.nationalgeographic.com/news/2006/08/060804-castro-legacy.html. Between 1900 and 1959, Cuba's forest and plant cover was reduced from 52% to somewhere between 8–14% as land was concentrated in the hands of a few private domestic and foreign companies. After the Revolution of 1959, the first reforestation programme was initiated. The increase in forest cover was modest, estimates are 18% in the 1980s, until the post–2000 decline of the sugar industry and intensive livestock programmes, and the launch of reforestation projects in the mountains which saw forest cover rise from 25% to 31% by 2016. For an environmental history of Cuba demonstrating the link between the sugar industry and deforestation see Reinaldo Funes Monzote, *From Rainforest to Cane Field in Cuba: an environmental history since 1492*, University of North Carolina Press, 2008. For a more general approach see: Enrique del Risco Rodriguez, *Los bosques de Cuba: historia y características*, Editorial Científico Tecnica, 1995.
23. 'Power of Community', 2006.
24. Cited by Lovgren, 'Castro the Conservationist', 2006.
25. In the 1770s, the French Physiocrats, identified *nature* as the source of all value. Their Scottish contemporary, Adam Smith, argued that *labour* was the source of value. Karl Marx's critique of political economy drew on both these notions to argue that labour, set to nature, was the source of all value. Thus, under capitalism both nature and workers are exploited in the interests of capital accumulation.
26. This hardly surprising given the increasing overlap between political and corporate interests globally. It also undermines the notion of 'green capitalism' and the idea that the free market and liberal democracies are the best systems for confronting climate change.
27. Judith A. Cherni and Yohan Hill, 'Energy and Policy Providing for Sustainable Rural Livelihoods in Remote Locations: The case of Cuba', in *Geoforum*, 40, 2009, 645–654.
28. There is an extensive bibliography, especially emerging after the collapse of the USSR and the socialist bloc, about environmental damage under socialist governments. For the Cuban case, see Sergio Díaz-Briquets and Jorge Pérez-López, *Conquering Nature: The Environmental Legacy of Socialism in Cuba*, University of Pittsburg Press, 2000.

29. Director, Directorate of Environmental Policy in CITMA, cited in Karen Bell, 'Environmental Justice in Cuba', *Critical Social Policy* 2011 31: 257.
30. US Department of Commerce, 'Investment in Cuba', 178 and 187.
31. US Department of Commerce, 'Investment in Cuba', 10.
32. Fidel Castro, 'History Will Absolve Me'. www.marxists.org/history/cuba/archive/castro/1953/10/16.htm.
33. Radio Rebelde. 'About us'. http://www.radiorebelde.cu/english/about-us/.
34. Bérriz, Interview in Havana, 5 July 2017.
35. Reduced from 23% to 3% according to Richard R. Fagen, *The Transformation of Political Culture in Cuba,* Stanford University Press, 1969, 45–47. Internationally, a country can be declared 'free from illiteracy' with a literacy rate of 96%.
36. Esther Gloria Armenteros Cárdenas, *Personal email correspondence,* 15 August 2017.
37. Guevara's examination of the documents of this, and similar US-owned companies, influenced the development of his Budgetary Finance System. See Yaffe, *Che Guevara,* 33–41.
38. Che Guevara, 'Discurso Clausura del Fórum de Energía Eléctrica', 20 November 1963, in *Escritos y Discursos,* Editorial de Ciencia Sociales, 1977. Vol 7. 1963, 135. https://www.youtube.com/watch?v=9FeuV8T7w34
39. The mission set out six months before the Cuban Revolution was declared 'socialist' in April 1961. Other agreements with the USSR included: the annual sale of 4 million tons of Cuban sugar at substantially higher than the world market prices, credit for purchasing capital and consumer goods, and Soviet assistance to adapt Cuban petrol refineries, with prospecting for Cuban oil and developing nickel mines.
40. Trueba, Ángel (2001), 'El MININD en la industrialización socialista de Cuba 1960–1965', in *40 Aniversario Ministerio de Industrias.* Editora Política, 2001, 34.
41. Sáenz, Interview in Havana, 7 January 2005.
42. Pre-1959, sugar workers in Cuba resisted the mechanisation of the industry so this process was introduced by the revolutionary government. For more on this see Yaffe, *Che Guevara,* 174–7; Cushion, *Hidden History.*
43. Bérriz, Interview in Havana, 5 July 2017.
44. 'Power of Community'. There is an extensive bibliography about the evolution of intensive agriculture in Cuba, including Armando Nova González, *La agricultura en Cuba: Evolución y trayectoria (1959–2005),* Editorial de Ciencias Sociales, 2006.
45. The following historical information draws largely from Bérriz, *Algunos Aspectos Del Desarrollo Histórico Del Uso De Las Fuentes Renovables De Energía En Cuba:* undated document; and Bérriz, Interview in Havana, 5 July 2017.
46. Rodríguez, Interview in Havana, 20 December 2016.
47. As discussed in Chapter 2 on the Special Period. By 2006, 80% of Cuba's agricultural production was organic and the annual use of chemical pesticides had fallen from 21,000 tonnes in the 1980s to 1,000 tonnes. See 'Power of Community'.
48. Bérriz, *Fuentes Renovables,* 7.
49. The Cubans were aided in this by Canadian company Sherrit; see Chapter 2 on the Special Period.
50. Wind was not considered to have significant energy value, and to only be useful in small windmills for pumping water. Bérriz, *Fuentes Renovables,* 7.
51. Another issue obstructing the expansion of renewable energy use in Cuba was the need for the technology to enable that energy to be fed into the national grid.
52. Bérriz, Interview in Havana, 5 July 2017.
53. Cubaenergía mainly works with the Ministry of Energy and Mines, but also the Ministry of Agriculture and Food Industry and CITMA.
54. The Island of Youth is 50 kilometres south of mainland Cuba, the seventh largest island in the Caribbean, with a population over 86,000.
55. Alfredo Curbelo Alonso, Interview in Havana, 5 July 2017. The Cubans hoped to purchase the small-scale plants they required from a Canadian company. However, under US blockade regulations, the equipment could not be imported, because it contained parts that were manufactured in the United States. Alternative equipment was imported from an Indian company, Ankur, that had developed a simple technology suitable for Cuban

conditions. Käkönen, et al., *Energy Revolution in Cuba: Pioneering for the Future?*, Finland Futures Research Centre, FFRC eBook 4, 2014, 22.

56. Cited anonymously in *Energy Revolution in Cuba*, 11.
57. The weekend before Hurricane Dennis hit Cuba, hundreds of thousands of Cubans had participated in Meteorology Exercise 2005, a national mobilisation to prepare for the tropical storms involving workers, farmers, students and specialists from the municipal Defence Councils, work centres, social institutions, grassroots organisations, the Ministry of the Interior and the Revolutionary Armed Forces. My report from the time is available here: Yaffe 'Hurricane Dennis: when the going gets tough . . .', *Fight Racism! Fight Imperialism!* 186, August/September 2005. http://www.revolutionarycommunist.org/.
58. See Chapter 7 on Cuba–US relations for more on this.
59. Bérriz, Interview in Havana, 5 July 2017. This may well be the case in Cuba, however, which Cherni and Hill point out, as the International Energy Agency projections suggest that, by the year 2030, 1.4 billion people will *still* lack electricity, around 17% of the world's total population. Cherni and Hill, 'Energy and Policy', 645.
60. Fidel Castro, 'Speech in the Aula Magna'.
61. Fidel Castro, 'Speech in the Aula Magna'.
62. Fidel Castro, 'Speech in the Aula Magna'.
63. Curbelo Alonso, Interview in Havana, 5 July 2017.
64. *Energy Revolution in Cuba*, 5; Dieter Seifried, 'Cuban Energy Revolution: A Model for Climate Protection?' Büro Ö-quadrat report, 2013. www.oe2.de/fileadmin/user_upload/download/Energierevolution_Cuba_eng.pdf.
65. 'Cuban Energy Revolution', 19; Curbelo Alonso, Interview in Havana, 5 July 2017. Seifried's report adds: 'At the same time, improvements in the transmission and distribution networks were made to reduce the transmission and distribution losses. While in 2007 the entire distribution and transport losses amounted to 15.7% of the produced electricity, they were successfully reduced to 14.8% by December 2008.'
66. Curbelo Alonso, Interview in Havana, 5 July 2017.
67. Bérriz, Interview in Havana, 5 July 2017.
68. Curbelo Alonso, Interview in Havana, 5 July 2017.
69. Mario Alberto Arrastía Avila, 'Distributed Generation in Cuba: Part of a Transition towards a New Energy Paradigm', in *Cogeneration and On-Site Power Production*, November–December 2008, 62.
70. Seifried, 'Cuban Energy Revolution', 3. In summer 2016, the Cuban government announced temporary restrictions on energy consumption as a result of falling oil imports from Venezuela and the government's decision to keep expenditure within the annual plan (avoiding additional imports), rather than technological capacity. There was no return to blackouts. The energy scarcity suffered in 2019 is discussed in Chapter 10.
71. Arrastía Avila 'Distributed Generation', 65.
72. Käkönen et al, *Energy Revolution in Cuba*, 4.
73. Laurie Guevara-Stone, 'La Revolucion Energetica: Cuba's Energy Revolution', 9 April 2009. www.renewableenergyworld.com/
74. Guevara-Stone, 'Revolucion Energetica', 6.
75. Arrastía Avila, 'Distributed generation', 62; Seifried, 'Cuban Energy Revolution', 7; Käkönen et al, *Energy Revolution in Cuba*, 14.
76. Seifried, 'Cuban Energy Revolution', 8. Once complaints emerged about the low quality of the energy-saving bulbs imported from China, the Cubans began producing and distributing LED bulbs. Curbelo Alonso, Interview in Havana, 5 July 2017.
77. Käkönen et al, *Energy Revolution in Cuba*, 14.
78. Seifried, 'Cuban Energy Revolution', 8. The average annual consumption of the old Soviet refrigerators was 800 kWh/unit, while the new Chinese equipment requires around 350 kWh.
79. Seifried, 'Cuban Energy Revolution', 8.
80. Käkönen et al, *Energy Revolution in Cuba*, 14.
81. Seifried, 'Cuban Energy Revolution', 8–9
82. Seifried, 'Cuban Energy Revolution', 8.

83. Juventud Rebelde, 'Banca cubana puede asumir todos los créditos para el pago de los equipos electrodomésticos', *Juventud Rebelde*, 4 December 2007, http://www.juventudrebelde.cu.
84. Centro de Estudios de Población y Desarrollo, *Salario En Cifras: Cuba 2010*, Oficina Nacional de Estadisticas, 2010, 3. www.one.cu/publicaciones/.
85. Seifried, 'Cuban Energy Revolution', 16.
86. Juventud Rebelde, 'Los Equipos Electrodomésticos'.
87. Seifried, 'Cuban Energy Revolution', 8 and 11. He adds: 'This exceptionally large advantage in favour of energy efficiency is partly due to the low efficiency standard before the Energy Revolution, and also to the high cost of power generation in the Cuban energy sector.'
88. Seifried, 'Cuban Energy Revolution', 10.
89. Fidel Castro, cited by Guevara-Stone, 'Revolucion Energetica', 3.
90. Arrastía Avila, 'Distributed Generation', 65; Seifried, 'Cuban Energy Revolution', 13.
91. Seifried, 'Cuban Energy Revolution', 13.
92. Curbelo Alonso, Interview in Havana, 5 July 2017.
93. Mario Alberto Arrastía Avila and Laurie Guevara-Stone, 'Teaching Cuba's Energy Revolution', *Solar Today*, January–February 2009, 31.
94. Guevara-Stone, 'Revolucion Energetica', 4–5.
95. Seifried, 'Cuban Energy Revolution', 21.
96. Michal Nachmany, Sam Fankhauser, Jana Davidová et al., *Climate Change Legislation in Cuba*, The 2015 Global Climate Legislation Study: A Review of Climate Change Legislation in 99 Countries, 6.
97. Arrastía Avila, 'Distributed Generation'; Käkönen et al, *Energy Revolution*, 16.
98. Käkönen et al, *Energy Revolution in Cuba*, 7, 16.
99. The National Environment Strategy replaced the 1997 National Programme on Environment and Development, first elaborated in 1993. Nachmany et al, *Climate Change Legislation in Cuba*, 5.
100. Curbelo Alonso, Interview in Havana, 5 July 2017.
101. Revista Eolica y de Vehiculo Electrico, *Cuba impulsa las energías renovables en Isla de la Juventud*, 9 October 2014, https://www.evwind.com/2014/10/09/isla-de-la-juventud-poligono-de-uso-de-energias-renovables/.
102. European Commission, *Suburban agriculture and cooperative building in 10 municipalities in the provinces of Camaguey, Las Tunas and Holguin*. No date. https://ec.europa.eu/europeaid/case-studies/suburban-agriculture-and-cooperative-building-10-municipalities-provinces-camaguey-la–0_en. The project involves experimentation in three municipalities: Los Palacios, a rice producing municipality; Güira, which produces principally fruit and vegetables; and a milk producing municipality in Camagüey. It supports 89 cooperatives, 'to reach 1,268,399 beneficiaries with improved access to healthy food and lower prices [and] to support women's initiatives'.
103. At the Experimental Station of Pastures and Forages Indio Hatuey, the first scientific research centre in the agricultural branch opened by the Revolution, in March 1959
104. Curbelo Alonso, Interview in Havana, 5 July 2017.
105. Bérriz, Interview in Havana, 5 July 2017.
106. See Klepak, *Raúl Castro and Cuba*.
107. Bérriz, 'Política Energética', June 2017.
108. For example, Katheryn Felipe, 'Cuba's Energy Strategy for 2017, in *Granma International*, 24 February 2017, 4.
109. Bérriz, Interview in Havana, 5 July 2017.
110. Information from the Office of Renewable Energies, Ministry of Energy and Mines, May 2017, cited in Bérriz, 'Política Energética', 2017.
111. Bérriz, Interview in Havana, 5 July 2017.
112. Induction cooking heats a cooking vessel by magnetic induction, instead of by thermal conduction from a flame or an electrical heating element.
113. Cuba, *Portfolio of Opportunities for Foreign Investment*, 2018–2019, 79.
114. The other five strategic areas are: effective, socialist government and social integration; productive transformation and international insertion; infrastructure; human potential – science, technology and innovation; human development, social justice and equity.

115. 'Plan Nacional De Desarrollo Económico Y Social Hasta 2030: Propuesta De Visión De La Nación, Ejes Y Sectores Estratégicos', *Documentos del 7mo. Congreso del Partido aprobados por el III Pleno del Comité Central del PCC el 18 de mayo de 2017 y respaldados por la Asamblea Nacional del Poder Popular el 1 de junio de 2017*, 20.
116. Bérriz, 'Política Energética', 2017.
117. *The Economist*, 'The Miracle of Marabú, Cuba's Wonderful Weed', 1 June 2017. www.economist.com/news/americas/.
118. See Alfredo Curbelo Alonso, Oscar Jimenez and Joel Suarez, for more on the potential: 'Biomass based gasifier for providing electricity and thermal energy to off-grid locations in Cuba. Conceptual design', in *Energy for Sustainable Development* 16, 2012, 98–102.
119. Curbelo Alonso, Interview in Havana, 5 July 2017.
120. Bérriz, 'Política Energética', 2017.
121. Bérriz, Interview in Havana, 5 July 2017.
122. The water heaters cost nearly 3,000 pesos. 'La Habana: Venderán calentadores solares de agua para el sector residencial', *Cubadebate,* 27 August 2019.
123. The 2016–17 *Portfolio of Opportunities for Foreign Investment* included 123 projects in energy and mining, nearly one-third of the total. Emilio Morales, 'Investment Report: Nickel, Oil, and Sustainable Energy', *Cubatrade*, 1 March 2017. www.cubatrademagazine.com/2637–2/
124. ProCuba, Center for the Promotion of Foreign Trade and Foreign Investment, *Foreign Investment Opportunities in Cuba*, 8 November 2017. http://www.procuba.cu/en/invertir/noticiasinver/MTY5OA==.
125. Morales, 'Investment report'.
126. In 2017, there were only 13 'totally foreign capital enterprises' in Cuba. See *Portfolio of Opportunities for Foreign Investment, 2018–2019*, 16.
127. Michael Voss, 'China, Cuba cooperate in developing renewable energy' CGTN, 26 September 2016, https://www.youtube.com/watch?v=ZbxECkx1J1k; Sarah Marsh, 'Lack of cash clouds Cuba's green energy outlook', *Reuters*, 31 March 2017. http://uk.reuters.com/article/us-cuba-energy-idUKKBN1720EB.
128. New Energy Events, 'Havana Energy announces second biomass plant in Cuba', 28 February 2018. http://newenergyevents.com/havana-energy-announces-second-biomass-plant-in-cuba/. The question is whether the tightening of the US blockade by the Trump administration will hinder Havana Energy's future plans.
129. Bérriz, Interview in Havana, 5 July 2017.
130. Bérriz, 'Política Energética'.

5. THE CURIOUS CASE OF CUBA'S BIOTECH REVOLUTION

1. The material in this chapter is similar to that in a previously published journal article, Helen Yaffe, 'The Curious Case of Cuba's Biotech Revolution' *History of Technology*, 34, 2019, 203–22.
2. Notable exceptions include work by historians of science Angelo Baracca and Rosella Franconi, for example 'Cuba: The Strategic Choice of Advanced Scientific Development, 1959–2014', *Sociology and Anthropology* 5:4, 2017, 290–302; political geographer, Simon M. Reid-Henry, *The Cuban Cure: Reason and Resistance in Global Science*, University of Chicago Press, 2010; and Marguerite Rose Jiménez, 'Cuba's Pharmaceutical Advantage', NACLA, 16 August 2011, https://nacla.org/article/cuba%E2%80%99s-pharmaceutical-advantage. Cuban medical scientists contribute to international journals, but these provide technical rather than historical accounts. Exceptions here include Andrés Cárdenas's work on innovation and economic development, for example *The Cuban Biotechnology Industry: Innovation and Universal Health Care*, Institute for Institutional Innovations Economics, University of Bremen, Germany, 2009; and an historical overview provided by Ernesto Lopez Mola, Ricardo Silva, Boris Acevedo et al., 'Biotechnology in Cuba: 20 years of scientific, social and economic progress', *Journal of Commercial Biotechnology*, 13, 1, 2006.
3. Cárdenas, *Cuban Biotechnology*, 7.
4. Lee, Interview via Skype, 3 October 2017.
5. Lee, Interview via Skype, 3 October 2017.

6. The Institute of Research in Chemistry (1848); the Observatory of Meteorology and Physics (1856); and the Royal Academy of Medical, Physics and Natural Sciences (1861), founded by the Spanish queen's decree. The word 'Royal' was dropped in 1902 with formal independence.
7. President Obama acknowledged Finlay's contribution when he announced rapprochement between the US and Cuba, 17 December 2014. 'Statement by the President on Cuba Policy Changes', The White House, Office of the Press Secretary. https://obamawhitehouse.archives.gov/the-press-office/2014/12/17/statement-president-cuba-policy-changes.
8. This and following information draws on MacDonald, *Hippocrates in Havana*, 15–79.
9. In 1910 Dr. Domínguez Roldan introduced radiotherapy equipment into Cuba. In 1947, nitrogen mustard was used by Professor Zoilo Marinello, who also installed the first cobalt therapy equipment in 1957. In 1945 the League against Cancer opened a dispensary providing consultations. In 1949, the construction of a new 'Curie' hospital was funded by the League against Cancer and the national lottery, with the state contributing the land. Idania Caballero Torres and Lien Lopez Matilla, 'La historia del CIM contada por sus trabajadores', unpublished paper, 2017, 3–4.
10. International Bank for Reconstruction and Development (IBRD) in collaboration with the government of Cuba, *Report of the Mission to Cuba*, Washington DC: Office of the President, 1951, 223.
11. 31% of Cubans over six years old had no schooling; another 29.4% had three years' schooling or less. In rural Cuba, 41.7% of over ten years old were illiterate.
12. This and following information from James W. McGuire and Laura B. Frankel, 'Mortality Decline in Cuba, 1900–1959: Patterns, Comparisons, and Causes', paper delivered at the Latin American Studies Association, Dallas, Texas, 27–29 March, 2003, 23–5.
13. McGuire and Frankel, 'Mortality Decline in Cuba', 23–4.
14. This and following information from MacDonald, *Hippocrates in Havana*.
15. MacDonald, *Hippocrates in Havana*, 46.
16. MacDonald, *Hippocrates in Havana*, 50.
17. US Department of Commerce, 'Investment in Cuba', 187.
18. MINSAP report 1969, cited in MacDonald, *Hippocrates in Havana*, 27.
19. Robert Huish, *Where No Doctor Has Gone Before: Cuba's Place in the Global Health Landscape*, Wilfrid Laurier University Press, 2013, 265.
20. The resulting linguistic problems were evident in the public health exam papers of 1961–2 according to MacDonald, *Hippocrates in Havana*, 57.
21. Fidel Castro, 'Discurso Pronunciado por Fidel Castro el 8 de Octubre de 1987', in David Deutschmann and Javier Salado (eds), *Ernesto Che Guevara: Gran Debate: Sobre la economía en Cuba 1963–1964*, Ciencias Sociales, 2003, 392.
22. There were up to 100,000 prostitutes in Cuba in 1958.
23. MacDonald, *Hippocrates in Havana*, 56
24. MacDonald, *Hippocrates in Havana*, 55–58
25. This and following information from C. William Keck and Gail A. Reed, 'The Curious Case of Cuba', *American Journal of Public Health*, 2012, 14.
26. Keck and Reed, 'Curious Case', 14.
27. Baracca and Franconi, 'Cuba: Strategic Choice', 9; MacDonald, *Hippocrates in Havana*, 28.
28. See Yaffe, *Che Guevara*, 163–98.
29. Tirso Sáenz, Interview in Havana, 20 February 2006.
30. The farm was called Ciro Redondo after a fallen Rebel Army captain from Guevara's column.
31. Yaffe, *Che Guevara*, 188–90.
32. In 1966 it was renamed the National Institute of Oncology and Radiobiology (INOR) and oncology became a speciality at the same level as surgery or internal medicine.
33. Juan Valdés Gravalosa, Interview in Havana, 22 February 2006.
34. This was pointed out to me by José Luis Rodríguez, former Minister of the Economy, Interview in Havana, 20 December 2016.
35. Mola et al., 'Biotechnology in Cuba', 2.
36. This and following information from Keck and Reed, 'Curious Case', 14.

37. Mass organisations refers to Cuban street committees, women and youth organisations, and trade unions.

38. Julie M Feinsilver wrote: 'From the outset of the revolution, Fidel has made the health of the individual a metaphor for the health of the body politic. Therefore, he made the achievement of developed country health indicators a national priority. Rather than compare Cuban health indicators with those of other countries at a similar level of development, he began to compare them to those of the United States,' *Cuban Medical Diplomacy: When the Left Has Got It Right*, 30 October 2006.

39. MacDonald, *Hippocrates in Havana*, 143.

40. The ratio has fallen in recent years due to both improving health outcomes and numbers of doctors serving abroad. Keck and Reed, 'Curious Case', 15.

41. Information from Keck and Reed, 'Curious Case', 16.

42. Uriarte, *Cuba: Social Policy*, 3.

43. Hannah Caller, 'Socialism is Healthier', *Fight Racism! Fight Imperialism!*, 208, April–May 2000. http://www.revolutionarycommunist.org/.

44. Uriarte, *Cuba: Social Policy*, 9.

45. United Nations cited by Keck and Reed, 'Curious Case', 18; Kofi Annan, Secretary General of the United Nations, 11 April 2000, cited by Uriarte, *Cuba: Social Policy*, 6.

46. Aleida Guevara, talk on 'Cuban Medical Internationalism', University College London, Institute for the Americas, 17 November 2017.

47. Keck and Reed, 'Curious Case'.

48. Nina Notman, 'Cuba's Cancer Treatments', *Chemistry World*, 16 March 2018.

49. Agustín Lage Dávila, Interview in Havana, 7 July 2017.

50. Genetech was founded in San Francisco in 1976 by venture capitalist Robert A. Swanson and biochemist Herbert Boyer. Then AMGen was set up in Los Angeles in 1980. Biotechnology took off in Europe in the 1990s, and subsequently in Japan, Singapore and China.

51. The focus here is biotechnology for human health care, not animal health care or agriculture, areas in which Cuba also boasts some innovative developments.

52. Simon Reid-Henry, *The Cuban Cure: Reason and Resistance in Global Science,* University of Chicago Press, 2010, 26. Biological sciences stagnated in the USSR from the 1920s to the mid-1960s, under the influence of Trofim Lysenko. In 1948, the study of genetics was outlawed.

53. Information from Baracca and Franconi, 'Cuba: Strategic Choice'; Caballero and Matilla, 'Historia del CIM'; Lage Dávila, Interview in Havana, 7 July 2017; and Reid-Henry, *Cuban Cure*.

54. *New York Times*, 'Epidemic in Cuba sets off dispute with US', 6 September, 1981. www.nytimes.com/1981/09/06/world/epidemic-in-cuba-sets-off-dispute-with-us.html.

55. Fidel Castro, 26 July 1981, cited by *New York Times*, 'Epidemic in Cuba'.

56. Marieta Cabrera, 'La ciencia desnuda un crimen contra Cuba', *Bohemia*, 29 January 2016. http://bohemia.cu/ciencia/2016/01/. The study states: 'Cuban researchers were able to amplify and sequence the full genome of the original strains obtained in different moments of the epidemic in 1981, using bioinformatic tools . . .'

57. Caballero and Matilla, 'Historia del CIM', 10.

58. Including Curie Institute (Paris), the Pasteur Institute (Paris), Heidelberg University (Heidelberg, Germany) and Harvard University (Cambridge, MA, USA). Thorsteinsdóttir, Saenz, Quach et al., 'Cuba: Innovation through Synergy', *Nature Biotechnology*, 22, December 2004, 23.

59. Reid-Henry, *Cuban Cure*, 47.

60. Meningococcal disease is one of a group of bacteria responsible for the life-threatening infections meningococcal meningitis and meningococcal septicaemia. Untreated, these conditions can kill within 24 hours. 10% of survivors suffer serious, long-term disabilities, including brain damage. Meningococcal disease is among the top ten global causes of death due to infection. There are 13 different forms of the disease but serogroups A, B and C are by far the most common. According to the World Health Organization there are up to 25,000 meningococcal deaths every year in Africa.

61. Dr Gustavo Sierra cited in 'Meningitis B: Cuba', documentary posted by Journeyman Pictures on 25 January 2008 www.youtube.com/watch?v=rgQZhTg04IM.

62. Despite this, Cuba's achievement has been ignored or censored in Britain. In September 2015 when the NHS introduced a new Meningitis B vaccine for babies it claimed the vaccine: 'makes England [sic] the first country in the world to offer a national, routine and publicly funded MenB vaccination programme'. NHS Choices, https://assets.publishing. service.gov.uk/. The then British Health Secretary Jeremy Hunt repeated the claim. In fact, until 2014, only Cuba had developed a safe and effective Meningitis B vaccine and millions of people in Cuba and around the world had benefited.

63. Lage Dávila, Interview in Havana, 7 July 2017.

64. This occurred during the period of Rectification from the mid-to-late-1980s, during which Fidel Castro pulled Cuba away from the Soviet economic management model, fostering innovative science and technologies instead of the heavy industries the Soviets' recommended (see Chapter 1).

65. Lara Marks' masterful 2015 history of the development of monoclonal antibodies (MABs) omits Cuban advances that have placed the island at the forefront of MAB-based immunology therapies. Lara V. Marks, *The Lock and Key of Medicine: Monoclonal Antibodies and the Transformation of Healthcare*, Yale University Press, 2015.

66. The first monoclonal antibody registered for cancer treatment in the United States was 1997.

67. Lage Dávila, Interview in Havana, 7 July 2017.

68. In the 1980s, almost 80% of world pharmaceutical production (estimated at USD 84 billion) came from industrialised capitalist countries; 19% from centrally planned socialist economies; 11% from Asia, Latin America and Africa (just 0.5%).

69. Cubadebate, 'Cuba promueve en China posibilidad de inversiones en biotecnología', 24 April 2014. http://www.cubadebate.cu/noticias/2014/.

70. Lage Dávila, Interview in Havana, 7 July 2017.

71. Helen Yaffe, 'Cuban Development: Inspiration to the ALBA-TCP' in Thomas Muhr (ed.), *Counter-Globalization and Socialism in the 21st Century: The Bolivarian Alliance for the Peoples of Our America*, Routledge, 2013, 101–118.

72. Recombinant human erythropoietin is used primarily to treat anaemia. By 2019, it had been used to treat 1 million patients in 20 years. CIM, *Presentacíon*, 2019.

73. The development of Vidatox is entwined with the life of Niurys Monzon, who was diagnosed with pancreatic cancer at the age of 11. In 1992, despite two years of chemotherapy, radiation treatment and three operations, the cancer had spread and hope was fading. Her father contacted a biologist from Guantanamo, Misael Bordier, who was experimenting with the scorpion venom on cancerous tumours in rats and dogs. The results were astonishing: 'The immune system of the benign cells increases, the malignant cells start dying and the tumors shrink or disappear' explained Bordier. 85% of the rats survived. Then aged 15, Niury's became the first Cuban patient to test the venom. When CNN reported on the story in 2003, Niurys was 28 years old and breeding 3,000 scorpions under Bordier's guidance to distribute the venom to other Cuban patients for free from her home. Lucia Newman, 'Scorpion venon: A cure for cancer?' CNN, 23 October 2003, http://edition.cnn.com/2003/HEALTH/10/23/cancer.scorpion.venom/.

74. Compatible with other oncological treatments, the formula has no contraindications. The product has been approved for sale in China and some Latin American countries.

75. For a longer discussion juxtaposing the emergence and characteristics of the biotechnology industry in the United States and advanced capitalist countries and Cuba see Yaffe, 'Cuba's Biotech Revolution'.

76. Christian Zeller, 'The Pharma-biotech Complex and Interconnected Regional Innovation Arenas', *Urban Studies* 47, 13, 2010, 2870.

77. Agustin Lage Dávila, *La Economia del Conocimiento y el Socialismo: Preguntas y Respuestas*, Editorial Academia, 2015, 17–19.

78. This question was addressed by Gary Pisano, *Science Business: The Promise, the Reality, and the Future of Biotech*, Harvard Business School Press, 2006. It was subsequently labelled the 'Pisano Puzzle'. See Lazonick and Tulum, 'US Biopharmaceutical Finance and the Sustainability of the Biotech Business Model', *Research Policy*, 40, 2011, 1170.

79. Joseph Cortright and Heike Mayer, *Signs of Life: The Growth of Biotechnology Centres in the US*, Brookings Institution, Center on Urban and Metropolitan Policy, 2002, 19.

80. Cortright and Mayer, *Signs of Life*, 9.
81. Lazonick and Tulum, 'US Biopharmaceutical Finance', 1172.
82. Lazonick and Tulum, 'US Biopharmaceutical Finance', 1180.
83. Lazonick and Tulum, 'US Biopharmaceutical Finance', 1176.
84. For example, the 1980 Bayh–Dolye Act gave universities and hospitals clear property rights to new knowledge that resulted from federally funded research. Also in 1980, the Supreme Court decision in Diamond vs. Chakrabarty ruled that genetically engineered life forms are patentable. The Orphan Drug Act of 1983 provided generous tax credits for pharmaceutical companies that develop drugs for rare diseases. By 2008, orphan drugs accounted for 74% of total revenues and 75% of product revenues of the six leading companies.
85. Cortright and Mayer, *Signs of Life*, 9.
86. Lage Dávila, Interview in Havana, 7 July 2017.
87. Lee contrasts this to the US, the UK and Europe, where typically a small start-up is established to investigate the science behind a 'great idea'. It is subsequently bought out by a larger company, sometimes twice, which might decide 'well, you developed this drug for a really rare disease but we're going to use it to treat lung cancer', and subsequently 'it really bombs and a great idea disappears'. Lee, Interview via Skype, 3 October 2017.
88. Lee, Interview via Skype, 3 October 2017.
89. EFE, 'Cuba comienza a entregar gratis la píldora preventiva del VIH', 3 April 2019. www.efe.com/efe/america/sociedad/.
90. Given this ratio, 52,000 amputations which take place annually in the US due to diabetic foot ulcers could be prevented.
91. Orfilio Peláez, 'The jewel that Fidel conceived', *Granma*, 7 September 2017, http://en.granma.cu/cuba/2017-09-07/.
92. Lage, Interview in Havana, 7 July 2017.
93. Sara Reardon, 'Can Cuban Science go Global?', in *Nature*, 29 September 2016.
94. *Haemophilus influenza* type b (Hib) is a bacteria responsible for severe pneumonia, meningitis and other invasive diseases almost exclusively in children aged under five.
95. Similarly to Heberprot-P, over 100,000 patients worldwide have benefited from using Itolizumab.
96. This pales into insignificance in comparison to the United States, however, where some 5,500 patents are awarded annually according to Cortright and Mayer, *Signs of Life*, 9.
97. Information from Reid-Henry, *Cuban Cure*, 99–100.
98. Subsequently, they sought a more efficient carrier for EGF.
99. Lee, Interview via Skype, 3 October 2017.
100. Reardon, 'Can Cuban Science Go Global?', 602. In Britain women make up only 12.8% in the science, technology, engineering and maths workforce. George Arnett, 'How well are women represented in UK science?', *Guardian*, 13 June 2015 www.theguardian.com/news/datablog/2015/.
101. This, and low salaries in Cuba, have prompted many Cuban medical scientists to seek employment overseas. However, there is no evidence that the 'brain drain' from Cuba is greater than in other developing countries. Thorsteinsdóttir et al., 'Cuba: Innovation', 22.
102. Lage Dávila, *La Economia del Conocimiento*.
103. Marguerite Jiménez, 'Epidemics and Opportunities for U.S.-Cuba Collaboration' *Science & Diplomacy*, 6 September 2014; Reid-Henry, *Cuban Cure*.
104. Lage Dávila, Interview in Havana, 7 July 2017.
105. Reid-Henry, *Cuban Cure*, 124. Under the Helms–Burton Act, implemented the following year, individual fines could go up to USD 250,000 plus ten years incarceration for trading with Cuba.
106. BBC, 'Cuba vaccine deal breaks embargo', 29 July 1999. http://news.bbc.co.uk/1/hi/world/americas/406780.stm. Other companies who approached Cuba's biopharma industries include: Amersham, Monsanto, Biovation and Biognosis. Reid-Henry, *Cuban Cure*.
107. See Reid-Henry, *Cuban Cure*, about the York Medical collaboration with CIM.
108. Idania Caballero, Interview in Havana, 7 July 2017.

109. York Medical invested USD 10 million over five years in CIMAB, CIM's business wing, and Lage was elected onto their board of directors.
110. Caballero, Interview in Havana, 7 July 2017.
111. John Bolton, speech at the Heritage Foundation, 'Beyond the Axis of Evil: Additional Threats from Weapons of Mass Destruction', 6 May 2002. https://www.heritage.org/defense/report/.
112. Fidel Castro, 'Respuesta Del Presidente De La República De Cuba A Las Declaraciones Del Gobierno De Los Estados Unidos Sobre Armas Biológicas', 10 May 2002, http://www.cuba.cu/gobierno/discursos/2002/esp/f100502e.html.
113. David Gonzalez, 'Carter and Powell Cast Doubt on Bioarms in Cuba', *New York Times*, 14 May 2002, www.nytimes.com/2002/05/14/world/carter-and-powell-cast-doubt-on-bioarms-in-cuba.html.
114. The gravity of the US threat to Cuba must be understood in the international context (invasion of Afghanistan) and the national context (open hostility between the Cuban government and US diplomats in Havana). See Chapter 7 on Cuba–US relations.
115. Reardon, 'Can Cuban Science go Global', 602
116. For more details on Cuban biotech deals in the developing world see Thorsteinsdóttir et al, 'Cuba: Innovation', 5.
117. Biotechpharma is a joint venture in Beijing employing 300 Chinese staff and 14 Cubans to produce monoclonal antibodies.
118. CIM, presentacíon general, 2019; Notman, 'Cuba's Cancer Treatments'.
119. Lee, Interview via Skype, 3 October 2017.
120. The extensive FDA application form required Roswell Park scientists to inspect all the manufacturing, research and development components of CIMAvax-EGF, a process which revealed 'how sophisticated, how carefully designed CIM's clinical trials are', according to Lee. On the 30-day deadline for a FDA response, Roswell Park received a two-line email giving them permission to proceed. Lee, Interview via Skype, 3 October 2017.
121. Lee, Interview via Skype, 3 October 2017.
122. Notman, 'Cuba's Cancer Treatments'.
123. 'CIMAvax is a b-cell vaccine. Its strength is to generate antibodies against epidermal growth factor, and those antibodies deplete epidermal growth factor in the serum. Cancers like lung cancer are very dependent on that growth factor so by depleting it with this immune response and neutralising the immune response, the cancer is starved. Opdivo, or Nivolumab is a T-cell immunomodulator. It activates the T-cells component of the immune system, and those T-cells see the tumour and kill it directly. So you have antibodies being generated by CIMAvax and activated T-lymphocytes being generated by Opdivo.' Lee, Interview via Skype, 3 October 2017.
124. Opdivo costs USD 10,000 a month, four times Cuba's annual health care expenditure per capita, which is around USD 2,500.
125. Lee, Interview via Skype, 3 October 2017.
126. Richard Stone, 'United States bans most government scientists from travel to Cuba', *Science,* 28 November 2017. https://www.sciencemag.org/news/2017/11/united-states-bans-most-government-scientists-travel-cuba.
127. Bill Haseltine, 'The Cuban Biotechnology Industry: A Report by Brookings Trustee Bill Haseltine', Brookings, 2012, 1–3.
128. 'There has been a global trend of increasing R&D (7.4 per cent annual increase of total capitalised costs) since 1980, as well as an increase in R&D expenditure per new drug (802 US millions/drug).' Mola et al, 'Biotechnology in Cuba', 3.
129. Rick Mullin, 'Tufts Study Finds Big Rise in Cost of Drug Development' 20 November 2014. https://cen.acs.org/articles/92/web/2014/11/Tufts-Study-Finds-Big-Rise.html
130. The 2017/18 portfolio of investment opportunities in Cuba states the biopharma sector aims: 'To promote projects in Cuba with strategic partners for manufacturing finished products and active drug ingredients for generic medicines. In the case of biotechnological products, we will be evaluating specific businesses that would complement domestic projects, thereby preserving [Cuban] intellectual property and looking out for the proper use of what may be jointly generated, as well as the creation or extension of production capacities.'

6. CUBAN MEDICAL INTERNATIONALISM: AN ARMY OF WHITE COATS

1. The pile of paperback books on the floor was the new English edition of Pérez Ávila's own book about AIDs in Cuba, *A Doctor and His Patients Talk about AIDS in Cuba*, Casa Editora Abril, 2016.
2. Pérez Ávila graduated with a master's in clinical pharmacology from McGill University in Canada. He studied in the Schools of Tropical Medicine in London and Liverpool and visited universities in Chicago, Cleveland and Ghana.
3. It resembles malaria, cholera, typhoid fever and meningitis. Between 1976 and 2013, the WHO reports a total of 24 outbreaks involving 1,716 cases.
4. The virus is at its most virulent shortly after death, so traditional burial rites involving bathing and embracing the deceased catalyse its spread.
5. USD 2.9 billion was pledged to the WHO by late 2014, but only a little over USD 1 billion was received. John M. Kirk and Chris Walker, 'Cuban Medical Internationalism: The Ebola Campaign of 2014–15', *International Journal of Cuban Studies*, 8:1, Spring 2016, 12.
6. Cited in WHO report, 'Cuban Medical Team Heading for Sierra Leone', September 2014. http://www.who.int/features/2014/cuban-ebola-team/en/.
7. The NGO Doctors without Borders had 225 international staff workers in three West African countries by March 2015, working alongside 2,560 locals. Their medics served for weeks at a time, not months like the Cubans.
8. Jorge Pérez Ávila, Interview in Havana, 6 July 2017.
9. Dr Leonardo Fernández, cited by Enrique Ubieta Gómez, 'Doctors Fighting Ebola: Completing Their Mission with Revolutionary and Medical Ethics', *Granma* online, 23 march 2015, Granma http://en.granma.cu/cuba/2015-03-23/doctors-fighting-ebola.
10. Kirk and Walker, 'The Ebola Campaign'.
11. Fernández, cited by Ubieta Gómez, 'Doctors Fighting Ebola'.
12. Pérez Ávila, cited by Gail Reed, 'Meet Cuban Ebola Fighters: Interview with Félix Baez and Jorge Pérez Ávila, 'A MEDICC Review Exclusive', *MEDICC Review*, 17: 1, Jan-Mar 2015.
13. Kirk and Walker, 'The Ebola Campaign'.
14. 'Cuba maintains fierce point-of-entry controls: mandatory prophylaxis if returning from a malaria-endemic region and quarantine if returning from Ebola-infected locations … routine follow-up actually occurs for travellers returning from any potential disease "hot spot". First, the neighbourhood doctor is notified of a recently returned passenger. The doctor is then obligated to follow up directly with that person both to allow for detection of any unusual symptoms and to ensure quick treatment where necessary as a means of avoiding onward transmission. In this way, the Cuban health system far outperforms any health system in the Global North.' Wexham and Kittlesen, 'Cuban Healthcare Offers Many Lessons for Global Health Security', Latin American and Caribbean centre blog, London School of Economics, 27 February 2019.
15. Kirk and Walker, 'The Ebola Campaign', 10.
16. Fernández, cited by Ubieta Gómez, 'Doctors Fighting Ebola'.
17. The Editorial Board, 'Cuba's Impressive Role on Ebola', *New York Times*, 19 October 2014. https://www.nytimes.com/2014/10/20/opinion/cubas-impressive-role-on-ebola.html.
18. Barak Obama, 'Statement by the President on Cuba Policy Changes', 17 December 2014. The White House, Office of the Press Secretary, https://obamawhitehouse.archives.gov/the-press-office/2014/12/17/. In Liberia, the Cubans worked in US-built centres and operated alongside US NGOs, such as Partners for Health. Felix Baéz was transported to Geneva on Phoenix Air, a company under contract to the US State Department.
19. John Kirk, 'Understanding Cuban Medical Internationalism', PowerPoint presentation, 2019.
20. John Kirk, *Healthcare Without Borders*, University Press of Florida, 2015, xii.
21. Margaret Randall, *Exporting Revolution: Cuba's Global Solidarity*, Duke University Press, 2017, 99.
22. Feinsilver, 'Cuban Medical Diplomacy'; Feinsilver, 'Fifty Years of Cuba's Medical Diplomacy: From Idealism to Pragmatism', *Cuban Studies*, 41, 2000, 96–7.
23. Wexham and Kettle, 'Cuban Healthcare'.
24. Robert Huish, 'Why Does Cuba "Care" So Much? Understanding the Epistemology of Solidarity in Global Health Outreach', *Public Health Ethics*, 7:3, 2014, 262–4.

25. In 1823, the Monroe Doctrine asserted the United States' control over the Americas at the exclusion of European powers, and the notion that Cuba should gravitate naturally to the United States when freed from Spain was articulated. In 1848, following the war with Mexico, the United States annexed one-third of Mexican territory and President James K. Polk offered to buy Cuba from Spain. Thus, the United States' emerging expansionist/imperialist character was already clear by the late 19th century.
26. See Isaac Saney 'Homeland of Humanity: Internationalism within the Cuban Revolution', in *Latin American Perspectives*, 164, 36:1, January 2009, 113.
27. Ernesto Domínguez López and Helen Yaffe, 'The Deep Historical Roots of Cuban Anti-imperialism', in *Third World Quarterly*, 38:11, 2017, 2517–2535.
28. Fidel Castro, cited by Kirk, *Healthcare Without Borders*, 20.
29. The Associacion Nacional de Economistas Cubanos calculates that the US blockade costs Cuba USD 12 million every day, which adds up to USD 4.4 billion annually. Since the mid-2000s, medical exports have earned the country USD 6 to 8 billion annually. However, those revenues do not deduct government expenditure on medical training and overseas missions. ANEC presentation, 2019.
30. The dangers faced by Cuban healthcare workers were underscored by the gun-point abduction of two Cuban medics – Dr Assel Herera Correa, a general physician, and Dr Landy Rodriguez, a surgeon – from Mandera, a town in north-east Kenya on 12 April 2019. They are believed to have been taken into Somalia and were still being held hostage in late 2019. The two were from a group of 100 Cuban medical specialists who first arrived in Kenya in May 2018 following an agreement signed between both countries' governments to improve Kenya's public health system.
31. Huish, 'Why Does Cuba Care', 266.
32. In 2018, infant mortality in Haiti was 41.5:1,000 by which time Haiti had been a beneficiary of Cuban medical assistance for two decades.
33. Cited by Kirk, *Healthcare Without Borders*, 52
34. Feinsilver, 'Cuban Medical Diplomacy'.
35. This title borrows from Kirk, *Healthcare Without Borders*, chapter 1.
36. Kirk points out that, in supporting the guerrillas, Fidel Castro risked the wrath of French President Charles de Gaulle who had resisted US pressure to break relations with Cuba. *Healthcare Without Borders*, 20.
37. Jose Ramon Ventura, cited in, Kirk, *Healthcare Without Borders*, 20.
38. Piero Gleijeses, 'Cuba and Africa: A History Worthy of Pride', *Socialist Voice*, 2004. http://www.socialistvoice.ca/?p=66.
39. Steve Brouwer, *Revolutionary Doctors: How Venezuela and Cuba are Changing the World's Conception of Health Care*, Monthly Review Press, 2011, 58.
40. Kirk, *Healthcare Without Borders*, 120.
41. Brouwer, *Revolutionary Doctors*, 46. Kirk, *Healthcare Without Borders*, 7; Huish, 'Why Does Cuba Care', 265.
42. Brouwer, *Revolutionary Doctors*, 185.
43. Kirk, *Healthcare Without Borders*, 24.
44. Piero Gleijeses, 'Moscow's Proxy? Cuba and Africa 1975–1988' *Journal of Cold War Studies*, 8:4, 2006, 105.
45. Gleijeses, 'Moscow's Proxy?' has more on Cuban interventions in Angola and Ethiopia.
46. See Kirk, *Healthcare Without Borders*, Table 5.1, 120.
47. Brouwer, *Revolutionary Doctors*, 48.
48. See Gleijeses, 'History Worth of Pride'; Saney, 'Homeland of Humanity'.
49. Kirk lists medical faculties established in Yemen 1976, Guyana 1984, Ethiopia 1984, Uganda 1986, Ghana 1991, The Gambia 1999, Equatorial Ghana 2000, Haiti 2001, Guinea Bissau 2004, Venezuela 2005 and Timor-Leste 2010. *Healthcare Without Borders*, Table 5.1, 27.
50. Pérez Ávila, Interview in Havana, 6 July 2017. Pérez himself developed a drug for a strain of malaria which had become resistant to Chloroquine and was affecting Cubans in Angola. See Flor de Paz, 'Jorge Pérez Ávila, director del IPK: Médico hasta sus nanopartículas', *Cubadebate*, 26 diciembre 2014. http://www.cubadebate.cu/noticias/2014/12/26/.

51. Gustavo Kourí, cited by Iramis Alonso and Bárbara Avendaño, 'Gustavo Kourí: Un hombre para la ciencia'. Bohemia, 23 December 2005. http://articulos.sld.cu/ipk/2005/12/24/.
52. Gustavo Kourí served as Vice Chair at the United Nation's TDR (tropical diseases) Special Programme for Research and Training in Tropical Diseases and was a member of WHO's Scientific and Technical Advisory Group for Neglected Tropical Diseases. For an account of his work see: TDR News, 'Remembering Gustavo Kourí', 7 May 2011. www.who.int/tdr/news/2011/in-memoriam-kouri/en/.
53. Pérez Ávila, Interview in Havana, 6 July 2017.
54. Kirk, *Healthcare Without Borders*, 26.
55. On a visit to the Island of Youth in 1995, my sister and I spent time with a group of Zimbabwean students in their fifth year of studying in various non-medical professions. Thousands of students were still hosted there.
56. Information from Kirk, *Healthcare Without Borders*, Table 5.1. 120.
57. Cited in Kirk, *Healthcare Without Borders*, 242–3.
58. The EU contributed USD 2 million to help affected children, while the European Bank for Reconstruction and Development donated EUR 550 million for a protective shell to be placed over Reactor 4. Several international NGOs ran projects to assist the victims, especially children. Kirk, *Healthcare Without Borders*, 237–40.
59. See Cuba and Chernobyl, Cuban Television documentary: https://www.youtube.com/watch?v=H10xE1CcKxQ.
60. Fidel Castro cited by Kirk, *Healthcare Without Borders*, 252.
61. 'Cuba and Chernobyl', Cuban Television documentary.
62. Pre-1959, Tarará was a holiday spot for the Cuban middle class. Subsequently it was turned into a camp for the Cuban pioneers organisation for 7- to 14-year-olds, and a polyclinic was set up. In the 1980s, during the dengue epidemic described in Chapter 6, the clinic was converted into a hospital. In 1990, it was converted into the Children of Chernobyl Camp.
63. A minority were Russian or Belarussian, but most Ukrainian. The travel costs were paid by their governments, or privately.
64. Some 3% of the children faced life-threatening conditions and stayed for long periods with a family member. 17% had chronic pathologies and stayed at the Tarará hospital. 60% were ambulatory and treated at primary healthcare facilites. 20% were relatively healthy but needed screening as they lived in contaminated zones. Kirk, *Healthcare Without Borders*, 245.
65. Kirk, *Healthcare Without Borders*, 249. Kirk estimates the costs to Cuba in billions of dollars, 249.
66. Both Ukrainian presidents are cited making this commitment by Kirk, *Healthcare Without Borders*, 250.
67. Gail Reed, 'Where to Train the World's Doctors? Cuba', TedMed talk, 1 October 2014. https://www.youtube.com/watch?v=rS_Ssisz2_M.
68. Diplomatic relations were restored with Guatemala in 1998, Honduras in 2002, Nicaragua in 2007, and El Salvador and Costa Rica in 2009.
69. Fidel Castro, 'Speech at the Closing Session of the 12th National Science and Technology Forum', 21 November 1998. www.fidelcastro.cu/en/discursos/speech-delivered-closing-session–12th-national-science-and-technology-forum
70. Kirk records that the Cuban government turned down Spanish investors proposing to establish a tourist complex with a golf course on the site. Kirk, *Healthcare Without Borders*, 43. The following information is drawn from Kirk, *Healthcare Without Borders*; Reed, 'Where to Train the World's Doctors?'; Brouwer, *Revolutionary Doctors*.
71. CubaDebate, 'La ELAM ha graduado en Cuba 170 médicos estadounidenses', CubaDebate, 2 August 2017. http://www.cubadebate.cu/noticias/2017/08/02/.
72. Margaret Chan, 'Remarks at the Latin American School of Medicine', World Health Organization, 27 October 2009. http://www.who.int/dg/speeches/2009/cuba_medical_20091027/en/.
73. Kirk, *Healthcare Without Borders*, 65.
74. Anyone who has sought medical treatment in Cuba is likely to have been attended to by an ELAM student.
75. Kirk, *Healthcare Without Borders*, 58.

76. Kirk, *Healthcare Without Borders*, 49. In addition, when foreign media has reported on ELAM it has often been to sensationalise some dispute between students and Cuban authorities, over accommodation conditions or food. In April 2019, some (social) media outlets sought mileage out of a protest by Congolese students angry about the failure of their own government to provide them with a stipend. Conflict is inevitable, given the sheer numbers of young people from diverse countries and cultures confined in one space under such an intense programme.

77. Reed, 'Where to Train the World's Doctors?'.

78. Even Cuba's world-leading biotechnology industry is catered towards providing low-cost treatment in a primary care setting, as Chapter 5 explains.

79. For more on this issue see Huish, *Where No Doctor Has Gone Before*.

80. Reed, 'Where to Train the World's Doctors?'.

81. For a discussion about the two-way flow of international solidarity see Gavin Brown and Helen Yaffe, *Youth Activism and Solidarity: The Non-Stop Picket Against Apartheid*, Routledge, 2018, 32–43.

82. Hugo Chávez, April 2010, cited by Kirk, *Healthcare Without Borders*, 187.

83. By 2014 an estimated 60,000 Venezuelans had been treated in Cuban hospitals.

84. Héctor Navarro, cited by Bouwer, *Revolutionary Doctors*, 76. Figures also from Brouwer, *Revolutionary Doctors*, 75–6.

85. Kirk, *Healthcare Without Borders*, 171.

86. It is also true that, at the height of this collaboration, many Cubans complained about the deterioration of Cuban healthcare provision at home, an indication of their extremely high expectations, given that Cuba retained the best patient to doctor ratio in the world. There was some subsequent effort by the Ministry of Public Health to address this issue.

87. For more on emergence and impact of the Cuba–Venezuela embrace see Helen Yaffe, 'Cuban Development,' 101–18.

88. Yaffe, 'Cuban Development'.

89. Brouwer, *Revolutionary Doctors*, 15

90. Kirk, 'Cuban Medical Internationalism'. In 2017 when the figure was 3.5 million, Telesur reported that 90% of the beneficiaries were Venezuelans and the rest were from 18 Latin American countries. www.telesurtv.net/english/news/. Among the beneficiaries was the former Bolivian soldier who shot Che Guevara in 1967.

91. A high proportion of graduates are women, 77% of graduates in 2012. Kirk, *Healthcare Without Borders*, 185.

92. Kirk, 'Understanding Cuban Medical Internationalism'.

93. Based on the number of patients who would normally have died if medical care had not been provided, according to previous data. Kirk, *Healthcare Without Borders*, 187.

94. This has risen slightly since Venezuela's economic and political crises from 2013. The mainstream media claimed a 30% rise in 2016, but the CIA estimate for that year was 12.5 per 1,000 live births, still lower than in 2010.

95. Fidel Castro, 'Speech at the Foundation Ceremony of the "Henry Reeve" International Contingent of Doctors Specialized in Disaster Situations and Serious Epidemics, and the National Graduation of Students of Medical Sciences, 19 September 2005'. Scoop Independent News World. http://www.scoop.co.nz/stories/WO0509/S00376.htm.

96. A friend of mine, a native of New Orleans working as a community organiser in Houston, helped out in the Houston Astrodome, which hosted tens of thousands of survivors. He described the desperation, disorganisation and 'circus of political opportunism and condescension' the survivors faced. He also told me that when the live TV news channels broadcast onto huge screens in the command centre showed the image of Fidel Castro with news of Cuba's offer to assist, the US military personnel and politicians awkwardly ignored it.

97. Fidel Castro, 'Speech, Foundation Ceremony of the "Henry Reeve"'.

98. Helen Yaffe, 'Internationalism in Practice: Cuban Doctors in the Mountains of Pakistan', *Fight Racism! Fight Imperialism!* 190, April–May 2006. http://www.revolutionarycommunist.org/americas/cuba/.

99. Over USD 6.5 billion was pledged internationally, of which a little over USD 1 billion was received by the Pakistani government.
100. Yaffe, 'Internationalism in Practice'.
101. Kirk, *Healthcare Without Borders*, 128–30
102. Yaffe, 'Internationalism in Practice'.
103. Jean Víctor Généus, cited by Kirk, *Healthcare Without Borders*, 207–8.
104. Randall, *Exporting Revolution*, 180.
105. Kirk, *Healthcare Without Borders,*199.
106. John Kirk and Emily Kirk examined media censorship of Cuba's role, 'Cuban Medical Aid to Cuba', *Counterpunch*, 1 April 2010. www.counterpunch.org/2010/04/01/cuban-medical-aid-to-haiti/.
107. Fidel Castro, 23 January 2010, cited by Kirk, *Healthcare Without Borders*, 198.
108. The November 1998 cooperation agreement included a literacy campaign, education, agriculture, tourism, sport and, principally, medical cooperation. One month later, the first Cuban doctors arrived in Haiti.
109. Kirk, *Healthcare Without Borders*, 194.
110. PAHO report cited by Kirk, *Healthcare Without Borders*, 196. Under-five infant mortality was reduced from 135 to 59.4 per 1,000. Kirk also describes how in September 2004, when 2,800 people died after flooding in the Haitian port city of Gonaïves, a 64-person medical brigade arrived from Cuba to support the 18 Cuban medics already worked there. They set up an additional network of six clinics and a public health education campaign to prevent epidemics. Kirk, *Healthcare Without Borders*, 191.
111. Kirk, *Healthcare Without Borders*, 193.
112. Many faced unemployment for lack of investment in the public healthcare sector as mentioned above.
113. Kirk, *Healthcare Without Borders*, 205–6
114. Cited by Kirk, *Healthcare Without Borders*, 213.
115. Kirk, *Healthcare Without Borders;* Huish, 'Going Where No Doctor Has Gone'; Randall, *Exporting Revolution*.
116. On Cuba's role in the South Pacific see John M. Kirk and Chris Walker, 'From Cooperation to Capacitation: Cuban Medical Internationalism in the South Pacific' in *International Journal of Cuban Studies*, 5.1 Spring 2013, 10–25; on assistance for the disabled see Kirk, *Healthcare Without Borders*, chapter 3. The programme was based on a similar programme developed in Cuba during the Battle of Ideas and discussed in Chapter 3. Kirk lists 20 Cuban international disaster responses between 2000 and 2010, most of which are not included in this chapter. Kirk, *Healthcare Without Borders*, Table 5.1, 120–22.
117. Fidel Castro, 'Speech, Foundation Ceremony of the "Henry Reeve"'.
118. Economist Intelligence Unit (EIU), 'Country Report, Cuba', 21 December 2017, 25–6.
119. Kirk, *Healthcare Without Borders*, 39.
120. EIU, 'Country Report', 25.
121. For example, the British government gave money to South Africa to help pay Cubans operating in Southern Africa, while France did likewise for its former African colonies.
122. Aleida Guevara, 'Cuban Medical Internationalism'.
123. While tourism earnings were only slightly higher in 2016 (USD 3.07 billion) medical exports had fallen from around USD 8.2 billion in 2016.
124. According to Cuban economist José Luis Rodríguez, cited in EIU, 'Country Report', 25. The EIU's own annual estimate for the same period is USD 2 billion lower.
125. Rob Baggot and George Lambie, 'Hard Currency, Solidarity, and Soft Power: The Motives, Implications, and Lessons of Cuban Health Internationalism', *International Journal of Health Services*, 49:1, 2019, 170.
126. From 1998 to early 2010, 6,494 Cuban doctors in Haiti had carried out 14 million medical consultations ($10 each = $140 million), 225,000 surgeries ($100 each = $225 million), 100,000 births ($50 each = $5 million), 47,273 eye operations ($25 each = $1 million). Plus 570 Haitian medical graduates ($5,000 each = $5.5 million) and 11 years of salaries ($500 monthly = $41 million). José Steinsleger, 'Haití, Cuba y la ley primera'. *La Jornada*, 3 February 2010. http://www.jornada.unam.mx/2010/02/03/opinion/019a1pol.

127. Kirk, *Healthcare Without Borders*, 34.
128. The 2018 figure was a forecast. EIU, 'Country Report', 25.
129. US sanctions on Venezuela were first implemented by Obama in 2015.
130. Kirk, *Cuban Medical Internationalism*.
131. Aleida Guevara, 'Cuban Medical Internationalism'.
132. A PAHO report also found that almost 70% of the Brazil's poor families had access to basic health care in 2017 through the More Doctors Programme. 'Brazil: Bolsonaro Ready to Terminate the "More Doctors" Program', Telesur, 7 February 2019, https://www.telesurenglish.net/news/
133. Telesur, 'Over 1,000 Physicians Give Up Bolsonaro's "More Doctors" Program', 4 April 2019 https://www.telesurenglish.net/news/.
134. For more on the Medical Parole Programme see H. Michael Erisman, 'Brain Drain Politics: The Cuban Medical Professional Parole Programme', *International Journal of Cuban Studies,* 4: 3/4, (Autumn/Winter 2012), 269–90.
135. Randall, *Exporting Revolution*, 162.
136. Erisman, 'Brain Drain Politics', 279.
137. Erisman, 'Brain Drain Politics', 282. Erisman also points out that Cuban medical professionals may be rendered ineligible as immigrants to the United States if they have been members of a communist party or affiliated organisations within ten years of their application.
138. The Editorial Board, 'A Cuban Brain Drain, Courtesy of the US', *New York Times*, 17 November 2014. https://www.nytimes.com/2014/11/17/.
139. With this avenue for defection ended, a group of 150 Cuban doctors in Brazil filed lawsuits in Brazilian courts, 'demanding to be treated as independent contractors who earn full salaries, not agents of the Cuban state' as reported by Ernesto Londoño, 'Cuban Doctors Revolt: "You Get Tired of Being a Slave"', 29 September 2017, *New York Times*. https://www.nytimes.com/2017/09/29/world/americas/brazil-cuban-doctors-revolt.html. If successful, they are unlikely to pay back the Cuban government for their training.
140. Among US programmes in Cuba have been efforts to set up 'private pharmacies' often stocked with medicines pilfered from government resources.
141. Pérez Ávila, Interview in Havana, 6 July 2017.
142. Guideline 70, 2016–21, 'Documentos de 7mo. Congreso'.
143. Guideline 84, 2016–21, 'Documentos de 7mo. Congreso'.
144. Cited by Kirk, *Healthcare Without Borders*, 276
145. Agencia Cubana de Noticias, 'Destaca Canciller cubano labor de médicos en Mozambique', 9 April 2019, *Escambray*, http://www.escambray.cu/2019/. On 14 March, Tropical Cyclone Idai hit Mozambique affecting 2 million people and killing at least 400.
146. Carlos Fernandez de Cossío, Cuba's General Director of US Affairs, interviewed by Andrea Mitchell, MSNBC, 3 May 2019. http://www.msnbc.com/andrea-mitchell-reports/
147. John Kirk, 'Cuban Foreign Policy from Raúl to Díaz-Canel', presentation on the panel 'Cuba After Castro: A New Model of "Prosperous and Sustainable" Socialism', Latin American Studies Association Annual Congress, Boston, 25 May 2019.

7. CUBA AND THE UNITED STATES: *PLUS ÇA CHANGE, PLUS C'EST LA MÊME CHOSE?*

1. This figure rises to over USD 933 billion when taking into account the depreciation of the dollar against the price of gold on the international market.
2. Carlos Fernandez de Cossío, Cuba's General Director of US Affairs in Cuba's Ministry of Foreign Relations, interviewed by Andrea Mitchell, MSNBC, 3 May 2019. http://www.msnbc.com/andrea-mitchell-reports/watch/.
3. John Bolton, 'Remarks by National Security Advisor Ambassador John R. Bolton on the Administration's Policies in Latin America', issued on 2 November 2018. https://www.whitehouse.gov/briefings-statements/. On 10 September 2019, Bolton was sacked by Trump as National Security Advisor, but claiming he had first resigned.

4. Ricardo Alarcón, Interview in Havana, 27 December 2016.

5. George W. Bush, 'President Bush Delivers Graduation Speech at West Point', United States Military Academy, West Point, New York, June 1, 2002. https://georgewbush-whitehouse. archives.gov/news/releases/2002/06/.

6. Fidel Castro, 'Discurso pronunciado en las honras fúnebres de las víctimas del bombardeo a distintos puntos de la república, efectuado en 23 y 12, frente al cementerio de Colón', 16 April 1961. http://www.cuba.cu/gobierno/discursos/1961/esp/f160461e.html.

7. Che Guevara cited by Kornbluh and LeoGrande, *Back Channel*, 85.

8. In 2016, Tracey Eaton revealed that: 'The State Department, the Agency for International Development and the National Endowment for Democracy have spent $304,300,000 on Cuba-related democracy programs since 1996. The Broadcasting Board of Governors, which oversees Radio & TV Martí, has spent another $700 million or so. That brings the total to around $1 billion [by 2015].' Tracey Eaton, 'Democracy Spending Down, but Controversy Remains', *Along the Malecón*, 1 October 2016. https://alongthemalecon. blogspot.co.uk/2016/10/.

9. See the Channel 4 documentary, '638 Ways to Kill Castro', directed by Dollan Cannell, 28 November 2006, about CIA attempts to assassinate Fidel Castro. https://www.youtube. com/watch?v=COd4fIvUBeI.

10. James Bamford, *Body of Secrets: Anatomy of the Ultra-Secret National Security Agency*, First Anchor, 2002, 77.

11. Tomás Diez Acosta, *Peligros y principios*. Editorial Verde Olivo, Cuba, 1992, 170.

12. The statement 'he may be a son of a bitch, but he's our son of a bitch' has been attributed to several US presidents referring to different foreign dictators. President Franklin D. Roosevelt allegedly said it about Anastasio Somoza in Nicaragua and/or Rafael Trujillo in the Dominican Republic.

13. Bardach, *Cuba Confidential*, 145.

14. Carriles, Bosch and Mas Canosa had died peacefully, at full liberty, in Miami. Rodriguez was still alive at the time of writing.

15. Kornbluh and LeoGrande, *Back Channel*, 112. For example, according to the *San Francisco Chronicle*, 'With at least the tacit backing of U.S. Central Intelligence Agency officials, operatives linked to anti-Castro terrorists introduced African swine fever virus into Cuba in 1971. Six weeks later an outbreak of the disease forced the slaughter of 500,000 pigs to prevent a nationwide animal epidemic.' '1971 Mystery', 10 January 1977. http://www. maebrussell.com/Health/CIA%20Pig%20Virus.html.

16. FBI veteran, cited by Bardach, *Cuba Confidential*, 116.

17. Carriles, cited by Bardach, *Cuba Confidential*, 175.

18. Carriles was granted Venezuelan citizenship, which explains why the Chávez government requested his extradition to Venezuela where he was wanted for the Cuban airline bombing mentioned later.

19. The so-called Archives of Terror uncovered in Paraguay in December 1992 revealed that at least 50,000 people had been killed, 30,000 'disappeared' and 400,000 arrested and imprisoned under Operation Condor.

20. Cuban researchers, academics and former agents have documented these activities in detail. Among the English language accounts are: Bardach, *Cuba Confidential*, and Hernando Calvo Ospina, *Bacardi: the Hidden War*, London: Pluto Press, 2000.

21. Bardach, *Cuba Confidential*, 179.

22. Note verbale datée du 24 novembre 2014, adressée au Secrétaire général par la Mission permanente de Cuba auprès de l'Organisation des Nations Unies, 2 March 2015, http:// tinyurl.com/y2e2ugwh

23. From 1973 to 1976 more than 100 politically motivated attacks in South Florida were directed by anti-Castro groups: businesses and media outlets were bombed, careers were destroyed and people were assassinated.

24. Bardach, *Cuba Confidential*, 117.

25. Bosch cited in the *Miami Herald*, 'Venezuelans Absolve Bosch in Bombing of Plane', 27 September 1980. http://www.latinamericanstudies.org/belligerence/bosch-absolved. htm.

26. Bardach, *Cuba Confidential*, 192.

27. Tina Griego, 'They Risked Everything to Open a Door to Cuba: They were Shunned for it', *The Washington Post*, 5 January 2005. www.washingtonpost.com/news/storyline/wp/2015/01/05/. The Brigade grew out of *Arieto*, a magazine published by New York-based exiles who supported the Cuban Revolution.
28. Griego, 'They Risked Everything'.
29. Kornbluh and LeoGrande, *Back Channel*, 179. On this first meeting with Fidel Castro in Havana, Benes apparently first joked that he had come to collect the USD 1 million the government of Cuba owed his family for expropriating their textile factory. Kornbluh and LeoGrande, *Back Channel*, 180.
30. Nelson Valdés, personal communication, 18 December 2018.
31. Kornbluh and LeoGrande, *Back Channel*, 195; Bardach, *Cuba Confidential*, 110; Griego, 'They Risked Everything'.
32. After 10,000 Cubans sought asylum in the Peruvian embassy in April 1980, Fidel Castro announced that any Cuban who wanted to leave the island could go to Mariel harbour and be picked up by Cuban-Americans.
33. Bardach, *Cuba Confidential*, 116.
34. 'Cuban Security discovered and identified a total of 179 officers, 27 polygraph (lie detector) technicians, 28 communications technicians and 18 CIA collaborators.' They included foreign recruits. Manuel A. González, 'Agentes encubiertos y oficiales descubiertos', *Razones de Cuba*, 4 mayo 2016. http://razonesdecuba.cubadebate.cu/articulos/agentes-encubiertos-y-oficiales-descubiertos/.
35. González, 'Agentes Encubiertos'.
36. Bardach, *Cuba Confidential*, 139–40.
37. Bardach, *Cuba Confidential*, 211.
38. Two bombs were placed on the flight by Venezuelans Freddy Lugo and Hernán Ricardo Lozano.
39. Eaton, 'Democracy Spending Down'.
40. Bolton, 'Remarks by National Security Advisor'.
41. Six months after Bolton's statement, on 5 May 2019, Secretary of State Mike Pompeo suggested that the Trump administration was talking to the Cuban government about the situation with Venezuela. David Jessop, 'Pompeo Indicates Dialogue may be Taking Place with Cuba on Venezuela', *Cuba Briefing*, 13 May 2019, 3.
42. This analysis draws from Kornbluh and LeoGrande, *Back Channel*. For a Cuban account see Elier Ramírez Cañedo and Esteban Morales Domínguez, *De la Confrontación a los Intentos de 'Normalización': La Política de los Estados Unidos hacia Cuba*, Editorial de Ciencias Sociales, 2014.
43. Kornbluh and LeoGrande, *Back Channel*, 44–45.
44. For fear of recriminations from the powerful Cuban exile community, US officials have often claimed that talks concerned a single issue. According to Alarcón, however, that was rarely the case: 'I have a hard time remembering the exceptional moments when we only talked about that one thing'. Alarcón, Interview in Havana, 27 December 2016.
45. Because he presided over the National Assembly, foreign commentators often referred to Ricardo Alarcón as the third-most powerful figure in Cuba. He also was a member of the Political Bureau of the Communist Party of Cuba until 2013. Today he is an adviser to the Council of State.
46. Alarcón, Interview in Havana, 27 December 2016.
47. Accompanying Alarcón on the Cuban team were José Antonio Arbezú, from the Cuban Communist Party's Americas Department, and Olga Miranda, Legal Adviser in the Ministry of Foreign Relations.
48. Alarcón, Interview in Havana, 27 December 2016.
49. Fidel Castro to Peter Tarnoff in 1977, cited in Kornbluh and LeoGrande, *Back Channel*, 201.
50. A point emphasised by Josefina Vidal, Interview in Havana, 28 December 2016.
51. Chile, Uruguay, Bolivia and Mexico voted against, but only Mexico defied the decision. According to Kornbluh and LeoGrande, before the OAS vote officials from the US, Brazil and Mexico made a secret pact to ensure that one OAS country would maintain relations

with Cuba; not even President Johnson knew about the deal orchestrated by Secretary of State Dean Rusk. Kornbluh and LeoGrande, *Back Channel*, 100.

52. Diplomatic relations with the Soviet Union, which had been broken after Batista's coup in 1952, were re-established in May 1960. The United States broke off diplomatic relations with Cuba on 3 January 1961.

53. Piero Gleijeses, *Conflicting Missions: Havana, Washington, and Africa, 1959–1976*, University of North Carolina Press. Gleijeses has researched and published many important works about Cuba's role in Africa. In 1973, 200 Cuban military advisers went to the People's Democratic Republic of Yemen, then the only 'socialist state' in the Arab World; Cubans trained revolutionaries in the Dhofar region of feudal Oman and sent troops to Syria. Between November 1973 and May 1974 Cubans using Soviet tanks directly engaged Israeli forces in the Golan Heights. Randall, *Exporting Revolution*, 71.

54. Piero Gleijeses, 'Moscow's Proxy?', 98.

55. An organisation for states not formally aligned to the capitalist or socialist world power blocs. The label 'Non-Aligned Movement' (NAM) was not adopted until the fifth conference in 1976. Havana went on to host NAM summits in 1979 and 2006.

56. This led to the foundation of the Organization for the Solidarity with the Peoples of Asia, Africa and Latin America (OSPAAL).

57. The four countries were Barbados, Guyana, Jamaica, and Trinidad and Tobago,

58. Allende, Interview in Havana, 4 January 2017.

59. Serrano, Interview in Havana, 4 April 2018. In 2018 there were 2,011 solidarity associations worldwide, which organised more than 3,800 activities in 131 countries. Nuria Barbosa León, 'Retos para el Movimiento de solidaridad con Cuba en el 2019', *Granma*, 25 January 2019. http://www.granma.cu/cuba/2019-01-25/.

60. When I attended the World Festival of Youth and Students in Cuba in 1997, the largest delegation was from the United States, with 850 members. By comparison, the British delegation had fewer than 100 members.

61. Bardach, *Cuba Confidential*, 127.

62. Cited by Jane Franklin, 'The Cuba Obsession', *The Progressive*, July 1993, http://andromeda. rutgers.edu/~hbf/canf.htm.

63. Bardach adds: 'that the one exemption written into the bill allowed US telecommunications firms to do business with Cuba and that Mas Canosa presided over one of the largest phone cable systems in Florida prompted Beltway wags to dub the legislation the "Jorge Mas Canosa Telecommunications Act".' Bardach, *Cuba Confidential*, 128.

64. Franklin, 'Cuba Obsession'.

65. Kornbluh and LeoGrande, *Back Channel*, 268.

66. See Bardach, *Cuba Confidential*, 128–30.

67. The Helms–Burton Act has four titles. Title I is concerned with 'strengthening international sanctions against the Castro government'; Title II contains measures of 'assistance to a free and independent Cuba'; Title III authorises US nationals with claims to confiscated property in Cuba to file suits in US courts against persons that may be 'trafficking' in that property; Title IV obliges US authorities to deny entry into the United States of foreigners owning or 'trafficking' in 'confiscated properties of United States nationals'. Cuban Liberty and Democratic Solidarity (Libertad) Act of 1996. https://www.treasury.gov/resource-center/sanctions/documents/libertad.pdf.

68. Stefaan Smis and Kim van der Borght, 'The EU-US Compromise on the Helms–Burton and D'Amato Acts', *American Journal of International Law*, 93:1, January 1999, 228.

69. 1997 Understanding, supra note 12, 36 ILM at 529, cited in Stefaan Smis and Kim van der Borght, 'EU-US Compromise', 232.

70. The EU's concern for Cuban human rights did not extend to the indiscriminate suffering inflicted by the US blockade.

71. The one exception I am aware of (prior to the enactment of Title III of the Helms–Burton Act) was in April 2016 when a district court in Dortmund, Germany, issued an order against PayPal for applying US laws in the country. See: http://misiones.minrex.gob.cu/en/articulo/cubas-report-resolution-705-united-nations-general-assembly-entitled-necessity-ending.

72. Roque said that the Brother's leader Basulto 'had asked him for information he could use to attack electric transmission towers in Ceinfuegos province'. Stephen Kimber, *What Lies Across the Water: The Real Story of the Cuban Five*, Fernwood Publishing, 2013, 109–10. See also: Asamblea Nacional de Poder Popular, *The Perfect Storm: The Case of the Cuban Five*, Editora Política, 2005.

73. The payment received in 2001 only applied to three of the deceased who had been US citizens. The family of the fourth was granted USD 3 million from the other recipients. 'Cuban pilots charged with murder', CNN, 22 August 2003, http://edition.cnn.com/2003/LAW/08/21/cuba.pilots/.

74. I was in Cuba in summer 1997, along with 12,000 young people from around the world participating in 14th World Festival of Youth and Students under the slogan, 'For Anti-Imperialist Solidarity, Peace and Friendship'.

75. Kimber, *The Cuban Five*, 199. Ten Cuban agents involved in the Wasp Network were arrested, but five of them struck deals with US authorities – lesser sentences in exchange for testifying against their compatriots.

76. They were convicted of false identification, conspiracy to commit espionage and, in Gerardo Hernández's case, conspiracy to commit murder, for passing information about the Brothers flight plans to Cuban intelligence prior to the shoot down. The Five were subjected to long stretches in isolation and denial of access to lawyers or family visits.

77. Cuba and Venezuela set up ALBA in 2004. Bolivia joined in 2006, Nicaragua in 2007, Honduras in 2008 (withdrawn after the 2009 coup against Manuel Zelaya), Dominica in 2008, Ecuador in 2009 (withdrawn in 2018), Antigua and Barbuda 2009 and Saint Vincent and the Grenadines in 2009, Saint Kitts and Nevis, Saint Lucia (2014) and Grenada 2014.

78. Helen Yaffe, 'Cuban Development', 101–18.

79. Cited by Philip Brenner and Marguerite Jimenez, 'US Policy on Cuba Beyond the Last Gasp', *NACLA Report on the Americas,* 39:4, 21.

80. Correa Delgado, Interview in London, 28 October 2009.

81. There were exceptions: Mexico has been a member of the North American Free Trade Area with the United States and Canada since 1994, and the Pacific Alliance established between Chile, Colombia, Mexico and Peru in 2011 was favourable towards the United States, arguably having been set up to counter the impact of the more radical trade and cooperation forums.

82. Ernesto Domínguez López and Helen Yaffe, 'The Deep Historical Roots of Cuban Anti-imperialism' in *Third World Quarterly*, 2017, 38:11, 2526.

83. Mireya Moscoso was a graduate of Miami Dade College which was established in 1959 largely for Cuban exiles. According to Canadian journalist Jean-Guy Allard, 'The pardon ... was negotiated in Miami by Ruby Moscoso, sister of the then Panamanian president Mireya Moscoso, for the sum of USD 4 million, according to documents published on the internet. It is also revealed that Posada Carriles used false documents provided by the US embassy in Panama to leave that country.' Special for *Granma International*, 7 April 2005. www.latinamericanstudies.org/posada/pardoning.htm.

84. Relations were restored by the incoming administration of Martín Torrijos.

85. Carol J. Williams, 'US Criticized as Cuban Exile is Freed', *Los Angeles Times*, 20 April 2007.

86. Democracy Now! Interview with Ann Louise Bardach, 2009, 'Cuban Exile Carriles and Her Book'.

87. George W. Bush, 'State of the Union Address', 21 September 2001, https://www.theguardian.com/world/2001/sep/21/september11.usa13.

88. John Bolton, Speech 'Beyond the Axis of Evil', 2000.

89. David Gonzalez, 'Carter and Powell Cast Doubt on Bioarms in Cuba', *New York Times*, 14 May 2002. www.nytimes.com/2002/05/14/world/carter-and-powell-cast-doubt-on-bioarms-in-cuba.html.

90. This was in contravention of the United Nations Declaration on the Inadmissibility of Intervention and Interference in the Internal Affairs of States. Resolution 36/103, 91st Plenary meeting, 9 December 1981.

91. See 'The "Diplomacy" of James Cason: Manual for Manufacturing Dissidents' for a chronological record of Cason's activities between 10 September 2002, when he arrived, to 14 March 2003. The final event listed on 14 March was a workshop on 'journalistic ethics' hosted at Cason's home with 34 Cubans of the 'independent press', 21 journalists from 10 foreign press agencies and 5 members of USIS. Even the content of the lunch is noted in the document. Cuba Socialista: https://web.archive.org/web/20040108232206/http://www.cubasocialista.cu/texto/csidisi1.htm.

92. Even some longstanding supporters of Cuba, such as US scholar Noam Chomsky, condemned Cuban government repression.

93. Phillip Agee, 'Terrorism and Civil Society as Instruments of US Policy in Cuba', *Counter Punch*, 8 August 2003. https://www.counterpunch.org/2003/08/08/.

94. James Petras, 'The Responsibility of the Intellectuals: Cuba, the US and Human Rights', 1 May 2003. https://www.canadiannetworkoncuba.ca/Documents/Petras-1may03.shtml. He adds: 'This is especially true of the U.S. where under Title 18, Section 951 of the U.S. Code, "anyone who agrees to operate within the United States subject to the direction or control of a foreign government or official would be subjected to criminal prosecution and a 10 year prison sentence".'

95. Felipe Pérez Roque, 'Cuban Foreign Minister Felipe Pérez Roque', press conference, 9 April 2003. https://www.canadiannetworkoncuba.ca/Documents/Roque-Dissidents-Apr03.shtml.

96. Rosa Miriam, *Los Dissidentes*, Editora Política, 2003, has testimonies from 12 Cuban state agents infiltrated into US-backed internal opposition. http://www.lajiribilla.co.cu/pdf/disidentes/parte1.pdf.

97. Witness statement by Néstor Baguer Sánchez Galarraga, footage shown at Roque, 'Press Conference'. The agent had helped lead the journalism ethics workshop at Cason's home on 14 March referred to earlier.

98. Witness statement by Odilia Collazo, footage shown at Roque, 'Press Conference'.

99. Roque, 'Press Conference'.

100. By March 2004, the US military was holding nearly 7,500 prisoners in Abu Ghraib prison in Iraq.

101. Roque, 'Press Conference'.

102. Roque, 'Press Conference'.

103. The label 'Ladies in White' is a wildly misplaced reference to the Argentinian Madres de la Plaza (Mothers of the Square), who emerged in Argentina to demand information about the 30,000 people 'disappeared' during the Dirty War, 1976 to 1983, under the US-backed military dictatorship.

104. See 'Laura Pollán, muerte de las damas de blanco, fracaso contra el pueblo de Cuba', 16 Oct 2011. *Razones de Cuba*. https://www.youtube.com/watch?v=IQ6689MU1ug. In November 2006, Álvarez was sentenced to four years in prison in the United States for conspiracy to stockpile weapons for use against Cuba. A few years earlier Álvarez's plans to bomb Havana's famous Tropicana night club were thwarted by a Cuban government intelligence agent he unwittingly offered to pay USD 10,000 per bomb.

105. Colin Powell, US Secretary of State, 'foreword', 'Commission for Assistance to a Free Cuba, Report to the President', May 2004. https://pdf.usaid.gov/pdf_docs/Pcaab192.pdf.

106. 'The program could draw on youth organizations in Central and Eastern Europe, especially in Poland, the Czech Republic, Albania, Serbia, to travel to Cuba to organize and conduct training, develop informational materials and conduct other outreach. Many of these groups have been successfully involved in similar efforts in other countries and have expressed a commitment to doing the same in Cuba'. 'Commission for Assistance', 23.

107. 'Commission for Assistance', Condoleezza Rice, Secretary of State, Chair; Carlos Gutierrez, Secretary of Commerce, Co-Chair, July 2006, 20. This USD 20 million annual 'investment' continued into the Obama era.

108. Alarcón cited by Suzanne Goldenberg, 'US has $80m plan for Cuba after Castro', *Guardian*, 4 July 2006. https://www.theguardian.com/world/2006/jul/04/usa.cuba.

109. Raúl Capote, *Enemigo*, Editorial José Martí, 2011.

110. Capote, *Enemigo*, 87–9.
111. Sánchez was also receiving a monthly salary of USD 10,000, paid by SIP IAPA (a group of Latin American big media corporations) and the Spanish daily *El Pais*. See Salim Lamrani, 'Conversaciones con la bloguera cubana Yoani Sánchez', *Rebelion*, 15 April 2010, available in English: http://internalreform.blogspot.com/2010/04/; and Helen Yaffe, 'The Grotesque Circus of Yoani Sanchez' *Fight Racism! Fight Imperialism!* April–May 2013. http://revolutionarycommunist.org/americas/cuba/2970-tg170413.
112. Jonathan Farrar, Cable, 15 April 2009. https://wikileaks.org/plusd/cables/09HAVANA221_a.html.
113. United States Government Accountability Office, Report to Congressional Requesters, Foreign Assistance US Democracy Assistance for Cuba, November 2006, 37. https://docs.google.com/file/d/0B6Mo1c2bIFLWODkxbWwwOGpaM0E/edit.
114. Miami exiles alleged that Cuba was laundering USD 3.9 billion with the Swiss bank.
115. Daniel W. Fisk 'Advancing the Day When Cuba Will Be Free', Deputy Assistant Secretary, Bureau of Western Hemisphere Affairs, Remarks to the Cuban American Veterans Association, Miami, Florida, 9 October 2004. https://2001-2009.state.gov/p/wha/rls/rm/37025.htm.
116. Allegedly, the OFAC group pursuing Cuban assets had many more members than the group set up to pursue the assets of Osama Bin Laden.
117. Chapter 3 has more information on this. The Cuban legislation did not criminalise the US dollar, which could be legally held or deposited in Cuban bank accounts.
118. 'Years of receiving perks and privileges from the government had established something of a détente between the Jewish community and the Castros – they even had some of the best access to technology like cell phones and email of anyone on the island.' Joshua Hersh, 'I Was Duped. I Was Used.' *BuzzFeed*, 1 July 2015. https://www.buzzfeed.com/joshuahersh/alan-gross-and-the-high-cost-of-democracy-in-cuba.
119. Gross was released on 17 December 2014.
120. See: 'Cubans Mobilise Against Imperialist Mercenaries and Terrorists', http://www.youtube.com/watch?v=FdiAx-HtLM0.
121. Orlando Zapata's criminal record involved: domestic violence (2003), possession of a weapon and assault (fracturing someone's cranium with a machete) (2000), fraud (2000), and public disorder (2002). John M. Kirk and Emily J. Kirk, 'Human Rights in Cuba and Honduras, 2010: The Spring of Discontent', *Cuba Analysis*, 19 May 2010. https://cuba-solidarity.org.uk/news/article/1851/human-rights-in-cuba-and-honduras-2010-the-spring-of-discontent.
122. French commentator Salim Lamrani points out: 'On the one hand AI [Amnesty International] characterises them as "prisoners of conscience" and on the other hand it admits they committed the serious crime of accepting "money or materials from the US government".' Salim Lamrani, 'The Suicide of Orlando Zapata Tamayo', *Voltaire Network*, 18 March 2010, http://www.voltairenet.org/article164489.html. Lamrani points out that in 2009 there were 122 suicides in French prisons and 60 in those of England and Wales, none of which were met with international outcry.
123. The day after his death, Zapata's mother declared: 'They finally murdered my son', and later called for the world to impose sanctions on Cuba. In response, Cuban national news aired footage of Zapata's mother thanking Cuban medical personnel: 'We have full confidence; we can see your concern and everything that is being done to save him.' She referred to 'the best doctors, trying to save his life'. The Cuban medics had a kidney for transplant standing by.
124. In 1995 Fariñas assaulted, battered and threatened to kill a woman doctor and hospital director. Sentenced to 3 years, he initiated his first hunger strike and joined the 'dissidence'. In 2002, an old woman he attacked with a walking stick needed emergency surgery. Sentenced to 5 to 10 years, Fariñas began a second hunger strike. His third hunger strike was to demand a television in the hospital wing where he was recovering from dehydration caused by the second. In December 2003, Cuban authorities released him because of his medical condition, but in 2006 Fariñas initiated a hunger strike to demand internet access from his home for his work as a reporter for *Radio Martí*. Salim Lamrani, 'The Inconvenient

Truth about Guillermo Fariñas', *Machetera*, https://machetera.wordpress.com/2010/11/11/the-inconvenient-truth-about-guillermo-farinas/. In 2016, Fariñas was among a handful of 'dissidents' who met President Obama at USIS in Havana.

125. Both programmes were exposed by Associated Press investigations. Those contracted were given 'quick pointers on how to evade Cuban intelligence and were paid as little as $5.41 an hour for work that could have easily landed them in prison'. Editorial, 'In Cuba, Misadventures in Regime Change', 9 November 2014, *New York Times*. https://www.nytimes.com/2014/11/10/opinion/in-cuba-misadventures-in-regime-change.html.

126. The official claim was that Gross's release was a humanitarian gesture and not part of the prisoner swop.

127. Vidal, Interview in Havana, 28 December 2016.

128. Cuba's resolution has received a majority vote in favour every year since it was first submitted in 1992. For several years, only the United States and Israel have opposed it.

129. In January 2015, after visiting Cuba the previous summer, Thomas Donohue, president of the influential US Chamber of Commerce, enthused about the prospects of trade with Cuba, pointing out that many countries were increasing trade with Cuba, including Russia and China. 'State of American Business News Conference', C-Span, https://www.c-span.org/video/?323778-2/. In early January 2015, some 30 US agricultural and food companies announced that they would pressure Congress to end the blockade.

130. Putin cited by Alexei Anishchuk and Daniel Trotta, 'Putin Pledges To Help Cuba Explore for Offshore Oil', Reuters, 11 July 2014. Russia was exploring for oil and gas in Cuban waters and assisting the Mariel port construction. Cuba agreed to host navigation stations for Russia's own satellite global positioning system, Glonass. Other economic, financial, military and intelligence projects between the two countries were underway.

131. Cuba's annual bilateral trade with China was worth almost USD 2 billion. China agreed to import Cuban nickel, sugar and cigars, digitalise the television system, upgrade communications and cyber security and cooperate in the health, education and science sectors. China offered to provide a USD 120 million loan and assistance with the construction of another new port and industrial development zone in Cuba's second city, Santiago de Cuba.

132. Barak Obama, 'Statement by the President on Cuba Policy Changes', The White House Office of the Press Secretary, 17 December 2014. https://obamawhitehouse.archives.gov/the-press-office/2014/12/17/statement-president-cuba-policy-changes.

133. Raúl Castro, 'President Raúl Castro speaks to Third CELAC Summit in Costa Rica', Granma, 29 January 2015.

134. Allende, Interview in Havana, 4 January 2017.

135. However, the Cuban Adjustment Act, which gives any Cuban permanent residency in the United States after one year in the country, has not been abrogated.

136. The deal with Google, which did not require a licence, is discussed in Chapter 10.

137. The one exception was a shipment of 40 tons of artisanal charcoal produced by Cuban cooperative farms and imported in January 2017 by Scott Gilbert, the attorney who represented US government contractor Alan Gross, released from prison in Cuba in 2014.

138. Alberto Navarro, Talk in Havana, March 2018. The High Representative is generally referred to as the EU 'Ambassador'.

139. Navarro, Talk in Havana, March 2018.

140. Karin Strohecker, 'Cuba creditors offer "very significant relief" in debt proposal', Reuters, 13 February 2018.

141. Granma News Staff, 'President Díaz-Canel Visits Major Works Underway in Mariel Special Development Zone', *Granma*, 14 January 2019. http://en.granma.cu/cuba/2019-01-14/president-diaz-canel-visits-major-works-underway-in-mariel-special-development-zone.

142. In 1958, Cuba's diplomatic relations were mostly with the Americas and Europe.

143. Eduardo Delgado Bermudez, presentation at the second seminar, London School of Economics (Latin America and Caribbean Centre) and University of Havana (FLACSO), Havana, 2 December 2018. In 1973, Cuba broke off diplomatic relations with Israel, the only country in the world to consistently support the US blockade of Cuba at the UN General Assembly.

8. RAÚL CASTRO'S REFORMS: SOCIALIST EFFICIENCY OR CAPITALIST OPENING?

1. The other government leaders were José Ramón Balaguer Cabrera, José Ramón Machado Ventura, Esteban Lazo Hernández and Carlos Lage Dávila.
2. For more about the Great Debate of the 1960s see Yaffe, *Che Guevara*, and Yaffe, 'Che Guevara and the Great Debate', 11–40.
3. See Mimi Whitefield, 'Contradictory Policies Mean One Step Forward and One Step Back for Cuba's Ailing Economy', citing retired US State Department official Gary Maybarduck, *Miami Herald*, 13 August 2018. www.miamiherald.com/news/nation-world/world/americas/cuba/.
4. Raúl Castro, closing remarks at the Sixth Congress of the Cuban Communist Party, 19 April 2011. http://en.cubadebate.cu/opinions/2011/04/21/closing-remarks-Raúl-castro-ruz-party-congress-cuba/.
5. Fidel Castro, 'Speech in the Aula Magna'. See Chapter 3 on the Battle of Ideas and Chapter 4 on the Energy Revolution.
6. Fidel Castro, 'Speech in the Aula Magna'.
7. Raúl Castro, speech in Camaguey, *Granma*, 26 July 2007. http://www.granma.cu/granmad/2007/07/27/nacional/artic01.html.
8. Cuban friends told me how they insisted on announcing their names and addresses when contributing their critique.
9. Raúl Castro, speech in Camaguey.
10. There was a 3% increase in tourist numbers, but an 11% decrease in revenue from the tourist industry.
11. The lack of hard currency was especially serious as Cuba was obliged to pay upfront and in cash for food imports from the United States, by then the fifth most important source of imports behind Canada, China, Spain and Venezuela. Following the damage to Cuba caused by Hurricane Michelle in November 2000, the Trade Sanctions Reform and Export Enhancement Act was passed in the United States, allowing US firms to sell agricultural and food products and medicine to Cuba, a one-directional 'humanitarian' exception to the United States blockade. Imports from the United States rose to the value of over USD 700,000 in 2008, partly because Cuba made emergency imports following the worst hurricane season on record in 2008 and partly because of global price rises. With the measures taken under Raúl Castro, purchases fell steadily to USD 340 million by 2011. See William A. Messina, Jr, 'U.S. Food and Agricultural Exports to Cuba: Progress, Problems and Prospects', Association for the Study of the Cuban Economy, 30 November 2012, https://www.ascecuba.org/asce_proceedings/u-s-food-and-agricultural-exports-to-cuba-progress-problems-and-prospects/.
12. International press headlines heralded the restoration of capitalism in Cuba, the 'low-key death knell of the "new socialist man"', and the 'egalitarian wage system', according to Rory Carroll, 'Cuban Workers To Get Bonuses for Extra Effort', *Guardian*, 13 June 2008. https://www.theguardian.com/world/2008/jun/13/cuba. Capped or not, bonus payments in Cuba are awarded for surpassing 'norms' in the production of physical goods or services, that is, in terms of use values, not in terms of exchange values.
13. Raúl Castro, speech at the close of the first ordinary period of sessions of the seventh legislature of the National Assembly, 11 July 2008. http://www.ratb.org.uk/Raúl-castro/.
14. New usufruct farmers received assistance from existing Credit and Service Cooperatives and the National Association of Small Farmers, a cooperative federation founded in 1961. By 2018, nearly a quarter of a million individuals and legal entities had received over 2 million hectares of idle land in usufruct and another half a million hectares were deemed available. Cuban News Agency, 'Over 2 Million Hectare of Land Granted in Usufruct in Cuba', 7 August 2018. http://www.cubanews.acn.cu/economy/. While falling short of expectations, the programme saw a 5.3% annual increase in food production.
15. The focus on teaching professionals was partly a response to public concerns about the lack of professionalism of the very young emergent teachers who poured into study centres during the Battle of Ideas in the effort to reduce class sizes to 20, as explained in Chapter 3.
16. Raúl Castro, 'Speech Delivered During the Closing Ceremony of the Sixth Session of the Seventh Legislature of the National People's Power Assembly', 18 December 2010. www.cuba.cu/gobierno/Raúldiscursos/2010/ing/r181210i.html. In January 2012 Raúl Castro stressed the need to fight corruption politically, starting in the ranks of the CCP. 'On many

occasions, those implicated in corruption cases were members of the Party, who clearly harboured double standards and used their status to secure positions in leadership bodies, flagrantly violating their responsibilities as Communists.' Raúl Castro, 'Discurso de Raúl Castro: "El rumbo ya ha sido trazado"' speech at the closing of the First National Conference of the CCP, 29 January 2012, *Cubadebate*. http://www.cubadebate.cu/opinion/2012/01/29/.

17. Economist Intelligence Report, *Cuba Country Report*, January 2010, 13.
18. Raúl Castro, 'No tenemos derecho a equivocarnos, afirma Raúl', Intervención del Presidente Raúl Castro en la Asamblea Nacional del Poder Popular', 20 Dcember 2009. *Cubadebate*. http://www.cubadebate.cu/opinion/2009/12/20/.
19. Economist Intelligence Report, *Cuba Country Report*, January 2010, 11.
20. Editorial, *Financial Times*, 17 September 2010.
21. Raúl Castro, Speech to the National Assembly, August 2010. http://www.cuba.cu/gobierno/Raúldiscursos/2010/esp/r010810e.html.
22. For example, workers in entities where production is paralysed by the failure of external supplies failed to arrive.
23. The implications of this are discussed in Chapter 9.
24. Raúl Castro, Speech to the National Assembly, 1 August 2010.
25. Ernesto Che Guevara, 'Reuniones Bimestrales', 10 March 1962, Ministerio de Azúcar. *El Che en la Revolución Cubana: Ministerio de Industrias*. Tomo VI, Ministerio de Azúcar, 1966, 208; Fidel Castro, 30 November 1986, cited in *Granma*, 15 July 2010, 1.
26. Ernesto Freire Cazañas, Interview in Havana, mid-September 2011.
27. In this period, President Obama was talking about squeezing Cuba until the regime fell and US Congresswoman Ileana Ros-Lehtinen, Chairman of the US Senate's Foreign Affairs Committee, had called for Cuba to be attacked as Libya had been.
28. The almost three-fold rise in the number of *carretilleros*, from 5,679 in May 2011 to 16,454 in November 2011, reflected both individuals legalising their previously informal occupations and the increase in agricultural production.
29. By 2015, the state sector had shrunk by 718,000 workers, 40% of the original target. In 2016, the end of dismissals from the state sector was announced in the 7th Congress of the CCP. Carmelo Mesa-Lago, *Voices of Change in Cuba: From the Non-state Sector*, University of Pittsburg Press, 2018, 6 and 144. Around this time, according to the CTC, nearly 70% of registered self-employed workers were previously in the informal (illegal) sector without rights.
30. CCP Congresses are supposed to be held every five years.
31. The 12 categories were: economic management; macroeconomic policies (including monetary, exchange, fiscal and pricing policies); external economic relations; investment; science, technology and innovation; social policy (education, health, sports, culture, social security, employment and wages); agroindustry; industry and energy; tourism; transport; construction, housing and water resources; and commerce.
32. *Guidelines for Updating the Economic and Social Model*, VI Congreso del Partido Comunista de Cuba, Republic of Cuba, 18 April 2011, 9.
33. *Guidelines for Updating the Economic and Social Model*, 10.
34. 16 guidelines were moved to other points, 94 remained unchanged, 181 were changed and 36 new guidelines were incorporated.
35. Raúl Castro, 'Central Report to the 6th Congress of the Communist Party of Cuba', 16 April 2011. http://www.granma.cu/ingles/cuba-i/16-abril-central.html.
36. On 1 January 2011, Havana Province had been divided into two new provinces, Artemisa and Mayabeque, where new experiments in more decentralised administration and political structures were carried out. This process of political decentralisation is endorsed and extended in the new Cuban Constitution, approved by national referendum in February 2019, which particularly strengthens the Municipal Assemblies.
37. Following the Congress elections, women made up 42% of the Central Committee, a tripling of the previous figure. The proportion of black and 'mixed-race' Cubans rose by 10% to 30%, slightly below their proportion of the Cuban population (officially 35%). Raúl Castro revealed that this improvement was the result of an active policy to promote those sectors. 'These are the children of the working class; they belong to the poorest segments of the population and have had a politically active life in students' organizations, the Union of Young Communists and the Party. Most of these youths accumulate 10, 15 or

20 years of experience working at the grassroots level without abandoning their jobs in the professions they studied, and the majority were proposed by their respective Party cells during the process leading up to the Congress.' Raúl Castro, speech to the 6th Congress.

38. 'The fortitude of the Party basically lies in its moral authority, its influence on the masses and the trust of the people . . . The fortitude of the State lies in its material authority, which consists of the strength of the institutions responsible for demanding that everyone comply with the legal regulations it enacts. The damage caused by the confusion of these two concepts is manifested, firstly, in the deterioration of the Party's political work and, secondly, in the decline of the authority of the state and the government as officials cease feeling responsible for their decisions.' Raúl Castro, 'Central Report to the 6th Congress'.

39. Raúl Castro, 'Central Report to the 6th Congress'. This process of differentiated and targeted social assistance was a feature of the Battle of Ideas discussed in Chapter 4.

40. As discussed in Chapter 2.

41. This restriction was strengthened in the updated *Guidelines* of April 2016 which added the prohibition of the concentration of wealth.

42. Recipients must use the subsidy for the specified job and the cheque is paid directly to the retail outlet or the named self-employed construction worker. The state subsidies were to be financed from the revenue collected by the local government from the retail sales of construction materials in each province.

43. These CNAs do not own the enterprise, but they can own equipment or other assets. Leases are for up to ten years, renewable for an equal term.

44. No more than 10% of work-days in any year may be performed by hired labour. These restrictions aim to prevent the cooperative from exploiting the self-employed worker.

45. BBC News, 'Cuba Claims Massive Oil Reserves', 17 October 2008. http://news.bbc.co.uk/1/hi/world/americas/7675234.stm.

46. US Department of Commerce, *Report on Foreign Policy-Based Export Controls*, 2008, cited by Amnesty International, *The US Embargo Against Cuba: Its Impact on Economic and Social Rights*, https://www.amnestyusa.org/pdfs/amr250072009eng.pdf. A 2006 World Security Institute report described the US Blockade as technology denial and 'successful in relegating Cuba's energy development schemes to less than world class'. https://cri.fiu.edu/research/commissioned-reports/oil-cuba-alvarado.pdf

47. Letter to Barack Obama from four Cuban-American congress members, cited by Jim Lobe, 'Cuba Plans Deep-water Oil Drilling', *Al Jazeera*, 6 Nov 2011. www.aljazeera.com/indepth/features/2011/11/201111511216261487.html.

48. On 9 November 2011, Democrat Senator Bill Nelson introduced a bill to allow claimants to sue foreign companies responsible for any oil spill without limit. Journalist John Paul Rathbone described this as 'not so much an environmental measure. It's more of a stick with which to beat Cuba – or rather, as the sponsors admit, to discourage companies from drilling for oil there'. John Paul Rathbone, 'The Cuban "oil crisis"', *Financial Times*, 22 November 2011.

49. Ros-Lehtinen and a bipartisan group of 34 representatives wrote to Repsol's chairman calling on him to 'reassess the risks inherent in partnering with the Castro dictatorship, including the risk to its commercial interests with the United States', warning that the company could face liability in US courts. The Obama administration also applied pressure on Repsol and the Spanish government. Lobe, 'Cuba Plans Deep-water Oil Drilling'.

50. Mark Frank, 'Cuba Insists It Has Oil; US Companies Still Uninterested' *Reuters*, 6 May 2015. In November 2018, Cuba announced it has oil and gas output potential equal to 22 million barrels a year, including more than 16 million barrels of crude and CUPET was preparing for a new round of international bids for exploration. 'Cuba Seeks Foreign Partners for Oil Exploration', *Xinhua*, 10 December 2018. http://www.xinhuanet.com/english/2018-12/10/c_137663419.htm. In December 2018, Australia's Melbana announced it would work to increase production from Cuba's Santa Cruz offshore field. Renzo Pipoli, 'Australia's Melbana agrees with Cuba on plan to expand island's offshore production', *UPI*, 5 December 2018. In April 2019, Cuba's Petroleum Company (CUPET) was working on several shallow offshore oil wells with equipment and expertise supplied through a joint venture with China's Great Wall Drilling Company, an affiliate of China National Petroleum Corporation. Xiang Bo 'Chinese Technology Helps Cuba Drill for Offshore Oil', *Xinhua*, 17 April 2019.

51. Damien Cave, 'Easing Path Out of Country, Cuba Is Dropping Exit Visas', *New York Times*, 16 October 2012; William Booth, 'Cuba To Ease Travel Abroad for Many Citizens', *Washington Post*, 16 October 2012.

52. Cubadebate, 'Cuba seguirá apostando por una emigración legal, ordenada y segura' *Cubadebate*, 25 October 2012. http://www.cubadebate.cu/especiales/2012/10/25/.

53. As discussed in Chapter 7 on Cuba and the United States.

54. In anticipation of the elimination of this legislation, thousands of Cubans travelled to Central America hoping to cross the border while they still could.

55. *Granma*, 'Nota Oficial', 22 March 2013, http://www.granma.cu/granmad/2013/10/22/nacional/artic07.html.

56. *Granma*, 'Nota Oficial'.

57. For an overview of the development of Cuba's two pesos and the impact on the Cuban economy see Chapter 2 on the Special Period.

58. Rodríguez, Interview in Havana, 20 December 2016.

59. Rodríguez, Interview in Havana, 20 December 2016.

60. Rodríguez, Interview in Havana, 20 December 2016.

61. Emily Morris, talk at the Cuba Research Forum event 'Getting Into and Understanding Cuba Today ', Canning House, 6 March 2017.

62. The figures in brackets indicate the total debt owed prior to any cancellations. In early 2018, the London Club presented a debt relief offer for Cuba's USD 1.4 billion debt. Karin Strohecker, 'Cuba Creditors Offer "very significant relief " in Debt Proposal', *Reuters*, 13 February 2018. No agreement had been yet been reached by May 2019.

63. Marc Frank and John Paul Rathbone, 'Cuba in Drive to Attract Foreign Investment', *Financial Times*, 8 May 2018. https://www.ft.com/content/9ef0f118-4fcd-11e8-a7a9-37318e776bab.

64. In 2012 Odebrecht USA sued the State of Florida over a state law banning trade with companies which have business ties to Cuba. Patricia Mazzei, 'Odebrecht Sues Florida Over New Law Banning Government Hiring of Firms Tied to Cuba', *Miami Herald*, 4 June 2012. https://www.miamiherald.com/latest-news/article1940369.html.

65. Mariel Port was set to benefit from the planned construction of the transoceanic Nicaragua Canal; however, in April 2018 the private Hong Kong Nicaragua Canal Development Investment Company, headed by Wang Jing, a Chinese billionaire, closed its offices after Jing lost 80% of his wealth in Chinese stock market turbulence in 2015–16. The project appears to have been abandoned.

66. Havana Port cannot be deepened because a vehicle tunnel runs beneath it. Mariel is also closer to the United States.

67. The interviewee requested anonymity so I have referred to him as 'general manager' or 'manager'.

68. General manager, Mariel TC, Interview in Havana, March 2018.

69. General manager, Interview in Havana, March 2018.

70. General manager, Interview in Havana, March 2018.

71. The main changes to the previous 1995 law include: a maximum 60-day waiting period for a response to any other foreign investment proposals (approval comes from the Ministry of Science, Technology and the Environment); halving taxes on the profits of most joint state–foreign enterprises from 30% to 15%; exemption from income tax and an eight-year tax exemption on profits for new investors, followed by a 50% tax on profits for most ventures; the tax limit on profits from new raw material enterprises will be reduced from 45% to 22%; exemption from customs taxes for the importation of any necessary equipment during the initial investment process; and exemption from direct labour taxes. The Cuban state retains the right to expropriate properties in case of public or social interest, with the obligation to pay compensation. These measures apply for foreign investors at Mariel SDZ who must also contribute 0.5% of their income to Mariel SDZ maintenance and development fund and pay a 1% sales or service tax for local transactions.

72. Steve Ludlam, 'What About the Workers?' Autumn 2014. https://cuba-solidarity.org.uk/cubasi/article/182/what-about-the-workers.

73. Ludlam, 'What About the Workers?'.

74. Echoing the previous Congress, new age and term restrictions were confirmed for key positions in the state and political organisations. The newly elected Central Committee

(142 members) had an average age of 54; 44% were women and 36% black and 'mixed-race' Cubans. Raúl Castro reflected: 'Higher than those of the previous Congress, but we are not satisfied'. Three of the five new members elected onto the 17-member Political Bureau were women. All 'from humble backgrounds, [who] worked in the grassroots'. Raúl insisted: 'there can be no preconceived leaders, everyone who graduates must work five years at least at the basic level in the speciality which they studied at university'. Raúl Castro, speech at the closure of the 7th Party Congress, 19 April 2016. http://www.cuba-venezuela.org/index.php/2016/04/22/.

75. Raúl Castro, 'Central Report to the 7th PCC Congress', 18 April 2016. Guideline 4 of the updated *Guidelines* for 2016–21 state that: 'In non-state management forms, the concentration of property and material and financial wealth in non-state natural or legal persons will not be allowed.'

76. Raúl Castro, 'Central Report to the 7th PCC Congress'.

77. There were complaints in the run-up to the 7th CCP Congress that the kind of national public consultation which preceded the 6th Congress in 2011 had not taken place. The CCP's official response was that this was unnecessary as the focus of the discussion were those same documents that had already been subject to national debate.

78. Juan Alejandro Triana Barros, 'Inclusion, Inequalities and Opportunities: A Glance to the Cuban Private Sector', on the panel 'Inclusion within the New Constitution: The Role of Social Entrepreneurship in Cuba', paper given at the Latin American Studies Association Congress, 24 May 2019.

79. Having studied first the draft and then the approved documents, I can verify the extent of changes which have taken place.

80. Raúl Castro, 'Speech during Second Extraordinary Session of the National Assembly of People's Power', 2 June 2017, *National Network on Cuba*. http://www.nnoc.info/5022-2/.

81. Jesus García Pastor Brigos, 'Cuba 2015: propiedad socialista y relaciones con Estados Unidos', unpublished paper, 2015.

82. 'Conceptualización del Modelo Económico Y Social Cubano de Desarrollo Socialista', July 2017, 3 and 12.

83. As Fidel Castro asserted in 1998 during the Special Period: 'Right now, we are basically defending the sovereignty and independence of our country and the achievements of socialism. If we can build a little bit of socialism we do it, but mainly we want to improve what we have done, to achieve excellence.'

84. 'Conceptualización del Modelo Económico', 10–12.

85. These include dignity, equality, and full human freedoms; the leading role of the CCP (a vanguard party, Martiana [followers of José Martí], Marxist, Leninist and Fidelista); socialist democracy based on the sovereign power of the people; the socialist state as the guarantor of freedom, independence, sovereignty, people's participation and control, rights and laws; and the people's socialist ownership of the fundamental means of production as the main form of national economic and socioeconomic system based on the real power of the workers and communal ownership via the state; socialist planning; national defence and security; equality of rights and duties of citizens. 'Conceptualización del Modelo Económico . . .', 14–17.

86. 'Conceptualización del Modelo Económico', 19.

87. 'Conceptualización del Modelo Económico', 32 and 33.

88. 'Conceptualización del Modelo Económico', 52.

89. 'Plan Nacional De Desarrollo Económico Y Social Hasta 2030: Propuesta De Visión De La Nación, Ejes Y Sectores Estratégicos', *Documentos del 7mo. Congreso del Partido aprobados por el III Pleno del Comité Central del PCC el 18 de mayo de 2017 y respaldados por la Asamblea Nacional del Poder Popular el 1 de junio de 2017*, 21–22. The actual sectors proposed as strategic are: construction; electro energy; telecommunications; transport, storage and trade logistics; logistics for network and hydraulic installations; tourism, including marine and nautical tourism; professional services, especially medical; non-sugar agroindustry and foodstuffs; pharmaceuticals, biotechnology and biomedical production; sugar-related agroindustry and derivatives; and light industry.

90. Raúl Castro, 'The Communist Party Will Resolutely Support and Back the New President', Speech to the National Assembly, Granma, 19 April 2018.

91. In July 2019, the salaries for state sector workers in the 'budgeted sector', which includes health and education, saw significant rises, fostering a return to state employment by some professionals who had left those sectors.
92. In the same period annual growth of agriculture was 0.9%, of manufacturing industry 1.4%, sugar industry 4.5%, construction 2.4%, investments 2.3%, the average salary rose 6.1%, consumer price index rose 2.1%, real salaries went up 4% and labour productivity was up 2.0%. Rodriguez, 'Política económica' (III), *Cubadebate*, 2 September 2018. www.cubadebate.cu/opinion/2018/09/05/
93. Rodríguez, 'Política económica' (I), *Cubadebate*, 28 July 2018. http://www.cubadebate.cu/opinion/2018/07/28/.
94. Rodriguez, 'Politica economica' (III), *Cubadebate*, 21 August 2018. http://www.cubadebate.cu/opinion/2018/08/21/.
95. Raúl Castro, *El rumbo Ya Ha Sido Trazado*.

9. THE CUBAN TIGHTROPE: BETWEEN THE PLAN AND THE MARKET

1. These are discussed in the previous chapter on Raúl's Reforms.
2. Fundora, Interview in Havana, 22 December 2016.
3. Munster, Interview in Havana, 28 March 2018. The main authors of these studies were Mayra Espina, Maria del Carmen Sabala, Dayma Echeverría and Luisa Íniguez who, together with UNICEF, worked on the *Child and Adolescent Atlas of Cuba*, to provide details about the living conditions of families in every municipality of the country.
4. Raúl Castro, 'Speech to the National Assembly of Peoples Power', 11 July 2008, http://www.cuba.cu/gobierno/Raúldiscursos/2008/esp/r110708e.html.
5. This differs from the principle of communism: 'from each according to their ability, to each according to their need.'
6. Oficina Nacional de Estadísticas e Información, 'Empleo y Salarios', *Anuario Estadístico de Cuba 2014*, table 7.15, 'Main indicators of the social welfare system', 18. www.onei.cu/aec2014/07%20Empleo%20y%20Salarios.pdf.
7. Jenny Morín Nenoff, *¿Quo vadis Cuba? El proceso de transformación cubano desde la perspectiva de los perdedores en el cambio*, 2015, 9.
8. Munster, Interview in Havana, 28 March, 2018.
9. Oscar Fernández Estrada, *El Modelo De Funcionamiento Económico En Cuba Y Sus Transformaciones. Seis Ejes Articuladores Para Su Análisis*, Observatorio de la Economía Latinoamericana, August 2011, 27 (fn 71). https://ideas.repec.org/a/erv/observ/y2011i1545.html.
10. For this view see work by Camila Piñeiro Harnecker, for example 'Cuba's Cooperatives: Their Contribution to Cuba's New Socialism', Cliff DuRand (ed.), *Moving Beyond Capitalism*, Routledge, 2016, 184–94.
11. Fundora, Interview in Havana, 22 December 2016.
12. During the Battle of Ideas, discussed in Chapter 3, Fidel Castro had promoted the decentralisation of education centres to each municipality, known as the municipalisation of higher education. But with precedence given to the drive for economic efficiency this municipalisation was rolled back. Fundora says: 'The Universities were becoming more white again, predominated by the children of the university graduates, and lost a little of their popular character.' From 2016, there was a return to decentralisation of higher learning facilities, she said, and university intake was set to increase again with many courses reopened. Fundora, Interview in Havana, 22 December 2016.
13. Ricardo Torres Pérez, 'Cuba's Emerging Economic Model' presentation on the panel 'Cuba After Castro: A New Model of "Prosperous and Sustainable" Socialism', Latin American Studies Association Congress, 25 May 2019.
14. For Che Guevara's analysis see Yaffe, *Che Guevara*, and Yaffe, 'Che Guevara and the Great Debate', 11–40.
15. Triana Barros, 'Inclusion, Inequalities', Latin American Studies Association Congress, 2019. When asked to identify successful examples of 'social entrepreneurship' applicable to Cuba, Triana and his fellow panellist Emily M. Medley were not forthcoming.

16. The students were members of the Grimshaw Club, a student society concerned with international relations at the London School of Economics (LSE). This trip was organised by Michael Maisel, who, prior to undertaking an MSc at LSE, worked for Engage Cuba in the United States, 'a national coalition of private companies, organizations, and local leaders dedicated to advancing federal legislation to lift the 55-year-old Cuba embargo in order to empower the Cuban people and open opportunities for US businesses'. https://www.engagecuba.org/.
17. Ricardo Torres, Talk in Havana, 30 March 2018.
18. The IMF economist wished to remain anonymous. Email correspondence, 1 October 2018.
19. Ricardo Torres, Talk in Havana, 30 March 2018.
20. Humberto Blanco, Interview in Havana, 20 December 2016.
21. Another economist from Cuba who would like the island to emulate Norway is Mauricio De Miranda Parrondo, 'Los problemas de la propiedad y el funcionamiento económico en la economía política de la reforma en la nueva Constitución cubana', at Latin American Studies Association Congress, 25 May 2019. He is a professor at the Pontificia Universidad Javeriana de Cali in Colombia, not at a Cuban institution.
22. Blanco, Interview in Havana, 20 December 2016.
23. García Brigos, 'Cuba 2015: propiedad socialista y relaciones con Estados Unidos', unpublished paper, 32.
24. Triana Barros, 'Inclusion, Inequalities'.
25. Yailenis Mulet Concepción, 'Self-employment in Cuba: Between Informality and Entrepreneurship: The Case of Shoe Manufacturing', *Third World Quarterly*, 37:9, 2016, 1715.
26. Assistants cannot legally perform their activities if the owners do not take part directly in the production or service – that includes when the owner is unavailable due to illness or maternity.
27. Consequently, the new Labour Code of 2014 gave contracted workers the right to written contracts, minimum salaries and maximum hours, rest periods and paid holidays, and health and safety at work. See Steve Ludlam, 'What About the Workers?'.
28. Constitution of the Republic of Cuba, 1976, Article 21. Thus the need to update the Constitution, to incorporate the legal and structural changes over the previous decades.
29. García Brigos, 'Cuba 2015', 13.
30. Fundora, Interview in Havana, 22 December 2016.
31. See Chapter 8 on the reforms under Raúl Castro on this announcement.
32. Freire Cazañas, Interview in Havana, September 2011.
33. Fundora, Interview in Havana, 22 December 2016.
34. Concepción, 'Self-employment', Figure 2, 1720. 'The research took six months of field study in five Cuban provinces. We interviewed 44 manufacturers (out of a total of 72) who have been operating for 10 to 20 years, and 10 production workshops were thoroughly studied. In addition, 120 workers were interviewed (including manufacturers, vendors and hired workers), as well as different workers in the state sector, central government officials, suppliers and clients.'
35. In May 2019, it was announced that nine new wholesale markets would be opened for non-agricultural cooperatives, some six and a half years after they were created. Vivian Bustamante Molina, 'Abrirán nuevos mercados para venta mayorista', *Granma*, 25 May 2019.
36. On 8 September 2018, in his well-known blog, *La Pupila Insomne*, Iroel Sanchez highlighted this not legal but apparently tolerated situation, describing how 15,000 apples were swept away within minutes by employees of a private business from a state store and transported in the store's own transport truck. https://lapupilainsomne.wordpress.com/2018/09/08/asalto-en-la-puntilla-hay-que-ir-mas-alla-por-iroel-sanchez/. Sanchez's exposé generated a vibrant debate within Cuba and those involved in this case were removed from their posts.
37. Concepción, 'Self-employment', 1716.
38. Alarcón, Interview in Havana, 27 December 2016.
39. Concepción, 'Self-employment', 1717.
40. Like many Cubans, when Concepción uses the term 'medium businesses' she is referring to enterprises which would mostly not qualify as 'medium-sized' in Britain.

41. Concepción, 'Self-employment', 1719.
42. 60% of interviewees had more than one point of sale; 84% would not like to become a cooperative; 64% have negative opinion towards relations with the state; 100% have not accessed state credit. Concepción, 'Self-employment', 1719–20. For similar data about the opinions of Cuban non-state sector workers, see Mesa-Lago, *Voices of Change*. However, Mesa Lago's survey is based on a smaller sample of interviews.
43. Concepción, 'Self-employment', 1726 (fn 11).
44. Concepción, 'Self-employment', 1715.
45. Morín Nenoff, *Quo Vadis Cuba?*, 8.
46. Morín Nenoff, *Quo Vadis Cuba?*, 6.
47. Munster, Interview in Havana, 28 March, 2018.
48. Mesa Lago, *Voices of Change*, 7.
49. Connor Gory, 'Empowering Cuban Women', interview with Marta Núñez, *International Journal of Cuban Health & Medicine*, 20: 3, July–September 2018, 1.
50. Conceptión, 'Self-employment', 1718.
51. Saira Pons Pérez, 'Tax Law Dilemmas for Self-employed Workers', 20 May 2015, Cuba Study Group, 3. http://cubastudygroup.org/from_the_island/issue-29-tax-law-dilemmas-for-self-employed-workers-2015. When a business has five or fewer employees, it does not pay a tax on the use of a labour force. From the sixth to the tenth employee the tax is equal to 150% of the average wage of the province where the business is registered; for the eleventh to the fifteenth worker it is 200% of this rate; and starting with sixteenth worker, 300% is taken. Pons Pérez left CEEC in July 2018.
52. Pons Pérez, 'Tax law dilemmas', 2, 6.
53. Guideline 4 of the 2016–2021 *Guidelines*.
54. Che Guevara, *Apuntes Críticos a la Economía Política*, Editorial de Ciencias Sociales, 2006, 10.
55. Raúl Castro, Speech at the close of the first ordinary period of sessions of the seventh legislature of the National Assembly, 11 July 2008. http://www.ratb.org.uk/Raúl-castro/149.
56. Miguel Díaz-Canel, 'Transcripción de la entrevista concedida por el Presidente cubano Miguel Díaz-Canel a Telesur', 19 September 2018. www.cubadebate.cu/especiales/2018/09/19/.
57. Morín Nenoff, *Quo Vadis Cuba?*, 11.
58. 'The Brookings Institution hosted a panel in February 2011 confirming the strategy to soften the blockade in areas that could be key for private sector expansion in Cuba.' Oscar Fernandez Estrada, Fernandez Estrada, Oscar. 'The Economic Transformation Process in Cuba after 2011', in C. Brundenius and R. Torres Pérez (eds), *No More Free Lunch*, Springer, 2014, 32, fn 11.
59. García Brigos, 'Cuba 2015', 68.
60. Barak Obama, 'Statement by the President on Cuba Policy Changes', White House Office of the Press Secretary, 17 December 2014.
61. See Camila Piñeiro Harnecker (ed.), *Cooperatives and Socialism: A View from Cuba*, Palgrave Macmillan, 2013. For a discussion of why Che Guevara did not regard cooperatives as a socialist form of production see Helen Yaffe, 'Che Guevara: Cooperatives and the Political Economy of Socialist Transition', in Harnecker (ed.) *Cooperatives and Socialism*, 115–42.
62. García Brigos, 'Cuba 2015', 36.
63. Cliff DuRand, 'Cuba's New Cooperatives', *Monthly Review*, 1 November 2017. https://monthlyreview.org/2017/11/01/cubas-new-cooperatives/.
64. García Brigos, 'Cuba 2015', 72.
65. García Brigos, 'Cuba 2015', 69.
66. Mesa-Lago, *Voices of Change*, 74.
67. Oscar Figueredo Reinaldo and María del Carmen Ramón, 'Cooperativas de la construcción, para que no haya grietas en sus cimientos', *Cubadebate*, 5 May 2016. www.cubadebate.cu/especiales/2016/05/05/.
68. Reinaldo and Ramón, 'Cooperativas de la construcción'.
69. The exchange rate in state-owned enterprises is gradually being adjusted to lower the value of the CUP against the CUC; for example, it has been lowered to 1 CUC to 10 CUP. This is discussed in Chapter 8.

70. Raúl Castro, 'Central Report to the 7th PCC Congress', 18 April 2016. http://en.cubadebate.cu/news/2016/04/18/7.
71. A position which the new Constitution changes to President of the Republic of Cuba.
72. Pons Pérez, 'Tax law dilemmas', 1.
73. Díaz-Canel, *Entrevista con Telesur*.
74. Article 82 of the approved Constitution states that Art 82 'Marriage is a social and legal institution. It is one of the organizational structures of families.' The 11th Special Provision at the end of the Constitution states that within two years of the Constitution taking effect there shall be 'a process of popular consultation and referendum for the Family Code programme, which must include the form that a marriage may take.' One influential Cuban policy-maker I spoke to believed it was a mistake to have included any specification about the character of marriage in the nation's Constitution – something which does not appear in many other countries' constitutions.
75. Article 5. 'The Communist Party of Cuba, unique, Martiano, Fidelista, and Marxist-Leninist, the organized vanguard of the Cuban nation, sustained in its democratic character as well as its permanent linkage to the people, is the superior driving force of the society and the State. It organizes and orients the communal forces towards the construction of socialism and its progress toward a communist society. It works to preserve and to fortify the patriotic unity of the Cuban people and to develop ethic, moral, and civic values.' Preamble, Constitution of the Republic of Cuba, 2019. www.constituteproject.org/constitution/Cuba_2019D.pdf?lang=en.
76. Preamble, Constitution of the Republic of Cuba.
77. Constitution of the Republic of Cuba, Article 19.
78. Constitution of the Republic of Cuba, Article 31.
79. Much foreign commentary suggested that private property and foreign investment were new features in socialist Cuba. Actually, the Constitution of 1976 left some 20% of arable land in the hands of small private farmers or agricultural cooperatives. In 1982, foreign investment was first approved for joint ventures with the Cuban state. In 1992, the Constitution was amended to state that mandatory state ownership applied only to the 'fundamental means of production'. The employment changes of 2010 created the conditions for the emergence of private businesses and significantly expanded the non-state sector workforce. In 2011 private markets were permitted for houses, cars and other goods. In 2014 a new Foreign Investment Law was implemented. Since 1993, 67% of agricultural production has been carried out in the non-state sector. Meanwhile, 85% of Cubans are homeowners, rising to 96% in Havana.
80. Constitution of the Republic of Cuba, Article 30.
81. Constitution of the Republic of Cuba, Article 42.
82. Constitution of the Republic of Cuba, Title VIII: Local Organs of People's Power.
83. David Jessop, *Cuba Briefing*, 25 February 2019, Issue 996, 3.
84. Editorial, 'Cuba Dijo Sí a la Nueva Constitución' Granma, 25 February 2019. http://www.granma.cu/reforma-constitucional/2019-02-25/cuba-dijo-si-por-la-nueva-constitucion-25-02-2019-16-02-47.
85. Che Guevara, 'Man and Socialism in Cuba', in Bertram Silverman (ed.), *Man and Socialism in Cuba: The Great Debate*, Atheneum, 1971, 343.
86. Alarcón, Interview in Havana, 27 December 2016.
87. García Brigos, 'Cuba 2015', 57.
88. Allende, Interview in Havana, 4 January 2017.
89. Redacción Nacional, 'La Habana llega con más del 80% de su recuperación constructiva al ejercicio Meteoro', *Granma*, 14 May 2019. http://www.granma.cu/cuba/2019-05-14/la-habana-llega-con-mas-del-80-de-su-recuperacion-constructiva-al-ejercicio-meteoro-14-05-2019-23-05-11.

10. SURVIVING INTO THE POST-RAPPROCHEMENT PERIOD

1. For more on Cuban expectations prior to Trump's mandate see Helen Yaffe and Jonathan Watts, 'Top diplomatic negotiator in Cuba warns Trump: "aggression doesn't work"', *Guardian*, 17 January 2017.

2. Donald Trump, interviewed by Jamie Weinstein, 7 September 2015, *Daily Caller*. https://dailycaller.com/2015/09/07/donald-trump-on-his-nuclear-doctrine-democracy-promotion-and-why-he-refuses-to-use-term-supreme-leader/. He added the inevitable qualifier about getting a better deal.
3. Trump cited by Jeremy Diamond, 'Trump Shifts on Cuba, Says He Would Reverse Obama's Deal', 17 September 2016, CNN. https://edition.cnn.com/2016/09/16/politics/donald-trump-cuba/.
4. Vidal, Interview in Havana, 28 December 2016.
5. Information from US lawyer Robert Muse, 'The Cuban Economy and US-Cuba Policy: An Update – Progress, Challenges and Opportunities', meeting organised by the Caribbean Council/Cuba Initiative, 30 November 2017. According to Muse, each action by the Trump administration on Cuba has occurred after a 'stimulus' from Rubio.
6. William LeoGrande, 'A Detour on the Road to Normalization: U.S.–Cuban Relations During Donald Trump's Presidency', presentation on the panel Más allá de Trump: Retos y oportunidades para el retorno al proceso hacia la normalización de relaciones Cuba-Estados Unidos at the Latin American Studies Association Annual Congress, 26 May 2019.
7. President Trump issued the National Security Presidential Memorandum NSPM–5 entitled "Strengthening the Policy of the United States Toward Cuba", 16 June 2017.
8. The US Embassy had been upgraded from an Interest Section two years earlier in July 2015.
9. Associated Press, 'Spies in Cuba Were Among First Victims of Mysterious Sonic "attacks"', *Guardian*, 2 October 2017. https://www.theguardian.com/world/2017/oct/02/cuba-sonic-attacks-us-spies. In late January 2019, the Canadian government followed suit, withdrawing half its embassy staff and shutting its consular services in Havana, while the cause of the 'Havana Syndrome' was under investigation. This action was apparently taken after Canadian diplomats threatened to take legal action against their government unless it responded more seriously to their plight. The investigation results are available here: https://www.medrxiv.org/content/medrxiv/early/2019/09/29/19007096.full.pdf. They point to neurotoxicity resulting from excessive fumigation to prevent the spread of the Zika virus in Cuba.
10. Additionally, in March 2019, the duration of the B2 visas issued for Cubans visiting the United States was drastically reduced from 5 years to 3 months.
11. LeoGrande, 'A Detour on the Road'.
12. The list, along with updates published 15 November 2018, 11 March 2019, 24 April 2019 and 26 July 2019 is available from: https://www.state.gov/cuba-sanctions/cuba-restricted-list/.
13. Muse, 'Cuban Economy and US-Cuba Policy'.
14. National Security Presidential Memorandum NSPM–5.
15. Cristina Escobar, Talk in Havana, 28 March 2018. However, in early September 2019, there was a reminder that, while the Cubans may participate in the internet and social media, they cannot control it. On 11 September, the accounts of the principle Cuban media outlets and several government Ministers were 'suspended' by Twitter, coinciding with a live televised announcement given to the nation by President Díaz-Canel concerning fuel scarcities resulting from US sanctions against Venezuela and Cuba.
16. This was revealed through the 2018/19 fiscal year budget documents of the Miami-based network, the Office of Cuba Broadcasting (OCB), an entity charged with overseeing the plans. The OCB manages the operations of Radio Martí and TV Martí, discussed in Chapter 8, and is a subsidiary of the state-owned Broadcasting Board of Governors (BBG), which owns and supervises other networks broadcasting pro-US propaganda overseas, including Voice of America and Radio Free Europe. www.miaminewtimes.com/news/us-planned-cuban-facebook-propaganda-on-radio-tv-marti–10625033.
17. Susana Antón, 'Nuevas regulaciones sobre el espectro radioeléctrico', *Granma*, 29 May 2019.
18. Margaret E Crahan, 'Trump and His Advisers: Impact on the Molding of US Foreign Policy', presentation on the panel Más allá de Trump: Retos y oportunidades para el retorno al proceso hacia la normalización de relaciones Cuba-Estados Unidos, LASA Congress, 26 May 2019.
19. LeoGrande, 'A Detour on the Road'.
20. David E. Sanger, 'With Bolton, Trump Creates a Hard-Line Foreign Policy Team', *New York Times*, 22 March 2018. https://www.nytimes.com/2018/03/22/us/politics/bolton-trump-hard-liners.html.

21. Like Rubio, despite a long career lobbying for a harsher US policy toward Cuba, Claver-Carone has apparently never visited the island. Global Americans, 'On Trump's Latin American team', 28 May 2019. https://theglobalamericans.org/2019/05/trumps-latin-america-team/. Claver-Carone founded and directed the US–Cuba Democracy PAC, one of the most pro-active pro-blockade groups in Washington.
22. Bolton, 'Remarks by National Security Advisor'.
23. LeoGrande, 'A Detour on the Road'.
24. In violation of international norms, the law includes those who were Cuban citizens at the time but subsequently received US citizenship.
25. LeoGrande, 'A Detour on the Road'.
26. Donald J Trump, tweet, 30 April 2019.
27. Bolton also blamed the Russian government for keeping Maduro in power. Chapter 6 on Cuban medical internationalism discusses the work of Cuban healthcare workers in Venezuela.
28. Bruno Rodríguez, tweet, 30 April 2019.
29. The claimants are Mickael Behn, whose US grandfather owned the Havana dock until 1960, and Javier García-Bengochea, a 'descendent' of the owners of dock facilities in Santiago de Cuba.
30. Video, 'Carnival Corp. is the First US Company Sued for Using "stolen property"'. *Miami Herald*, 2 May 2019, https://www.miamiherald.com/news/local/article229952669.html. The US Foreign Claims Settlement Commission in 1971 certified that the Havana Docks Corporation had a claim against the Cuban government. The commission found that the value of the properties in 1971 was $8,684,360.18, the equivalent of about $54.5 million in today's dollars. Daniel Rivero, 'First Lawsuit Against Company Operating in Cuba is Filed under Title III' *WLRN*, 2 May 2019.
31. Rivero, 'First Lawsuit'.
32. Cuban Liberty and Democratic Solidarity (Libertad) [Helms–Burton] Act of 1996. https://www.treasury.gov/resource-center/sanctions/documents/libertad.pdf.
33. LeoGrande, 'A Detour on the Road'.
34. The government imports some USD 2 billion worth of foodstuffs annually, a proportion of which is from the United States.
35. This was the view presented by Jose Luis Rodriguez, former Economy Minister between 1994 and 2008, in a podcast interview with the Vice President of the Union of Journalists, Ariel Terrero. 'Cuba regresará al periodo especial?' *Cubadebate*, 9 May 2019. http://www.cubadebate.cu/especiales/2019/05/09/.
36. Speaking in a personal capacity, the Google employee wished to remain anonymous. Interview, 14 May 2019. 'There have been articles speculating that that means a subsea fibre optic cable', he told me, 'and that certainly is one of the infrastructure options that would likely be explored, but that's not the only one.' Cuba could also connect to an existing local optic fibre cable or build a cable through a consortium. Cuba is currently connected to the Venezuelan-owned ALBA 1 optic fibre underwater cable, but the performance has been disappointing and unable to meet demand. Prior to that, Cubans relied on expensive, slow satellite connections, which largely explained the 'rationing' and high charges for internet access. ETECSA has been working with a Chinese company to build up the internal infrastructure, something in which Google is not currently involved.
37. Previously, content on Google apps such as YouTube had to travel long distances to be accessed on the island, meaning long waits while material buffered.
38. Google employee, Interview, 14 May 2019.
39. Associated Press, 'Cuba Signs Deal with Google To Connect to Modern Internet', CBC News, 29 March 2019. https://www.cbc.ca/news/technology/cuba-google-internet-1.5076587.
40. Chapter 7 has more on Jorge Mas Canosa and his role in influencing the United States' Cuba policy.
41. For example, 'Project Shield' an app to protect sites against cyber-attacks, according to John Paul Rathbone, 'Google Strikes Deal To Bring Faster Web Content to Cuba', *Financial Times*, 28 March 2019. The Google–ETECSA deal includes a freedom of information clause which provides against data censorship.
42. Pedro Freye, cited by Rathbone, 'Google Strikes Deal'.

43. Google employee, Interview, 14 May 2019.
44. To put this in perspective, Cuba was expecting 5.1 million international visitors in 2019, and this was revised down to 4.3 million (84.3%) as a result of the US government restrictions. The biggest group of visitors to Cuba are Canadians.
45. Cuba Educational Travel, 'Statement on New Cuban Travel Restrictions', 4 June 2019. https://www.cubaeducationaltravel.com/press-release-june-4-2019.
46. Navarro, Talk in Havana, March 2018. His formal title is 'High Representative' for the EU.
47. Navarro, Talk in Havana, March 2018.
48. In late May 2019, Spanish hotel firm Meliá became the first foreign company to have a case filed against it under Title III. The claim was made by the heirs of the Mata family and concerns the San Carlos Hotel (now the Meliá San Carlos), which is managed in a joint venture with Gran Caribe. The hotel was nationalised in December 1961 by the Cuban government. The law suit also names CIMEX, Cubanacán and Gaviota. Jessop, *Cuba Briefing*, 27 May 2019, 6.
49. European Union, 'Joint Statement by High Representative/Vice President Federica Mogherini, Minister of Foreign Affairs of Canada Chrystia Freeland and EU Commissioner for Trade Cecilia Malmström on the Decision of the United States To Further Activate Title III of the Helms Burton (Libertad) Act', 17 April 2019. https://eeas.europa.eu/delegations/united-states-america/61181/.
50. European Union, 'Declaration by the High Representative on Behalf of the EU on the Full Activation of the Helms–Burton (LIBERTAD) Act by the United States', 2 May 2019. https://www.consilium.europa.eu/en/press/press-releases/2019/05/02/.
51. In Britain, for example, the Minister of International Trade, George Hollingbery, told Parliament that the EU 'blocking' legislation of 1996, 'makes it illegal to comply with the extraterritorial effects of the embargo'. The 1980 UK Protection of Trading Interests Act states that 'it is illegal for UK companies to comply with extraterritorial legislation such as the US embargo'. The Act contains a provision for fines to be levied against companies and individuals that fail to comply with this stipulation. https://www.gov.uk/government/publications/exporting-to-cuba/.
52. The Canadians and Cubans discussed working together 'to defend Canadians conducting legitimate trade and investment in Cuba in light of the United States ending the suspension of Title III of the Helms–Burton Act'. Chrystia Freeland, cited by Jessop, *Cuba Briefing*, 20 May 2019, 4.
53. The Cuban government has also stated that any agreement on the payment of such compensation will need to include compensation for damages to the Cuban economy inflicted by the US blockade. In an unprecedented move, in August 2019, Cuba said it would defend its interests in US courts, through US-based law firms, in cases filed under Title III against Cuban state enterprises CUPET and CIMEX. Jessop, *Cuba Briefing*, 2 September 2019.
54. The trip took place in June 2019, organised by Cuba Initiative, which was set up in 1995 at the request of the British and Cuban governments to strengthen bilateral relations.
55. For example, in late May 2019, a Caribbean Customs Organisation was established in Havana, to circumvent US actions that prevent Cuban participation in discussions over international customs issues including border security and trade facilitation. Jessop, *Cuba Briefing*, 27 May 2019, 6. A delegation from Cuba's Ministry of Public Health visited India to expand ties with Indian institutions researching traditional and natural medicines; cooperation between Cuban and Chinese publishing houses was extended; an Action Plan for increasing bilateral trade was established between Cuba and Vietnam; and Bolivia was contracted to increase the food exports to Cuba to meet shortages. Meanwhile, the Canadian chain Blue Diamond signed two contracts with Cuban enterprise Gran Caribe to manage two hotels in Cayo Coco and Varadero, adding to the 19 it already manages. Jessop, *Cuba Briefing*, 13 May 2019, 5.
56. In many countries the ambassador and their partner *are* the embassy, according to Eduardo Delgado Bermudez, presentation at the 2nd seminar London School of Economics (Latin America and Caribbean Centre) and University of Havana (FLACSO), Havana, 2 December 2018.
57. Allende, Interview in Havana, 4 January 2017. The four embassies belong to Australia, Cuba, New Zealand and Taiwan.

58. 'The court ruled that Spain does not have international jurisdiction for its courts to resolve lawsuits on properties located outside its territory . . . In dismissing the case the judge ordered the plaintiff to pay the costs.' Jessop, *Cuba Briefing*, 9 September 2019, Issue 1019, 5.

59. Cuba's state sector employs over 3 million workers, compared to some 1.4 million in the non-state sector (agricultural and urban cooperatives, private farmers, usufruct farmers, the self-employed and small businesses). Of the state sector workforce, 52%, or 1.6 million workers, are in the 'enterprise sector', consisting of productive and commercial entities which sell, trade and receive revenues. Since 2014, many workers in the enterprise sector have benefited from incentives to increase production, linking pay to performance, removing salary caps, and providing payment in hard currency.

60. Salaries in the budgeted sector are capped at CUP 3,000; only those earning over CUP 2,500 pay individual income tax. All employees will now pay towards social security, 2.5% for those earning less than CUP 500 and 5% for those above. Social security payments, including some pensions, were last raised in November 2018; pensions were raised again to a minimum of CUP 280 and all those with pensions under CUP 500 see incomes rise.

61. Information on the salary rise and forthcoming economic reforms, along with the citations from President Díaz-Canel and Minister of the Economy, Alejandro Gil, are from: 'Cuban President and Several Ministers Report on Measures Recently Approved To Boost the Economy', *Granma International*, 2 July 2019; *Mesa Redonda*, 'Medidas para potenciar la economía del país en las condiciones actuales e incremento salarial', broadcast on 2 July 2019, www.youtube.com/watch?v=zpV9nx13guo; and 3 July 2019, www.youtube.com/watch?v=5ZYkYtyTmBk.

62. Groups of workers in the budgeted sector, including health care workers, received a pay rise in recent years, but others, including in the education sector, were left behind. Workers in the political organisations of People's Power and a group in public administration had not received a pay rise since 2005. Following the announcement, thousands of Cubans sought (re)employment in the state sector, including 8,000 (former) teachers who returned to Cuban classrooms by the new school year. This almost resolves the island's chronic lack of teachers. In other sectors, however, ministers warned against a return to inflated state sector payrolls stating that only essential workers should be recruited.

63. In a market economy, inflation is caused by increasing the supply of money without a concomitant increase in the value of the goods and services produced.

64. Provincial administrations are responsible for setting maximum retail and wholesale prices and reviewing them on a regular basis in an effort to prevent inflation. The cap applies to all products except those imported and distributed by the state which have a fixed price structure. David Jessop, 'New Controls on Prices and Non-state Enterprises Announced', *Cuba Briefing*, 2 September 2019, issue 1018, 1.

65. Instead of prohibiting this, the economy will be directed to meet the demand for such goods and services domestically.

66. However, as the salary and pension rises began halfway through the year, the cost in 2019 is half the annual cost.

67. The new measures aim to 'break the pattern of turning to imports to foster our national industry', said Gil, adding that nothing should be imported that could be produced domestically.

68. State enterprises whose exports exceed the plan will retain all or part of the extra hard currency earnings (after meeting obligations to the state) and can use those funds for essential imports or to pay other national producers. Similarly, non-exporting state enterprises can retain surplus revenues, after payments due to the central fund, and decide how to invest those, including in projects with domestic non-state enterprises and foreign companies. Restrictions on relations between these entities will be removed. Cuban enterprises which supply domestic products and services to foreign businesses operating in the Mariel Special Development Zone will be permitted to retain 50% of their profits. State enterprises will be allowed to sell excess production over their plan in the domestic market. Non-state enterprises may be facilitated to export through arrangements with state entities. The proposed reforms appear similar to the Soviet Planning and Management System implemented in Cuba in the 1970s until Rectification in the mid-1980s.

69. Accordingly, enterprises will be responsible for paying off their own debt to FINATUR.
70. It has been estimated that 10,000 Cubans are already using cryptocurrencies for personal transactions. Sarah Marsh, 'Skirting U.S. Sanctions, Cubans Flock to Cryptocurrency To Shop Online Send Funds', *Reuters*, 12 September 2019.
71. US Department of the Treasury, 'Treasury Issues Changes to Strengthen Cuba Sanctions Rules', 6 September 2019. https://home.treasury.gov/news/press-releases/sm770
72. Remittances are illegal if the recipient is a member of the Cuban Communist Party or to close family member of 'prohibited Cuban officials'. Authorisation for 'donative remittances' to non-family members was eliminated. These were the measures announced on 17 April 2019 but not yet enacted.
73. Steve Mnuchin, 'The United States holds the Cuban regime accountable for its oppression of the Cuban people and support of other dictatorships throughout the region, such as the illegitimate Maduro regime. Through these regulatory amendments, Treasury is denying Cuba access to hard currency, and we are curbing the Cuban government's bad behavior while continuing to support the long-suffering people of Cuba.' US Department of the Treasury, 'Cuba Sanctions Rules'.
74. The reality of the socialist countries' trade relations was strongly criticised by Ernesto 'Che' Guevara for failing to deliver in this regard. 'There should be no more talk about developing mutually beneficial trade based on prices forced on the backward countries by the law of value and the international relations of unequal exchange that result from the law of value . . . The socialist countries have the moral duty to put an end to their tacit complicity with the exploiting countries of the West.' Ernesto Che Guevara, 'At the Afro Asian Conference in Algeria', 24 February 1964. https://www.marxists.org/archive/guevara/1965/02/24.htm.
75. *Mesa Redonda*, 'Medidas para potenciar la economía del país en las condiciones actuales e incremento salarial', broadcast on 3 July 2019. www.youtube.com/watch?v=5ZYkYtyTmBk
76. This is not meant to imply that these institutions and apparatus were introduced in the 1990s; most of them were not. The ration book, for example, was introduced as a temporary measure in 1962 and never removed. While both Fidel and Raúl Castro stated their wish to eliminate the ration book once conditions permitted, its continuation has proven useful, for example in handling the sudden scarcity of basic foodstuffs occurring in spring 2019.
77. CubaDebate, '¿Qué sucede en la Tribuna Antimperialista?' 23 May 2019. http://www.cubadebate.cu/noticias/2019/05/23/.
78. William R. Rhodes, 'Venezuela's Healthcare Crisis Needs Emergency Attention', *Financial Times*, 8 February 2019. https://www.ft.com/content/f1d3b414-2af2-11e9-88a4-c32129756dd8. Nonetheless, in early June 2019, Cuba was struggling to maintain a stable supply of some medicines and of the raw materials and other inputs for its biopharma industry, following the tightening of the US blockade. Jessop, *Cuba Briefing*, 10 June 2019, 2.
79. ACN, 'Cuba: US Government Earmarks Millions To Hinder Cuban Medical Cooperation', Radio Rebelde, 29 August 2019, http://www.radiorebelde.cu/english/news/cuba-us-government-earmarks-millions-to-hinder-cuban-medical-cooperation-20190829/.
80. Vidal, Interview in Havana, 28 December 2016.

FURTHER READING

Rather than a full bibliography, this is a list of publications on which I have drawn and/or which readers may wish to consult for further information and analysis.

Alhama Belamaric, Rafael, Jesús Pastor García Brigos, Roberto Jesús Lima Ferrer and Daniel Rafuls Pineda. *Cuba: Propiedad Social y Construcción Socialista*, Nuevo Milenio, 2019.

Allahar, Anton L. and Nelson P. Valdés. 'The Bureaucratic Imperative: Economic and Political Challenges to Cuban Socialism in the Early 21st Century', *The CLR James Journal*, 19:1/2, 2013.

Álvarez, Mavis, Martin Bourque, Fernando Funes, Lucy Martin, Armando Nova and Peter Rosset. 'Surviving the Crisis in Cuba: The Second Agrarian Reform and Sustainable Agriculture', in Peter Rosset, Raj Patel and Michael Courville (eds.), *Promised Land: Competing Visions of Agrarian Reform*, Food First Books, 2006.

American Association for World Health. *Denial of Food and Medicine: The Impact of the US Embargo on Health and Nutrition in Cuba*, March 1997.

Angotti, Thomas. 'The Cuban Revolution: A New Turn', in *Nature, Society, and Thought*, 1:4, 1988, 527–49.

Aponte-García, Maribel. 'Foreign Investment and Trade in Cuban Development: A 50-Year Reassessment with Emphasis on the Post-1990 Period', *Bulletin of Latin American Research*, 28:4, 2009, 480–96.

Arrastía Avila, Mario Alberto. 'Distributed Generation in Cuba: Part of a Transition towards a New Energy Paradigm', in *Cogeneration and On-Site Power Production*, November–December 2008, 62–5.

Arrastía Avila, Mario Alberto and Laurie Guevara-Stone. 'Teaching Cuba's Energy Revolution', *Solar Today*, January–February 2009, 30–3.

August, Arnold. *Cuba and Its Neighbours: Democracy in Motion*, Zed Books, 2013.

August, Arnold. *Cuba–U.S. Relations: Obama and Beyond*, Fernwood Publishing, 2017.

Ayes, G.N. *Revolución Energética: Un Desafío Para el Desarrollo*, Editorial Científico-Técnica, 2008.

Azicri, Max. 'The Castro-Chávez Alliance', *Latin American Perspectives*, 36, 2009, 99–110.

Babbitt, Susan E. *José Martí, Ernesto "Che" Guevara, and Global Development Ethics: The Battle for Ideas*, Palgrave Macmillan, 2014.

Badella, Alessandro. 'Between Carter and Clinton: Obama's Policy Towards Cuba', *Caribbean Journal of International Relations & Diplomacy*, 2:2, June 2014, 29–59.

Baggot, Rob and George Lambie. 'Hard Currency, Solidarity, and Soft Power: The Motives, Implications, and Lessons of Cuban Health Internationalism', in *International Journal of Health Services*, 49:1, 2019.

Baracca, Angelo and Rosella Franconi. 'Cuba: The Strategic Choice of Advanced Scientific Development, 1959–2014', *Sociology and Anthropology* 5:4, 2017.

Baracca, Angelo and Rosella Franconi. *Subalternity vs. Hegemony: Cuba's Outstanding Achievements in Science and Biotechnology, 1959–2014*, Springer Briefs in History of Science and Technology, 2016.

Bardach, Ann Louise. *Cuba Confidential: Love and Vengeance in Miami and Havana*, Vintage Books, 2002.

Bolender, Keith. *Cuba Under Siege: American Policy, the Revolution and Its People*, Palgrave Macmillan, 2012.

Bolender, Keith. *Manufacturing the Enemy: The Media War Against Cuba*, Pluto Press, 2019.

Boorstein, Edward. *The Economic Transformation of Cuba: A First-Hand Account*, Modern Reader Paperback, 1969.

Brenner, Philip and Peter Eisner. *Cuba Libre: A 500-Year Quest for Independence*, Rowman and Littlefield, 2018.

Brouwer, Steve. *Revolutionary Doctors: How Venezuela and Cuba are Changing the World's Conception of Health Care*, Monthly Review Press, 2011.

Brundenius, Claes. *Revolutionary Cuba: The Challenge of Economic Growth with Equity*, Westview Press, 1984.

Brundenius, Claes. 'Whither the Cuban Economy after Recovery? The Reform Process, Upgrading Strategies and the Question of Transition', *Journal of Latin American Studies*, 2002.

Bustamante, Michael J. and Jennifer L. Lambe. *The Revolution from Within: Cuba, 1959–1980*, Duke University Press, 2019.

Calvo Ospina, Hernando. *Bacardi: The Hidden War*, Pluto Press, 2000.

Campbell, Al (ed.). *Cuban Economists on the Cuban Economy*, University Press of Florida, 2013.

Campbell, Al. 'Updating Cuba's Economic Model: Socialism, Human Development, Markets and Capitalism', *Socialism and Democracy*, 30:1, 2016.

Campos, Carlos Olivia and Gary Prevost. 'Cuba's Relations with Latin America', *Social Research: An International Quarterly*, 84:2, 2017.

Capote, Raúl. *Enemigo*, Editorial José Martí, 2011.

Cárdenas Andrés. *The Cuban Biotechnology Industry: Innovation and Universal Health Care*, Institute for Institutional Innovations Economics, University of Bremen, 2009.

Castro Díaz-Balart, Fidel. 'Global Challenges in Science and Innovation for Sustainable Development: Remarks from a Cuban Perspective', *Caribbean Journal of International Relations and Diplomacy*, 2:4, 2014.

Castro Ruz, Fidel. *History Will Absolve Me*, 1953, https://www.marxists.org/history/cuba/archive/castro/1953/10/16.htm.

Castro Ruz, Fidel. 'Discurso pronunciado por el Comandante en Jefe Fidel Castro Ruz . . . por el XX Aniversario de la caída en combate del comandante Ernesto Che Guevara', 8 October 1987, Council of State, Republic of Cuba.

Castro Ruz, Fidel. 'Tomorrow Will be Too Late', speech delivered at the Rio Summit, 1992.

Castro Ruz, Fidel. Speech delivered by Dr Fidel Castro Ruz, President of the Republic of Cuba, at the Commemoration of the 60th Anniversary of his admission to University of Havana, in the Aula Magna of the University of Havana, 17 November 2005, Council of State, Republic of Cuba.

Castro Ruz, Fidel. *My Life*. Ignacio Ramonet (ed.), Allen Lane, 2007. (Trans. Andrew Hurley)

Castro Ruz, Raúl. Speech delivered in Camaguey, 26 July 2007, *Granma*.

Cherni, Judith A. and Yohan Hill. 'Energy and Policy Providing for Sustainable Rural Livelihoods in Remote Locations: The Case of Cuba', *Geoforum*, 40, 2009.

Chilote, Ronald H. (ed). *The Cuban Revolution into the 1990s*, Latin American Perspectives Series, 10, Westview Press, 1992. (Trans. Anibal Yanez)

Chomsky, Aviva, Barry Carr and Pamela María Smorkaloff. *The Cuba Reader: History, Culture, Politics*, Duke University Press, 2004.

Colhoun, Jack. *Gangsterismo: The United States, Cuba and the Mafia, 1933 to 1966*, Or Books, 2013.

Cuba, Republic of. *Constitution of the Republic of Cuba*, 2019.

Curbelo Alonso, Alfredo, Oscar Jimenez and Joel Suarez. 'Biomass-based Gasifier for Providing Electricity and Thermal Energy to Off-grid Locations in Cuba: Conceptual Design', *Energy for Sustainable Development*, 16, 2012.

Cushion, Steve. *A Hidden History of the Cuban Revolution: How the Working Class Shaped the Guerrilla Victory*, Monthly Review Press, 2016.

Díaz Briquets, Sergio and Jorge Pérez López. *Conquering Nature: The Environmental Legacy of Socialism in Cuba*, University of Pittsburgh Press, 2000.

Díaz-Canel, Miguel. *Transcripción de la entrevista concedida por el Presidente cubano Miguel Díaz-Canel a Telesur*, 19 September 2018, *CubaDebate*.

Diez Acosta, Tomás. *Peligros y Principios*, Editorial Verde Olivo, Cuba, 1992.

Domínguez López, Ernesto and Helen Yaffe. 'The Deep Historical Roots of Cuban Anti-imperialism', *Third World Quarterly*, 38:11, 2017.

Dye, Alan D. 'The US Sugar Program and the Cuban Revolution', *Journal of Economic History*, 64:3, 2004.

Erisman, H. Michael. *Cuba's Foreign Relations in a Post-Soviet World*, University Press of Florida, 2000.

Erisman, H. Michael. 'Brain Drain Politics: The Cuban Medical Professional Parole Programme', *International Journal of Cuban Studies*, 4:3/4, 2012.

Erisman, H. Michael and John M. Kirk. *Cuban Foreign Policy: Transformation under Raúl Castro*, Rowman & Littlefield, 2018.

Espina, Mayra. 'Viejas y Nuevas Desigualdades en Cuba: Ambivalencias y perspectivas de la reestratificación social', *Nueva Sociedad*, 216, julio–agosto, 2008.

Fagen, Richard R. *The Transformation of Political Culture in Cuba*, Stanford University Press, 1969.

Feinsilver, Julie M. 'Fifty Years of Cuba's Medical Diplomacy: From Idealism to Pragmatism', *Cuban Studies*, 41, 2000.

Feinsilver, Julie M. *Cuban Medical Diplomacy: When the Left Has Got It Right*, Council on Hemispheric Affairs, 2006.

Fernandez Estrada, Oscar. 'The Economic Transformation Process in Cuba after 2011', in C. Brundenius and R. Torres Pérez (eds), *No More Free Lunch*, Springer, 2014.

Foner, Philip. *A History of Cuba and its Relations with the United States*, International Publishers, 1962.

Font, Mauricio (ed). *Changing Cuba/Changing World*, The Cuba Project, Bildner Center for Western Hemisphere Studies, 2008.

Franklin, Jane. 'The Cuba Obsession', *The Progressive*, July 1993.

Franklin, Jane. *Cuba and the United States: A Chronological History*, Ocean Press, 1997.

Funes Aguilar, Fernando and Luis L. Vázquez Moreno (eds). *Avances de la Agroecología en Cuba*, Estación Experimental de Pastos y Forrajes Indio Hatuey, 2016.

Funes Aguilar, Fernando, L. García, M. Bourque, N. Pérez and P. Rosset. *Transformando el Campo Cubano: Avances de la Agricultura Sostenible*, ACTAF-Food First-Ceas, 2001.

Funes Monzote, Reinaldo. *From Rainforest to Cane Field in Cuba: An Environmental History since 1492*, University of North Carolina Press, 2008.

Gasperini, Lavinia. 'The Cuban Education System: Lessons and Dilemmas', *Country Studies: Education Reform and Management Publication Series*, 1:5, 2000.

Gillespie, Richard (ed). *Cuba after Thirty Years: Rectification and the Revolution*, Frank Cass, 1990.

Gleijeses, Piero. *Conflicting Missions: Havana, Washington, and Africa, 1959–1976*, University of North Carolina Press, 2003.

Gleijeses, Piero. 'Cuba and Africa: A History Worthy of Pride', *Socialist Voice*, 2004.

Gleijeses, Piero. 'Moscow's Proxy? Cuba and Africa 1975–1988', *Journal of Cold War Studies*, 8:4, 2006.

Gleijeses, Piero. 'Cuba and the Independence of Namibia', *Cold War History*, 7:2, 2007, 285–303.

Gott, Richard. *Cuba: A New History*, Yale University Press, 2004.

Guevara, Ernesto 'Che'. *Apuntes Críticos a la Economía Política*, Editorial de Ciencias Sociales, 2006.

Guevara-Stone, Laurie. 'La Revolucion Energetica: Cuba's Energy Revolution', *Renewable Energy World*, 9 April 2009.

Guzmán, María G. 'Thirty Years after the Cuban Hemorrhagic Dengue Epidemic of 1981', *MEDICC Review*, 14:2, 2012.

Hamilton, Douglas. 'Whither Cuban Socialism: The Changing Political Economy of the Cuban Revolution', *Latin American Perspectives*, 29:3, 2002.

Hansing, Katrin and Bert Hoffman. 'Cuba's New Social Structure: Assessing the Re-stratification of Cuban Society 60 Years after Revolution', *GIGA Research Programme*, 315, February 2019.

Hernández, Rafael. 'Looking at Cuba: Notes towards a Discussion', *Boundary 2*, 29:3, 2002. (Trans. Dick Cluster)

Hernández-Reguant, A. (ed). *Cuba in the Special Period: Culture and Ideology in the 1990s*, Palgrave Macmillan, 2009.

Hershberg, Eric and William M. LeoGrande (eds.). *A New Chapter in US-Cuba Relations: Social, Political, and Economic Implications*, Palgrave Macmillan, 2016.

Huish, Robert. *Where No Doctor Has Gone Before: Cuba's Place in the Global Health Landscape*, Wilfrid Laurier University Press, 2013.

Huish, Robert. 'Why Does Cuba "Care" So Much? Understanding the Epistemology of Solidarity in Global Health Outreach', *Public Health Ethics*, 7:3, 2014.

International Atomic Energy Agency. *Cuba: A Country Profile on Sustainable Energy Development*, International Atomic Energy Agency, 2008.

International Bank for Reconstruction and Development. 'Report of the Mission to Cuba, July 1951'. Washington, DC, Office of the President.

Jiménez, Marguerite Rose. 'Cuba's Pharmaceutical Advantage', North American Congress on Latin America (NACLA), 16 August 2011.

Jiménez, Marguerite Rose. 'Epidemics and Opportunities for U.S.–Cuba Collaboration', *Science & Diplomacy*, June 2014.

Käkönen, Mira, Hanna Kaisti and Jyrki Luukkanen. *Energy Revolution in Cuba: Pioneering for the Future?*, Finland Futures Research Centre, FFRC eBook 4, 2014.

Kapcia, Antoni. *Cuba: Island of Dreams*, Berg, 2000.

Kapcia, Antoni. 'Educational Revolution and Revolutionary Morality in Cuba: The "New Man", Youth and the New "Battle of Ideas"', *Journal of Moral Education*, 34:4, 2005.

Kapur, Teddy and Alastair Smith. *Housing Policy in Castro's Cuba*, Joint Center for Housing Studies, 2002.

Keck, C. William and Gail A. Reed. 'The Curious Case of Cuba', *American Journal of Public Health*, 102:8, 2012.

Kimber, Stephen. *What Lies Across the Water: The Real Story of the Cuban Five*, Fernwood Publishing, 2013.

Kirk, Emily. *Cuba's Gay Revolution: Normalizing Sexual Diversity through a Health-Based Approach*, Lexington Books, 2017.

Kirk, John M. *Healthcare Without Borders*, University Press of Florida, 2015.

Kirk, John M. and Chris Walker. 'From Cooperation to Capacitation: Cuban Medical Internationalism in the South Pacific', *International Journal of Cuban Studies*, 5:1, 2013.

Kirk, John M. and Chris Walker. 'Cuban Medical Internationalism: The Ebola Campaign of 2014–15', *International Journal of Cuban Studies*, 8:1, 2016.

Kirk, John M. and H. Michael Erisman. *Cuban Medical Internationalism: Origins, Evolution, and Goals*, Rutgers University Press, 2002.

Klepak, Hal. *Raúl Castro and Cuba: A Military Story*, Studies of the Americas, Palgrave Macmillan, 2012.

Koont, Sinan. 'The Urban Agriculture of Havana', *Monthly Review*, 60:8, 2009.

Koont, Sinan. *Sustainable Urban Agriculture in Cuba*, University Press of Florida, 2011.

Lage Dávila, Agustín. *La Economia del Conocimiento y el Socialismo: Preguntas y Respuestas*, Editorial Academia, 2015.

Lamrani, Salim. *The Economic War Against Cuba: A Historical and Legal Perspective on the U.S. Blockade*, Monthly Review Press, 2013.

Lamrani, Salim. *Cuba, the Media, and the Challenge of Impartiality*, Monthly Review Press, 2015.

Latner, Teishan A. '"Agrarians or anarchists?" The Venceremos Brigades to Cuba, State Surveillance, and the FBI as Biographer and Archivist', *Journal of Transnational American Studies*, 9:1, 2018.

Ledón-Naranjo, Nuris, Adolfo Castilo-Vitlloch, Idania Caballero-Torres and Agustín Lage Dávila. 'Gestión de Desarrollo de Productos en la Industria Biotecnológica', *VACCI Monitor*, 26:1, 2016.

LeoGrande, William M. and Julie M. Thomas. 'Cuba's Quest for Economic Independence', *Journal of Latin American Studies*, 34, 2002.

LeoGrande, William M. and Peter Kornbluh. *Back Channel to Cuba: The Hidden History of Negotiations between Washington and Havana*, University of North Carolina Press, 2014.

León Cotayo, Nicanor. *El Plan Bush: Cuba, Made In USA*, Editorial Unicornio, 2006.

López Matilla, Lien and Idania Caballero Torres and Raimundo Ubieta Gómez. 'Innovation Management in the Main Biotech Companies in Cuba', *Technology Transfer and Entrepreneurship*, 3, 2016.

López Mola, Ernesto, Ricardo Silva, Boris Acevedo, José A Buxadó, Angel Aguilera and Luis Herrera. 'Biotechnology in Cuba: 20 Years of Scientific, Social and Economic Progress', *Journal of Commercial Biotechnology*, 13:1, 2006.

Lovgren, Stefan. 'Castro the Conservationist? By Default or Design, Cuba Largely Pristine', *National Geographic*, 6 August 2006.

Ludlam, Steve. 'Regime Change and Human Rights: A Perspective on the Cuba Polemic', *Bulletin of Latin American Research*, 31:S1, 2012.

Ludlam, Steve. 'Reordenamiento, Lineamientos Arriba: Legitimacy and Political Culture in Cuba's Reform Strategy', *International Journal of Cuban Studies*, 4:3/4, 2012.

Luke, Anne. *Youth and the Cuban Revolution: Youth Culture and Politics in 1960s Cuba*, Lexington Books, 2018.

MacDonald, Theodore. *Hippocrates in Havana: An Analytical and Expository Account of the Development of the Cuban System of Healthcare from the Revolution to the Present Day*, Bolivar Books, 1995.

MacDonald, Theodore. *The Education Revolution: Cuba's Alternative to Neoliberalism*, Manifesto Press, 2009.

Mack Arien and William LeoGrande (eds.). 'Cuba: Looking Toward the Future', *Social Research, An International Quarterly*, 84:2, 2017.

Mesa-Lago, Carmelo. 'Cuba's Economic Counter-reform (rectificatión): Causes, Policies and Effects', *Journal of Communist Studies*, 5:4, 1989.

Mesa-Lago, Carmelo. *Voices of Change in Cuba: From the Non-state Sector*, University of Pittsburg Press, 2018.

Ministerio de Ciencia, Tecnología y el Medio Ambiente. 'Enfrentamiento al Cambio Climático en la República de Cuba: Tarea Vida', May 2017, https://bit.ly/2PDtzs9.

Miriam, Rosa. *Los Dissidentes*, Editora Política, 2003.

Molina Díaz, Elda. 'Cuba: Economic Restructuring, Recent Trends and Major Challenges', *Monthly Review* online, 13 April 2009.

Moran, Daniel D., Mathis Wackernagel, Justin A. Kitzes, Steven H. Goldfinger and Aurélien Boutaud. 'Measuring Sustainable Development: Nation by Nation', *Ecological Economics*, 64:3, 2007.

Moreno Fraginals, Manuel. *The Sugarmill: The Socioeconomic Complex of Sugar 1790–1869.* Monthly Review Press, 1976.

Moreno Fraginals, Manuel. 'Plantation Economies and Societies in the Spanish Caribbean, 1860–1930', in Leslie Bethell (ed) *The Cambridge History of Latin America*, 4, 1986.

Morín Nenoff, Jenny. 'Los perdedores del proceso de actualización del modelo socioeconómico cubano: los cuentapropistas contra su voluntad', *Historia, Voces y Memoria*, 11, 2017.

Morris, Emily. 'Unexpected Cuba', *New Left Review*, 88, July–August 2014.

Mulet Concepción, Yailenis. 'Self-employment in Cuba: Between Informality and Entrepreneurship, The Case of Shoe Manufacturing', *Third World Quarterly*, 37:9, 2016.

Notman, Nina. 'Cuba's Cancer Treatments', *Chemistry World*, 16 March 2018.

Nova González, Armando. *La Agricultura En Cuba. Evolución y Trayectoria (1959–2005)*, Editorial de Ciencias Sociales, 2006.

Olalde Font, Raúl, Taymi Gonzalez Morera, Lianet Herrera González, Judith Cherni, Antonio Urbina Yereguí and Lucia Serrano Luján. 'Innovacion Tecnologica Energética en Comunidades Rurales: Caso de Estudio Comunidad de "Manantiales", Villa Clara, Cuba', *Centro Agricola*, 43:3, 2016.

Pérez Ávila, Jorge. *A Doctor and His Patients Talk about AIDS in Cuba*, Casa Editora Abril, 2016.

Pérez Casabona, Hassan. *Palabra en Combate: Uno Más*, Casa Editora Abril, 2001.

Pérez, Jr., Louis A. *Cuba and the United States: Ties of Singular Intimacy*, University of Georgia Press, 2003.

Pérez, Jr., Louis A. *Rice in the Time of Sugar*, University of North Carolina Press, 2019.

Piñiero Harnecker, Camila (ed). *Cooperatives y Socialism: A View from Cuba*, Palgrave Macmillan, 2013.

Piñeiro Harnecker, Camila. 'Cuba's Cooperatives: Their Contribution to Cuba's New Socialism', in Cliff DuRand (ed.), *Moving Beyond Capitalism*, Routledge, 2016.

Pollitt, Brian H. and G.B. Hagelberg. 'The Cuban Sugar Economy in the Soviet Era and After', *Cambridge Journal of Economics*, 18:6, 1994.

Pollitt, Brian H. 'The Rise and Fall of the Cuban Sugar Economy', *Journal of Latin American Studies*, 36, 2004.

Pons Pérez, Saira. 'Tax Law Dilemmas for Self-employed Workers', Cuba Study Group, 20 May 2015.

Premat, Adriana. 'Small-Scale Urban Agriculture in Havana and the Reproduction of the "New Man" in Contemporary Cuba', *Revista Europea de Estudios Latinoamericanos y del Caribe*, 75, 2003.

Pruna Goodgall, Pedro M. *Historia de la Ciencia y La Tecnología en Cuba*, Editorial Científico-Técnica, 2006.

Raby, D.L, *Democracy and Revolution: Latin America and Socialism Today*, Pluto Press, 2006.

Ramírez Cañedo, Elier and Esteban Morales Domínguez. *De la Confrontación a los Intentos de "Normalización": La Política de los Estados Unidos hacia Cuba*, Editorial de Ciencias Sociales, 2014.

Randall, Margaret. *Exporting Revolution: Cuba's Global Solidarity*, Duke University Press, 2017.

Reardon, Sara. 'Can Cuban Science Go Global?', *Nature*, 29 September 2016.

Reid-Henry, Simon M. *The Cuban Cure: Reason and Resistance in Global Science*, The University of Chicago Press, 2010.

del Risco Rodríguez, Enrique. *Los Bosques de Cuba: Historia y Características*, Editorial Científico Tecnica, 1995.

Roman, Peter. 'Electing Cuba's National Assembly Deputies: Proposals, Selections, Nominations and Campaigns', *European Review of Latin American and Caribbean Studies*, 82, 2007, 69–87.

Roman, Peter. *People's Power: Cuba's Experience with Representative Government*, Roman and Littlefield, 2003.

Romanò, Sara and Davide Barrera. 'The Impact of Market-orientated Reforms on Inequality in Transitional Countries: New Evidence from Cuba', *Socio-Economic Review*, 2019.

Rosset, Peter and Medea Benjamin. *The Greening of the Revolution: Cuba's Experiment with Organic Agriculture*, Ocean Press, 1994.

Saney, Isaac. *Cuba: A Revolution in Motion*, Zed Books, 2004.

Seifried, Dieter. *Cuban Energy Revolution: A Model for Climate Protection?* Büro Ö-quadrat report, 2013.

Smis, Stefaan and Kim van der Borght. 'The EU-US Compromise on the Helms–Burton and D'Amato Acts', *American Journal of International Law*, 93:1, 1999.

Smith, Rosi. *Education, Citizenship, and Cuban Identity*, Palgrave Macmillan, 2016.

Stone, Richard. 'Cuba Embarks on a 100-year Plan to Protect Itself from Climate Change', *Science*, 10 January 2018.

Sweig, Julia. *Inside the Cuban Revolution: Fidel Castro and the Urban Underground*, Harvard University Press, 2002.

Sweig, Julia. *What Everyone Needs to Know about Cuba*, Oxford University Press, 2009.

Thorsteinsdóttir, Halla, Tirso Saenz, Uyen Quach, Abdallah S. Daar and Peter A. Singer. 'Cuba: Innovation through Synergy', *Nature Biotechnology*, 22, 2004.

Torres, Ricardo and Victoria J. Furio. 'Transformations in the Cuban Economic Model Context, General Proposal, and Challenges', *Latin American Perspectives*, 41:4, 2014.

Uriarte, Miren. *Cuba: Social Policy at the Crossroads: Maintaining Priorities, Transforming Practice*, An Oxfam America Report, 2002.

United States Government. Cuban Liberty and Democratic Solidarity (Libertad) Act of 1996. https://www.treasury.gov/resource-center/sanctions/documents/libertad.pdf

United States Government. *Commission for Assistance to a Free Cuba: Report to the President*, May 2004.

United States Government. *Commission for Assistance to a Free Cuba: Report to the President*, July 2006.

US Department of Commerce. *Investment in Cuba: Information for United States Businessmen*, Washington, DC, GPO, July 1956.

Valdés, Orlando. *Historia de la Reforma Agraria en Cuba*, Ciencias Sociales, 2003.

Walker, Chris and Emily J. Kirk. 'Alternatives? Pitfalls of Polarized Internationalism: Protest against Cuban Medical Solidarity', *Studies in Political Economy*, 98:1, 2017.

White, Nigel D. 'Ending the US Embargo of Cuba: International Law in Dispute', *Journal of Latin American Studies*, 51:1, 2019.

Whittle, Daniel and Orlando Rey Santos. *Protecting Cuba's Environment: Efforts to Design and Implement Effective Environmental Laws and Policies in Cuba*, University of Pittsburgh Press, 2006.

World Wide Fund For Nature, *Living Planet Report*, 2006.

Wright, Julia E. *Sustainable Agriculture and Food Security in an Era of Oil Scarcity: Lessons from Cuba*, Earthscan, 2009.

Yaffe, Helen. *Che Guevara: The Economics of Revolution*, Palgrave Macmillan, 2009.

Yaffe, Helen. 'Che Guevara and the Great Debate: Past and Present', *Science & Society*, 76:1, 2012.

Yaffe, Helen. 'Che Guevara: Cooperatives and the Political Economy of Socialist Transition', in Camila Piñeiro Harnecker (ed.), *Cooperatives and Socialism*, Palgrave Macmillan, 2013.

Yaffe, Helen. 'Cuban Development: Inspiration to the ALBA-TCP' in Thomas Muhr (ed.), *Counter-Globalization and Socialism in the 21st Century: The Bolivarian Alliance for the Peoples of Our America*, Routledge, 2013.

Yaffe, Helen. 'The Curious Case of Cuba's Biotech Revolution', *History of Technology*, 34, 2019.

Yordi García, Mirtha, Enrique J. Gómez Cabezas and María Teresa Caballero Rivacoba. *El Trabajo Social en Cuba: Retos de la Profesión en el Siglo XXI*, Editorial Unión, 2012.

Zabala Arguelles, María del Carmen, Susset Fuentes Reverón, Geydis Fundora Nevot, Danay Camejo Figueredo, David Díaz Pérez, Vilma Hidalgo López-Chávez and Marta Rosa Munoz Campos. 'Referentes Teóricos para el Estudio de las Desigualdades Sociales en Cuba: Reflexiones sobre su Pertinencia', *Revista Estudios del Desarrollo Social: Cuba y América Latina*, 6:1, 2018.

Zanetti, Oscar. *Esplendor y Decadencia del Azúcar en las Antillas hispanas*, Editorial de Ciencias Sociales, 2012.

Zimbalist, Andrew (ed.). *Cuban Political Economy: Controversies in Cubanology*, Westview Press, 1988.

Zimbalist, Andrew and Claes Brundenius. *The Cuban Economy: Measurement and Analysis of Socialist Performance*, John Hopkins University Press, 1989.

INDEX